St. Catherines:
The Untold History of People and Place

Also by George J. Armelagos

Mesolithic Populations from Wadi Halfa (with David L. Greene)

Demographic Anthropology (with Alan C. Swedlund)

Consuming Passions: The Anthropology of Eating (with Peter Farb)

Paleopathology at the Origins of Agriculture (edited with Mark N. Cohen)

Anthropologie Des Coutumes Alimentaires Translation of *Consuming Passions The Anthropology of Eating* (with Peter Farb)

Populations in Transition: Anthropological and Epidemiological Perspective (edited with Alan C. Swedlund)

Black Mesa Anazazi: Reconstructing Life from Patterns of Disease (with Debra Martin, Alan H. Goodman and Ann Magennis)

In Memory of
Holly Katherine Woods and Glenise "Gee" Little
and for
Bonny Katherine Woods and Ollie Paul Sibley

Acknowledgements

Nicole Naar provided extraordinary advice on editorial matters and design in the final stages of the book's development of the book. Katherine Woods was a source of valuable information about life on St. Catherines. In addition, she read the entire manuscript and provided editorial comments on many versions of the book. Susan Armelagos provided editorial comment on the entire manuscript. Walter Meeks' remembrances of his role in the reburial of Billy Harris were invaluable to the chapter about life on Colonels Island. Glenise (Gee) Little provided many photographs that were used in the book, and was particularly helpful in reconstructing her experiences during the Coast Guard "occupation" of the island. Glen and David Little, Gee's sons, provided recent photographs from the island. The Chapman brothers (George, Ralph, and Ben) provided unique information on growing up on the island. Ben's long friendship with John Woods, Jr, helped to flesh out the richness of the St. Catherines experience. The Rowey Woods' family provided recollections that added to the description of visits to the island. Duke Chapman and "Skipper" Chapman Duffy provided information about their father (Alger) and about their remembrances about their visits to St. Catherines. Sonny Timmons, oyster man extraordinaire, added to our discussion of life "in the creek." Billy Bland was a helpful in finding individuals who were part of the St. Catherines' story. Whitney Easton's insights into the forgotten century of enslavement provided useful information on this neglected topic. Pete Clark was an important source for information on Local Dignitary Hunt on St. Catherine. Kevin Meckes, an expert on wound healing, provided insights into the burn injury suffered by John Woods, Jr.

A special thanks to Amy Benson Brown, Director of the Author Development Program in the Center for Faculty Development at Emory University, who read the earliest versions and made important suggestions that helped to structure the book. Robin Doyon, R.E. D. Design developed and executed the cover design. Emory University provided time and resources to complete the project. Debra Keyes provided suggestions for cover design. Trang and Tom Black and their children, Taryn and Eli, were wonderful neighbors who listened to my endless descriptions of what I was working on at any given time.

St. Catherines Island

The Untold History of People and Place

By George J. Armelagos and John Toby Woods, Jr

John T. Woods Jr.

Colonels Island Press
Atlanta, Georgia

xv

Colonels Island Press
1327 Peachtree St. NE, Suite 504
Atlanta, Georgia 30309

This book was published in 2012
© George J Armelagos and John T. Woods, Jr.
978-0-9853455-0-1

Contents

1
Introduction

St. Catherines: An Untold History of People and Place

"Lindy, Anne Thought Honeymooning on Georgia Isle" blared the page-one headline of the *Atlanta Constitution*, with the sub-headline, "Romantic St. Catherines Island Believed Hiding Place of Famous Bridal Couple" (AC 1929d). There was no need for the *Constitution* to more clearly identify Charles Lindbergh and Anne Morrow, who *Time Magazine* described 50 years later as "one of America's first celebrity couples in a media-crazy century" (Smith 1999). Romance and mystery have been a part of St. Catherines' history for centuries. Nearly 300 years earlier, the island was the place where John Wesley, the founder of Methodism, romanced Sophy Hopkey at the start of their ill-fated relationship. The Lindberghs were to be guests of their friends C. M. and Indiola Keys. The Keys had bought the island that year to create their own "hunter's paradise" and personal playground. Even with a horde of newspapermen on their trail, the elusive couple was never found on the "little semi tropical island …a spot as secluded and steeped in legend as may be found on the entire Atlantic coast" (AC 1929d). This publicity added to the romance of St. Catherines, an image that the Keys encouraged. *The New York Times* (McMullen 1930) reported how "men weary of the city crowds" sought the solitude of island life (see Figures 1 and 2). The *Times* (McMullen 1930) described an idyllic setting in which "Mr. Keys arrives by plane to his own landing strip and lives in Button Gwinnett's remodeled house, putting his guests in converted slave quarters." Interestingly, the Keys never built a landing strip, Button Gwinnett never lived in the house that bears his name, and the guests never stayed in "converted" slave cabins.

Figure 1. Beach on St. Catherines Island.

The acquisition of St. Catherines by three industrialists – Howard Coffin, James Willson and C.M. Keys – is consistent with the cloud of mystery and ambiguity the characterizes the history of St. Catherines. The trio formed a corporation solely to purchase the island, hiding each individual's role in the venture. This evasion reflects a pattern of presenting St. Catherines in a way that highlights its historic beginnings as the home of prominent Americans while avoiding less appealing details of its history. For example, Mary Musgrove, the remarkable daughter of a Native American mother and an English father, played a critical role in the birth of the Georgia Colony. Button Gwinnett, who purchased St. Catherines from Musgrove, was a key figure in the birth of the nation. However, Musgrove illegally brought the first enslaved people to St. Catherines, and in later years Gwinnett "legally" increased their presence on the island. Under the direction of the Waldburg family and with the labor of enslaved black populations, the Sea Island cotton plantation defined St. Catherines for the next century. This part of the story has received little scholarly attention.

Given the important role of St. Catherines in the early history of this nation, surprisingly little is known about this Sea Island off of the Georgia coast, especially in comparison to its sister islands: Ossabaw, Sapelo, St. Simons, Jekyll and Cumberland. In the untold history of the island, John Toby Woods, II—who with his father were superintendents of the island for a half a century— and I tell the story of the island's various owners and the Woods' role as the island's stewards. John Toby Woods, II and I use more recent history to delve into the island's past, removing the cloak of myth and mystery. In particular, we provide the first detailed look at the "captains of industry," such as C. M. Keys and Edward J. Noble of Life Saver fame, who both molded and were molded by St. Catherines.

Figure 2. North Beach, St. Catherines Island.

John Toby Woods, II and his father provide a unique perspective on life on the island. John Woods is probably the last living individual who knew members of the Rauers family, the Keys, and Edward J. Noble. Using John's remembrance, his father's daybooks, court records, census tracts, slave registers, unpublished maps, documents, unpublished photographs, and letters that he and his father saved, we have reconstructed the untold history of St. Catherines. For example, in the early 1930s John Woods' sole playmate on St. Catherines was Eutherle Austin, a member of the last black family to live on island. To understand how the Austins came to be the last black family on the island requires understanding the history of black populations on the island. While Woods brings the an essential eyewitness perspective to this history, my own training as an anthropologist allows me to approach the story of St. Catherines with the accuracy and interpretative skills it requires.

Public knowledge of the island has been informed by superficial presentations that provided a distorted image of place. The promotion of St. Catherines Island to the public is a practice in myth building. For example, the Georgia Public Broadcasting's well-regarded documentary on the barrier islands, *Secret Seashore*, highlights St. Catherines' zoological conservation program, the excavated Spanish Mission, the role that St. Catherine played as the center of the free black state, and the Button Gwinnett House and "portrait." Images of the Gwinnett house are shown as his portrait scrolls in the foreground. The portrait, however, is a figment of an artist's imagination. Even the designation of St. Catherines on the National Historic Landmark register features a picture of the Button Gwinnett house on its website. There are no known images of Gwinnett produced during his lifetime and there are no descriptions of his likeness from that time. The portraits were commissioned a century after his death to enhance a valuable autograph collection. Although the portrait was qualified as a "suppositive" likeness in the 1900s, it has now become the authentic depiction of Gwinnett. It is fitting that a fabricated image of Gwinnett is used to support the notion that Gwinnett built the "Gwinnett House." So the story goes.

While myth and mystery envelopes the owners and occupants of the island, St. Catherines remains a natural treasure of relatively unspoiled beauty. The island, which has been privately owned for much of its history and is now controlled by a non-profit foundation, has withstood many attempts at commercial development. It was the home of the Guale people over 2000 years ago and in the 1570s was the site of the Santa Catalina de Guale, the first Spanish Mission in America. The story of the Native American habitation and the founding of the Mission is well known (Thomas 1987; Thomas, et al. 1978).

Figure 3. Tunis Campbell.

Interestingly, the knowledge of the last two centuries of history on St. Catherines is surprisingly shallow. It is this untold history that is the subject of this book. The most complete modern history of the island (Durham and Thomas, 1978) mentions the Waldburgs' plantation that grew Sea Island cotton for most of the 19th century on the backs of an enslaved population. There has been little effort to unravel the complex history of Jacob Waldburg and his sons, Jacob and George, and their exploitation of the enslaved population on the island. We provide the first use of the Slave Registers, census tracts and court documents to reconstruct the changes in population structure from enslavement to freedom. St. Catherines played a central role in the post-emancipation era when General William Tecumseh Sherman issued Field Order 15 and established a freed black state with its capitol on the island. Tunis Campbell's role as governor of the freed black state is well known, but the role that St. Catherines played during this period in American history remains to be told. Campbell (Figure 3) was vilified by Southern historians as an exploiter of the inhabitants of the island after emancipation. We reveal a more balanced view of the emergence of Tunis Campbell.

With emancipation and the loss of forced labor, St. Catherines was transformed into one of the finest privately owned hunting preserves in America. A key player in this phase of the island's history was Jacob Rauers, a Savannah businessman who purchased the island from Anna Rodriquez in 1876. The Rauers' mansion, built on the banks of Waldburg Creek, was considered one of coastal Low Country's premier homes. We show how Rauers used a hunt by Admiral Winifred Schley, hero of the Spanish American War, to launch St. Catherines to national prominence as one America's foremost hunting locations. We document the decline of the hunting preserve and the transition to the oyster business led by Augustus Oemler, Rauers' son-in-law. Previous histories of the island only mention "a Capt. Umbler" who established an oyster factory after World War I. We have documented in detail the founding of the Oemler enterprise long before the First World War, and have documented its impact on the black populations of St. Catherines. The island became a company town, and but once it declined the black families left the island.

Moving forward in time, Clement Melville and Indiola Keys were giants in their respective worlds. In the 1920s, Keys was the "father of civil aviation" and Indiola was a popular singer who starred on Broadway. To Toby Woods and his family, they were just "Mr. and Mrs. Keys," and they never used or referred to them by their given names. In fact, Durham and

Thomas (1978) identify them only as "the Keys" who were "New York investors" without delving into their fascinating history. C. M. Keys, a newspaperman turned financier, controlled 26 airplane companies at one time. As an industrialist, Keys laid the foundation of what has become commercial aviation in America. His wife Indiola Arnold Keys was a comedic opera star who made headlines in her earlier life when she became the sixth wife of boxing champion "Kid McCoy" (the real McCoy).

We document C. M. and Indiola Keys' million-dollar transformation of the island into their private playground. They nurtured the myth that the Waldburg home overlooking Waldburg

Creek was the original residence of Button Gwinnett on St. Catherines (Figure 4). It was reported that C. M. Keys' health concerns led to his retirement (WSJ 1932) and eventual recuperation on St. Catherines. But there was trouble in paradise. Keys had been forced to retire from the aviation business when it was

Figure 4. The so-called Button Gwinnett house.

revealed that he had secretly borrowed $14 million dollars from his company and invested it in his own stocks. When the market crashed in the early 1930s, he was wiped out financially. His colleagues and business associates never revealed his unethical behavior. Even with this economic setback, Keys was able to invest in a $1 million dollar renovation of the island that changed its face forever; though his funds were eventually depleted (Figure 5). The Rauers eventually foreclosed the mortgage on St. Catherines in 1938 and the island returned to them. From 1939 to 1943, with the island under the control of the Rauers family, much of the virgin forests were harvested for timber.

Edward J. Noble's purchase of St. Catherines in 1943 received national attention. Noble was a legendary entrepreneur who owned the Life Saver Company and the American Broadcasting Corporation. He was known in the business world as a "wonder boy" for purchasing the Life Saver Company and transforming it into a million dollar business. He eventually bought the island and all of its buildings for less than $11 an acre. We provide the first complete picture of how he transformed St. Catherines into a cattle "ranch" and personal retreat. When Noble stepped on St. Catherines, however, he was greeted by U.S. Army forces and later the U.S. Coast Guard, all sent to protect St. Catherines from the threat of U-Boat incursions from Germany. We provide the only detailed descriptions of the armed forces' presence on St. Catherines in the mid-20th century, and how they became "members" of Toby Woods' family.

Noble had an interesting relationship with Toby Woods, who was then superintendent of the island. Mr. Noble was known for selecting the best people to run his businesses so that he could enjoy his free time. Most of those on the island who knew Mr. Noble describe him as a carefree owner who knew how to enjoy himself. In truth, Mr. Noble ruled St. Catherines with a tight fist. While on the island, Mr. Noble would spend his time in a restored slave cabin and only went to the "big house" for meals or to entertain guests. Behind the scenes, Mr. Noble managed Toby Woods in a manner that belies his public image. Their interaction brings up issues of class and regional bias. We have unpublished letters, interviews with many of those who worked on the island, Toby Woods' daybooks, and other documents that provide a unique perspective on how St. Catherines functioned under Mr. Noble's ownership. After the death of Mr. Noble, St. Catherines was in flux while the executor of his estate, Alger Chapman, determined what would be the best course of action. There were maps to show how a bridge could be built to develop St. Catherines in much the same way as Hilton Head. There were even inquiries by NASA to acquire it as part of a series of launch sites in the 1960s. Today it remains a part of a trust that preserves its scientific and historical significance.

Figure 5. St. Catherines Island homestead. Ca. 1930

Will there be pressure to develop St. Catherines Island? The Survival Center for exotic animals has downsized and questions about the island's future have been raised. Neighboring Jekyll Island, which is protected by the state of Georgia, is in the process of considerably controversial development. Can St. Catherines' past help to plan for its future?

St. Catherines: An Untold History of Place and People moves beyond a travel book depicting the exoticism and luxury of the island. It is the most complete account of the island, and is of significance to not only to those interested in the Sea Islands and the social history of the coastal Low Country, but also to a more general audience that is attracted to the issues of class, race and regionalism. Other island biographies, such as that of Fripp Island by Page Miller (2006), reveal the making of a residential community out of a once sleepy resort when a bridge was built. While the ownership histories of Ossabaw, Sapelo, St. Simons, Jekyll and Cumberland Islands by northern businessmen are well known, Jacob Rauers, C. M. Keys, and Edward J. Noble's occupation of St. Catherines has received scant treatment. We provide biographic background on the owners that enlightens us about those who shaped the island and how the island shaped them.

2

John's Story

In 1997, Lynn Sibley and I visited Billy Harris Point on Colonels Island, Georgia, in search of a place that would provide a retreat from the bustle of our condominium on Peachtree Street in Midtown Atlanta. Lynn, who "loves" the water, was attracted to the possibility of living near the ocean and the opportunity to sea kayak. Lynn searched the *Atlanta Journal Constitution* classified ads and found David Ginn's ad for a house on the edge of the 700-foot marsh lining the Sunbury Creek. The house on Billy Harris Point is a scant 45-minute kayak trip to St. Catherines Island, which boldly marks the horizon to the south.

Before we bought the house, we met our future next-door neighbors and friends, Will and Tweet Darsey. Will Darsey, born and raised in Liberty County, would be our guide to the Low Country that he loved. Will was drawn to Billy Harris Point by its people and irresistible beauty. Will talked about one of our soon-to-be-neighbors whom he described a "wonderful character." Mr. Woods, he told me, was usually seen on his bike riding down the 528-foot dock leading to the Sunbury Creek and the *Papa T*, his son's shrimp boat. He relayed that Mr. Woods was the harbinger of spring. While some people see the robin as the sign first sign of spring, Will said that Mr. Woods would herald its arrival by removing his shirt and not replacing it until the fall when the sun set lower in the sky (Figure 6).

John Woods is a complex character who is just as much at ease working shirtless in his yard as he is in a suit running the meeting of the electricity Co-op[1]. He served on the Co-op board for 40 years, and as its president for 21 years. He was comfortable talking to me about fishing even when I asked him, "What is bait and tackle?" John, who some friends called "Captain John," is one of the most knowledgeable navigators of the waters near Colonels Island. It is as if he possesses an internal GPS that can instantly recall a sandbar and how it shifts during the season. Aboard his Cobbtown Skiff[2], we have visited the nooks and crannies of Factory Creek on St. Catherines. We have circled Ossabaw Island and Bradley Creek on its north end. He knows the complex McQueens Inlet – described as one of the most notoriously difficult areas to navigate – as if there was a map on the back of his hand.

John is a veritable encyclopedia of the social and natural history of Colonels and St. Catherines Islands. He has a memory that keeps every detail intact to be recalled when needed. He would tell me a story so rich in detail that when I found a document describing the same event, I was shocked by his phenomenal accuracy. However, John is modest about his ability to reveal the untold story of St. Catherines and Colonels Islands. After a long and detailed story, he would smile and say with a twinkle in his eye, "That's the truth," and with a short pause, "as far as I know it." He would hand me a sixty-year-old letter from E. J. Noble that would confirm a "fact" that he had told me and he would say the document was, "better than my memory."

Almost from the beginning, I was drawn to the possibility of writing about John and his relationship to St. Catherines. I am an anthropologist who has specialized in the evolution of diet and disease in prehistory. I am more comfortable writing about skeletons that have been in the ground for thousands of years. While I realized that it would be a stretch to write a biography of

Figure 6. John, with Bonny Kate Woods riding in the basket, on his dock at Billy Harris Point. Photo taken 1997.

Figure 7. The "official" photograph of John Toby Woods as President of Coastal Electric Membership.

John Woods, I felt driven to do it. I soon realized that to understand John, the person, it would be necessary to understand the places that shaped him: St. Catherines Island, Colonels Island and even Sunbury Creek. For example, John told me that his sole playmate on St. Catherines was Eutherle Austin, the adopted daughter of Aaron and Nancy Austin, the last permanent black family on St Catherines. I thought that I would find a history of the black populations on St. Catherines, but I was dismayed to find that no such definitive history existed.

With John's help, I have corrected this shortcoming and provided one of the first comprehensive descriptions of enslaved blacks brought illegally by Mary Musgrove, and later legally by Button Gwinnett in the late 1700s. Even though it was well known that Jacob Waldburg harvested Sea Island cotton on the backs of enslaved blacks, there seemed to be little interest in providing the specifics of how he exploited these populations. If one is to understand the history of St. Catherines, this period of history must be discussed. It is not at all uncommon for someone relating the history of St. Catherines to move from the Button Gwinnett era to Tunis Campbell's leadership of the freed black state, completing skipping the Waldburg era. For John Woods and others on St. Catherines, there are constant reminders of this period. The remains of slave cabins are found near the big house, and the south end of the island contains many visual reminders of the past. Green Seed and Sams Field, the source of whose names has been lost to history, were cleared by families in bondage. The ditches they dug to define the fields can still be faintly seen as John rides around the island on roads named by the Waldburgs. The mortal remains of many enslaved individuals remain entombed in simple graves in an unmarked but well-known cemetery. John is "proud" to know every piece of St. Catherines. To John, to be "proud" is to be "pleased".

John is one of the "proudest" people I have met. He is proud that he has never bought bait for his many fishing trips, and he is proud to share his "catch" with you. He is proud that he has never accepted a "tip" from any of the stranded fishermen that he has towed home. John is proud that in his forty years as a member of the Electric Membership Cooperative (EMC) board he has never missed or arrived late to a meeting (Figure 7). He is proud of his family and their role in managing St. Catherines for half a century. While he was modest about talking about himself, when it came to his family

John was aglow describing their rich contributions. In fact, John was thrilled to sing the praises of his family's deeds. By the time I moved to Colonels Island, John's father had died. I lamented to John that we had missed an opportunity to record his remembrances. But we still had his mother who could provide us details of her life on the island. I felt that we had time to write the story; but I procrastinated too long. John's mother, his Uncle Albert, and his sisters Clel and Gee died within a few years. We could wait no longer, and so I began the story.

John Toby Woods' life has been anchored in three historic places on the coast of Low Country Georgia: Colonels Island, Sunbury, and St. Catherines Island (Figure 8). John was born on Colonels Island, and moved to St. Catherines when he was three days old. Since retirement, he has spent his time on Colonels Island. Colonels Island represents "book ends" marking his birth and his "retirement" – a span of over three-quarters of a century. His activity during the last 25 years would make most people think that retirement was a euphemism for even more hard work than before.

Under the stewardship of the Woods family, St. Catherines remained a hidden jewel for a half a century. Just as family treasures are put away for safekeeping and rarely seen, St. Catherines historic links to Liberty County are deep and invisible to all but a few of its residents. Those who live in Liberty County will likely never see any of the million artifacts from the excavations on St. Catherines. The artifacts[3] are housed at the Fernbank Museum in Atlanta, Georgia, a four and half hour trip from Liberty County. From my office at Emory University, it takes less than fifteen minutes for me to visit the collections. Some of the most important figures in American archeology – Charles Colcok Jones (1883)[4], Clarence Bloomfield Moore (1998), Lewis Larsen, Joseph Caldwell (Schneider and Crusoe 1976) and David Hurst Thomas – have excavated on St. Catherines. Moore (Aten and Milanich. 2003), a wealthy businessman, outfitted his steamship the *Gopher* and traveled the waterways of the southeast. He excavated seven mounds on St. Catherines from 1896 to 1897 and spent the summers producing well-illustrated reports that generated interest in southeastern archeology (Moore 1898; Moore 1903; Moore and Larson 1998; Moore and Nadaillac 1897). At a time when the mounds were thought to be the work of aliens, the lost tribes of Israel or populations from Atlantis, Moore did much to focus attention on the Native Americans that were the true mound builders.

Even the best studies of Colonels Island and its surroundings give short shrift to St. Catherines. As John says, books such as *Children of Pride* (Jones and Myers 1984), *Dr. Bullie's Notes* (Holmes and Presley 1976), and the highly acclaimed *Dwelling Place* (Clarke 2005) give St. Catherines only a glancing mention.

While St. Catherines may have avoided the gaze of writers, it was always on John's mind. The first day that I met John in June 1997, we began a discussion of St. Catherines that continues to this day. On that summer afternoon, I was visiting John's home to see the grave of W. J. L. "Billy Joe" Harris that lies in John's yard. Billy Harris was the son of prominent planter and physician, Dr. Raymond Harris, and his wife Mary. The plantation included the land where John's house now stands. It is a mystery why Billy was buried on the family plantation and not in the cemetery burial plots in Walthourville, Georgia after his death in December 1859. John shared a publication (Thomas, et al. 1977) that told the story of the excavation of Billy Joe Harris' remains. The grave had been neglected for a century and John helped stabilize it with the famed archaeologist Davis Hurst Thomas. In that publication, Davis Hurst Thomas and his team compared the recovered remains of Billy Joe Harris to those found in graves of enslaved individuals buried in the Middle Settlement mound on St. Catherines Island. Billy Joe Harris was the family's "closeted" mentally challenged son. The story of the enslaved individuals buried on St. Catherines began our discussion of the island.

I was aware of St. Catherines and knew that it was the site of a Spanish mission and the home of one of Liberty County's signers of the *Declaration of Independence*. I had read about the mission and had read the reports on the skeletons recovered and reported by Clark Spenser Larson, a fellow biological anthropologist and good friend. I knew that Button Gwinnett once lived on the island and that his house still stood on Waldburg Creek. John challenged this "fact" and revealed the depth of his knowledge and his commitment to an accurate history of the island. He commented, "Marmaduke Floyd on page 46 in *Georgia's Disputed Ruins* argues that most of the tabby construction on St. Catherines dates back to the Waldburg times." After finding a copy of the book and seeing that he was correct in his citation, I was duly impressed. I still was not too concerned about the myth of the Button Gwinnett house as a serious issue. But, as John pointed out to me, this myth has dominated interest in the island and obscured more important aspects of St. Catherines' history. For example, Georgia Public Broadcasting's well-regarded documentary on the barrier islands, *Secret Seashore*, highlights the zoological conservation program, the excavated Spanish Mission[5], the role that St. Catherines played as the center of the freed black state, and the Button Gwinnett House and "portrait." The portrait is actually a figment of the artist's imagination, as there are no known images of Gwinnett or descriptions of his likeness from that time. The portraits were commissioned a century after his death to enhance a valuable collection.

John has traversed all of the high ground on St. Catherines and knows many of the mounds containing the 4000-year-old remains of the Guale Indians. John was a source of valuable information on the extensive archeological excavations revealing the island's past. The first recorded history of the island began in the 1500s when the Spanish Mission was established. Our story discusses Mary Musgrove who, with her husband Thomas Bosomworth, established a plantation on the island in the 1700s. The contentious negotiations with the Georgia Colony began with the establishment of the plantation. The Bosomworths moved to St. Catherines in 1748, and after eleven years of bitter struggle were given title to the island by the Georgia Colony. In 1765, Bosomworth sold the island to Button Gwinnett.

Sunbury is the once famous port that played an important role in the Revolutionary War. It was a major center of commerce, politics and learning until it was eclipsed after the Civil War and became one of the lost towns of Georgia (Jones 1878; McIlvaine 1971). John lived in Sunbury from 1960 to 1976, and his son Johnny still lives in the house that Toby Woods, John's father, built during his own retirement. Sunbury has experienced a resurgence as people rediscover the port city. Recently, a restaurant featuring crab and shrimp has attracted patrons from as far as Savannah. Most guests drive the 40-minute trip by car, but it is also possible to dock at the restaurant along the port.

If he could have had a choice, it would be hard to for John to have found three locations as interesting and as unique as these places. In many ways, the memories of Toby and John Woods are stories of place as well as person. John:

> In September 1936, I moved from St. Catherines to Colonel's Island along with my two older sisters to live with my Grandmother Rogers [and] to go to school. The house originally had three rooms; Daddy had a fourth room built on for us. We had running water in the kitchen but not inside the bathroom. We had a wood stove and a fireplace. There was no electricity

until 1940. We then had one sixty-watt light in each room. My grandmother wanted only one room lighted at a time. The light bill never got over the two dollar minimum.

Even with electricity, they still didn't have a refrigerator, electric iron, or washing machine. His father gave Grandmother Rogers a jersey cow and she had chickens and a small garden. John describes his school years,

> We went to the elementary school at Dorchester Village (the school had three teachers for seven grades). The school bus route was over 10 miles each way on dirt roads. If we had a real high spring tide, we would have to wait to get back to Colonels Island. There was a causeway and bridge that joined Colonels Island to the mainland.

John's great-grandmother died when his grandmother was just five days old, and she was raised later by her stepmother who eventually had nine other children. His great-grandfather had 21 children. John relates,

> Although her brothers were schoolteachers, farmers or businessmen, my grandmother had only a fourth grade education. She married John Rogers, who was an orphan raised by Uncle Luke to help work on the farm. She had five children; the youngest, Jimpsey, was mentally challenged due to an early illness. As a small boy he was burned real badly. His clothes caught fire when he got too close to fire heating the outside wash pot used to boil the clothes that were being washed.

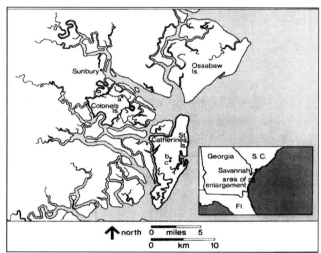

Figure 8. Map of St. Catherines Island, Colonels Island and Sunbury. From Durham and Thomas (1978)

John told me that his grandmother's husband died at 48 from a ruptured appendix. As he told me the story, he said, "If it wasn't for bad luck, she would not have had any luck at all." While the line was frequently used to describe the fortune of those who seemed to always face hardships, Grandmother Rogers seemed to epitomize the saying. John describes her as "a small woman, not quite 5 feet tall" who he "found tough to live with." While John respected her difficulties, he said sadly, "she never seemed to have any tender words."

John described how his father would go to Savannah one Friday a month to get supplies for St. Catherines. He said, "Daddy would come by Grandmother's house and leave us some groceries; sugar, flour canned goods. If we were lucky, he would take us to the island for the weekend." There were problems keeping the pantry well stocked. John said,

Since we didn't have a refrigerator to keep meats and I was always hungry, when I got home from school, in the winter months, I would take the single shot 22 rifle that my daddy had took from somebody hunting on St. Catherines and go squirrel hunting hoping to get 2 or 3 squirrels for dinner. If I could get a good shot at them, I would shoot it in the head. I didn't miss much as bullets were valuable.

As a teenager, John was always searching for ways to help bring food to the table, not always with success. Most of these "projects" involved his relatives and produced conflict and disappointment. He tells the story about the time when he was hired to trap hogs:

One winter, one of Uncle Hoke's relatives came to trap hogs on Colonels Island as it was open ranges at the time. We didn't have a fence law until about 1953. His relative told me if I would help him catch the hogs after school, when he had caught a load to sell, he would give me a "pretty." That sounded good to me since I could take my rifle and kill me a squirrel at the same time.

He had a tractor and a sled that he would pull through the trails in the woods to the trap pens that he had built. I would ride on the sled with my rifle. When we got to the pens, we pulled the sledge up to the pen door. If we had a hog to sell, we would put it in the sled. If it was a sow with pigs, we would castrate the male pigs and turn them loose for the next year. Finally after several weeks, he had a load to take to the market. When he had sold the hogs, he came by to give me my "pretty", a box of 22 rifle bullets.

John's time on the mainland was, in his view, a necessity. Life on the island was too confining and he needed the experience from the mainland. However, he was always drawn to St. Catherines and knew that he would return one day.

3

On the Trail of the Elusive Button Gwinnett

John was proud of his dog Button, a terrier mix that Mrs. Keys had given to his dad in the 1930s. Soon after his arrival on St. Catherines, Button was riding on the fender of Mrs. Keys' fine convertible (Figure 9). Button was some dog. In addition to being skilled at remaining seated on the fender as the car turned on St. Catherines' bumpy roads, Button was also a 'gator killer. Ben Chapman, John's cousin, reminded him of the time when John, age twelve at the time, caught and kept a three-foot alligator as a pet. Since 'gators are not known to like the company of people, he housed it in large tub for safekeeping. Button saw John catch the 'gator and watched him play with it for a couple of days. One morning, John's mother woke before him and discovered a deadly deed. She came into the house and announced, "John, Button has killed your 'gator." John said, "I went outside, saw the bloody remains of my 'gator and saw Button sitting there with a smile on his face."

When I saw the picture of Button on the fender of the car, I told John that he was justifiably proud of his dog's agility (Figure 10). John replied that he was most proud of Button because, "he never lied." I had heard of dogs that would fake a limp long after an injury healed

to gain their owner's sympathy, but I never considered that lying. I asked John to explain what he meant by championing Button's veracity. "George, he never barked on the trail and when he did bark, you had yourself a 'coon.'" He explained that a dog that barks on the trail of a raccoon keeps the animal on the move. To John, the "coon is playing tag with the dog," and the canine becomes so confused that he barks up a tree that the 'coon left long ago. That, to John, was a lying dog. The dog was literally, "barking up the wrong tree."

John described how on a 'coon hunt Button would silently circle around him, always keeping a 100-yard distance as he moved on the trail. Catching raccoons was one of Button's missions in life. Button hated raccoons since his first encounter with one that "about drowned him when he was a puppy." John said, "I had to haul him out of the water." According to John, he never got into a predicament like that again.[1] "Button was a smart dog. If you picked up a gun, he knew you were going hunting. If you moved toward

Figure 9. John and his dog Button. Ca. 1940.

the car, he knew that you were going for a ride. And he loved to do both," John recalls. Like a sentinel, Button preferred to stay outside of the house waiting for a driver. He was so fast that he was often on the left fender (his preferred perch) before anyone had a chance to open the car door.

John said that "the number of 'coons that Button killed was unreal. Back then, the meat and hides were valuable. Now you can't legally sell wild meat and the fur is worthless. That's all that I can say about Button." But John had plenty to say about hunting as it is practiced now. Now, hunting is a social event. The hunters with their yapping dogs are part of the ritual. A team of hunters takes great pleasure in identifying their dog's bark. "That's old yeller in the pasture," one hunter shouts to the others, pleased that he recognizes the howl. John commented that after the mainland hunt, many of the dogs would stray in search of other prey and hunters would leave the cages in their pickup trucks open awaiting a hopeful reunion. In John's day, people hunted for food to eat or sell.

Figure 10. Button perched on the fender of Mrs. C. M. Keys' 1928 Model A convertible. Mrs. Keys is driving and C. M. Keys is the passenger in the rear seat. Ca. 1932

Long before I moved to Colonels Island, I knew that Button Gwinnett, the dog's namesake, was one of the three signers of the *Declaration of Independence* from Georgia, and that he had died following a duel with General Macintosh. After living on the coast a while, you learn that Gwinnett once owned St. Catherines Island, that he was supposedly buried there, and that the Button Gwinnett house remains a lasting legacy of his link to coastal Georgia. When I asked John about the Button Gwinnett house, I was surprised at his reluctance to talk about it. John, I soon realized, had a convincing case regarding the inauthenticity of the house reputed to be the home of Button Gwinnett (Figure 11).

According to John, that story was the imaginative creation of one of St. Catherines' previous owners. I soon realized that John had researched Gwinnett extensively, and he told me the story behind the myths unnecessarily created to enhance Gwinnett's greatness.

Button Gwinnett is certainly one of the more interesting characters in American history. While he lived only 12 years in the United States, he left an indelible mark on our history. He was born in Gloucestershire, England in 1735, married Anne Bourne in 1757, had three children, and arrived in Savannah in 1765 (Deaton 2006; Jenkins 1926).[2] After failing as a merchant in Charlestown and Savannah, he went further into debt to purchase St. Catherines in hopes of living as a gentleman farmer (Durham and Thomas 1978:219). By February 1773, Gwinnett's empire had collapsed and his interests were sold for £5250. While his personal fortune declined, his role in politics rose dramatically. He was appointed the second President (Governor) of Georgia following the death of Archibald Bulloch, but lost his bid for reelection two months later. He made an arrangement with his creditors that allowed him to remain on the island[3] until his infamous death in the duel with Brigadier General Lachlan McIntosh on May 19, 1777. Their feud began when McIntosh received a military appointment that Gwinnett had expected to receive. The grudge was further fueled when Gwinnett brought charges against George McIntosh, Lachlan's brother, accusing him of collaborating with the British. An incensed General McIntosh berated Gwinnett in front of the Georgia Assembly, calling him a "scoundrel and a lying rascal." When McIntosh would not apologize for those fighting words, Gwinnett challenged him to a duel.[4] The duelers, facing each other from just 10 feet away, did the gentlemanly thing and shot towards the lower part of the body. Both were injured, but Gwinnett's gunshot wound to his left knee (a fact that played a role in later attempts to identify his remains) became infected and he died twelve days later. He was the second signer of the *Declaration of Independence* to die (Malone 1954). The mystery begins soon after his death. While there was a burial and a grave marker, both were soon lost to history.

The interest in Gwinnett's bones began in 1848 when the citizens of Augusta, Georgia erected the Signers' Monument dedicated on July 4th of that year. They had the remains of Lyman Hall and George Walton reinterred beneath the marker that sits on the 500 block of Greene Street in Augusta. The hope was that, when Gwinnett's bones were found, he too would be reinterred there.[5] Unfortunately for the Augustans, Gwinnett's remains seemed to have disappeared.

Then in 1943, Arthur J. Funk, a retired Savannah school principal on a trip to the nation's capital, became intrigued with John Turnbull's painting of *The Declaration of Independence*[6] in the Rotunda. The mural depicts 42 of the 56 signers of the Declaration. Funk was surprised not to find Button Gwinnett among them. He asked why and was told that no likeness or descriptions of Gwinnett existed. Funk made it his mission to correct that shortcoming, and for the rest of his life he searched through documents in hopes of finding a likeness of Gwinnett.

Figure 11. The alleged Button Gwinnett house, after renovations by the Keys and Noble Foundation

In 1957, while searching through the accounts of Gwinnett's executor, he came across an entry accounting for a payment of 49 schillings and 6 pence to a Sexton who was in charge of the church and cemetery, and another accounting for a memorial. Without a portrait or a description of Button Gwinnett, Funk turned his attention to finding his grave. Surmising that the only Sexton in Savannah at that time was at the Christ Church, he felt that that he would have been buried there. The burial ground associated with the Church had been deeded to the city of Savannah and is now known as the Colonial Park Cemetery at E. Oglethorpe and Abercorn (Piechocinski 1999). Funk found a headstone that was obliterated except for a G or C, T and a 7. With the help of the Georgia Historical Commission, archaeologist Lewis H. Larsen, Jr. excavated the burial. The exciting discovery of a hole in the left femur (Figures 12 and 13) led Larson to conclude that he had found Button Gwinnett. Then the fun really began.

If there is an antagonist in this tale, it is A. (Antonio) J. Waring, a physician with an interest in archaeology. He witnessed the exhumation in 1957 and immediately ridiculed the idea that these were Button Gwinnett's bones. Indeed, upon viewing the burial, he exclaimed, "That looks like a woman's skeleton to me." He claimed that the damage to the left femur was caused be post-mortem processes. To settle the issue once and for all, Waring sent the femur to the

Smithsonian Institution to have bone examined (Williams 1966). Marshall T. Newman, a biological anthropologist,[7] studied the femur and concluded that the damaged area was not caused by bullet shot and that the bone belonged to a woman who was five feet two inches tall. Waring asked Newman if it were possible that the femur was that of a six-foot man with a musket wound (Figures 12 and 13). He relied on Sanderson's (1822) *Biography of the Signers of the Declaration of Independence*, which claimed that Gwinnett was over six feet tall.[8] It was unusual that Waring sent only the femur for examination, and that Newman made his assessment on the basis of a single bone. His willingness to base his assessment on such limited evidence is not what one would expect of a professional anthropologist. Faced with an impasse, they threw the issue to Mayor W. Lee Mingledorff, who – like any good bureaucrat – passed the issue on to the Savannah-Chatham County Historic Site and Monument Commission. The Commission issued their report, *The Burial Place of Button Gwinnett: A Report to the Mayor and Alderman of the City of Savannah* on September 19, 1959 (Frazier, et al. 1959).

John provided me with a 34-page yellowing photocopy of the report. In a quasi-judicial style, the committee examined all of the evidence and came to the unsurprising conclusion that they indeed had the remains of Gwinnett. The Commission's report is a point-by-point refutation of Marshall T. Newman's one-page analysis.

I am a reluctant critic of Newman's assessment, since I have not had a chance to examine the bones myself. I usually chastise my students for analyzing bones from photographs, but I had no alternative. First, I am relatively confident that the remains from the burial are those of a male. The angle that the head and neck of femur make in relationship to the shaft is large (nearly 120°). In females, the neck and head make a more acute angle to accommodate their wider hips. The squareness of the anterior portion of the mandible (lower jaw) also suggests that the remains are those of a male. The molar teeth were lost during the individual's lifetime, and the jawbone healed (resorbed), leaving no evidence of the tooth sockets that once housed the molar tooth roots. This pattern suggests these were the bones of a mature individual in his late thirties or early forties.

It is likely that in Waring's discussions with Newman, he asked specifically if this bone could have belonged to a six-foot male. There is a formula for assessing stature from a single bone (White and Folkens 2005:398-399). In archeological excavation, reconstructing stature provides important information for assessing the health of a population. Skeletal biologists have studied the bones of living people and developed a formula for estimating stature from the long bones of an individual. This formula (2.38 x femur length in cm + 61.41 ± 3.27) takes the length of the femur (44 cm), multiplies it by the constant (2.38), and then adds the constant (61.41) to get the stature in centimeters 166.13 cm (5'5''). The 3.27 cm is the range of variability within the living populations from which this formula was derived. Applying this equation to the femur in question, we get a range from 162.9 cm to 169.4 cm. This suggests that the individual was between 5'4" and 5'6".

In the search for any piece of evidence to support their case, Frazier and colleagues (1959:23) went to the *Encyclopedia Britannica* to show that Gwinnett was shorter than originally claimed. They found an entry on the "Welch" (Gwinnett's ancestry) and found that "the Welch are predominately a little people of slender build." So much for science. Each side was willing to pick and choose any and all random facts to support their case.

Does the damage to the lower end of femur suggest a musket wound, or bone deterioration after death? Professor Lenore Barbian, formally a curator at the National Museum of Medicine and now a Professor of Anthropology at Edinburgh University of Pennsylvania, has provided me with photographs of century-old bones with musket wounds (Figures 14 and 15). If the musket shot hit the shaft of the bone, it would have caused a fracture that splits the bone in two (one of Antonio Waring's contentions). However, if the musket shot hit the spongy bone above the knee, the result would be a fracture radiating away from the wound with the femur remaining intact. The photograph of the purported Button Gwinnett femur is inconclusive. There is obvious evidence of changes that occurred after death, making any definitive conclusion suspect. The radial fractures indicative of a musket wound are not evident on the femur from the "Gwinnett burial," but, again, the photograph is not clear enough to make a definitive evaluation. My conclusion that it is a mature male, and that it may or may not be Gwinnett. I have to rely on the testimony of the people who viewed the actual photographs and the X-rays of the femur. Lacking my own visual confirmation, I have to reluctantly accept the assessment of other experts that there was evidence of a musket wound.

Figure 12. The purported left femur of Button Gwinnett. Note the damage above the joint surface of the knee.

One of the experts was Mr. Herb Glass, ballistics consultant for *True Magazine*. This credential seemed to the impress commission, which accepted his findings with enthusiasm. As John had pointed out to me earlier, it is not likely that either Gwinnett or McIntosh used a full charge in their guns, which might explain the lack of a circular wound in the femur under consideration.

Just when you think that this story could not get any more complicated, you discover a new twist. One would have expected that bones from the burial would have been stored in a museum while these issues were being decided, but this was not the case. Funk kept the bones in his possession. For six years, he had them stored in a copper-lined coffin that he kept in his guest room. Given the fact that the guest room prominently housed a coffin, it is not surprising that few of Funk's friends took advantage of his offer of hospitality to share the room with a signer of the *Declaration of Independence*.

The New York Times (NYT 1960) reported that Mayor W. Lee Mingledorff refused one last request from Augusta's mayor, Millard A. Beckum, for the reburial of Gwinnett's bones at the Signers Monument. The search for Button Gwinnett's bone has some bizarre episodes. John brought me an aging copy of the *Atlanta Journal and* The *Atlanta Constitution Magazine*, which proudly announced on its mast-head that the paper "covers Dixie like the dew." Andrew Sparks (1955) describes a trip to St. Catherines in search of the grave site of Button Gwinnett. Sparks received a "lead" from a Savannah fireman who claimed to guide hunting and fishing parties to the island for John Monroe, the fire chief of Savannah at the time. The informant gave Sparks a map in the tradition of a typical scavenger hunt, with an "X" marking the spot of the slave burial ground near the big house. The informant told Sparks, "You won't have any trouble finding the grave" (Sparks 1955:6). Driving from Savannah on U.S. 17 (I-95 was not yet built) and turning on State Route 38, Sparks reached the dead-end at Yellow Bluff fishing camp. Sparks had not made any reservations. He figured that with all of the boats leaving Yellow Bluff, he could easily get a lift to St. Catherines.

Sparks quickly encountered Arthur Goodman, the owner of Yellow Bluff, and told him about his mission to St. Catherines in search of Button Gwinnett's grave. Goodman had been in the Army and married Mildred Bell, Roger Youman's niece by marriage. In 1951, Arthur and Mildred Goodman bought Yellow Bluff. Goodman, a relative newcomer to Liberty County responded, "You're looking for who? Buttons Gwinnett? Why I never heard of him." After Sparks gave Goodman a brief course in American history and Liberty County's links to Gwinnett and Lyman Hall, Goodman said, "I have been at Yellow Bluff for five years, but I didn't know we had so much history here. What do you know! Two signers of the *Declaration of Independence* lived right here in this county" (Sparks 1955:7).

As Sparks tells the story, an intrigued Arthur Goodman was tempted to join his quest, but had bait to sell, boats to launch, and cabins to prepare for northern Georgia fisherman scheduled to arrive that night. Arthur suggested that Sparks contact Hoke Youmans, who was taking a group of fisherman to the island the next morning. For directions, he recommended Toby Woods, John's father. "If anyone can tell you where Buttons is buried, he can. He knows every inch of the island," said Goodman. Others at Yellow Bluff were drawn to the conversation and the strange quest. L. L. "Pop" Durden, a relative of John's and a former watchman of the southern end of St. Catherines, was at the Bluff that day. "Pop" related a recent discovery that Toby had made of an old building at "Graveyard Swash[9]" and suggested that they look there. Everyone seemed to know where to find Button's bones.

At their first meeting, Uncle Hoke[10] told Sparks,

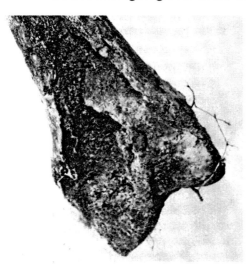

Figure 13. The damaged area of the knee. Close-up view of femur.

I have been going over to St. Catherines for 32 years and I guess that I've taken two or three parties over every year looking for the grave. I wouldn't get my hopes too high. But I'll tell you this. A man who knows the history of the Georgia Coast better than anyone was Marmaduke Floyd, of Savannah. He's dead now, but he told me once that from the information he had, he thought the grave would be found along a ridge you cross on the road to McQueen's Inlet. I pass it every morning taking fisherman to the inlet. You can see part of a chimney and the foundation of an old building. I've never had time to stop and investigate, but someday when I have time I'm going to follow the ridge to the river. That's where you'll find the grave if it's on the island (Sparks 1955:11).

Figure 14. Musket wounds to the shaft of the femur, resulting in a fracture of the bone. Courtesy of the Smithsonian Institution.

The next morning, Uncle Hoke took the McQueen fishing party and Sparks' group to St. Catherines aboard *The Wye Goodie*.[11] Sparks and his crew were driven by truck to John's father's house where they learned that Toby had gone to Thunderbolt to have a boat repaired (Woods 1955b: June 8th).[12] John said, "Daddy had little time for that foolishness." John's mom, Gladys, was enlisted to guide the expedition in her husband's absence. She was a worthy guide, and knew the island almost as well as her husband. Gladys Woods was also a skeptical guide: "You won't find the grave there; those are all slave graves, according to what we were told by old-time Negroes. And only a few stones are left." Before returning to "telephone sitting,"[13] she took them to Graveyard Swash, Graveyard Gulch or Graveyard Ridge, as the area had been named by the enslaved populations whose descendants left the island for the mainland. Although Gladys helped Sparks find the site that Uncle Hoke mentioned, they found no marker and Sparks speculated that the loose bricks they found might be part of a "brick enclosed tomb." This was an unwarranted speculation, according to John, since those remains were part of a house that had long ago fallen into disrepair. Sparks was unsuccessful in his treasure hunt, but he had hope that others would soon be on the trail,

> Hoke Youmans said he was going to make a search himself, and Arthur Goodman, whose curiosity was aroused, said he was going to look, too. Possibly, they are there this weekend searching for the lost grave of one of Georgia's signers of the *Declaration*.

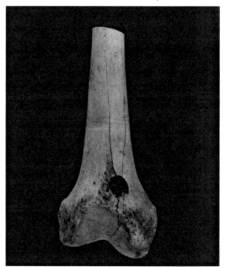

Figure 15. Musket wound to the spongy bone of the femur, in which the shot is absorbed and the outline is maintained.

John chuckled at the thought of Uncle Hoke and Arthur Goodman traipsing along Cemetery Ridge looking for Button's bones. It was Fourth of July weekend, and John was sure that they had "bigger fish to fry."

All that is left of Button Gwinnett's earthly remains are the bones that have been attributed to him, his autographs, and the house that he allegedly built on St Catherines. The debate surrounding Gwinnett's burial in Savannah's Colonial Cemetery continues to this day. John believes that the evidence is convincing. I am not so sure. Why is finding Button's bones so important? If Button Gwinnett never even saw the house named after him, and if the bones in the "Gwinnett" grave are not his, then what do we have left?

There are only 36 Button Gwinnett signatures in existence (Robertson 1946).[14] Gwinnett's autograph is one of the most sought after autographs in the world. In 1983, it was thought to be worth about $100,000 (Harvey 1983), and is now suggested to be worth $250,000 dollars (Deaton 2006). There is the copy on the *Declaration of Independence*, and 20 signatures are housed in institutions. Gwinnett was a relatively obscure figure and he died shortly after signing the document (Duffus 1926).[15] Collectors who focus on corralling all those who signed the document have driven the price up.

Early biographical accounts lamented the lack of a likeness or even a description of the elusive Mr. Gwinnett. However, in 1958, the Fulton Federal Savings and Loan Association purchased a portrait of Gwinnett attributed to Jeremiah Theus from a New York gallery for $5000 (Williams 1966). The Director of the Atlanta Art Institute immediately called it a fake. There is no mention of a portrait in the probate of the estate, and the portrait is dated to 1769. Its location is written as Charleston, SC, even though during the time Button Gwinnett was alive the city was known as Charles Town and 'S' was not used as an abbreviation for South. Despite these facts, the portrait has become part of the myth. Even reputable history sources, such as *The New Georgia Encyclopedia,* publish pictures that are supposedly authentic portraits of Gwinnett.[16]

Thus, we are left only with the Gwinnett house on St. Catherines as part of Button Gwinnett's heritage, and now even this is in question. John has three lines of evidence that have convinced him that, although Button Gwinnett may have lived on St. Catherines, the house attributed to him was not there before. John is sure that, " C. M. Keyes and his wife started the myth that the big house on St. Catherine's belonged to Button Gwinnett when they had the house restored in 1929-1930."

The renovation began shortly after the 150th anniversary of the signing of the *Declaration of Independence,* which prompted a renewed interest in Button Gwinnett. John is so sure of this that he issued me a challenge: find a mention of the Button Gwinnett house earlier than 1929, when the Keys began their renovation and sowed the seeds of the myth by referring to it as the Button Gwinnett house. "I can find nowhere that the house is called the Button house before 1929." He goes on to say,

> My grandfather, John Rogers, and his two sons bought fish from the black
> people on St. Catherines all through the 1920s. They never referred to the
> house as being the Button Gwinnett house. At that time, it was mostly
> referred to as the hunting house or the old house and it's where the hunters
> who were guests of the Rauers stayed while hunting deer and other animals.
> The huge magnolia tree on the north side of the house with a large limb
> parallel to the ground was where the hunters cleaned their game.

In 1905, an article in the *Atlanta Constitution* pictured the purported Button Gwinnett house with the caption, "Overseer's Residence." The article goes on to state that,

> The old Waldburg home, constructed of tabby, was relegated to the use of
> the island's overseer after the estate was obtained by Mr. Rauers, and the
> new owner built a handsome house at the north end of the island, and had
> beautiful grounds laid out by a landscape gardener (AC 1905c:8).

Charles Francis Jenkins (1926), who was the first true authority on Gwinnett, planted the seeds of the myth when he went searching for Gwinnett's dwelling on St. Catherines. Jenkins (1926:43) wrote,

> It is not if this dwelling was the home of Button Gwinnett, but it was undoubtedly the location of his home. There are no dates on the buildings and no one apparently knows when they were constructed. Most of the buildings look old enough to date back to Gwinnett's time, and in the absence of proof to the contrary, it is the writer's opinion that this was, at least, the site of Gwinnett's home on the island of St. Catherines.

Looking "old" and the "absence of proof to the contrary" are not valid criteria for making such an assessment. In addition, Jenkins may not have been an objective observer. Charles Francis Jenkins and his brother, Arthur H. Jenkins, were nephews of Wilmer Atkinson founder of *Farm Journal*. Both of the Jenkins brothers worked for the corporation (McMillem Ms). Jenkins's biography of Gwinnett was one of his many projects. He had collected one of the few complete sets of autographs of the signers of the *Declaration of Independence*. On his Germantown estate, he developed one of the largest collections of hemlock species. In his garden he constructed the Signers' Walk (Jenkins 1946), which included a stone from the home of each of the signers of *The Declaration of Independence*. Jenkins was especially interested in getting a memorial for Button Gwinnet, since it was the last stone needed to complete the Signer's Walk (Jenkins ND).

Jenkins made a concerted effort to get material from St. Catherines, and was specifically interested in "tabby, a cement block made of oyster shell" from one of "the ruins of the slave houses…" (Jenkins ND). As early as 1939, Jenkins wrote to Rauers Cunningham (Jenkins 1939a; Jenkins 1939b; Jenkins 1941) requesting a stone from St. Catherines. While Cunningham wrote that he would send the stone (Cunningham 1939) and any other relic that Jenkins might want, he never sent the stone. In his account, Jenkins was disappointed. Jenkins (Jenkins ND) wrote,

> Mr. Rauers Cunningham, a representative of the Rauers family in Savannah, has made numerous promises to get me a stone. At one time, I mailed him $5.00 bill to give to his colored superintendent for boxing and trouble but Mr. Cunningham never said "boo."

Jenkins renewed his interest in securing a memorial from St. Catherines after its purchase by Edward J. Noble (Jenkins 1943a; Jenkins 1943b; Jenkins 1943c). He met with success when Noble agreed to send a stone (Noble 1943a), and Toby wrote to Jenkins that a 254-pound stone (SALR 1943) was on its way. John said that the 12 x 12 x 24-inch block was from the foundation of the Rauers' mansion that was torn down by the Keys. Jenkins desire to find a memorial suggests that he may not have been an objective observer in his assessment of the Gwinnett house.

John's mother – who lived on Colonels Island for most of her life, spent many years on St. Catherines, knew the Rauers and Oemlers, and had many friends in the black community – told John, in private, that the big house was never referred to as the Button Gwinnett house by herself or her black friends. His mother mentioned that only after the Keys purchased St. Catherines was it referred to as the Button Gwinnett house. Other frequent visitors to St.

Catherines were silent on Button Gwinnett's house as a presence on the island. John cited Marmaduke Floyd (1937:16) as evidence when he said,

> Miss Julia , who lived on Colonels Island until 1935 or 1936 across from St. Catherines, 'stated that her uncles were frequent guests of Mr. Waldburg and often visited the 'Mary Musgrove house.'[17] They were interested in "its unusual construction" of wattle work and lime plaster with wide piazzas that stood until about 1860.

Miss King related that Waldburg, "was positive in his identification of that house, as well as of numerous other places of historical interest on the island and there was never mention of a Button Gwinnett house."

John provided evidence of earlier sources referring to the house as the Waldburg's residence. In the *Early Days on the Georgia Tidewater*, Buddy Sullivan (1990:313) refers to the November 1863 passage of the Navy ship *The Seneca* when naval surgeon, Dr. Samuel Boyer, was quoted saying, "We are passing the Waldburg Mansion on the island passage." John noted that Jacob Waldburg's home was on the northwest coast of St Catherines, overlooking the island waterway. There was no mention of Gwinnett.

Gwinnett's enterprises on St. Catherines did not prosper. He spent a great deal of time at Sunbury, and was deeply involved with the politics of the independence movement. During that time, he was heavily in debt and building a house would have been an additional burden. It is difficult to imagine that he would have had time to build the house attributed to him. I asked John where he thought Gwinnett lived when he moved to the island. John said that the Musgrove house would have been the most likely place.

There are also structural inconsistencies that would argue against Button Gwinnett having built the house that now bears his name. John said that, "the rafters in the big house are the same style as the ones in the tabby horse barn and the wall-to-wall support rod that spans the width of the big house are the same as in the Cotton Gin building.[18] These links suggest that these buildings were constructed during the Waldburg era, a fact that is especially important to John's argument.

John shared this conclusion with Robert Groover who wrote a history of Liberty County. John recalls,

> In 1991, Groover wrote in the *Coastal Courier* [19] that it was only after a myth began in this century that the big house on St. Catherines belonged to Button Gwinnett. Frank McCall, a gentleman from Moultrie, Georgia who was famous for restoring old houses, was the architect on the big house when it was restored in the early 1970s. He told me, privately, that the house did not date back far enough to belong to Button Gwinnett.

Earlier, Groover (1987:10) claimed that Gwinnett lived in the Bosomworth (Musgrove) house. If Button Gwinnett did not build the house, then who did? John's research shows that the Waldburgs were the most likely builders. In *Georgia's Disputed Ruins* (Coulter 1937), Marmaduke Floyd (1937:46) states that that most of the tabby construction on St. Catherines dates back to the Waldburg ownership. In 1829, the Musgrove-Bosomworth house was still standing (White 1849:379),

> Twenty years since, the mansion in which Bosomworth and his queen resided
> was standing. It was singular in its construction and appearance, being
> wattled with hickory twigs, and plastered within and without with mortar
> made of lime and sand and surrounded by spacious piazzas.

John seems particularly disturbed by the incorrect attribution of the "big" house as the Button Gwinnett house, and by the fact that the myth has become perceived as reality. I did a quick Google search and found that he was correct. Most interesting was an obituary posted from the *Savannah News* reporting the death of Mrs. Gladys Hall Chapman, age 90, on January 8, 2006. Mrs. Chapman was the mother of Ben Chapman, a cousin and lifelong friend of John. It states that, "She was a native of Emanuel County, moving to Vidalia in 1981 and was a retired caretaker of the Button Gwinnett House on Saint Catherines Island." John spoke frequently of Mrs. Chapman, his aunt, who was affectionately known as Snooker. Her son, Ben, was John's friend and he described him as a "brother to me."

I found other references to the Button Gwinnett house on St. Catherines in my Google search. The St. Catherines Sea Turtle Conservation Program's history of the island mentions the renovation of the Button Gwinnett house. It states that,

> Extensive renovations accomplished between 1929 and 1931, with the
> raising of the Rauers house and renovation of the Button Gwinnett[20] House
> and current scientific compound before the Great Depression terminated
> further development.

Even with convincing evidence that Button Gwinnett did not live in the Button Gwinnett house, will it change how his alleged ownership of the house is viewed? We are not likely to see an abandoning of the myth. We have unimpeachable sources maintaining that there are no likenesses of Gwinnett. Yet pictures that were originally labeled as "an artist's conception"[21] or "suppositive portraits" (Robertson 1946)[22] have now become "authentic." That is how history is written and rewritten.

Epilogue

In this chapter, John said "that is all there is to say about Button." Well, that is not exactly the case. I remember a number of conversations when John would provide me with more tidbits about Button, the dog. He sang his praises as an exceptional squirrel hunter. At the time, I had assumed that a dog adept at hunting raccoons would be a good squirrel dog. I now know that is not the case. Some dogs do raccoons and some dogs do squirrels, but Button did both. John recounted, "I remember the day we buried Button. My family was there and there wasn't a dry eye among us." He said that even though more than sixty years had passed, "I can take to you the spot where we buried him and we could dig up his bones if we wished." I was struck by the incredible irony. Button Gwinnett, a statesman with a marked grave, was lost for many years. Button, a dog buried by 15-year-old John Toby Woods in an unmarked grave, remains known to him more sixty years later.

4

Mary Musgrove and the Reverend Bosomworth: Life on St. Catherines Island, 1680-1782

It is a myth that Button Gwinnett built the house on St. Catherines that bears his name. Yet, the search for the myth's origin is as elusive as the search for Gwinnet's bones. The lack of Gwinnett's worldly remains likely fueled acceptance of even the flimsiest claims by Georgians seeking to reconstruct the state's history. Therefore, it is not surprising that the "Gwinnett House" became a shrine commemorating the founding of the Republic and Gwinnett's link to St. Catherines.

The assertion that Gwinnett built the big house on St. Catherines lies in stark contrast to

the paucity of his material legacy. His thirty or so known signatures on existing documents carry a commanding price. Putting on my anthropologist's hat, there are a number of issues to address. Why does holding a piece of paper with a signature hold such power? There is a widely held belief that inanimate objects have power because someone has touched them. The mere fact that Gwinnett signed the document imbues it with a special "force." The value of the autograph is simply an economic matter of supply and demand. Gwinnett lived hard and died young. Since there are so few of his signatures available, the price has risen dramatically.[1]

The irony of this fixation on Gwinnett is that it overshadows the contributions of Mary Musgrove and her ties to the island and its history. In reality, Mary Musgrove's role in establishing the Georgia Colony was a substantial contribution to making of the South and the nation. Her ownership of St. Catherines, obtained as a gift from Creek chief Tomochichi, was contested for decades.

Figure 16. Mary Musgrove and the Reverend Thomas Bosomworth with 200 Creek Indians confronting Georgia officials in Savannah.

Unraveling the ownership of St. Catherines from the time of Mary Musgrove, the Reverend Thomas Bosomworth and Button Gwinnett is a challenge (Figure 16). After the Spanish abandoned St. Catherines in 1680, the written record of the island's ownership remained silent for half a century (Durham and Thomas 1978). In May 1733, General James Edward Oglethorpe, with Mary Musgrove as his interpreter, signed a treaty in which the Creek Indians[2] ceded the land between Savannah and the Altamaha Rivers, from the ocean to the headwaters of the rivers. The Creek retained St. Catherines and the other nearby Sea Islands for their own use (BevenMs 1733). It was through her work for Oglethorpe and other founders of the Georgia Colony that Mary Musgrove's came to lay claim to St. Catherines and the other Sea Islands. How did this happen?

Mary Musgrove, known as Coosaponakeesa[3] to the Creek, was born in at Creek village at the beginning of 17th century. Her birth resulted from a union between Edward Griffin, an English trader, and a Creek woman who Mary claimed was closely related to the *mico*s, or Creek chiefs. In 1715, when Mary was seven years old, she was taken to Pon Pon[4] in what is now South Carolina. She spent the remainder of her formative years there, learning English and converting to Christianity (Baine 1992; Bosomworth 1747; Jones 1883). Mary Musgrove was a unique character in American history whose persona has assumed mythical proportions on two levels (Baine 1992). On one level she earned her reputation by forging a relationship between the Native Americans and the English. Describing her role as that of a mere interpreter belies her importance, since Mary used her knowledge of both Creek and English to function as a "culture broker" (Braund 1991; Sweet 2005:248).[5] Mary Musgrove became Oglethorpe's interpreter and liaison, and played a crucial role in mediating the interactions between the colonists and the Native Americans (Frank 2004).

On the second level of myth creation, Mary claimed that she was born of royal blood in Coweta Town. Mary said that her mother was a sister to "old Chichilli" and his brother Brims, *micos* whose power base was Coweta Town (Baine 1992:428). According to Baine (1992), she was born in Tuckabachee Town with no direct "blood line" to the *micos*. Mary and her then husband, the Reverend Thomas Bosomworth, created the fiction of royal descent in 1746 or 1747 soon after Oglethorpe left Georgia.[6] The myth of a royal blood line played an important role in the Bosomworths' claim of ownership of St. Catherines, Ossabaw and Sapelo Islands (Baine 1992). Whatever the reality, Mary Musgrove was able to develop an intimate relationship with the Creek leadership in Tuckabachee and Coweta, and received strong support from both groups. The Creek *mico* Malatchi eventually referred to himself "by the paternal line[7]; being the son of the old Emperor Rightful and natural prince of the upper and lower Creek nation," and recognized Mary as a "princess with authority to negotiate over lands"[8] (Juricek 1989: for documents). In a sense, this fiction allowed Mary and the Creek leadership to manipulate the British government's notions of royalty.

Mary Musgrove straddled the worlds of the Creek and the English colonists, and was therefore was well placed to mediate both groups' interests in the Georgia Colony. She was a familiar figure in the Wind Clan[9] at Coweta Town, the Creek Village near Columbus, Georgia, as well as the English settlements. Her understanding of English and Creek culture allowed her to navigate sensitive issues and assist with negotiations between the two groups. Her acceptance in both English and Creek societies positioned her to be seen as advocate for each side. She was able to manipulate issues so that both the Creek and the English saw her as being on "their side," thus ensuring her role as a "culture broker." Musgrove's accomplishments cannot be underestimated, and they attest to her ability to work both sides of her heritage effectively.

With the formation of the Georgia Colony in 1733, John and Mary Musgrove established their position as frontier traders. Their role as interpreters during the negotiations helped expand the Musgroves' business interests. To an extent, the meeting between General Oglethorpe and the Musgroves was inevitable. The Musgroves' trading post, Cowpen, was on the Savannah River where the Tallmadge Bridge now stands, and close to where General Oglethorpe (Figure 17) established the Georgia Colony. Mary Musgrove's service as an interpreter was immediately needed. The Musgroves' influence was so important that John Musgrove accompanied a group of Creeks who traveled with Oglethorpe to England (Figure 19) in

Figure 17. James Oglethorpe. By Alfred Edmund Dyer.

1734[10] (Frank 2004). The Georgia Trustees gave the Musgroves a tract of land on Yamacraw Bluff (Frank 2004), four miles west of Savannah along the Savannah River.[11] When John Musgrove died in 1735, Mary moved Cowpen to Yamacraw Bluff where it soon became the center of the English-Indian deerskin trade.[12]

Given Mary's role, it was essential that she be married. As a trader, interpreter and liaison between the Creek and the English, Mary traveled frequently and often hosted dignitaries. For example, Charles and John Wesley, founders of the Methodist Church in search of potential converts among the Creek Indians, frequently visited. John Wesley even attended the funeral of Ned, Mary Musgrove's last surviving child, in November 1736 (Fisher 1998:81). Being an unmarried woman in this role would have reduced Mary's status and prompted questions about her morality (Gillespie 1997). The fact that she remained a widow for years, a relatively long period for a woman in her position, attests to her power. While a widow, Mary had access to 1400 acres in Georgia and Carolina that would ultimately be inherited by her son (Fisher 1998). According to colonial law at that time, property could only be inherited through the male line.[13] Although Mary had use of the land, she could not sell any of the 1400 acres.

Figure 18. Chief Tomochichi and his nephew.

On March 15, 1737, Mary wed Captain Jacob Matthews, a former indentured servant who served with Oglethorpe's militia, and they established a trading post at Port Venture on the Altamaha River.[14] Mary and Jacob were deeply in debt and considered moving to Carolina to avoid their debtors. However, this was a poor option since she owed Charles Town merchants at least £1000 (Fisher 1998).[15] Later that year, at a dinner attended by Colonial Secretary William Stevens, Chief Tomochichi (Figure 18) granted Mary and Jacob 300 acres near their Yamacraw holdings.[16] This was problematic gift for the Trustees because land could only be transferred to the crown, not to individuals. As an English subject, Jacob could not become a major landholder without government authority, because it would weaken the crown's power. The Trustees had to deal with this situation strategically to avoid offending Mary, who they still depended on and to whom they owed so much.[17]

The Trustees first tried to completely avoid the issue. By 1739, the Trustees relaxed the tenure requirements and allowed women to own Trustee land. Colonist were permitted to inherit up to 2000 acres of land that they would be allowed to lease on a long term basis (Fisher 1998:122). However, as late as 1742, the Matthews were still petitioning to take control of the land granted to them in 1737. After an extended illness, Jacob Mathews died on June 6, 1742 at Cowpen. Adding to these difficult times, Oglethorpe, one of Mary's strongest supporters, left Georgia for the last time on July 1743 and never returned. Mary felt the void after her husband's death and Oglethorpe's departure once the Trustees began reneging on promises made to them.[18]

Popular publications often refer to Mary Musgrove as a "princess" (Todd 1981), or "Empress and Queen of the Upper and Lower Creeks"[19] (Bauer-Mueller 2007; Coulter 1927). From an anthropological perspective, the existence of an empress or queen in Creek culture is unlikely since the concept was not part of their worldview. Mary was likely considered a "beloved woman," one of the most honorific terms in Creek culture. As the Creek leadership became more involved with the Trustees of the Georgia Colony, they begin using terms that gave her (and them) special standing. Titles such as "empress" or "queen" fit the hierarchy of European royalty much better than "beloved woman." As an anthropologist, I learned a lesson about how cultures can adapt by adopting kinship terms that allow them to communicate effectively in cross-cultural situations.

Mary's legendary status was further elevated by an event that shocked the Georgia Colony. On July 8, 1744 at Fort Frederica on St. Simons Island, Mary Musgrove Matthews married the well-known Reverend Thomas Bosomworth. The marriage was met with disbelief by Georgians, many of whom thought it was a joke. Bosomworth, a member of the Church of England, came to the Georgia Colony as a missionary and was the Chaplain for Oglethorpe's regiment. This marriage resulted in a significant rise in Mary's social status (Frank 2004), and the ambitious couple became a formidable team.

In mid-1700, the Creeks were under considerable pressure from unrest between English settlers and other Indian groups and forced a small band of Yamacraw who lived near Savannah to move their village to St. Catherines,[20] which had been reserved for Indian use (Fisher 1998:170). In 1745 the Bosomworths were still trying to get recognition of the land Tomochichi had granted to Mary (Fisher 1998:172). While awaiting a response to their requests, they set up a plantation on St. Catherines in 1745.[21] Bosomworth brought six slaves from Carolina to St. Catherines, incensing the Trustees who were trying to enforce a prohibition of slavery in the colony. Then in 1748, Malatchi, the Lower Creek chief, granted the Bosomworths three islands under his control – Ossabaw, St. Catherines and Sapelo[22] – but reserved fishing, planting and hunting rights on St. Catherines for the Creek. Again, the British responded by claiming that land could only be granted or ceded to other nations. Even with the land ownership in dispute, the Bosomworths offered the land for sale. In 1751, the Trustees amended the laws to allow slavery (Wood 1974; Wood 1984; Wood 2002; Wood and Gray 1976). However, the issues of individual ownership and the 2000-acre limit remained.

By 1748, the Bosomworths had a plantation boat and moved to and from the mainland and St. Catherines. Some claim that they built their house at Persimmon Point and operated from there. John Toby Woods, Jr. has convinced me that the site of their house was instead further to the north on Waldburg Creek, near the house now claimed to be the home of Button Gwinnett. John Woods found a map of coastal Georgia[23] from February 1, 1780 that clearly shows a house in this area attributed to the Bosomworths (Figure 20). Significantly, there is no reference to Gwinnett on the map. A map drawn so close to the date of Gwinnett's notorious death surely would have noted his house if it had existed. The Bosomworths' house, which was still standing in 1860, was a prominent building with an "unusual construction" of wattle work and lime plaster, and had large rooms surrounded by a wide piazza.

In an attempt to resolve the issue of their ownership of St. Catherines, the Bosomworths, led a group of 200 Indians to Savannah in 1749 (Figure 19). This confrontation raised major concerns among the citizens of Savannah and made the Bosomworths a feared couple. The event is immortalized in a well-known print entitled, "The Bosomworths Invade Savannah."[24] It depicts the Reverend Thomas Bosomworth in full religious regalia with Mary at his side and the Creek Indians lined behind them.[25] Mary even traveled to England to plead her case, armed with a document created in 1750 that ceded the land to her. Eventually, in 1754, the Board of Trade referred the case to the courts in Georgia.

On October 14, 1754, the Bosomworths sold a half share of interest in St Catherines, Ossabow, and Sapelo to the London merchant, Isaac Levy, for £1000.[26] Two years later, Bosomworth contacted Levy in Philadelphia to come to Georgia to protect his investment.

Figure 19. James Oglethorpe presenting Yamacraw Indians to the Georgia Trustees in England. Oil by William Vevelst.

Squatters were overrunning St. Catherines,[27] and the original deed was necessary to remove them from the island.

Finally, Governor Henry Ellis was able to convince the Trustees to adopt a plan that would settle the land claims of the Bosomworths. After many petitions and two decades of conflict (1747,[28] 1748,[29] 1750,[30] 1752,[31] 1753[32]), the English had a plan to resolve the conflict. The Colony would pay the Bosomworths £2100 sterling (what they would have obtained from selling Sapelo and Ossabaw), and give them title to St. Catherines. The agreement was finalized on July 24, 1759, and one year later the land was reverted back to Mary Bosomworth. The next day, on June 14, 1760, she conveyed the island to Grey Elliott (Savannah) by trust. This act may have been an attempt to protect the land from claims by Isaac Levy.

Mary died on St. Catherines sometime after 1763.[33] Her exact burial place on the island has not been determined, and her remains have never been found. John Woods believes that she was probably buried near or in what is now known as Mary's Mound. John remembers when

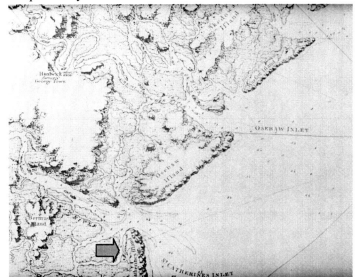

Figure 20. The Des Barres map (1780), showing the location of the Bosomworths' house. In 1780, given the recent death of Button Gwinnett in 1777, his house would have been noted if it existed.

Joseph Caldwell, an archeologist from the University of Georgia, dug a test pit (Todd 1981, pictures the test pit) in the mound and determined that it predated Mary's death. It is possible that Mary, or Coosaponakeesa as she often referred to herself, chose to be buried in an existing Indian burial mound befitting of a person with her status and background.

In 1765, the year that he married Sarah, a chambermaid in his service, Thomas Bosomworth placed an advertisement in the *Georgia Gazette* offering St. Catherines for lease. Button Gwinnett had moved from Charleston to Savannah in October of that year, and he responded to the advertisement

Figure 21. "Suppositive" portrait of Button Gwinnett. There were no known likenesses made during his lifetime. The portraits are fictive representations and were made to enhance autograph collections. National Park Service.

(Figure 21). He obtained St. Catherines from Reverend Bosomworth, his new wife Sarah, and Grey Elliot through a long-term lease. Gwinnett appears to have bought the island on October 30, 1765, and by 1770 he began placing mortgages on the island. As previously mentioned, the question of where Gwinnett lived on the island has become a matter of debate. The romantic view is that he built what is now referred to as the Button Gwinnett house during his ownership of the island. It is more likely, however, that he lived in the Bosomworth house – which by all accounts was an impressive structure. Given his difficulty running the plantation, his political activities, and the lack of labor, constructing the "big" house would have been a formidable task for Gwinnett.

Gwinnett did not succeed in making the plantation profitable. By February 1773, Gwinnett's creditors, led by Alexander Rose from Charleston and Robert Porteus from Beaufort, sold St Catherines for £5250 and used the funds to pay off Gwinnett's debts. The ownership changed a number of times in 1776 and the following year. At least half of St. Catherines' ownership reverted back to Bosomworth, who later returned to St. Catherines with his family. Button Gwinnett died following his duel with McIntosh in May, 1777 (Figure 22). In 1782, Bosomworth was forced to sell land and slaves at a Marshall's sale. He died later that year, although Sarah survived him for a number of years. It is not clear what happened to the estate after Sarah's death.

Durham and Thomas (1978:222) report that a court ordered division of St. Catherines was enforced on February 17, 1786. By July 1, 1797, Owen Owen and David Johnson owned an undivided half interest on St. Catherines comprised of re-confiscated estates from the southern half of the island. Again by court order, half of the island was deeded to John McQueen[34] and one-fourth each to Henry Putnam and Nathan Brownson.[35] On September 4, 1790, Henry Putnam deeded his quarter to Thomas Bourke (Burke). Bourke obtained the northern half of the island from Commissioner of Reverted Estates by January 14, 1796. Alexander Rose, who had purchased the island from Gwinnett, sold his interest to Anthony White and eventually the land was confiscated. On November 26, 1799, Ardanus Burke (Bourke) deeded one-fourth of the north end of St. Catherines. These changes set the stage for the transformation of the island into the region's largest plantation growing Sea Island cotton with enslaved populations.

Figure 22. This lithograph is a fanciful depiction of the Gwinnett- McIntosh duel. Probably by Ferris and published in William Brotherhead's *Book of the Signers*.

5

The Plantation Years:
Sea Island Cotton, Enslavement, and the Waldburgs

Thomas Bourke conveyed some holdings on St. Catherines to John Morel and others. On July 9, 1800 executors of the Bourke estate conveyed the northern half to Jacob Waldburger. Owen Owen owned the southern half. In March 1802, Owen Owen laid a conflicting claim through John Milledge the executor of Waldburger's estate. By 1812 the Waldburgs owned the entire island.

The Waldburgs

Jacob Waldburger (Waldburg), originally from South Carolina, was a rather obscure figure in Georgia history and was difficult to track. In many instances, it was necessary to determine whether we were dealing with the father or the son. To add to the confusion, there were different ways of spelling the surname. Waldburg was previously spelled Waldburger; the – 'er' was dropped by Jacob Waldburger's children. Waldburger's sons built on their father's purchase of St. Catherines to produce the greatest transformation in the island's history, and it was a challenge to determine when the sons began their control of St. Catherines. Finally, there was the matter of Jacob's brother George, who shared ownership of the island but is rarely mentioned despite his active role in the political and economic affairs of Savannah. George M. Waldburg had a son, George M. Waldburg Jr., who was born in 1822 but never married.

One of the elder Jacob Waldburger's major claims to fame was his relationship with James Jackson (Foster 1960; Lamplugh 1989; Lamplugh 2006), who was described as Savannah's most famous duelist (Gamble 1923). Although he is better known for his "political career studded with duels and bloody street brawls (Lamplugh 2006)," Jackson was an astute politician that left his mark on Georgia for decades after his death (Figure 23). He was a revolutionary war hero, the leader of the Jeffersonian party in Georgia, a United States Senator, and a Governor of the State of Georgia. Jackson was also a leader in rescinding the Yazoo Act, which sold 35,000,000 acres of the western frontier, included what is now Alabama and Mississippi, for $500,000. Jackson resigned from the U.S. Senate so that he could return to Georgia to fight what he considered a land give away. He was later elected to the Georgia legislature, where he skillfully overturned the Yazoo Act.

Regarding duels, Jackson was said to have declined only one challenge, and that was from Jacob Waldburger. Waldburger was placed in Jackson's law office in 1783 and lived with his family during the four years that he was training to be a lawyer (Green 2001). After completing his practice, Waldburger seemed to "turn on" his mentor. He claimed that Jackson's combative style offended too many Georgians. In the course of his movement away from Jackson, Waldburger began embracing Jackson's enemies. Jackson viewed this as a betrayal.

Rather that confronting Waldburger with a challenge to a duel, Jackson chastised him in a series of newspaper letters signed Gracchus.[1] The practice of anonymous public debate in the newspapers was a common practice at that time. Jackson characterized Waldburger as "a little boy" who he provided with "the best of my house," and who repaid him by joining, "with a little a (political) party to break my character and reputation (Gamble 1923:55)." Waldburger was incensed and wrote that since Jackson had, "utterly refused to receive a challenge, or give me that satisfaction due one gentleman to another, I therefore pronounce General James Jackson an ASSASIN of reputation AND A COWARD (Gamble 1923:55). The debate continued until Waldburger was near death, but it never reached the level of physical confrontation.[2] Gamble claims that this was the only time that Jackson refused to respond to a challenge.

In one exchange, Jackson stated that Waldburger was a person of little means when he took him in to train for the law. This characterization was especially offensive for Waldburger, who responded by saying that his mother was a woman of substantial wealth and that his income as a lawyer reached £3000 a year. As a lawyer, he was a wealthy man. After the Revolutionary War (1776-1785), the senior Jacob Waldburg (Waldburgh) and his family were recorded in the history of Bryan County as planters with substantial land holdings. Waldburg had acquired the confiscated 500-acre plantation of Lieutenant John Gordon. The land became part of Waldburg's Cottenham Plantation on Redbird Creek near the Ogeechee River. Jacob Waldburg (listed as Waldburger) married Catharine Millen on August 5, 1790 (Georgia Historical Society 1993b:30).[3] They had two sons, Jacob Waldburg, Jr., born in September 1793, and George Millen Waldburg, born in 1795.

Jacob senior, though in ill health, believed that remarriage was harmful to the children. He instructed his executors – John Morel,[4] John Milledge,[5] Donal (Donald) McLeod and James Jones[6] – to take charge and remove George and Jacob from their mother's care in the event that she remarry. George and Jacob would have to reside in a state at least 500 miles away from their mother, Catharine, and they were not to see their mother unless the four executors agreed. In 1797, Jacob Waldburg succumbed to tuberculosis (Gamble 1923:56) and died in the Bahamas. The care of the children and their mother was placed in hands of the executors.

The children were sent away while Catharine remained in Savannah and the executors controlled their spending. For example, Catharine would go to a merchant and purchase something and the merchant would have to bill the estate. Catharine Millen Waldburg eventually remarried. John H. Morel (Georgia Historical Society 1993b:59) who was an executor of the estate,[7] in June, 1803. Thirty-six year old Catharine Morel was married to Morel less than five years when she died from consumption[8] on January 6, 1809 (Georgia

Figure 23. James Jackson. Courtesy the Hargett Rare Book and Manuscript Library. University of Georgia Libraries.

Historical Society 1984).[9] She died at her townhouse in Heathcote Ward, and her remains were conveyed to and deposited in the country (Georgia Historical Society 1984: 56).[10] Morel married Sarah M. Alger, a widow, on November 11, 1812 (Georgia Historical Society 1993a:69).

John H. Morel was George and Jacob Waldburg's stepfather for six years. Morel played an infamous role in American history. He was a Navy Agent in 1818 (NWR 1819:23) and United States Marshall for the District of Georgia for a four-year term beginning in January 1818. Although John Quincy Adams and President James Monroe had reservations about Morel, he was reappointed for another term in 1822. Morel, described as a "coarse" character (Noonan 1977:43), was an independent force who was "a thorn in the side of two presidents, James

Monroe and John Quincy Adams…" but was appointed for a term by each of them (Orren 1998:351). It was his role as a Marshall that led to his infamy.

It began on June 29, 1820, when federal agents aboard the U.S. revenue cutter *The Dallas,* under the command of John Jackson, spotted a ship off the coast of the northern coast of Florida. The agents boarded the ship, *The Antelope*, and found 300 Africans held in chains for sale as slaves (Noonan 1977).Congress had made the importation of slaves illegal in 1808.[11] On March 2, 1819, Congress reinforced the prohibition of slave importation with the "Act in Addition to the Acts Prohibiting the Slave Trade." Jackson was acting on this legislation, which gave the President the authority to apprehend slaver traders, and remove and protect their captives so that they could eventually be repatriated to Africa. With the capture of *The Antelope*, the enslaved individuals were brought to Savannah and were placed in the custody of Morel. Savannah, known for its sympathy for slavery, had a population of 7000 at that time, half of whom were enslaved individuals. Morel was a ruthless hater of Africans who had been accused of the "most atrocious" murder of a Negro.

Morel's treatment of the slaves was well known. He was a brutal "protector" who worked some of the captives on his own plantation and putting them to work on public projects for the city of Savannah, all while charging the United States for their upkeep. Their treatment under the protection of the U.S. Government was no different from that of enslaved individuals working the plantations. In October 1822, Eleazar Early, Postmaster of Savannah, went to Washington and relayed his concerns about Morel's behavior to another Southerner, John Calhoun, Secretary of War. Though Early did not have "hard evidence," his accusations were taken seriously enough that Adams relayed them to a meeting of the President's cabinet (Noonan 1977:79),

> … The Marshal for the District of Georgia was now accumulating a fortune of at least thirty thousand a year by working a number of African negroes who are in his possession as Marshal of the District, while at the same time he is making the most enormous charges against the public for maintenance of the very same negroes; that he makes it his own boast that he holds the office of Marshal for no other purpose and that he intends to *swamp* the negroes—that is, to work them to death—before they be finally adjudicated out of his possession. Mr. Early adds that his cruelty to negroes is universally known [and] that he did commit the murder of the black man for which he was tried and acquitted. The principal witnesses against him were *spirited* away. Early declares himself to be of the same political party with Marshal (Crawford's),[12] but is so horror-struck at the character and conduct of the man that he feels it to be his duty to denounce him.

Despite his tarnished reputation and questions about his moral authority, Morel was appointed by two United States presidents. In his diary, Secretary of State John Quincy Adams described Morel as having, "the ineffaceable stain of blood upon his hands." Yet, neither Adams nor Madison was willing to stand up to him.

The constitutionality of the law making the slave trade an act of privacy eventually reached the Supreme Court and the case was decided in 1825. John Marshal wrote a well-crafted opinion for the majority that addressed the immorality of slavery, and claimed that although the slave trade was no longer legal in the United States, the U.S. was bound to accept the laws of other nations. As the case moved slowly through the judicial system, politics was always a consideration. The case was delayed by a concern to maintain support for the Missouri compromise and the opinion was written to satisfy those on both sides of issue (Johnson 1997; Smith 1996; Smith 2001).

After more than 2500 days in Morel's custody, 120 of the Africans had died, two were missing, 39 were enslaved in the United States, and 142 were released and repatriated to Liberia on June 18, 1827. Many of those repatriated took the names of individuals who were important participants in the case. Peter Habersham,[13] July Habersham, Edward Berrin,[14] George Marshall,[15] and even a Boston Walburg[16] were sent to Liberia. Even with all of his problems, John H. Morel was again nominated for another term as U.S. Marshall. This time, President Andrew Jackson made the nomination on January 15, 1834. Only in death was John H. Morel removed as Marshall of Georgia. He died on June 3, 1834 of "gout"[17] (Georgia Historical Society 1989:17),[18] and was buried in Colonial Park cemetery in Savannah.

The Waldburgs on St. Catherines

By 1812, the Waldburgs owned all of St. Catherines. On land well suited for growing indigo, rice and cotton, the War of 1812 made cotton king. The war cut off the supplies of cotton imported from England, and the South was ready to fill the void. St. Catherines' environment is ideally suited for the long fiber cotton that was in demand and sold at a premium price, and the island soon became an important source of cotton. The labor-intensive demands of cotton spawned the institution of enslavement, and the Waldburgs soon possessed the largest number of enslaved individuals in Liberty County.

While the war would eventually make cotton king and the Waldburgs even wealthier planters, it did disrupt their lives in some instances. Sixty-one years after the War of 1812, J.H.C (J.H.C. 1873:6) relates an account providing insight into life on St. Catherines,

> Two young gentlemen of wealth and intelligence (Jacob and George
> Waldburg) owned a major portion of St. Catherine's Island, where they
> cultivated an extensive cotton plantation. They were exceedingly
> hospitable-kept bachelors' ball- and were frequently visited by friends from
> Savannah and other points on the mainland, who would spend days
> together, boating and fishing. While entertaining a party of gentlemen in a
> most sumptuous manner, on the 4th of July, 1814, they were suddenly
> interrupted by the landing of two barges within fifty yards of their
> residence. No alternative was left them but to scamper to the thickets, which
> fortunately was near at hand – leaving their hot dinner steaming on the
> board. The British helped themselves bountifully, not only to dinner, but to
> the French brandy and wines which they found on hand; under the influence
> they committed acts of vandalism, *approaching* those perpetuated by the
> Yankee cousins in the late war-with the differences in favor of the British,
> that they did not burn down the house in which they found such good fare,
> nor destroy the provisions, nor steal the silver spoons. The only harm they
> did was the breaking of some crockery and glassware, and hacking elegant
> tables with their swords. This was bad enough in all conscience and it was
> said they sent an apology to the Waldburgs for their unsoldierly conduct.

During that time there was a concerted effort to establish a church for the enslaved populations, but this was opposed by the Waldburg or their agents. George D. Sweet (1815:4) from The Great Ogeechee Church[19] wrote to his missionary board of success in establishing a church on St. Catherines "after much opposition,"

> *First Lord's day in May, 1814.* Having had a call to preach on the Island of
> St. Catherines some time ago, the Lord was graciously pleased to pour out
> his spirit and this morning the Lord opened the hearts of many, who gave
> strong evidence of converting grace; the ordinance of baptism was
> administered to *twenty-eight* hopeful converts, and a church was planted
> here, after much opposition.

In 1819, George and Jacob were reported to have divided property that was part of their father's estate. The division of the property awaited George Waldburg's return to Savannah following his studies at Princeton. He received a Master of Art degree conferred on September 29, 1820 (American 1820). The property in Savannah was worth about $12,500 for each brother. Two years later (1821), Jacob Waldburg married Elizabeth Lawrence Higbe who he had met in Trenton, New Jersey. The Waldburgs built a home on the corner of Barnard St. and South Broad Street (now Oglethorpe) and lived there for the next 50 years. The house was considered one of Savannah's most impressive mansions (Harden 1969). The Norton house, as it was then known, was described as,

> ... an example of that substantial style of architecture used by men of
> wealth in a former age, when timber was plentiful, and veneer was
> unknown. The walls of the house are more than two feet thick, and the brick
> of which it is built is all rosined as are the hardwood floors. The ceilings,
> walls, partitions and other inside woodwork are all of the costliest and most
> durable materials. The interior furnishings, decorations and the wonderful
> chandeliers were all imported from Europe and most of these still remain to
> add to the artistic beauty of the house itself. A delightful garden on the
> Barnard street side of the house is in keeping with the rest, and on the west
> side is another garden which affords a charming playground for the
> children. The property has one hundred and twenty feet of frontage on
> Oglethorpe Avenue, and from a financial standpoint is one of the most
> valuable in the city. The house is built with two stories and a basement,
> containing many rooms of the generous proportions that our ancestors
> enjoyed. It cost $55,000 and required three years and a half in building.

The home on West Oglethorpe anchored Jacob Waldburg's and his family's social life in Savannah. A daughter, Elizabeth Lewis Waldburg, was born in 1825 and spent most of her life at the house in Savannah. As a child she was said to have spent considerable time on St. Catherines. George M. Waldburg, named for his father, was born on July 26, 1822.[20]

On August 6, 1826, the brothers divided St. Catherines. They both held the northern part of the island in common. George maintained hunting and timber rights on the south of the "pasture fence."[21] C. Powers, the surveyor of the island, was assigned to resolve any conflict that the brothers may have had. In 1830, the Waldburg estate with Thomas Olden[22] as agent (Anon.

1924)[23] was listed as a plantation with an absentee planter and with 85 enslaved individuals. In the 1830 census,[24] Thomas Olden listed Jacob Waldburg as living on St. Catherines. George M. Waldburg was also listed as residing on the island. Paul H. Wilkins and Mary E. Wilkins were also listed as residents. Jacob was listed as having 79 slaves, and his brother, George, as having 38 slaves. Wilkins was recorded as having 89 slaves[25] (see Figure 24 for an example of the census).

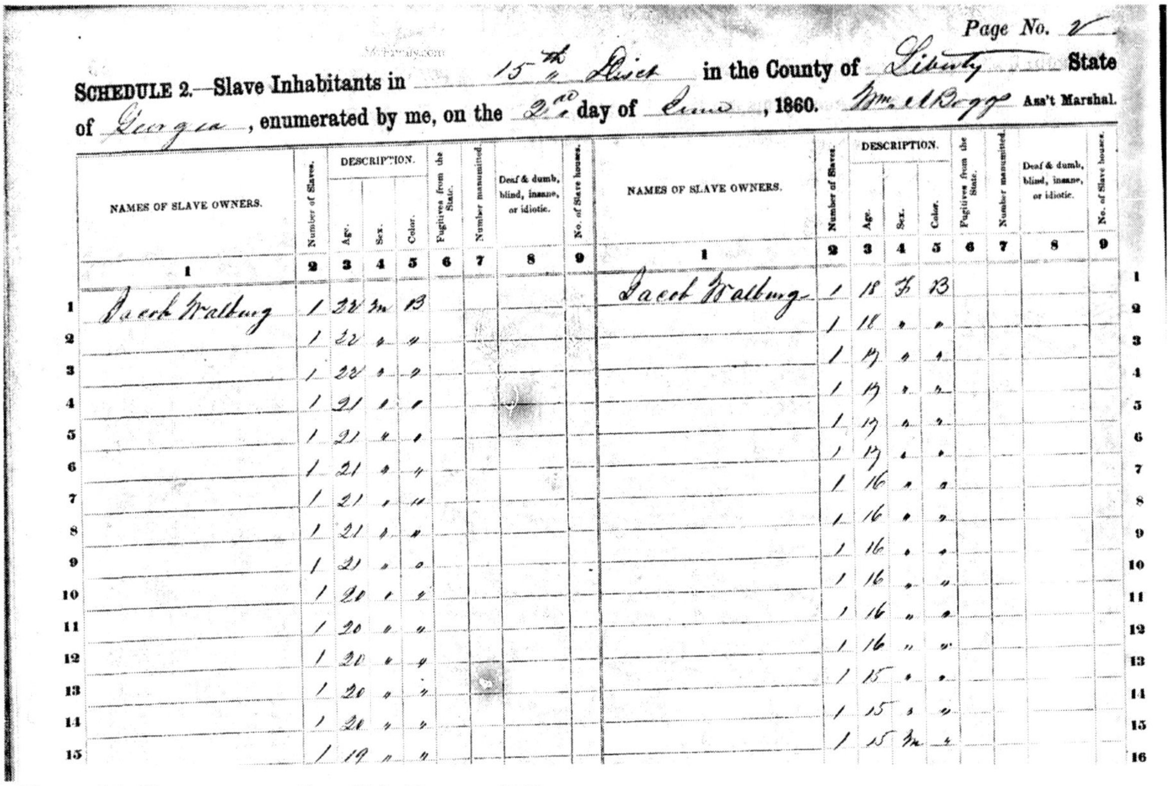
Page No. 2

SCHEDULE 2.—Slave Inhabitants in 15th Dist in the County of Liberty State of Georgia, enumerated by me, on the 2nd day of June, 1860. Wm. el Boggs Ass't Marshal.

	Names of Slave Owners	Number of Slaves	Age	Sex	Color	Fugitives from the State	Number manumitted	Deaf & dumb, blind, insane, or idiotic	No. of Slave houses	Names of Slave Owners	Number of Slaves	Age	Sex	Color	Fugitives from the State	Number manumitted	Deaf & dumb, blind, insane, or idiotic	No. of Slave houses	
	1	2	3	4	5	6	7	8	9	1	2	3	4	5	6	7	8	9	
1	Jacob Waldburg	1	22	m	B					Jacob Waldburg	1	18	F	B					1
2		1	22								1	18							2
3		1	22								1	17							3
4		1	21								1	17							4
5		1	21								1	17							5
6		1	21								1	17							6
7		1	21								1	16							7
8		1	21								1	16							8
9		1	21								1	16							9
10		1	20								1	16							10
11		1	20								1	16							11
12		1	20								1	16							12
13		1	20								1	15							13
14		1	20								1	15							14
15		1	19								1	15	m						15
																			16

Figure 24. Slave enumeration. U.S. Census. 1860.

Durham and Thomas (1978:223) remark that the first fifty years of Waldburg habitation on St. Catherines are relatively cloudy. Furthermore, they claim that the main house and other buildings are from the Gwinnett era.

> Waldburg continued to operate the plantation on St. Catherines' north end, utilizing the tabby house generally considered to have been Gwinnett's home. A regular complex of shop buildings, stables, barns and slave quarters grew in the area using many of the old tabby buildings from Gwinnett's operations...[26]
>
> The south end of the Island was also given over to cotton production. Another complex of buildings, slave quarters, etc., was established and a large "mansion" built, which overlooked the marsh near the intracoastal waterway.

John Woods has never found evidence of a mansion on the south end of St. Catherines. We have surmised that there was some confusion because of the alterations that made to the

Oemler house on the south end. Van Marter (1904:448) provides a description of the South End Plantation in 1904:

> The whole day was one long round of surprises, beautiful views, mingled with unexpected pauses to allow for some more deer shooting, or occasional stops in which to give the negroes a chance to kill another coon. After exploring the southern end and lunching in a grassy field dotted with graceful palmettos, we turned our heads homeward, passing first through a marshy region dotted with hammocks, veritable haunts of deer, and, I regret to add, of snakes; thence, climbing up on high ground, we traveled what had once been cultivated land in the golden days, now overgrown, but still very pretty; and finally reached the ruins of the old South End Plantation house and the adjacent slave houses.

Van Marter's photograph clearly indicates the tabby plantation house (Figure 25) that was later used by the African Baptist Church until 1930 (Durham and Thomas 1978a:238). Waldburg's two plantations dramatically changed the landscape of St. Catherines. In 1850, Jacob Waldburg had 119 slaves and was taxed on 2000 acres; George Waldburg had 97 slaves. George Waldburg died on St. Catherines on August 5, 1856 of "congestive chills,"[27] and left his entire estate to his brother Jacob. His son, George M. Waldburg, Jr. died nine years earlier on July 28, 1847. The

Figure 25. Old "tabby" slave houses with adjacent "plantation house" (VanMarter 1904:446). John Woods indicates that from this description, it appears that they took the southern exit off South Beach Road across Fiddlers Flat (the marshy region dotted by hammocks) just south of Uncle Aaron's house and the turned north, presenting the view seen above.

probated will[28] listed assets totaling $51,955.00, which included 92 slaves individually valued between $5.00 and $900, with a total value of $47,750.00.

After inheriting George's slaves, Jacob controlled 255 slaves on land valued at $193,000 (Duncan 1986:4), and an estate valued at $383,000 (Duncan 1986: 28). On the northern end of the island, Waldburg built the "big" House, frequently referred to in modern times as the Button Gwinnett house,[29] and 21 slave cabins (Figures 27 and 28). He constructed a cotton gin (Figure 26) that attracted the attention of his neighbors on the mainland.[30] The map at the end of the chapter charting the antebellum fields on the island bears testament to the transformation of St. Catherines by Waldburg and the populations he enslaved (Figure 30). There were at least 24 fields, prepared for rice, indigo or cotton, depending on changing market demand.

The Waldburgs' social and political world was centered in the city of Savannah. Jacob's and George's father wanted them to be educated so that they would have meaningful lives. In the 1850s, Jacob served on the board of directors of the Savannah Gas Company. In 1850, he was the Union and Southern Rights[31] Candidate for the Alderman position in Savannah. The next year, he wrote the constitution for the newly formed Chatham Mutual Loan Association. He remained on their board of directors until his death. Jacob was also a strong supporter of the Georgia Historical Society located in Savannah. In addition to the plantations on St. Catherines, Jacob also had a 4300-acre plantation in Lowndes County near Valdosta, Georgia (MWT 1865).

George Millen Waldburg was also an important figure in the political and financial life of Savannah. He had significant stock holdings in the Central Railroad and Banking Company, and the Savannah Gas-Light Company. He served on the grand jury that increased fines for selling liquor to enslaved individuals. In 1853, he began collecting money to help people that caught the fever.[32] As the fever epidemic continued, over 1000 citizens of Savannah perished. George Waldburg solicited donations from merchants and contributed $1000 of his own funds. Waldburg Street in Savannah attests to the community's esteem for the family. George Waldburg's son[33] remains a mystery. It is reported (Georgia Historical Society 1989:255) that a George Waldbourg (Waldburg) was buried on July 29, 1847. He was attended by Dr. Arnold and died from "Dropsy[34] & Dis. Of Heart." at "S. Broad/hethcote." He is buried in the family plot at St. Bonaventure.[35]

Elizabeth Lewis Waldburg, Jacob's daughter, married John

Figure 26. Cotton gin built by the Waldburgs.

Houston McIntosh Clinch on May 31, 1854 (Georgia Historical Society 1993b:322). Clinch was a member of the Duncan L. Clinch family that owned Refuge Plantation on the Santilla River near St. Mary's, Georgia.[36] After graduating from the University of North Carolina in 1844, John Houston McIntosh Clinch returned to operate the rice plantation. After their marriage, the Clinches lived on Refuge Plantation.

The Civil War wreaked havoc for many planters in the South. The plantation owners of the Sea Islands were especially vulnerable. The Confederacy could not defend the Sea Islands, and as early as 1862 the Union Navy was bombarding them, forcing many of the planters to abandon some of the islands when they could not control their slaves. General William Tecumseh Sherman ended his march through Georgia by ravaging the coast.

On January 16,1865, Sherman issued Field Order 15 (Berlin 1990), which he believed would solve the problem posed by a growing number of displaced emancipated Blacks. The Order is better known as the document that gave emancipated slave "40 acres and a mule." It granted the "negro" population "the sole and exclusive management of affairs, subject only to the U.S. military and the laws of U. S. Congress." It also allowed

Figure 27. The ruins of the corn grinding mill and remains of another tabby cabin.

Figure 28. Corn mill with cabin six in the background.

emancipated Blacks to use the abandoned rice populations from the Atlantic Coast up to the Ogeechee and Altamaha Rivers, and the Sea Islands along the Georgia coast. St. Catherines became the capital of the freed slaves, marking a major shift in the island's history and clouding the ownership of St. Catherines.

Tunis Campbell, the leader of freedmen state, is one of the most interesting figures in the history of the South (Drago 1982; Duncan 1986; Duncan 2004). Under Tunis Campbell's leadership, the freed Blacks formed a "separatist democracy with a constitution, a congress, a supreme court and an armed militia" (Cimbala 1989: 601). Campbell was appointed by Rufus Saxton, assistant commissioner for the Freedmen's bureau, to be superintendent of the Sea Islands. Previously, his title was "governor" of Burnside, Ausaba (Ossabaw), St. Catherines, Sapelo, and Colonels Islands (Duncan 1986:20). By April 26, 1865, the St. Catherines government had a constitution, an eight-man senate, a twenty-man house, a judicial system with its own supreme court, and a militia of 275 citizen-soldiers (Duncan 1986:22-23). Tunis Campbell believed that "order is Heaven's first law" (Duncan 1986:22), and was described as a "well meaning and benevolent" "autocrat of the island"[37] (Duncan 1986:23). Campbell believed that the experience of self-government was essential for teaching the freedmen the lessons of democracy, and for preparing them for the right to vote whenever it was given to them.

In June 1865, as Campbell was settling 200 adults and 117 children on St. Catherines, Jacob Waldburg attempted to regain ownership of the island and was rebuffed. In the American Experience series *Reconstruction: The Second Civil War* (Deane and Rios 2004), Smith (2004) claims that Waldburg demanded that Campbell return his land and leave his island Figure 29). Waldburg is portrayed as waving deeds to the island that dated back 150 and 200 years, and shouting that he had a constitutional right to his land and that Tunis Campbell had only "a possessory

Figure 29. Sketch by A. R. Waud (1868) illustrating difficulties faced by Freedmen's Bureau. White planters confront emancipated slaves. Courtesy of the Library of Congress, Print and Photograph Division.

title given…in a time of war for abandoned lands." Campbell gave Waldburg an emphatic answer to his request. The St. Catherines Congress, under Campbell's control, passed a law that forbade any white person from stepping on the soil of the island. The 275-man militia, also under the control of Campbell, was ready to enforce the law and to resist encroachment by whites.

Ultimately, the plantations were returned to their previous owners. The freedmen assumed that they had been given title to the land, but Paul A. Cimbala (1989) notes that Order 15 gave the freedman "possessory title" to enjoy the fruits of their labor but did not give them ownership. After the assassination of President Lincoln in 1866, Andrew Johnson quickly rescinded the Special Field Order 15, allowing Southern plantation owners to reclaim their land. With the assassination of Lincoln, Reconstruction – as it was originally intended – came to an end. Reconstruction, described "as a failure, but a splendid failure," did not officially end, however, until the Presidency of Rutherford B. Hayes in 1877. On June 28, 1865, Waldburg's application to reclaim St. Catherines was approved by the military provost court. The Administrators of the Freedmen's Bureau felt that the court had acted in error and intervened during Waldburg's attempt to return to St. Catherines and reclaim his land. The ruling of the military provost court generated fear among the freed Blacks who would have their land taken away.

On October 19, 1865, Johnson ordered Commissioner Oliver O. Howard to arrange a plan that the planters and the freedmen would find mutually agreeable (Cimbala 1989:608). Andrew Johnson was never considered a friend of black Americans, and showed little concern for the freed black population's welfare. In the spring of 1867, ownership of St. Catherines was restored to Jacob Waldburg (MWT 1867)., but the fight in him was gone. He sold the island, three years later. The *Atlanta Constitution* wrote that St. Catherines was sold to Anna Rodriquez in 1870 for $80,000 and a piece of property in Brooklyn (AC 1905c:8).[38]

Jacob Waldburg filed a will on February 26, 1872 with special provisions for his servants, Charles Morel and Mary Casson. The summer of 1872 was spent in Ritchfield Springs, New York, as was his usual practice. There, on September 2, 1872, Jacob Waldburg died from "diseases of the heart" and his body was returned to Savannah for burial in St. Bonaventure Cemetery (Lot 25 and 26-C) a few days later on September 10.

Elizabeth Higbe Waldburg out-lived her husband by nearly a decade. In 1880, she was living in the house on Oglethorpe with her daughter and son-in-law.[39] Mrs. Waldburg died of "acute pleuritis" on February 17, 1881 and was buried in St. Bonaventure Cemetery (Bonaventure Historical Society 2000: 30).[40] After her death, Elizabeth Waldburg Clinch and her husband John Houston McIntosh Clinch administered the estate. The documents recoding the sale of the St. Catherines from Rodriquez to the Rauers (Liberty County 1876) report that Rodriquez purchased the island from the estate of Elizabeth H. Waldburg (Liberty County 1872). In 1900, Elizabeth and John were still living in the house on Oglethorpe.[41] Elizabeth died in 1903 and was buried in St. Bonaventure Cemetery (Bonaventure Historical Society 2000 253).[42] Her husband died a year later and was buried with his wife.[43]

With the death of Elizabeth Waldburg Clinch, the biological legacy of Jacob and George M. Waldburg came to an end. The material accumulation of their estate, totaling $235,287.15, was given to charity. The Bishop of Georgia Trustees, Fund to Support of Indigent Widows and Orphans of Deceased Clergymen of the Episcopal Diocese of Georgia, Orphans Home, St Paul's Free Episcopal Church and Widows Society each received $39, 214.52 (Cox 1979).

The Interlude between the Waldburgs and the Rauers

There was speculation about the deposition of St. Catherines after its sale to Anna Rodriquez. In April 1869, the *Atlanta Constitution* reported interest in the island from a "small company of capitalists" headed by Signor Joseph Borra, "an intelligent Italian" who was interested in purchasing St. Catherines or another sea island for $5 an acre (AC 1869). The plan was to import Italian workers to the island to initially engage in agriculture, and then "introduce certain manufacturers of great importance to the southern people." Borra was specifically interested in an island since he was concerned about racial mixing and an island would allow for better control of that possibility. Ultimately, Anna Rodriguez sold St, Catherines to Jacob Rauers, a prominent Savannah businessman in 1876.

Figure 30. Antebellum fields after the Waldburgs' tenure on the island. From Durham and Thomas (1978)

6

The Forgotten Century:
The Black Populations on St. Catherines Island from the Bosomworths, to the Waldburgs, to Freedom

When Aaron, Nancy and Eutherle Austin left St. Catherines in 1941, they were the last black family to have lived on St. Catherines. This is a remarkable fact given the history of St. Catherines. For 175 years, black populations – enslaved and freed – were a major presence on the island. Throughout the course of history, from Mary Musgrove and the Reverend Thomas Bosomworth's years of contentious ownership, to Button Gwinnett's short tenure, to the half a century of Waldburg family control, to the rise of Tunis Campbell and the Freedmen State, and finally to 75 years of the post-slavery era, St. Catherines has experienced dramatic changes in the "complexion" and composition of its inhabitants.

The 1930 census (Fifteenth Census of the United States: 1930, Militia District 1359, Liberty County) lists 45-year-old Aaron Austin, his wife Nancy (age 35)[1] and Sussana Jones, a 48-year-old boarder whose occupation was listed as a servant for a private estate. The private island estate had been recently purchased by C. M. Keys, James Willson,[2] and Howard Coffin. Keys proudly announced that the "...island would be used by its owners as a personal playground (AC 1929a:6)." John did not know the number of black families living on the island when the change in ownership occurred. He does remember his father saying that families that were not working for the Keys were not encouraged to remain on the island.

The Keys were in the throes of a major renovation of the buildings on the Island. The superintendent of the renovations, Arthur Wilson,[3] lived with his wife Anna, their four children (Josephine, age 8; John, age 7; Mary, age 5; and Margaret, age 2). A relative, George Wilson, was listed as a boarder and occupied one of the houses on the island. Arthur was supervising the extensive renovation of the main house and the slave quarters. This was a major undertaking, and the renovations were extensive. The project took almost two years to complete, and cost one million dollars.

John's father, John Toby Woods, had married six years earlier and was 29-years-old at the time of the census. Gladys Woods was in her early 20s and had three children in tow. Clel,[4] Gee,[5] and John, who were four, two and four months old, respectively. John Toby was listed as the foreman of the "private estate."

Sea Island Cotton on St. Catherines

There were many events that led to the changes on St. Catherines. The island's ecology was well suited for the planting of Sea Island cotton, but it requires intensive labor. For many years, the South relied on the labor of enslaved populations to meet those demands. The Civil War, emancipation, and Reconstruction had dramatic impacts on the island's population. The final phase in St. Catherines' history was its ownership by wealthy Northerners who considered the island their private playground. The *New York Times* reported that millionaire Northerners, with the exception of Jacob Rauers[6] (NYT 1892), now owned of all the Atlantic Coast islands, where, *The Times* said, " they have their own boats, horses, dogs, and clubhouses, and live in elegant style."

The Beginnings

For many tumultuous years, Mary and Thomas Bosomworth petitioned for recognition of their ownership of the land at Yamacraw. In 1745, they moved livestock and Indian and black slaves to St. Catherines and established a plantation.[7] The Trustees of the Georgia Colony were not happy with their relocation to the island, and were even less pleased that the Bosomworths had brought six Negro and a number of Indian slaves to St. Catherines (Fisher 1990: 183). According to Braund (1991), the Creek practiced the enslavement of both Native Americans and Africans prior to the founding of the Georgia Colony.[8] As the colony became more well established and the prohibition against slavery was repealed, the Creek's view of slavery began to evolve into that of the planters.

Button Gwinnett purchased St. Catherines from Reverend Thomas Bosomworth in 1765. Still in debt from his position as a merchant, he relied on credit to purchase[9] the island and to purchase six or seven slaves to work the land. Months before he acquired St. Catherines, the Colonial Council meeting in Savannah tied the granting of land to the ability to exploit it (Jenkins 1926:26). Grants of 50 acres could be secured for each family member or "Negro" to work the land. In 1766, Gwinnett petitioned the Council and received 800 acres of land, claiming himself, his wife and child, and 14 Negroes as evidence of his ability to exploit the land. Three years later, claiming that he had 25 Negroes, he petitioned for an additional 1,450 acres and was granted 1,350 acres (Jenkins 1926:47).[10] Faced with rising debt, Gwinnett mortgaged six enslaved[11] individuals, and a few months later he was forced to sell eight of them.[12] By February 1773, Gwinnett was forced to sell his interest in the island for £5250.

Waldburg and St. Catherines

Jacob Waldburg[13] became the owner of one of the largest populations of enslaved individuals in Liberty County. At a time when land was relatively cheap, wealth was measured by the number of enslaved people owned a by a planter. On July 9, 1800, Waldburg was listed as owner of the northern half of St. Catherines.[14] In 1812, the Waldburgs purchased the southern half of the island from David Johnson. Jacob Waldburg, Sr. had been dead for 15 years, and his wife for three years, when this transaction took place. Is it possible that his children executed these transactions? In 1812, Jacob, Jr. would have been 19-years-old and his brother George was 17-years-old. The transaction was likely undertaken by the executor of their father's estate. It is possible that Jacob, Jr. was a precocious businessman at age 19, but that is unlikely. Jacob and George had to wait until 1819 before receiving property from their father's estate. It was not until August 6, 1826 that the brothers divided St. Catherines. They shared parts of the northern end of the Island. George Waldburg retained hunting and timber rights in the southern end, south of the "pasture fence."[15] By the middle of the century, the Waldburg brothers had amassed major land resources on the back of an enslaved population.

The 1851 tax digest from Liberty County (Groover 1987:146) shows that Jacob Waldburg was assessed on his 2000 acres of land and 120 slaves, making him as one of the largest slave holders in Liberty County. T. B. Barnard had the same number of slaves,[16] but G. W. Walthour (233), Joseph Lane (192), and Roswell King, Jr. (167) each owned more enslaved individuals than Waldburg.

Liberty County enumerated the enslaved individuals owned by each planter. The 1850 slave schedule[17] lists the race, age and gender of each individual. This nameless list reflects the role that slavery played in Southern society. Their labor was the only concern, and a record of who they were as individuals was of little interest. The slave schedule for Jacob Waldburg listed 119 individuals,[18] equally divided by gender (60 females and 59 males). Nearly thirty percent (29.4%) of the group was under 15 years of age, and 4.2% were over 60 years of age. Individuals between 15 and 60 years of age represented 65.5% of the population. George M. Waldburg, who shared ownership of St. Catherines with his brother Jacob, had 97 enslaved individuals listed in the 1850 slave schedule.[19] George M. Waldburg's slaves schedule included 57 females (59%) and 40 males (41%). Of the total, 36.1% were under age 15, 55.7% were between ages 15 and 60, and 8.2% were 60 years or older. George died in 1856 and left his entire estate to his brother Jacob. The probated will[20] totaled $51,955.00, and included 92 slaves valued between $5.00 and $900 with a total value of $47,750.00.

The 1860 slave census[21] showed that Jacob Waldburg had accumulated 255 enslaved individuals (128 females and 127 males). Not counting the 92 inherited enslaved individuals he inherited from his brother, Jacob acquired an additional 44 individuals. The segment of the population under 15 years of age was 45.9%, and those 65 years or older make up only 2.4% of the population. The group between 15 and 65 years of age comprised 51.7 % of the group. There was a 211% increase in the number of enslaved individual in the decade between the two censuses. Eighty-four percent of the increase can be attributed to his inheritance. The segment of the population under 15 years of age increases from 29.4% to 45.9%, indicating an increase in the reproductive growth of the population.

Both immediately before and after the Civil War, St. Catherines and the other Sea Islands experienced an influx of freed Blacks. As war approached St. Catherines, Waldburg moved to the mainland with his "slaves." Mohr (1979) states that by the spring of 1862, the Union naval guns forced the owners off their islands. Many of the slaves sought refuge on St. Catherines, and Waldburg, unhappy with this turn of events, tried to retrieve them. The New York Times (E.P.B. 1862) reported,

> There was quite a commotion on St. Catherine's Island, near which was then our station,[22] last week, on account of a rebel raid among the darkies. An overseer of Mr. Waldburg, who owns the island, came over in the night for the purpose of securing some of his valuable hands, whom he supposed had escaped from the mainland to their former home on the island. After shooting two, and wounding another who tried to escape, they captured four of the most likely ones and left.

The same report described the influx of Blacks to St. Simons Island.

> On this island (St. Simons) there are about 500 fugitives, with constant additions from the mainland who are governed by an army captain whose headquarters are at the mansion of T. Butler King. He has a large number of acres under cultivation and has established schools where the ideas of young darkies are taught to shoot. A large part of the exercise seems to consist in singing the celebrated song, in which it is promised to hang JEFF. DAVIS on

a sour apple tree.

There were reports in the Northern press that St. Catherines was abandoned by the Confederate Army on November 21, 1862 (Liberator 1862).[23] Two Negroes that refused to go with the rebels were shot. The influx continued during the war, and once the war ended the island was reserved for the enslaved individuals that had been emancipated.

St. Catherines as the Capital of Freed Blacks

With the onset of the Civil War, it became more difficult to control the slaves and as early as 1861 the Waldburgs became vulnerable on St. Catherines (Mohr 1979). By the spring of 1862, guns from the Union Navy forced the planters, overseers and most of the enslaved people off of the island and onto the mainland. However, the Sea Island plantations became a refuge for Blacks escaping enslavement (Cimbala 1989:598; Mohr 1979). Towards the end 1864, General William Tecumseh Sherman ended his march through Georgia by ravaging its coastal region. On January 16,1865, Sherman issued Field Order 15 (Berlin 1990), which granted the "negro" population "the sole and exclusive management of affairs, subject only to the U.S. military and the laws of U. S. Congress," and the use of abandoned rice plantations from the coast up the Ogeechee and Altamaha rivers and the Sea Islands. Special Field Order 15 was said to promise forty acres and a mule to each of the freed Blacks.[24] Sherman appointed Brigadier General Rufus Saxton (Figure 31) to execute and administer the Order, and to establish the Freedmen's Bureau. He and his assistant, Brigadier General David Tillson, were deeply committed to the program and believed that it would transform the economic prospects of the emancipated Blacks in the South. Saxton believed that once the freedmen were given their 40 acres, they would prosper. Tillson believed that their ticket to prosperity was as wage laborers for large agricultural farms run by Yankee entrepreneurs. Ultimately, their efforts were doomed to fail. As Paul A. Cimbala (1989) notes, Order 15 only gave the Freedmen "possessory title" to enjoy the fruits of their labor, not ownership of the land – a technicality that was not made clear to the Bureau or the freedmen. Nevertheless, nearly a half-million acres were "given" to the freed Blacks[25] and St Catherines became as the capital of the freedmen state, marking a major shift in the island's history.

Figure 31. Rufus Saxton. Courtesy Library of Congress, Prints and Document Division

Tunis Campbell, the leader of the freedmen state, is one of the most interesting figures in the history of the South (Drago 1982; Duncan 1986; Duncan 2004). In 1863, as former enslaved individuals were gathering and as the Civil War was intensifying, the U.S. Secretary of War commissioned Campbell to work with freed slaves in South Carolina. At the time, Campbell was 51-years-old and a Methodist convert. General Tillson, who dealt with land claims and the resettlement for The Freedmen's Bureau, described Tunis Campbell as a person of "great plausibility; and remarkable cunning" (Cimbala 1989:617).

St. Catherines was established as the capital and the other Sea Islands became the center of resettlement. As capital of the freed Black nation, St. Catherines had 369 settlers claiming 4000 acres of improved and unimproved land (Cimbala 1989: 601). The freedmen lived in fifty-five dwellings that once housed Waldburg's slaves. The freed Blacks formed a "separatist democracy with a constitution, a congress, a supreme court and an armed militia." It was a unique setting for the emancipated Blacks who had never experienced such freedom and power.

The experiment of land redistribution on St. Catherines was fraught with difficulties. There were only nineteen freedmen[26] who applied officially for their 40 acres on St. Catherines through the Freedmen Bureau. A large number were given "possessory title" by Tunis Campbell, claiming that he had Sherman's "verbal authority" to allocate the land on St. Catherines (Cimbala 1989:614).[27]

The freedmen who returned to the island were not interested in growing cotton. Only 300 of the 2,500 acres of cleared were planted with cotton (Cimbala 1989: 604).[28] Over 200 freedmen from St. Catherines returned "in very destitute condition" and arrived too late to receive land; Campbell had already distributed land to 369 Freedmen (Cimbala 1989:610). Many of these landless freedmen survived by hunting, crabbing, killing deer and cutting wood for the Savannah market, and by planting small gardens of corn and sweet potatoes for their own use (Cimbala 1989:604). Some maintained their homes on St. Catherines and went to the mainland as wage laborers. Another problem that they faced was the change in work patterns. Under slavery, they had worked under the "task" system and had developed a cooperative work ethic. Now they were allowed to focus on their own needs once their tasks were completed (Morgan 1982).

Tunis Campbell and his wife Harriet used their own funds to recruit teachers from the North. On St. Catherines, there were eighty adults and children attending Campbell's academies. Nearly 1000 students were taught in Campbell's school throughout the South.

Many Northern white entrepreneurs became entangled in the politics and economics of the freedmen's relocation, creating confusion and conflict. St. Catherines was the initial effort to bring Northern economic capital to the South. General Tillson, anxious to create an independent work force, actually devalued the 40-acre grants approved by Campbell and reduced landholdings to ten to fifteen acres. Tillson then invited entrepreneurs from the North to plant the "unclaimed" land; enter the mysterious Captain John F. Winchester.

For many years, the owners of St. Catherines had puzzled over a headstone found in a post-Civil War cemetery located about 100 meters northeast of the manor house. In that cemetery, John and his dad found the resting place of ten individuals. The site was described as a black cemetery and had headstones marking the burials of Reverend George Waring, Dinah Sarah Young, and Richard Shead, plus one enigmatic headstone for a Captain John F. Winchester. John recalls his father describing Winchester as white (Durham and Thomas 1978a:234). The stone was inscribed:

CAPT. JOHN F. WINCHESTER
Died
Oct. 21st 1867
Aged
48 yrs. 2 mos. & 1 day

John did not have any other information about Winchester, who was obviously an obscure figure. A *New York Times* article published on August 13, 1866 with the headline "Georgia,

Miscellaneous Matters-The Blacks and Whites," was essentially a racist rant and had a reference to a Captain Winchester. The correspondent for the *New York Times* (NYT 1866) reported from Savannah:

> The city continues cool, healthy and pleasant. The cholera is dying out at Tybee, and no cases have originated yet in town ...Additional information received confirms my statement that our cotton crop will be about 200,000 bales, and I hear cheering news about our rice crop. I met last week in town Capt. Winchester, of the firm of Schuler Co., of New York, who bought St. Catherines Island, and he spoke very hopefully of their prospects. They have 700 acres of healthy flourishing Sea Island cotton. The negroes are working well, giving no trouble, and his factor estimates the value of his crop at between $80,000 and $90,000. The Captain, who is a Massachusetts man is delighted with their purchase and his residence among us, and laughs heartily at stories circulated by the Radical Abolition Press, of discourtesy and injuries to which, they say, Northern men are subjected.[29]

This was the first instance that we had come across Winchester's name and the assertion that he once owned St. Catherines. John was also surprised about his purported ownership of the island, and doubted the truth of the assertion. Armed with the clue that he was involved in St. Catherines after emancipation, I began researching the island's post-Civil War records. I doubted that Winchester would have been allowed to even purchase land on St. Catherines given that it was the capital of the Freedmen State. Paul A. Cimbala (1983; 1989) had the answers in a dissertation that he had completed in 1983 at Emory University.

Winchester was engaged in a scheme where he would lease 700 acres of "unclaimed" land. Tillson was committed to transforming the freedmen into a labor force for Yankee entrepreneurs who saw a unique opportunity to grow cotton on land that could be rented and had a large labor force. Tillson believed that black families working 40-acre farms would not be productive enough to transform the Southern economy, and he did what he could to discourage them. Tillson instituted a plan that he believed would create a labor force. Instead of providing them the 40 acres stipulated by Order 15, he gave them between 10 and 20 acres. This action had the effect of producing land for Winchester and his partner to rent, and produced a labor force for them.

The path that brought John F. Winchester to St. Catherines has not been clearly established. Winchester was born in Massachusetts and he and his family were living in Lynn, Massachusetts in 1860.[30] We know that Winchester was a Civil War naval officer with considerable experience in battle. He was Acting Master of the steamship *U.S.S. Monticello* that participated in the Atlantic Blockade (Rawson and Woods 1897:127). On August 28, 1861, the *Monticello* supported troops landing at Hatteras Inlet in North Carolina where they took a few hits from the Fort Clark and Fort Hatteras protecting the inlet from the Confederacy [see the report made at the time (USG 1861:53)]. The action at Hatteras Inlet was the first significant Union victory of the Civil War.

Winchester played another noteworthy role in the Civil War. In 1863, as Acting Master of the *U.S.S. Sumpter*, he was assigned to tow the *U.S.S. Alligator*,[31] the Union Navy's first submarine, to Port Royal, South Carolina (Smith 2006) (Figure 32). The *Alligator* was a green, 47-foot, riveted, iron-plated submersible vessel (SEP 1861) commissioned in 1861 for the purpose of attaching explosives to Confederate ships. It failed that task, and was redesigned with a hand screw. On April 3 1863, with the *Alligator* in tow, the *Sumpter* was caught in a storm near Cape Hatteras and Winchester was forced to cut the line and send the *Alligator* adrift. The wreckage has never been found.[32]

Figure 32. The *U.S.S. Sumpter* prepares to tow the *USS Alligator*. Watercolor by Jim Christey.

Winchester and his partner, Mr. Schuyler, approached Tillson before he arrived in Savannah to assume his role in the Freedmen Bureau and they discussed their plans with him.[33] They rented land on St. Catherines site unseen and were not aware of Tunis Campbell and his plans for the Island (Cimbala 1983:246). As Cimbala suggests, Tillson, a Northerner, had faith that Yankee initiatives would make St. Catherines bloom again.

Winchester contracted labor from the freed Blacks and experienced short-lived success (Cimbala 1989). In November 1866, there were 147 freedmen working for Winchester and Schuyler.[34] On the south end of St. Catherines, 420 freedmen were planting their own crops (Cimbala 1983:260). During that summer and fall, rations were given to some of the freedmen. Their cotton production was disappointing, and did not approach that of the Yankees.

Despite Winchester's optimistic interview with the *New York Times* where he claimed a cotton crop valued at $90,000, labor troubles precipitated by contact labor made the system unprofitable. The freedmen forced Winchester and Schuyler to make many concessions. For example, they had access to Winchester's equipment and were able to act as "factors" on the island. Schuyler and Winchester were bankrupt by the end of the year. Winchester died in bankruptcy[35] of unknown causes.[36] Winchester and his great experiment only lasted fourteen months.

In June 1865, Jacob Waldburg attempted to regain his land. Campbell gave Waldburg an emphatic answer to his request by prompting the St. Catherines Congress to pass a law forbidding any white person from stepping on the soil of the island. A militia of 275 men under the control of Titus Campbell was ready to enforce the law and to resist encroachment by Whites.

That same year, Jacob Waldburg advertised the sale of his 4300 acre plantation in Lowndes County in the *Macon Weekly Telegraph* (MWT 1865),

For Sale
My plantation, situated in the county of Lowndes, ten miles from Valdosta, the county town, and two miles from Ayattuh. The tract contains four thousand three hundred acres. Fourteen hundred are in cultivation, not surpassed in fertility in the county of which eleven hundred have been cleared within four years. The climate is decidedly healthy and the settlement eligibly situated. Attached to the plantation is a substantial grist

and sawmill, entirely new. The buildings are commodious and well
constructed. The quarters for the laborers are comfortable and capable of
accommodating upwards of two hundred. There are two large cotton and
gin houses upon the plantation. All the stock will be sold with it, consisting
of mules, cattle, hogs and sheep- possession to be give on or before January.
J. Waldburg, Savannah

After the assassination of President Lincoln in 1866, Andrew Johnson quickly rescinded the Special Field Order 15 and allowed the previous owners to reclaim the land. Andrew Johnson showed little concern for the freed black population's welfare. According to Eric Foner, Johnson was instead more interested in uniting the Southern whites and the Northern whites. The freed Blacks in Johnson's post-war South "would be landless ...rightless... plantation laborers" (Alexander 2004). After the reversal of Sherman's directive by Congress, there was a population decline on St. Catherines and Campbell left the island. The Freedmen's Bureau restored St. Catherines to Jacob Waldburg in April of 1867 (MWT 1867).

As a Republican leader, Tunis Campbell was able to purchase 1250 acres in McIntosh County (Bellville) and established a black landowner's support group. He later became involved in politics and served as a state senator representing Liberty, McIntosh and Tattnall counties. While in office Campbell pushed for equal education, integrated juries, homestead exemptions, voting rights, public access and the abolition of debtor's prison (Duncan 1986).

By 1871, the Democrats who controlled state politics began attacking Reconstruction and, by extension, Tunis Campbell. In 1876, even though the Attorney General's office tried to free him, Campbell was tried and found guilty of malfeasance in office and was leased out to serve his time in a convict labor camp, a euphemism for a chain gang.

The Rauers and the Black Families

On January 26, 1876, Jacob Rauers purchased St. Catherines Island to serve as a hunting preserve and country estate when he was not interested in being a planter.[37] In the 1880 census[38], there were 145 individuals living on the island. The extended Rauer's household included thirteen members: Jacob Rauers (age 43), his wife, Joanna (age 43), their four children (Elise, age 4; John Jacob, age 2; and the twins, Catherine and Fredricka, age 1), and Catherine Urguhart (age 58), an "aunt-in law." The household was supported by six domestic employees. Irish-born Mady Carlson (age 45) was the housekeeper. Tending the four children were Emma Minor, an 18-year-old black nurse, and Susan Luke, a 40-year-old black[39] nurse with a son Benjamin. John Richards (age 21), who was identified in the census as a mulatto, served as the butler. Finally, Patrick Farley (age 45) was the gardener.

There were only three other Whites listed in the 1880 census of the island. Thomas Fergerson (age 32), an Irish farm manager, and his wife Clara (age 28) formed a domestic unit along with their cook, Jane Richard (black, age 19). Finally, Thomas Sayess (age 29) was a married teacher living among the black farmers. It is not clear whom Sayess was teaching, and his wife was not living on the island.

There were 133 freed Blacks (72 females and 61 males) living on St. Catherines at the time of the census. Forty-six percent of the black population was under age 1,5 and 4.5% were older than age 65. The productive[40] segment of the population (15 to 65 years of age) comprised over fifty percent of the population (54.9). Thirty-nine percent of the population was involved in farm activity[41] of some type. There was also a Baptist minister, George Waring; a cook, Jane Albany; a washerwoman, Diannah Bowen; a hostler,[42] Andrew Mungin; and a carpenter, James Richards. Warings's tombstone reads

SACRED
in the memory of
REV. GEORGE WARING
BORN
Nov. 22, 1817
Died
October 1,1887.
He became a Minister of the
Gospel of Christ in the
Year 1878, he liveth up to the
faith to his death.
Blessed are the dead which
die in the Lord, from henceforth
you saith the spirit that they
shall rest from their labors
and their work do follow them.
Thou will show me the path of
life in thy Presence is fullness of
Joy at thy Right hand there are
pleasures for evermore.

The Rauers provided the most supportive environment for the black populations in the island's history. Their commitment to developing the best hunting reserve in the nation discouraged any large-scale agricultural activity. They did allow the Blacks living on the island to plant small gardens for their own use. After three decades, there was another dramatic shift in the island's use. Jacob Rauers died on May 4, 1905. He suggested in his will that the island be kept in the family, but left the final decision to the executors of the estate. He did not want the estate divided until the children were 30 years of age. Six years after the death of Jacob Rauers, Augustus Oemler married into the Rauers family and later established an oyster factory at Factory Creek.

Augustus Oemler on St. Catherines

The Oemler[43] house played a significant role in the Woods family's early years on the island. The Woods moved into the Oemler house on the south end of the island. A previous history of the island (Durham and Thomas 1978b) refers to "a Capt. Umbler" who married into the Rauers family and began an oyster business on the island's southern complex after World War I. The house, according to Durham and Thomas, was built on the foundation of the remains of an old mansion, and the old chimney was used in the construction.[44]

John and I have been able to construct a more complete picture of the island's history from this period. Augustus Oemler (age 52) married Frieda Rauers (age 31) on March 4, 1911

(AC 1911). Under the banner of "Savannah Social News," the *Atlanta Constitution* reported that "The marriage of Miss Frieda Rauers to Mr. Oemler took place Thursday morning at the home of the bride's mother in the presence of the immediate family ... The bride was attended by her twin sister, Mrs. Wayne Cunningham. Mr. and Mrs. Oemler left immediately for the Rauers plantation, St. Catherine's Island, and will make their home there."

Figure 33. Watercolor of the Oemler oyster factory on Back Creek. Artist was probably Frieda Omler's daughter and given to Gladys Woods by the Oemlers.

Augustus Oemler expanded his oyster business from Wilmington Island to St. Catherines. The 1920 U.S. census shed some light on the experience of black families[45] on St. Catherines during this period. There were 54 individuals living in 30 domestic units on the island. Oemler was listed as the factory owner. No other member of the Oemler family was listed as living on the island. William Huces, whose occupation was listed as storekeeper, was the only other individual categorized as white. Hayes Campbell, a 49-year-old cook and head of a household, was categorized as mulatto. His fifteen year old unemployed daughter (Agnes) was living with him. The only other individual categorized as a mulatto was Eliza, a laborer.

The oyster factory (Figure 33) employed 47 individuals that comprised 28 families, only five of which had a total of eight children living with them. Richard and Susan Horks, had three children living with them; the five other families had a single child. Two of the Horks' teenage sons, William and Sam, were also working in the factory. Only five children in the census were younger than 10 years of age.

Figure 34. The remains of one of the three oyster boilers from the Oemler oyster factory. This boiler is at Back Creek landing site. The Black workers lived one mile away in the South End Plantation tabby cabins that once housed the Waldburg slaves. The oyster house and artesian well were to the left of the boiler. The bank of the creek has eroded nearly 100 feet since the Oemlers left the island. The woods in the background are behind Cracker Tom Creek.

The community on St. Catherines had become a factory village with only a few of the amenities that would have been found on the mainland (see Figure 34 for the remains of the boiler). The factory store was the only source of necessities on the island. Forty percent of the households (twelve) had only a single member, reflecting the special nature of the community. It attracted many individuals that did not have dependents. In just a decade, the only remaining households were the Austins and Sussana Jones, the Keys' family servant. Neither the Austins nor Jones were listed in the 1920 census. John remembers his father Toby telling him that in the 1920s, he and his father-in-law, John Rogers, would buy fish from the black families on St. Catherines and resell the fish in inland towns near the coast, such as Hinesville, Glenville, and Ludowici.

Data from the 1850, 1860, 1880 and 1920 censuses illustrate three very distinct phases of the island's habitation by black families. Population pyramids from these three periods show interesting changes in the dependency ratios (percent age 0-14.9 + percent age 65 and over divided by the percent age 15-64.9 X 100). The dependency ratio is a useful measure of the "productive members of a population" and the number of people that they are supporting. The ratios of the enslaved population change dramatically: 45.1% to 94.5% from 1850 to 1860. In 1880 the ratio drops to 74.8%, and to 12.9% in 1920 when families working in the oyster factory occupied the island. These changes suggest that there was significant population growth through reproduction. While the dependency ratio declined in the period when freed Blacks were living on the island with the Rauers, the population seemed to be doing well. Rauers proudly stated that St. Catherines was a natural hunting retreat with no agricultural activity other than the "small patches" of the Negro tenants (AC 1905c).

An understanding of St. Catherines' history provides insights on how the island was used, and the role that black Americans played in its history. This aspect of the island's history has been neglected.[46] John Toby Woods and his father provide an important link to the past by revealing this aspect of the history of St. Catherines, and the region in general.

7

How St. Catherines Got Her Groove Back:
The Rauers' Nimrod Paradise, 1876-1929

Newspapers nationwide reported detailed accounts of a hunt on St. Catherines Island (CDT 1902a) that captured the public's interest. The hunting party included Admiral Winifred S. Schley, the hero of the Spanish American War. Twenty deer were killed, and Schley himself killed one, wounded another and missed two shots (AC 1902b). After Schely's first kill, each member of the hunting party performed the "inviolate custom" of placing their hands in the bleeding wound and smearing the slain buck's blood on Schley's face (AC 1902b).[1] It became a national story (CD 1902a) and the public could not get enough of their hero and his first deer hunt. The publicity put St. Catherines on the map as a hunter's paradise.

Jacob Rauers purchased St. Catherines Island for $40,000[2] from Anna Rodriguez on January 26, 1876 (Liberty County 1876), with the express goal of making it the nation's finest hunting preserve and country estate. Rauers was so insistent about this goal that he compelled the 1880 census taker to change his listed occupation from "merchant planter" to simply "merchant."

The purchase of the estate from Anna Rodriguez is shrouded in mystery. We know little about the transaction. The *Atlanta Constitution* reported that Jacob Waldburg's widow, who outlived her husband by a decade, eventually sold St. Catherines to Rodriguez in 1870 for $80,000 and for a piece of property in Brooklyn (AC 1905d:8). Twenty-nine years after purchasing the island, a feature article in the *Atlanta Constitution* recounted the Rodriguez's purchase of St. Catherines, suggesting that she had ulterior motives. The *Constitution* surmised (AC 1905d:8), that

> the Cubans wanted it [St. Catherines], it was said, as a base for filibustering
> expeditions on behalf of his [Rodriguez's] country, and traditions have it
> that outfits left the little island on the Georgia coast for the Queen of the
> Antilles, which had been rising for years in periodical revolt against the
> yoke of Spain, which was only broken when the power of the United States
> came to the aid of the Cubans.[3]

It appears that Anna M. Rodriquez purchased St. Catherines from the Estate of Elizabeth Waldburg in 1872 (Liberty County 1872) and lived on St. Catherines until she sold it to the Rauers. Rather than serving to foment political unrest in the Caribbean, after the Rauers' purchased St. Catherines, it became a quiet estate disrupted only by the occasional gunfire of hunters is search of wild game.

The Rauers family certainly left their imprint on the island (Figures 36 and 37). In 1880, the extended Rauers household included thirteen of the 145 individuals living on the island.

Jacob Rauers and his wife, Joanna, anchored the family. Their four children,[4] Elise, John Jacob, and twins Catherine and Frieda,[5] were all four years of age or younger and were surely a handful to care for. There was family help, however, from Catherine Urquhart, an "aunt in law" and member of the extended family. The family expanded by two members in the next five years. Alexander McDonald was born on August 23, 1883, and another son, , on November 21, 1885.

The household also included six domestic employees who provided support for the family. Mady Carlson was the housekeeper. Tending the toddlers were two nurses: Susan Luke and Emma Minor. John Richard served as the butler, and Patrick Farley was the gardener. Thomas Fergerson and his wife, Clara, managed the estate. Jane Richards, the cook, living in an adjacent house formed another domestic unit. Thomas Sayess, a teacher, was living among the black farmers. It is not clear whom Sayess' was teaching.

The Rauers provided a supportive environment for the 133 freed Blacks population on St. Catherines (Figure 35). Their commitment to developing the best hunting reserve in the nation discouraged any large-scale agricultural activity (AC 1905d; VanMarter 1904).In fact, Rauers' obituary (AC 1904c:4) stated that he "was the owner of St. Catherines with its valuable game preserve which has been visited by some of the most prominent men in the country."

Figure 35. Family on St. Catherines in the 1880s. Hargrett Rare Book and Manuscript Library, University of Georgia Libraries.

The Rauers did allow the black families living on the island to plant small gardens for their own use. The close relationship between the black families and the Rauers[6] is evident from a report of Catherine Rauers' wedding to Clifford Wayne Cunningham[7] (AC 1901: 11). The December 19th wedding was described as

> the most prominent society wedding of the season. … A feature of the wedding was the attendance of nearly all the colored population of St. Catherines Island, which is owned by Mr. Jacob Rauers, father of the bride, who chartered a steamer especially to bring them to Savannah for the wedding.

The patriarch, Jacob Rauers, was born in Bremen Germany on December 15, 1837 and immigrated to the United States in 1857. He was involved in banking and traveled extensively to Latin America. After the Civil War, Rauers worked as a cotton merchant and exporter until 1881, when he retired from business (Harden 1969:611). Rauers served as the German Consul for thirty-five years (AC 1904b).[8] When he was appointed Consul in 1868, his commission was signed by Emperor William I and countersigned by President Ulysses Grant. Rauers was also very involved in the social and civic life of Savannah. He was elected Vice Commodore of the Savannah Yacht Club in 1880. On land, Jacob Rauers was involved with the Savannah Jockey Club, and served as a judge at many horseracing events.

Jacob Rauers was one of Savannah's most important business leaders. He was a key figure in the development of the De Soto Hotel. When the hotel opened on January 1, 1890, over a half a million dollars had been spent on the building and its furnishings. He helped organize the Savannah Brewing Company. The Brewery specialized in producing a Pilsner beer[9] based on a recipe from his native Germany. Rauers was also involved in a number of Savannah's key businesses, including the Savannah Gas and Light Company, the Tyler Cotton Press Company, the Baldwin Fertilizer Company, and the Skidaway Shell Road Company.

John Jacob Rauers, his son, was born in 1877 and learned the lessons of his father well. He became a junior member of Williamson and Rauers, a major steamship and forwarding company. He was also director of the Savannah Trust Company, vice-president of the Savannah Hotel Corporation, vice-president of the Southern Fertilizer and Chemical Company, director of the Hull Vehicle Manufacturing Company, and director of the Savannah Brewing Company (Harden 1969).

The Rauers' ownership of St. Catherines Island cemented the island's reputation as a hunting reserve. Rauers' commitment to this end and is reflected in his conflict with the government over the construction of a lighthouse. He was determined to maintain control over the use of the island and believed that a lighthouse would be an intrusion. Even the occasional ship that was blown into the island's marshes created a crisis for Jacob Rauers. He was eager to sue a ship owner for damages to the marshes on his beloved island (AC 1893a; AC 1893 c). After Rauers' death in 1904, St. Catherines maintained its cache as a hunting paradise. In his will, he asked that his estate not be divided until the death of his wife Joanna, and until his children reached age 30. He also asked that St. Catherines Island be kept as a family asset, but left the final decision up to the executors of the will.

Joanna McDonald Rauers died on February 26, 1913. Her son, McDonald, died the next year at age 31. By this time, dramatic changes had already taken place on St. Catherines at the behest of Augustus Oemler, who had married into the family in 1911. Oemler established a thriving oyster business that employed the about fifty of the Blacks that remained on the island by the 1920s.

Hunting: How St. Catherines Got Her Groove Back

By 1893, St. Catherines Island was receiving notice as America's premier game preserve,[10] just as Rauers had hoped. The *Atlanta Constitution* (AC 1893b: 15) reported,

> A deer hunt on St. Catherine, the queen of the Sea Islands. ... The party[11] was the guests of Mr. Rauers who owns the island. A house which brings all the comforts of home in close touch with the wildness of nature gives Mr. Rauers an opportunity to display his qualities as a charming and skillful host [Figures 36-38]. Deer were plentiful and eight fell before the deadly aim of the sportsmen. ... The party all returned with glowing reports of this island paradise, and with a fund of jokes and anecdotes to last them a lifetime.

Figure 37. The tower of the Rauers' mansion in 1929.

Figure 36. The Rauers' mansion, considered one of the finest homes on the American coast. The foundation was made of tabby blocks that can be seen on the right side of the structure. Ca. 1929

Figure 38. The Rauers' freight dock to the north of the main dock. It was used to bring supplies and building materials for their house. There was a narrow gauge railroad, one small steam engine and a flatbed that ran from the dock to the site of the mansion. The private dock led to the entrance of the "big" house that the Keys referred to as the Button Gwinnett house.

Outing, an influential magazine during its time, was even more glowing in its description of the island's uniqueness. In the magazine, James Gilbert Van Marter (1904: 441) was ecstatic in his description of the St. Catherines,

> Down the coast of Georgia, very far from the Florida line, is an island, St. Catherine's by name some twenty-five miles long by five in width,[12] primitive, even primeval, off the beaten track, a kingdom in itself, devoted to the cult of Venery.[13] The Atlantic Ocean is on one side; vast marshes, deep inlets and navigable tidal streams on the other. Here are no tourists, no cheap sportsmen, no guides, no hotels, but instead a genuine wilderness,

> where roam countless deer; an island where everything is subordinated to sport. Unlike Jekyll Island, the millionaires' club, unlike any other numberless sea islands which dot the coast from Virginia to Florida, it is the property of a single man; one who appreciates and makes the most of his island kingdom. Here the Virginia deer thrive amazingly. Towns and cities are far away, and there are no troublesome neighbors with their dogs.

The Rauers and St. Catherines were well connected, and there were always powerful men who were interested in hunting. The *Washington Post* (WP 1894) reports that 200 of the 356 Congressmen and two-thirds of the 88 Senators were hunters and fisherman. The article profiled Savannah Congressman Rufus E. Lester,

> Lester has a weakness for the rifle, which he uses when hunting deer. St. Catherines Island, twenty miles out in the Atlantic Ocean[14] from Savannah, is his favorite hunting ground. This island is the property of Col. Rauers; It contains 23,000 acres, and is stocked with deer and other game, making it one of the best sporting lodges in America.

Entertaining the "rich and famous" as well as the "rich and powerful" has become a well-known pattern at St. Catherines, beginning during the time of the Rauers and continuing up to the present. Congressman N. C. Blanchard, who chaired the Congressional Rivers and Harbor Committee, arrived in Savannah to check out the $1M project to deepen the Savannah Harbor to a depth of 26 feet. Blanchard found enough time to spend the 1893 Christmas holiday on St. Catherines. His hunting party successfully bagged nine deer (AC 1894). While the success of the congressman certainly enhanced the island's reputation as a hunting resort, a war hero pushed its fame to a sublime level.

Everyone who had a chance would find a reason to visit the St. Catherines Island. W. W. Kimball, Lieutenant Commander of the newly commissioned (September 1897) *U.S.S. Du Pont*, the flagship of a torpedo flotilla moving from Savannah to Brunswick, took the inside route to get soundings on Doboy Sound and Waldburg Creek. "Surprisingly", Kimball found time "to allow the officers some shooting" on St. Catherines (AC 1897a: 3). The next year the *Du Pont* would play an important role in the Spanish American War.

Admiral Winfield S. Schley (Figure 39), a controversial hero of the Spanish American War[15] (Graham and Schley 1902), and General W. W. Gordon, another war hero who was hosting Schley in Savannah, arrived on the *W. F. McCauley*[16] tug. Ships along the way acknowledged the war heroes with demonstrations on their vessels (AC 1902d). Schley was the toast of Savannah. The planners organized a family reunion (CD 1902d), he was given the key to the city (CD 1902b), attended services at an historic church (CDT 1902b), cheered "wildly at a theater (CD 1902b), spoke to the local black college (WP 1902), and attended a number of public receptions in his honor. However, the big event was the hunt. The grand hunt for Admiral Schley and General W. W. Gordon,[17] with Jacob Rauers as host, was planned and announced in advance in the national press (CD

Figure 39. Admiral Winfield S. Schley.

1902c). Schley was to be given the most promising "stand," ensuring his success (AC 1902d). Page 1 of *The New York Times* reported the successful hunt (NYT 1902).

> "Until one has eaten bacon in camp under such circumstances," said the Rear Admiral, "he has no idea of its possible flavor. It is sliced by a deft darky,[18] a switch sharpened at one end, is struck through it with the other end in the earth, tipping the bacon toward the campfire. A piece of cornbread is laid on a stone just under the sizzling bacon, so it can catch the dripping grease, and with the flavor of the fat through the this bread the combination of bacon and corn pone is hard to beat" (CDT 1902a:5).

The reports of the hunt provide a vivid picture of what it entailed. The allure of the hunt was enhanced by Schley's detailed descriptions of his camping experience (CDT 1902a:5).[19]

Schley was willing to tell the world about the wonders of St. Catherines. He praised the abundance of the game; the birds, he said, "were exceedingly remarkable." Even a "heavy squall" on the second night of camping didn't dampen Schley's spirits. It only reinforced the magic of St. Catherines, since the excellent shelter allowed them to sleep unaware of what was transpiring in the night storm. There was also room for hyperbole. By mutual consent to avoid controversy, no discussion of the scores was to be given out to the public. However, they did provide information about the rifle used by the Admiral and his marksmanship was compared to the accuracy of the guns on his ship, *The Brooklyn*, which helped end the Spanish American War.

Schley used a twelve-gauge shotgun with two sets of barrels (one pair full choke and the other pair modified choke)[20] that he borrowed from William Schley, a relative from Savannah. However, W. W. Gordon broke the vow of silence to reassure the public of Schley's prowess with hunting weapons. Gordon said, "He shot with some of the best marksmen in this part of the state, and it is due him to say his record was not exceeded by anyone in the party (CDT 1902a:5)." In addition to the deer slain by Schley, they reported that he shot a raccoon that everybody agreed was the "one of the largest animals of its kind ever seen by any member of the party (CDT 1902a:5)."

Figure 40. Rauers hunting party with the twins in the mule wagon at the rear. Note deer at the left.

There were other accounts of hunts on St. Catherine that provide insights into the complexity of a hunt (Figure 40). James Gilbert Van Marter's article in *Outing* magazine,[21] "an Illustrated Monthly Magazine of Recreation," provided a description of a deer hunt on St. Catherines (VanMarter 1904). Van Marter arrived on St. Catherines with a bias about how deer should be hunted. He was more familiar with the northern deer hunt, in which the prey is stalked in the woods. Given the growth of underbrush and abundance of snakes, hunting on St. Catherines required the use of dogs and beaters. On St. Catherines, the beaters were black inhabitants who rode horses and had a team of dogs to flush the deer to the hunters.[22] John Woods pointed out that during hunts when E. J. Noble owned the island, beaters and dogs were still used, but not horses. Instead Noble's employees would act as beaters and those invited to the hunt would bring their own dogs to aid in driving out the deer. John found the dogs more trouble than they were worth, and he said that he and his coworkers would often have to round up dogs that could not stay on task once they had seen the deer. Even Van Marter said that had the beaters not been using a "stout whip", the dogs would have destroyed the animals after the kill.

Van Marter's hunt took place on the favored northern half of the island. He said, "We drove for an hour through the needle carpeted forest, horses and wheels scarce breaking the primeval stillness, until, reaching a group of horsemen, we halted hard by an Indian mound,[23] last vestige of a perished race." The hunters were placed in their "stands "about 150 yards apart and given specific instructions on where to shoot. The hunters with shotguns[24] waited while the beaters on horseback and the dogs drove the deer toward them. The deer appeared quickly and the hunters shot as they approached. After the first drive, they moved to another area, established their stands and waited about 15 minutes for the sound of the dogs and beaters signaling the arrival of the deer. He related the excitement of the moment (VanMarter 1904: 444),

> It requires good judgment, a quick eye, alert senses, and a total absence of buck fever to make a kill. To my way of thinking, the long drawn out pleasure of an open stalk in a mountainous country is much to be preferred to the intense momentary excitement of this snap shooting; but, of course, each method has its warm advocates. To one in search of soul-stirring excitement, I recommend this southern deer shooting.

> This time the drive went with a wild rush, passing well to my left; nothing seen, only heard, and ending in a veritable fusillade. Six, perhaps more, shots were fired, followed by a noisy altercation with the hounds, who, poor beasts, would persist in following their prey, owing probably to drops of blood from a wounded animal. Persuaded by a stout whip to obey their masters, the hounds were soon rounded up; the recall was blown on the horn, and we assembled to gaze upon a small buck, sole product of the fusillade. It seemed that eight deer, in one bunch, had passed between two stands, and afforded close but difficult shots; only one had fallen, and that one was hit by both standers.

On the second day of hunting, the Rauers provided Van Marter (1902:446) the opportunity to experience a hunt on the beach at the southern end of St. Catherines, which has a totally different ecology. He recounts,

> On the ocean side of St. Catherine's are to be found two or three small islands, called "hammocks," covered with a nearly impenetrable growth of scrub vegetation, consisting mostly of palmettos. The largest of these hammocks is connected at low tide with the main island by a broad beach and offers no avenue of escape to the deer who are unfortunate enough to seek refuge thereon. True, sometimes, but not often, they take to the water, and by hard swimming escape to the more distant islets.

Based on the above description, John said that most likely place described by Van Marter was the beach below McQueens Inlet.

It is not difficult to see why both the public and politicians were enthralled by St. Catherines. The island drew many more politicians to its shores (AC 1906d), but these visits did not make the *Washington Post*, the *New York Times* or the *Chicago Daily Tribune*. The hunts were now reported as minor social events. In the *Atlanta Constitution*, under the heading "Capitol Gossip"(AC 1906c), it was reported that Governor Joseph Meriwether Terrell and his wife Jessie Lee Spivey Terrell had a "royal time" hunting and fishing on St. Catherines as the guests of McDonald Rauers.[25] The Governor proudly praised his wife's success at fishing, "Mrs. Terrell easily bore the honors as a fisherman, her catches far exceeding that of any other member of the party"(AC 1906c). He was also quick to point out that he had "the good fortune to bring down a magnificent buck with his seventh shot." Another account of the event describes the Terrell party aboard the 100-foot steamer yacht, *Jessie,*[26] moored to St. Catherines' wharf and riding out a "West Indian hurricane" (AC 1906a).

The "Capital Hunt" continued, but controversy arose in 1917 when rumors spread that the hunt had actually taken place on Blackbeard Island, a Georgia state preserve supervised by Captain A. Oemler, "keeper of the game preserve." The *Atlanta Constitution* (AC 1917:18) reassured the public that the "now famous state house hunting party" hosted by Sam J. Slate, State Game Commissioner, took place on St. Catherines and not Blackbeard Island.

In 1918, the Rauers' relationship with the Georgia state legislature paid dividends. The State of Georgia passed a law restricting the use of rivers that end in government or private game preserves (State of Georgia 1918). It stated any saltwater creeks, streams, estuaries or bays on Georgia's Sea Islands that are maintained in whole or in part as private or public game preserves were off limits to anyone without permission of the owner. The law specified that this pertained to waterways on islands that were owned entirely by a single individual, family or estate. It sounded as if the law was written just for Rauers and St. Catherines; and, in fact, it was. If there were any question as to how the Rauers turned these hunts to their advantage, there is a hand-written letter to Jack Rauers from Samuel B. Adams, his lawyer and friend, who was a retired Supreme Court Justice (Adams 1927) with many friends in Atlanta. In the note, Adams attached two copies of the 1918 Act. Adams wrote, "[t]he enclosed law passed in 1918 – to which Maj. Tempkin[27] called your attention was prepared by us. Pratt[28] made two trips to Atlanta to look after its passage." Adams suggested that one of the two copies be given to Capt. Oemler. To ensure that the marshes were included in the interpretation of this act, in 1918 the Rauers registered an agreement made in 1900 that rented oyster rights to Augustus Oemler (Liberty County 1918).

In the modern era, politicians were frequent visitors to St. Catherines. Herbert Hoover (NYT 1932), Dwight D. Eisenhower, and Richard Nixon (CDT 1958) were afforded the island's hospitality, but in a quieter fashion. During the Noble era, the State, County and Superintendent's hunts were frequent events on the island.

While Rauers was establishing St. Catherines as a premier hunting site, he was tenaciously battling the U.S. Government's attempts to purchase land to build a lighthouse on the north end of the island.

Jacob Rauers Makes Heavy Work with the Lighthouse

The readers of the December 12, 1891 *Atlanta Constitution* (AC 1891) would have likely missed the report from Charles Foster, the Secretary of the Treasury, announcing that the federal government was appropriating $20,000 of the 1892 budget to purchase five acres of land on St. Catherines to build a light house overlooking Ossabaw[29] Sound. The readers were more likely drawn to news of one of Georgia's favorite sons, Charles Frederick Crisp. Crisp was a politician from Americus and the newly elected Speaker of the House. He would be staying overnight in Atlanta, and then returning for a visit to his hometown. The page one story bore the headline "Crisp is a Busy Man," and profiled his activity as one of Washington, D.C.'s most powerful persons. According to newspaper accounts, Crisp was besieged by House members seeking political positions and constituents sending over 100 letters a day. There was even a paragraph in the story about a pipe exploding in the Speaker's office in Washington. Everyone in the office was scared, except Crisp, who was too busy to be distracted and did not hear the commotion.

Buried in the ninth paragraph of the story, Foster's reported other expenditures that dwarfed the amount of funds needed to purchase land for the St. Catherines lighthouse. The Oconee River and Savannah River projects were scheduled to receive $50,000 and $75,000, respectively, for improvements. The $1,000,000 expenditure for the Savannah Harbor was of more interest simply because of its magnitude. Jacob Rauers, who had owned St. Catherines Island for over a decade, would have been keenly interested in the government's plan. While he was strongly opposed to any intrusion on his island, he could not have imagined that the issue would occupy him for the 12 remaining years of his life, and would not be settled until a nearly a year after his death. It is not clear from the newspaper accounts what exactly transpired between the 1891 announcement and the actual appropriation and subsequent lawsuit to condemn the land. Rauers claimed that the federal government never entered into negotiations to buy the land from him, and instead resorted to the court house (AC 1902c).

Rauers firmly believed that St. Catherines should remain pristine. The value of his holdings depended on the island's reputation as a hunting reserve, and this required a uniquely natural and undisturbed setting (AC 1902c:4). He was concerned that the lighthouse and its infrastructure would have a negative impact on the island's ecology. In contrast, the government viewed assumed that since they were only interested in just five acres as a miniscule part of the 23,000 acre island. Given this discrepancy in perspectives, it is not surprising that a prolonged legal battle ensued.

In 1898, the government reinstituted an earlier lawsuit that had been dismissed because the district attorney had failed to identify the statute allowing the condemnation to proceed (AC 1898). The *Atlanta Constitution* described Rauers as a "determined citizen in possession" of the island. Rauers claimed that the lighthouse would destroy the island as a game preserve, and therefore requested a settlement of $200,000. In 1899, the lawsuit was withdrawn again after the Board of Appraisers reported to the Savannah District Court that the five acres of land was worth $100,000, and that the St. Catherines game preserve was worth $200,000 (AC 1899a; AC 1899b; (AC 1899c). Interesting, St. Catherines Island was "returned for taxation at $35,000" in 1899 (AC 1899a: 3), and valued at $60,000 in 1905 (AC 1905f).[30] Three years later, Rauers filed suit against the government, demanding payment of $200,000 or that the government "cease its efforts to take from him part of his island and to disturb and harass him by different proceedings" (AC 1902c: 4). Three years later, 11 months after Jacob Rauers' death, the case was dismissed by Judge Emory Speers (AC 1905b). Anticipating defeat, the government decided instead to build the lighthouse on Blackbeard Island, adjacent to Sapelo Island (AC 1905a).

The lighthouse was not the only issue that landed the Rauers in court. In 1893, a hurricane (AC 1893f) damaged or destroyed 30 ships and drove the *Beatrice McLean,* captained by Matthew Balmer, onto St. Catherines Island (AC 1893d).[31] The ship had been ordered to the quarantine station on Blackbeard Island[32] (Sullivan 1990; Sullivan 2003), but sought safe harbor on the west side of St. Catherines and ended up being "drawn high up in the woods"[33] on the west side of St. Catherines" during the hurricane (AC 1893d: 1). Jacob Rauers demanded $500 for the damage to the marsh on the island (AC 1893a), and his demand was upheld by the court (AC 1893c).[34] It is not clear what had happened after Judge Falligant's decree, but the *Beatrice McLean* did sail again, only to sink in the Gulf of Mexico two years later (Garrison, et al. 1989).

Augustus Oemler on St. Catherines

The last phase in the use of St. Catherines prior to its sale to Clement Melville Keys and associates was the Oemler's oyster business on the island. There are some indications that Oemler had a presence on St. Catherines before he married into the Rauers family,The *Atlanta Constitution* (AC 1904a: 2) reported that Augustus Oemler transported a corpse and the assailant to Liberty County[35] aboard his sailboat. Louis Hamilton, a black farmer, struck Willie Lagree, a fellow farmer, with an axe and killed him. It appears that Lagree went to Hamilton's house on St. Catherines, broke down the door, and rushed into the house. Hamilton's wife threw her arms around Lagree and her husband smashed his head with an axe.

Oemler was also involved in harvesting oysters around the island. In October 1900, he and Jacob Rauers entered into a five-year agreement in which Oemler was given the right to harvest oysters on the lands surrounding St. Catherines for an annual rent of $600 (Liberty County 1918).[36] Oemler was to select "two acres of ground" on Seaside Field to "erect thereon all such buildings, structures, shed, machinery, etc., as he may desire in the prosecution of the oyster industry"[37] (Figure 41). The agreement also gave Oemler permission to build a wharf "out of the Negro quarters" on the west side of St. Catherines overlooking Waldburg Creek. Finally, he was allowed "to quarter" the ninety employees needed for the oyster factory on two acres for up to three months. Oemler was to restrict employees to the adjacent 100 acres and needed Rauers'

Figure 41. The Oemlers used concrete barrels as planters and placed them on the side of the stairs. He also used these barrels for food storage.

permission to move beyond this area. He was also allowed to cut the dry wood necessary to run the boilers for fifty-cents a cord. Oemlers' employees were not allowed to hunt or fish on the land, and Oemler was required to remove anyone who violated this rule from the island. In 1905, Oemler's canning factory on Wilmington Island produced (Bruce 1905: 108) 1,400,000 cans of oysters.

In discussing the Woods family's ties to St. Catherines, the Oemler[38] home played a significant role in their early years on the island (Figure 42). The Woods moved into the Oemler house on the south end of the island. It is claimed that the house was built on the foundation of an old mansion, but John is not aware of any evidence of a mansion on the south end. He suggests that the chimney remaining from the Oemler house may have been misinterpreted as remains from an earlier structure because of the tabby blocks (Figure 43). The tabby is similar to the concrete that Oemler used to manufacture materials for his house and other items.

Figure 42. The Oemler house as it stood in 2007.

Figure 43. Remains of the chimney.

John and I have been able to reconstruct a more complete history of this period of the island (for scenes from this period, see Figures 44-47). Fifty-two-year-old Augustus Oemler married thirty-one-year-old Frieda Rauers on March 4, 1911 (AC 1911). Under the banner of "Savannah Social News," the *Atlanta Constitution* reported that:

> The marriage of Miss Frieda Rauers to Mr. Augustus Oemler took place Thursday morning at the home of the bride's mother in the presence of the immediate family… The bride was attended by her twin sister, Mrs. Wayne Cunningham. Mr. and Mrs. Oemler left immediately for the Rauers plantation, St. Catherine's Island, and will make their home there.

Figure 44. The Oemlers and guests on South Beach. To the far left is Mrs. Oemler's convertible.[39] Note the two wagons that were used to transport some of the guests. Ca. 1930.

Figure 45. Another scene from South Beach. The twins with friends.

Figure 46. Mrs. Frieda Oemler in her convertible touring St. Catherines with distinguished guest, Mrs. H. N. Torrey, seated next to her. Her sister Elizather and brother-in-law Wayne Cunningham are next to Torrey. The Torreys were the owners of Ossabaw Island. The car is in front of the outside kitchen of the "big" house. To the right is the smoke house, and behind that is the magnolia that served as the skinning tree. To the right of the smoke house is the grape orchard surrounded by pecan trees. When John left the island in 1982, a few pecan trees were still standing.

Figure 47. On each side of the steps are planters that used wood barrels as molds. A number of the out-buildings are visible to the right. The corral is on the far right. The company store (not in the picture) was west (to the far left).

Augustus Oemler's ties to the oyster business went back many years. Oemler was 40-years-old when his father, Arminius Oemler, died in Savannah. The *Atlanta Constitution* reported in an obituary (AC 1897b) that, "Dr. A. Oemler, aged seventy-one, died tonight from the effects of being overheated."[40] Oemler was described as "a well-known scientist and practically the father of the oyster industry in this part of Georgia." The obituary noted that the senior Oemler headed a "big canning factory on Wilmington Island which ships" thousands of cans of vegetables and oysters north every year.

Arminius Oemler is credited with founding two of Georgia's most important industries: truck farming and the oyster industry. He began his study of medicine in Savannah with Stephen N. Harris (Barnett 1928-1936), Billy Joe Harris's brother, and completed his M.D. at the City University of New York. He left medicine because the "…strain on his sympathies affected his health." Instead, Oemler introduced "scientific diversified farming" to the South. Arminius Oemler's book on truck farming was published in four editions (1883, 1888, 1900, 1903). His essay on the oyster industry (Oemler 1889) stimulated its growth in Georgia. Even though the Oemler Oyster Company failed (AC 1893e), he led the fight for what is now known as the "Georgia Oyster Law" (AC 1889), which permitted deep water oystering.

Augustus Oemler was involved in a number of other activities that tied him to the Sea Islands. He was the keeper of the state game preserve on Blackbeards Island. In 1917, there were reports that a State House Thanksgiving holiday hunting party hosted by Sam Slate, Georgia's Game Commissioner, had taken place on Blackbeard Island. The *Atlanta Constitution* (1917:18) reported that Captain Oemler assured the public that the hunt took place on St. Catherines.

The decline of the oyster industry marked the last phase of the Rauers' control of St. Catherines. There were other issues that arose in the last five years of their ownership of the island. In 1918,[41] the state of Georgia legislated a tick eradication program that set the stage for the development of the cattle industry in the Georgia (Haygood 1986). Using the same tactics that brought them success enforcing the fish and game laws and in fighting liquor smuggling, the state purchased a 30-foot cabin cruiser to enhance their "fight" against the cattle tick (AC 1924c).

After a "sensational fight in the courts" to halt the eradication program on the Islands, the battle against the cattle tick began in earnest. State veterinarian Dr. Peter F. Behnsen,[42] two deputies and 20 mounted men began their efforts on Ossabaw Island where Detroiter Dr. H. N. Torrey was in the process of building his $1,000,000 mansion (AC 1924c). As if they were mounting a military campaign, the team was scoured the island's 30,000 acres in search of the 500 cattle that were to be dipped. Once they finished with Ossabaw, Dr. Behnsen said that the other islands would be "hunted". As early as January 1924, island owners were threatening legal action to overturn the dipping law (AC 1924d).

The Rauers were concerned that efforts to dip the island's 1000 wild cattle and 100 wild horses would result in damage to the land and its animals (AC 1924d). They were not on firm legal ground, however. State Legislator Lee J. Langley sent inquiries to Dr. Peter F. Behnsen about the extent of the tick eradication program as described in the law. Behnsen quoted Attorney General George Napier. who wrote that, since St. Catherines was in Liberty County, the law did indeed apply to the island (AC 1924d: 10),

> Since St. Catherine's Island is part of the state of Georgia, and since tick eradication is required in every part of the state, it necessarily follows that it is your duty as veterinarian, charged with the duty of enforcing the law, to see that ticks are eradicated on St. Catherines Island as well as in any part of the state.

Langley asked Savannah attorney Samuel B. Adams[43] for his opinion on Napier's response. In seeking the counsel of Adams, Langley was seeking advice from one of Georgia's best legal minds. Adams was elected to fill a short term on the Georgia Supreme Court (AC 1902a), and later headed the Georgia Bar (AC 1907). In a letter to Langley, Judge Adams[44] affirms the legal opinion of the Attorney General, but suggested other factors to consider saying (AC 1924d: 10),

> The opinion of the attorney general, assuming that his legal construction is correct, does not seem to take into consideration the great loss and damage to the owners from the destruction of property and game animals that the campaign would involve. Cattle and horses would have to be driven from retreats by fire, killed and then dipped.

Adams repeats the fears that the Rauers family had about the program. In his letter to Langley, he continues,

> St. Catherine's Island is a magnificent game preserve, the finest by far in the United States. The owners refused a cash offer of $600,000 for it from a northern man, who desired a game preserve with exclusive ownership for him. Summer homes of the owners are on the island and for that reason and because they themselves want to protect it as a game preserve. I understand that quite a number of adventurous spirits on the mainland are with the prospect of hunting wild cattle on the island and would be willing to protract hunting indefinitely.

At the end of July 1924, there was an attempt by Representatives Langley (Floyd County) and Way (Liberty County) to amend the law (AC 1924b). They convinced the Agriculture Committee No. 1 to amend the act passed on August 17, 1918, preventing the shipment of tick infested cattle into, out of, or through the state of Georgia (AC 1924b). They justified their action

Figure 48. Outside of the chimney, with wooden shingles at the top.

by saying that St. Catherines was so far from the mainland that there was no possibility that the wild cattle or horses[45] would ever escape to the mainland.

The issue came to a head in 1925 when Judge Peter F. Meldrim issued an injunction against dipping accepting the claims that dipping represented a danger to the stock (AC 1925). J. A. Langford, agent for state veterinarian Peter F. Behnsen, refused to cease dipping cattle, horses and mules on St. Catherines and was arrested, adjudged in contempt of court, fined $500, and given a 30 days sentence. As quickly as the issue appeared, it disappeared from the gaze of the press. The *Atlanta Constitution* did not report on cattle dipping again. Soon after, the Rauers family left the island for what they thought would be the last time.

John Woods remembered his father telling him about how he and his father-in-law, John Rogers, would go to the island to buy fish and animal hides to sell in Savannah and nearby towns during the 1920s. This provided the Woods' first ties to the islands. In 1929, the island was sold to C. M. Keyes, James C. Willson, and Howard Coffin. One of Toby Woods' first duties as superintendent was to remove the Oemler's furniture from their former home. Thus began the next chapter of the history of St. Catherines Island and the Woods family.

When part of the Oemler home developed a leaking roof, the interior of part of the house was damaged beyond repair. John Toby demolished the rooms, leaving the chimney above (Figure 48). The house was built on wooden blocks that have long since disappeared after demolition, but the base of the chimney was built on tabby block to support its weight. These blocks are similar to those used to construct the foundation of the Rauers mansion.[46] Durham and Thomas (1978:237) claim that the Oemler house was built on the foundation of a mansion. They say, "He rebuilt a house there utilizing the foundation blocks and one of the chimneys of the old 'mansion' which had stood there before." It is likely that they did not realize that the chimney remained from a more recent renovation.

8

St. Catherines' Resurrection and Fall from Grace:
The Decade of the Keys, 1929-1939

When I first heard about Mr. and Mrs. Keys, John Woods described them as New York hotel owners and stock investors. Roger S. Durham and David Hurst Thomas (1978), in their history of the island, mention the one time owners of St. Catherines as "the Keys" without identifying them by their "given" names. It took persistence to establish that "the Keys" were C. M. Keys and Mrs. Keys. Mrs. Keys always signed her letters and notes to the Woods as "Mrs. C. M. Keys." Months into my research, I found that Mrs. Keys was born Indiola Arnold.[1]

I was not prepared for the complex and interesting biography of these two talented individuals. Clement Melville Keys (Figure 49) was born in Toronto, Canada on April 8, 1876. He was a hockey player, poet, journalist, investor, and has been rightly described as "the father of commercial aviation." After graduating from the University of Toronto in 1897, he wanted to enter the business world. However, during an economic depression was not the time to begin a career in commerce. Instead, Keys taught classics at Ridley College in St. Catherines, Canada for three years (Young 1992). He immigrated to the United States in 1901 and became a citizen in 1924. Keys worked as a freelance writer and frequently reported for the *New York Times.* He then worked as a reporter (1901-1903) and as railroad editor (1903-1905) for the *Wall Street Journal* until he was hired as the financial editor of *World's Work* (1905-1911).Keys was such a talented and influential writer and analyst that he was selected as one of the top one hundred Business Journalist Luminaries of the last century.[2]

Such an outstanding journalist could have literally written himself into a career as an editor of a major business magazine. He was a versatile writer and his columns touched on diverse topics, including business advice for the investor (Keys 1913a), the role of the railroad president in vitalizing transportation (Keys 1902c), winter sea birds (Keys 1902d), bird nests (Keys 1902a), pets of the poor (Keys 1901), light verse (Keys 1902b; Keys 1904), biographical essays on railroad tycoons (Keys 1907), and even pamphlets on how to build a small house (Keys 1913b). In fact, in 1911, he was offered the editor-in-chief position of *World's Work*, but opted instead to form C. M. Keys & Company, an investment advisory company. Keys understood the complexity of the financial system and had the ability to explain its intricacies in print and as a speaker. Moreover, he showed a remarkable ability to apply what he had learned as a business writer.

If you have not heard of C. M. Keys, you are not alone. While reviewing J. M. Corn's (1985) *The Winged Gospel: America's Romance with Aviation, 1900–1950*, Gore Vidal (1985) notes Corn's failure to recognize Keys' role in transcontinental flight[3] in a book that claims to celebrate it:

> I was twice footnote to the history of aviation. On July 7, 1929, still on
> the sunny side of four years old, I flew in the first commercially
> scheduled airliner (a Ford Tri-Motor) across the United States, from
> New York to Los Angeles in forty-eight hours. Aviation was now so

safe that even a little child could fly in comfort. I remember only two things about the flight: the lurid flames from the exhaust through the window, then a sudden loss of altitude over Los Angeles, during which my eardrums burst. Always the trouper, I was later posed, smiling, for the rotogravure sections of the newspapers, blood trickling from tiny lobes. Among my supporting cast that day were my father, the assistant general manager of the company (Transcontinental Air Transport), his great and good friend, as the never great, never good *Time Magazine* would say, Amelia Earhart, as well as Anne Morrow Lindbergh, whose husband Charles was my pilot. Both Lindbergh and Amelia had been hired by the line's promoter, one C.M. Keys (not even a footnote now but then known as the czar of aviation), to publicize TAT, popularly known as 'The Lindbergh Line.'

It has been claimed that Keys' success in the aviation was due to his understanding of how railroad owners constantly improved their vision of transportation. He recognized the importance of a vertically integrated aviation company that could control all aspects of the market (Eltscher and Young 1998:3). In 1916, he informally advised Curtis Aeroplane and Motor Company about financial and organizational matters. Keys' advice was so helpful that they made him an unpaid Vice President. Within four years, Keys had purchased a controlling interest in the company. His leadership at Curtis was phenomenally successful. He took Curtis from the brink of bankruptcy to a merger with Wright Aeronautical Corporation, which was Curtis' most formable competitor at the time in 1929. He led the merged Curtis-Wright

Corporation for the next three years as its president. Keys' companies were vertically integrated, manufactured planes and their engines, and transported mail, people and military supplies (Eltscher and Young 1998:38). During this time, Keys leveraged himself to become the president of 26 companies, including Curtis-Wright, North American Aviation, National Aviation and Transcontinental & Western Air Transport[4] (Eltscher and Young 1998; Van der Linden 2002).

For all except the most ardent aviation "buffs," Keys' role in the development of passenger airplane travel appears to have been unsuccessful in retrospect, since within three years the service was abolished. The 48-hour transcontinental trip cut the travel time by a day (Hopkins 1975). The service, which was described as if "railroad took to the air," was simultaneously Spartan and luxurious.

Figure 49. C. M. Keyes. Portrait from Smithsonian Institution Air Museum

Passengers were portrayed as "both brave and hardy" (Hopkins 1975). They were served meals with table cloths and tableware, but exposed to an environment that forced some passengers to wear coveralls to protect their clothes (Dubin 2003). The plane, a Ford Tri-Motor (Figure 50), was known as the "Tin Goose" because of its uninsulated skin of corrugated aluminum. Its three 300-horse-power Wright J6-9 (R975-1) engines provided ample power for its trips. There were ten wicker seats for nine passengers who each paid 16 cents per mile for the trip (the radio operator had the first seat on the right side of the plane with his radio equipment on a table attached to the bulkhead). The plane had a cabin heater that maintained a "comfortable" temperature of 60 degrees at an altitude of 8000 feet.

Three factors led to the cessation of the service in the early 1930s: the collapse of the stock market, a $3 million loss running the service,[5] and the crash of one of its planes. The *City of San Francisco* slammed into Mount Taylor in New Mexico on September 4, 1929, and that misfortune drove passengers away (Hopkins 1975). Business travelers soon felt that the safety issues and inconvenience were not worth the 24 hours saved by the transcontinental air-rail service.

Keys went as far as having his employees fly as passengers to keep up the appearance of success. While he may have lost his fight for air travel at that time, he did win the war. The realization that passenger service could not be profitable led U.S. Postmaster General Brown to increase the subsidization of mail transported by airplanes (Hopkins 1975; Van der Linden 2002), which was essential for the survival of the industry. Air travel would eventually become an important part of American travel. Keys' imprint on the aviation industry is like an indelible watermark that is only apparent under careful examination.

Figure 50. Ford Tri-Motor at the Grand Central Terminal in Glendale California. Photo taken after NAT merged with Transcontinental, forming what eventually became TWA.

C. M. Keys was an accomplished businessman, even with a relatively light work schedule. He was well known for his habit of leaving the office at 4:00 PM every afternoon and avoiding work on the weekends. Keys work ethic and accomplishments, given what many consider to be a short workweek, has become a subject of conjecture. Robert Updegraff (1999), writing to support the powers of the subconscious for the website *Dreams Alive* comments,

> Coming down to contemporary man, C. M. Keys, president of a number of concerns, including the Curtis Aircraft Corporation, in one year recently spent five months fishing, golfing, and playing tennis in Cuba, Florida, and Europe. Mr. Keys always leaves his office at four o'clock and has not worked on Saturdays for five years. His home is on Fifth Avenue, where he spends much time rereading the classics and history.

> Competing with him are many men who work eight and 10 hours a day, day in and day out, and they wonder why they cannot catch up. The simple

reason is that Mr. Keys has taken his subconscious mind into his business, whereas they have not. He does the biggest part of his work 'tirelessly.'

Figure 51. The Woods family and friends out for a ride in Mrs. Keys' convertible. John is on the left front seat next to his mother. In the back are Bill Riddle, Gee, Curtis Lee and Clel.

Toby and Gladys Woods and their children revered Mrs. C. M. Keys, an intriguing character in her own right. Gee[6] remembers that when there was work to be done Mrs. Keys would be there helping "by getting her hands in the dirt." John's mother told him about the time when he was an infant and "peed" on Mrs. Keys while she was holding him. Gladys Woods was terribly embarrassed about the leaky diaper and she apologized profusely. Mrs. Keys just smiled and handed her a twenty-dollar bill, as if the accident were a good luck omen. In my exploration of her history, I found Mrs. Keys to be an exotic and mysterious figure; but, to John and his sisters, there was no mystery. She was just as an incredibly kind friend to them and their parents.

Gee still remembers Mrs. Keys' generosity. There were frequent convertible rides (Figure 51), and cherished gifts of hats, gloves, stockings, or other items from Mrs. Keys; and there were also some surprises. John described the time when Mrs. Keys gave him a doll. It seemed that John had not been kind to the dolls that Mrs. Keys had given Gee and Clel. John would drag their dolls on the cement floor of the porch, damaging the dolls' noses and soiling their dresses. As a three-year-old, John had a fascination with the dolls' eyes, and he would poke his finger into their orbits. In her infinite wisdom, Mrs. Keys knew how to resolve the issue. She presented John with his own doll; actually, she presented John's mom with John's doll. While John remembers the doll and played with it for a short time, he never knew what happened to it.

Figure 52. The doll that was a gift from Mrs. C. M. Keys to John Woods.

According to Gee, John's mother put it away for safekeeping once John's interests turned to alligators, raccoons and other wild animals in the menagerie that was St. Catherines. Recently, when Gee was preparing to move from Colonels Island to Brunswick, Georgia, she decided that John had matured enough to take care of the doll and presented it to him (Figure 52). In 2006, 72 years later, John was reunited with his first and only doll. However, for John, the most memorable gift from Mrs. Keys was Button, the terrier mix that became such an important part of their family (see Chapter 2).

In an earlier life, Mrs. Keys (Figure 53), born Indiola Arnold on October 23, 1885, was a comedic operetta singer who played "The Good Witch of the North" in the early stage productions of the *Wizard of Oz* (TrentonTimes 1905). The play opened in Chicago at the Grand Opera House on January 16, 1902.[7] In New York, she played the role of *"Ethylle"* in Victor Herbert's "It Happened in Norland," which

opened at the Lew M. Fields Theater on December 5, 1904.
The play ran for 254 performances over a two-year period
(12/5/1904-4/29/1905 and 8/31/1905-11/25/1905). Mrs.
Arnold's next role was in *His Majesty*, which opened at the
Majestic Theater on March 19, 1906. The play was produced
by Nelson Roberts and directed by Richard Carroll, and closed
after only 24 performances.[8]

On December 13, 1903, in New York City, 18-year-old
Indiola married 30-yearold Norman Selby (Los Angeles Times
1904). The event would have received little attention, had
Norman Selby not been better known as Charles "Kid"
McCoy, an outstanding boxer with a record of 200 victories.
McCoy was a well-known playboy who some say was the
fabled "real McCoy."[9] McCoy, who held the Welterweight
Championship, was known for his pugilistic skills as well as
his frequent trips to the altar. Indiola Arnold was his sixth
bride,[10] and their marriage was brief. In a report in the *Chicago
Daily Tribune* (1905), Indiola Arnold said that she was sorry
that she married Kid McCoy. She claims that she was deceived
into the marriage, recounting (Boston Globe 1905),

**Figure 53. Portrait of Mrs. C. M.
Keys. A gift to Gladys Woods.**

> I was married to Mr. Selby at Providence Rhode Island, December 13,
> 1903. I subsequently discovered that I had been inveigled into a ceremony
> by fraud and deception. Therefore, I commenced an action in the courts of
> Rhode Island to annul this marriage. This action has just been determined,
> the Supreme Court of Rhode Island holding that I should have brought an
> action for divorce. Therefore, under the law, I am, to my deep regret, the
> wife of Norman E. Selby. My attorneys however are now engaged in
> preparing papers which will enable me to sue for an absolute divorce.

They were divorced on the 5th of April, 1905, after a protracted legal battle (BostonGlobe
1905). If the divorce affected Kid McCoy, it was short lived. Seven weeks later, *The New York
Times* headlines read, "Mr. M'Coy, Engaged, Now Reads Chaucer; Tennyson, Longfellow, and
Browning Also Delight the Pugilist (NYT 1905)." McCoy was also well known for his love of
drink is quoted (NYT 1905:9),

> I haven't taken a drink and am not thinking fight any more. As a matter of
> fact I have taken to reading. I am fond of my books now. My Chaucer,
> Tennyson and Longfellow and Browning are great sources of delight to me.
> Poetry is fine.

Mrs. Lillian Estelle Earle Ellis, a widow who had inherited five million dollars, would soon
become his seventh wife.

In the 1920,[11] Clement Keys, 43, was living in Glen Ridge, New Jersey with his first
wife, Florence E. Hayes Keys, 38, whom he had married in 1905, and their two children: Edith,
13, and Florence, 12.[12] The marriage ended in divorce. C. M. Keys then became an American

citizen and married Indiola Arnold Reilly in 1924 (Ingham 1983:712). I found a passenger list of *The S. S. Saratoga* traveling to and from Cuba in 1912 with Indiola Reilly as a passenger. Her companion on one of those trips was Hugh J. Reilly, Jr.,[13] the executive of a New York railroad construction company owned by his father. In the summer of 1929, Indiola and Clement Keys were together on St. Catherines supervising the renovation (Figure 54).

Even in unraveling the sale of St. Catherines to Clement Keys and associates, confusion reigns. The *New York Times* reported that James Wilson[14] purchased the 23,000 acre island for a million dollars (NYT 1929).[15] Other sources claim it was the triumvirate of Keys, Howard Coffin and James Willson (AC 1929e; CSM 1929) who were co-owners. Howard E. Coffin was the owner of Sapelo Island and a major force in the development of the Georgia coast (Courson 1999; Courson 2003).[16] Willson, who was a financier from Louisville, Kentucky, teamed with Coffin and Keys to fund the merger of the Curtis and Wright airplane companies (NYT 1948).

Figure 54. The "big house" as it was when the Keys stepped onto St. Catherines Island. This picture, from Jenkins (1926), shows the front porch that the Keys replaced with an enclosed sun porch. It was later restored when the Noble Foundation renovated the house in 1971.

Willson was the "front person" for the St. Catherines Corporation that was formed in Atlanta. He was indentured to the corporation, making him and his partners liable for the contract (New York State 1929). Willson then signed the for the Bond of Deed for the Corporation[17] (Liberty County 1929a). The details of the sale were transmitted to M. B. Lane on March 28, 1929 and accepted by Willson on March 29, 1929. The deed called for six yearly payments with an interest of six percent paid semiannually for the reported $1M sale price. Covenants in the Bond of Deed prevented the St. Catherines Corporation from cutting timber on the island.

The *Christian Science Monitor* (CSM 1929:4) ran an article with the headline, "St. Catherine's Once Owned by Button Gwinnett, Signer of the *Declaration of Independence*, Believed Saved from Spoliation," heralding the sale. The *Monitor* (1929:4) went on to say,

> It is anticipated the new owners will spend much money in putting modern conveniences on the island. One of the things it will soon have will be a wide and adequate landing

field for flying machines. Each of the new purchasers is a 'flying" enthusiast. They believe firmly that the air is to furnish the field for the greatest advances in quick transportation methods that the world has ever known, and they are going to fit out a section of St. Catherines to share this development.

Flying into St. Catherines was an image that the Keys encouraged. The *New York Times* (McMullen 1930) described how men weary of the city crowds sought the solitude of island life. Discussing Keys' ownership of St Catherines, they describe how, "Mr. Keys arrives there by plane at his own landing strip and lives in Button Gwinnett's remodeled house, putting his guests in converted slave quarters"[18] (McMullen 1930:X11). The Keys never built a landing strip.[19] John's mother and father said that the Keys would take the train or "motor down" from New York to Maxwelton Estate on Colonels Island owned by the King family, where they would be picked up. Later, the Keys leased a lot from the Brown family, owners of Half Moon Marina, and they would dock there. E. J. Noble later purchased the dock lot after he bought St. Catherines, and it remains the takeoff point to the island.

While there were reports of a partnership in the purchase of St. Catherines, the presence of Coffin and Willson[20] on the island was minimal. There are pictures of Coffin visiting the island in the early 1930s. Willson's co-ownership was of a relatively short duration, less than 18 months. In a petition of separation,[21] Eda Turner Willson claimed that her husband's $10 million net worth included $125,000 from the sale of his share of St. Catherines Island (NYT 1930:22). H. E. Coffin was living on nearby Sapelo Island. If he was involved with St. Catherines, he was working behind the scenes. He was never an active participant in the renovations on the island. When the full impact of the Depression hit, Howard Coffin suffered financial reversals in 1934 and he was forced to sell Sapelo Island to R.J. Reynolds Jr., the cigarette tycoon (Sullivan 2002). Coffin died by his own hand in late November of 1937 (NYT 1937b:1).

On St. Catherines, it was clear who was in charge. The Keys were making the decisions, and Toby Woods was interested in working for them. As John tells the story,

My daddy also applied for work,[22] but the only position available was captain of the tugboat, "Egg Island."[23] He took it and brought the building materials from Savannah to the island. The biggest boat daddy had operated before was a rowboat and my mother taught him how to row that. The tug didn't have much power pulling one barge. He often could not make any headway against a strong tide. He would just keep churning until the tide slackened. Once he blew for the Thunderbolt bridge to open; it didn't, and he couldn't stop, ran into it and lost several pieces of timber off the barge, which he tied to the barge so that they could be towed to the island. One big cypress beam in the main house living room that he had tied on to tow still molds in damp weather.[24]

Figure. 55. *The Guale*. The boat was built with white cedar and the bottom was covered with canvas.

When John Toby began to work for the Keys, they owned *The Nautilus* and *The Guale* (pronounce with a hard G ("Gwalee"). The Keys did not know that "Guale" was pronounced "walley." Even when they were aware of the pronunciation, it did not matter. Forevermore, it was pronounced "Guale" with a "G". *The Guale* was powered by a 22-horse-power Johnson motor (Figure 55). The cabin at the bow of the boat was the only protection from the elements. The pilot operated the boat from the stern. John described the many times that the kids huddle together in the cabin while their dad faced the elements as he took them to their destination during a storm. Gee remembers a frightful night in hurricane force winds when she was in the cabin bailing out water while her father took off his raincoat to protect the motor from being swamped.

The Nautilus was a formidable vessel. It was a 34-foot boat with a cabin for passengers and an open pilot cabin on the side of the boat. With two 157-horse-power Universal engines, *The Nautilus* could reach a speed of 30 knots. A trip to the Half Moon dock (Figure 56) took about 20 minutes, compared to the hour-long trip each way with the tug. The Keys thought that such a substantial vessel needed a captain that everyone could see, so they bought John's father a summer and winter captain's uniform (Figure 57).

Figure 56. St. Catherines dock at Half Moon River. The two couples on the deck are Waldo Floyd and his wife, and Mr. and Mrs. Hancock. On the freight boat, John is on the far right and his dad is to his left. In the background on the left is J. H. Morgan's oyster and crab dock. Ca. 1945.

Figure 57. John Toby in his winter uniform at the helm of The Nautilus. Mr. and Mrs. Keys and guests are being transported to St. Catherines.

The Keys and the Revitalization of St. Catherines.

John describes the extensive renovations that were occurring on St. Catherines,

The Keys spent $1,000,000 restoring the "big" house, restoring one of the slave cabins,[25] building six guest cabins, three employee cottages, the superintendent's house with a cellar, the powerhouse and the main shop, a total remodel of the "big" house with the addition of a large living room, a servant quarters' wing and two cellars, renovated the horse barn, built a dock with boat house, and a swimming pool. The swimming pool was built just to the south of the "big" house. A telephone line was laid from the mainland to the island. The telephone line was connected to the mainland line where John Stevens lived. The Keys had a 6-foot high wire fence on one side of the 43-acre residential area that extended down one side of Rock Field.[26]

The plan involved changes to two major sections on the island. The "big" house complex included buildings that were built during the Waldburg period, such as the "big" house, the horse barn, and a number of cabins built to house enslaved individuals (Figure 58). The Rauers built their mansion and a freight dock on the north part of the complex (Figure 59). The employee complex was built south of the "big" house complex. The link between the "big" house complex and employee complex was a bridge with cedar railings. The bridge was built by the Keys and renovated and widened later. While the bridge may have been altered, the original cedar railings remain (Figure 60). The employee complex included the superintendent's house, the power plant, the main dock and three employees' cabins.

Figure 58. The extent of the renovation of the "big" house complex can be seen in this photo taken during renovation. The dock in the foreground is the original dock to the "big" house and the Rauers' mansion. In this view, the mansion had already been demolished. To the north is the supply dock used by the Rauers. To the far right is the horse barn and behind that and to the left is the ruin of the cotton gin. Below the dock are two rows of tabby cabins. The cleared area at the top of the photograph is Sams Field.

Figure 59. The private dock that led to the "big" house and the Rauers mansion. Toby Woods is in the foreground. The sign above the dock was made during the Noble Era. Talley Easterland built the frame and hand cut the letters out of cedar. The dock is no longer in use, but it remains a wonderful spot to watch the sunset and boat traffic on Waldburg Creek.

Figure 60. The bridge with the red cedar rails. Number 4 cabin is on the left of the bridge (cabins 2 and 3 are also visible). Part of Cabin 4 serves as a research kitchen. This more recent photos shows that the bridge has been widened while maintaining the cedar railings.

The jewel in their remodeling efforts was the "big" house, which they began referring to as the "Button Gwinnett" house. The "big" house was built next to the Rauers mansion. The Keys demolished the Rauers mansion that was considered one of the finest coastal homes when it was built. They used the lumber and the tabby-like cement blocks in the foundation to build other structures on the island.[27]

One particular cement tabby-like block from the Rauers mansion's foundation was sent by E. J. Noble to Charles Francis Jenkins in 1944 or 1945. Jenkins was the source for the claim that the Waldburg House was that of Button Gwinnett (Jenkins 1926). Jenkins' "Signers Walk" was his monument to the signers of the *Declaration of Independence*. It included stepping stones that were "connected closely with the life of a signer." The "Walk" in his garden at "Far Country" in the Hemlock arboretum of his estate at Germantown, Pennsylvania had a block from the Rauers' mansion foundation as one of the stepping stones (step 52) (Jenkins 1946). The "close connection" with Gwinnett was that it was from St. Catherines Island. It was made by the Rauers nearly a century after Gwinnett's death.

Arthur Wilson lived in the Rauers house with his wife Anna and their four children, Josephine, John, Mary, and Margaret while supervising the renovations on the island and the construction of the superintendent's house. George Wilson, a relative, occupied one of the employee cabins on the island. Arthur Wilson was not a well-liked boss. He seemed to offend not only the employees, but the sub-contractors as well. John described why Arthur Wilson was referred to unaffectionately as "Oh Hell."[28] They called him as "Oh Hell" because no matter how well you completed a task, his first words upon seeing the finished project were "Oh Hell." John also told me about the time when Uncle Otis Edenfield and other workers were rolling two 5,000-gallon water tanks that his dad had brought from Savannah off the barge and up the dock. They were having trouble pushing the tanks up the steep riverbank. Wilson, seeing the workers straining to push the water tanks up the bank, yelled, "Oh hell, one Yankee could push the tanks up by himself." Uncle Otis was not one to take what he considered unjustified criticism easily. He had a short fuse and was easily offended. John describes it,

Otis said that he didn't work on the island long. He told me about helping move the cotton gin steam engine off the island. But his problems started when he came face-to-face with an alligator. There was a big alligator in the water down by the dock. Otis got a gun and killed it. "Oh Hell" saw him kill the gator and picked up a stick and started toward him. Otis told him that if he didn't put the stick down, he would kill him too and I believe that he would have. So, "Oh Hell" fired Otis.

There was considerable infrastructure that needed be completed before the renovation of the buildings could be finished. John Rogers, Toby's father-in-law, was contracted to bring plumbing to all the buildings that were being renovated and constructed on the north end of the island (Figure 61) . This was a major undertaking, and there were always family members who could be found to help. John relates,

> My uncle Albert Rogers, as a boy, was hired by my grandfather, John
> Rogers, to dig a trench with a shovel. "Oh Hell" came up, took the shovel
> out of his hands, stuck the shovel deep in the ground and brought out a piled
> up shovel of dirt and said, "this is the way to dig, boy".

Arthur Wilson had struck again. Nevertheless, the work did get done. While the Keys implied that they renovated all of the "slave cabins," only one was renovated. The six guest cabins and three employee cabins were built in "the style of a slave cabin"[29] (Figure 62). John describes that the simulated tabby composed of cement embedded with shells was used extensively,

> We used cement mixed with oyster shells instead of rock or gravel for this
> work. We used oyster shells off the island and riverbanks to mix with the
> cement. We also plastered all of the building walls with cement mixed with
> oyster shells that had the look of tabby. Until I left the island in 1982, we
> still mixed oyster shells with the cement on everything we built.

Figure 61. The ditch dug under the supervision of John Rogers, who was contracted to bring plumbing to the buildings on the north end of St. Catherines.

Figure 62. The employee cabin under construction. To the left is a worker mixing the "cement tabby." The porch faces Waldburg Creek. Ca. 1929.

Figure 63. The front view of the Wilson house that was built by the Keys in 1930. This picture was taken early in E.J. Noble era.

The demolition of the Rauers mansion was a major operation. They salvaged many of the furnishings, such as mantles and mirrors, recycled lumber from the mansion, and recycled many of the cement tabby blocks that were used in the foundation. Some of the debris and unusable materials from the Rauers' mansion were dumped on the banks of Waldburg Creek to serve as rip-rap. Wood recovered from the demolition was used to build the dock in the superintendent's complex. The Keys built the Wilson House (Figure 63), which would eventually become the Woods' home when his dad, Toby, became superintendent. John's family lived there from 1943 until he left the island in September 1982.

The Bridge

The bridge between the "big" house complex and the employee complex was an important physical and symbolic presence (Figures 64 and 65). The bridge became a necessity when the Keys built an artesian well. As John tells it,

> Just south of the number 4 guest cottage at the end of the lawn was a ditch that drained a swamp area into Waldburg Creek when the Keys had an eight- inch artesian well drilled in 1930. The top of the well was reduced to four inches creating a flow that at the high tide exceeded six feet at spring tide. The overflow from the well was piped underground to that ditch.

> Just below the overflow pipe, the Keys had a bridge built. The handrails on the bridge were built with red cedar limbs that still are on the bridge today. The bridge was sort of a dividing

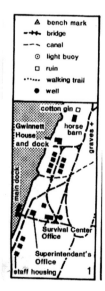

Figure 64. Map of bridge.

line between the wealthy owners and the hired help.

Figure 65. John, Clel and Gee on the bridge, with the corn grinder ruin in the background. Ca. 1932.

Figure 66. Toby Woods and C.M. Keys in a bateaux at St. Catherines (Date1935-1938).

The bridge connects the
the superintendent's home,
and other buildings such as
and the main freight dock

John said that his father (Figure 66) built a dam just off the riverbank across the ditch that drained the overflow from the artesian well, providing him and his friends with what he has called "a nice little lake." He goes on,

They used some of the tabby cement blocks that had been removed from under the Rauers house to make an overflow spill way. The dammed-in area made a nice little lake. My father caught sheephead and mullet and put them in the lake. To my dad's surprise, they lived even though it was fresh water. We liked to watch the fish from the bridge

Later in the year 1940 when I was 10 years old, my friend Jack Coleman, who was 11 years old, his father worked at the sawmills that were cutting lumber on the north end at the time. We drove an old Diamond T truck with solid tires and wooden spokes to the saw mills and picked up some wide rough boards and brought them back and built our first boat that was eight foot long and three feet wide, a flat bottom boat with a wide bow and stern. We corked the cracks with cotton. We could play in the little lake – chasing the fish and whatever.

In 1961, when my son Johnny was two years old, we were cleaning and mowing the lawn and Johnny was playing on the bridge. He was looking through the handrail and he fell into the foot deep water below. My daddy was walking across the bridge and heard the noise below. Johnny was trying to climb out of the steep ditch. Daddy rescued him and brought him to his mother, who cleaned him up in the deep kitchen sink in the superintendent's house.[30]

"big" house complex to
the employees' cabins,
the power plant house
(Figure 67).

re 67. The main dock was built using
er from the demolished Rauers house. It
to the superintendent's complex. . Ca.
s.

83

The Power Plant and Shop

The most important part of the infrastructure on the south side of the bridge was the power plant house and shop that was about 500 feet from the superintendent's house. The electrical equipment on the island – the lights, fans, and refrigerators – was run on 120-volt D. C. (direct current). John describes the power plant and the process for generating power,

> The light plant powered by a Fairbanks-Morse engine was in the power plant house and shop. It was a two-cycle, two cylinder, crankcase compression type diesel engine, that had to be started by air pressure, after the two cylinders were preheated with a cord soaked in fuel oil, lighted and screwed into each cylinder to preheat the air.
>
> The air compressor engine had to be cranked by hand and the air pressure had to be 90-100 lbs. to start the engine. The engine turned about 800 rpm per minute and it had a 15-kilowatt D.C. generator that charged a bank of batteries in 60 glass jars.[31] Each glass jar battery was one cell, which was equal to two volts. My father operated and maintained this light plant from 1930 until about 1946.[32]
>
> The electric wires were all underground. There was always a battle to keep the engine running. While the system was reliable, Daddy could have parts for the Fairbanks Morse diesel engine rebuilt or replaced. When there was one of the infrequent problems, he was able to purchase new parts from the Motor Supply Company at the west end of Broughton Street across West Broad Street. Motor Supply Company also had a machine shop that they could turn crankshafts. When the journals got worn or out of round, they would also grind valves and valves seats.
>
> Daddy usually ran the light plant in the afternoons, so that the employees could wash their clothes with the ringer type washing machines with a converter changing the current from D.C. to A.C. It was only in the 1950s after another light plant was installed that they had TVs to watch. He also ran the light plant at night with the converter attached until he was ready to go to bed, so that everybody could watch TV. He would then have to go out and shut the light plant down.
>
> They would then have to turn their converters off.[33] And only use the lights that would draw off the batteries. It wasn't unusual for my mother to run up the water pressure or turn off the light plant. My daddy liked to tell a new employee that he had hired, that they would need to buy some extra DC light bulbs for their house. They would go to Savannah and try to buy DC lights. There is no such thing. Light bulbs will work with either DC or AC current. It's only the voltage (120 volts) and wattage (100 watt) that are relevant in purchasing light bulbs.

Another important part of the power plant was a water pump that sent water to all the buildings on the island. John said that the water pump would build up 40 lbs. of pressure in the two 5,000-gallon water tanks. The water pump had to be operated by hand and did not have an automatic switch. When the pressure dropped below 20 lbs., the light plant had to be running to bring the pressure up to 40 lbs. to ensure the flow of water.

From the 1930 to 1946, the Fairbanks-Morse system worked as well as could have been expected. John recalls,

> My father bought a set of glass Exide batteries in 1946 when the Fairbanks Morse diesel light plant engine was replaced by two Hallett light plant engines.[34] These two diesel engines were always trouble. He used these Exide glass batteries until about 1956, then he talked Mr. Noble into purchasing a new 2-cylinder 71 series 54 hp at 1800 rpm 2 cycle General Motors diesel engine with a 15 KW DC generator attached. The unit was bought from Morgan's Inc. I was a master mechanic working for Morgan's at that time. My father installed the unit in the light plant powerhouse on the island, and I made the initial start up inspection on it.
>
> With this unit he bought a set of plastic Willard batteries. This light plant diesel [engine] was trouble free; we ran it until 1961. Then we replaced it with a R.E.A. underground cable running to the island. My father maintained these glass jar batteries all those years. He melted the sealing tar out of the top edge and rebuilt them when they went bad.

The "Big" House

The "big" house (Figures 68-70) became the jewel of the renovation project. In 1926, Charles Francis Jenkins included a printed a picture (opposite page 31 of his book) of the "Old Tabby Plantation House" in his definitive biography of Button Gwinnett (Jenkins 1926). He describes the complex near the "big" house and comments that Bosomworth and his "queen" had a house that was located a mile north of the present complex near her purported burial ground, what is now known as Mary's Mound. Visually surveying the area he described (Jenkins 1926: 42-43),

> west and overlooking the bay, is what has been the owner's house. It is a modest but comfortable dwelling built of tabby, a mixture of lime, sand and shells, as all the other houses and buildings nearby. Through the middle runs a wide hall with rooms opening off it on either side. The walls are of a considerable thickness; a porch is across the front. At the rear toward the north, is a square building which was the smoke house, and to the south is the outdoor kitchen, not far away from the rear entrance.
>
> To the south east of the mansion were the slave quarters, a regular village consisting of three rows of double cabins, seven in each row, the two rows

to the east facing a wide open common. Many of these have almost completely disappeared. At each end of the common are the ruins of square buildings which were used by the Negro women to grind corn. The church was destroyed some years ago, so that one of the double cabins had a steeple added and converted to a chapel. Two of the cabins are occupied by coloured folks who have been on the island for at least four generations, this being as far back as they had knowledge. Northeastwardly, from the rear of the mansion house, and in a general way balancing the slave quarters, are the large barn and ruins of the cotton gin.

Figure 68. Front view of the "big" house (on the left) and the tower of the Rauers mansion (on the right). By this time, the Keys had removed the outside kitchen of the "big" house and had constructed the big living room. The tower would later be demolished, but the smoke house remained. Photo 1929.

Figure 69. Side view of the "big" house.

Figure 70. The rear view of the "big" house showing the large living room with awning and walls covered with fig vine.

The acceptance of the "big" house as the Gwinnett House by the Keys is not surprising. They were nurturing the image of powerful people flying to the island to visit the house that was once the home of a powerful politician and signer of the *Declaration of Independence*. Staying in "restored slave cabins" was a unique experience available only to a few individuals. It was a much more impressive image than saying that you flew to St. Catherines and were entertained in the house of Jacob Waldburg, one of the Georgia's largest slave owners, and stayed in one of Waldburg's restored slave cabins.

The willingness of the academic community to accept Jenkins' and the Keys' speculation is quite surprising. The Gwinnett myth, however, is a central theme in "selling" the uniqueness of St. Catherines to the public. It has become one of the primary attractions on an island that few people will ever have a chance to visit. Selling the "big" house as that of Button Gwinnett required special attention to its renovation, special attention that it received. According to John's research,[35] the basic structure of the house was solid. The heart pine floors were in good enough shape and did not need much repair. They re-plastered some of the inside walls, and the outside walls were repaired with "St. Catherines cement"[36] (cement mixed with shell to make it look like tabby) in some places. Of course, it was necessary to completely rewire electrical service in the house. A state of the art heating system was replaced in the basement that could be fired by wood, coal or oil. There were substantial additions to the house and significant renovations of the original structures. John describes the changes made in the house from top to bottom,

Figure 71. Windows of the glassed in porch. Uncle Woodrow Rogers is in the foreground.

The house was re-roofed using Ludowici tiles that were manufactured and purchased from the factory in Ludowici, Georgia. Each of the non-interlocking clay red tiles had a rough bark-like texture and weighed 5¼ lbs. each.[37] They were installed on the roof of the original "big" house and over the roof of the big living room and the servant's quarters that were added to the original house. Only the side porch was covered with galvanized crimped tin.

All windows and doors in the house were replaced. The front porch was removed and a wide enclosed glass sun porch with a nice tiled floor was added (Figure 71). The cypress wood shingles on the roof were removed along with the board sheeting under them. New 2" x 6" foot rafters were installed in between the approximate 4"x 6" hand hewed rafters that were on 24" centers.

There were two ceramic tile bathrooms added behind the two back bedrooms on the first floor. A door was added in the wall that divided the front and back bedrooms, so that the front bedroom guests could go through from the back bedroom to the bathroom. All the plumbing fixtures and tile in one bathroom on the north side were green (Figure 72) and the south bathroom was furnished with lavender fixtures.

Figure 72. The green bathroom on first floor.

A larger walk-in closet with cedar line storage doors was added between the back bedroom and bathroom. In the down stairs bedrooms, there were fire wood storage closets next to the fireplaces and a closet with drawers next to that. The wide hall dividing the bedrooms at the east end on the north side had big walk-in linen closets, across the hall was a bar room with sink and storage shelves and a secret panel to the cellar. The stairs, to make the secret passage to the cellar, were never built.

The renovation involved major changes on the second floor. The four upstairs bedrooms were converted to two bedrooms in front, and two storage rooms with closets and counters with built in drawers in the back. To accommodate the changes in the upstairs bedrooms, the middle of the three dormers was widened so that a shared bathroom could be installed between the front bedrooms. Adding to the expanded quarters was a comfortable library that John described,

> Upstairs, over the hall and downstairs bathrooms, a nice library with double sliding doors was added. A skylight was installed over the library. The room was paneled with cypress boards and inset bookshelves. One sliding door opened to a balcony overlooking the huge living room with a stairway leading down from the balcony to the living room at the north end of the balcony.

From the balcony on the second floor there was a commanding view of the first floor. At the bottom of the stairs was an outside door and, just east of that, a half-bathroom. Across the room under the balcony was a door that led to the side porch with an entrance to the kitchen and servants quarters. Just east of the living room, a door led to the cellar underneath the bar and to the north side of the house. A door on the west side of the cellar opened up under the "big" house. A big furnace distributed heat throughout the house.

The key to the renovation was the addition of a large living room that required the removal of the outside tabby kitchen (Figure 73).

> The large living room was installed joining the "big" house on the back. It had wide oak floors with false wooden pegs at the end of each of the boards. It had exposed cypress support beams with a cypress ceiling and windows through the roof. A huge cypress beam was over the large fireplace that was floored with tile. Across the living is another huge cypress beam embedded in the wall over the extension to the living room that accents a sitting area. This huge cypress beam is the one my father towed home after running into the Thunderbolt Bridge.

> There is a large picture window on the east end of the living room with a large outside awning to shade the window from the morning sun. Just south of the picture window is a swinging door that led to the servant's pantry where all the guest dishes, glasses, and silver was kept in glass in shelves, drawers, and cabinets. There is also a large sink in the pantry. As you walked through the swinging door that led to the kitchen, a large pantry and refrigerator room were on your right. The kitchen was outfitted with a large counter topped with wide oak boards and cabinets and drawers underneath. On the east side of the kitchen was a double sink with a big wood stove on

the south side of the room. A table and chairs where the hired help ate completed the kitchen furnishings.

On the southwest end of the kitchen was a door leading to the side porch and to the servant's quarters. That led to a gunroom on the west side. That had glassed-in gun shelves (or cases) with drawers and a storage cabinet that could be locked. The gunroom had a door leading to the side porch.

All the floors throughout the servant's wing of the house were concrete covered with linoleum. The Keys left an old musket gun in the gun room, and it was still there when I retired.

Just south of the gunroom was a game room with cabinets, drawers and a double copper sink with counters on both sides. To the east of the gunroom and game room, a room that sometimes was used as a bedroom. Between the gun room and the bedroom is a stairway that leads to the three rooms in the servant's quarters that could be used as bedrooms. There was one bathroom upstairs.

Downstairs just south of the game room is a screened-in back porch with a half-bathroom on the east side. On that side of the porch are stairs leading down to the end cellar. The cellar had a laundry storage and a wine and liquor storage room. There was an opening to get under the big living room.

Both cellars had ground level windows. There was a laundry chute in the hall of the servant's quarters where you could drop laundry down to the cellar to be washed. There was a room service devise in the kitchen that buzzed and gave the room number of the room to be served, by mashing a button in the guest rooms.

There was a telephone in the kitchen and also in the guest part of the house so that you could call the superintendent's house or connect with the telephone company on the on the mainland. You had to hand-crank the phone to get your call through.

Between the side porch and the kitchen was an enclosed garden area for flowers and shrubbery, and also a path to carry wood to a wood storage area. The wood could be passed to the huge fireplace in the living room through a small area with a door inside. The wood would be cut into lengths of approximately four feet. They used fat lighter splinters to start the fire. We then added heart pine split logs and topped them off with split oak logs. There was a trap steel door in the bottom to catch the ashes, and it could be removed from the outside. In the huge cypress beam over the fireplace area was a carved poem signed by C.M. Keys (Figure 74).

Another feature of the house was a two-and-a-half-foot concrete side porch topped with thin granite. Just to the right, as you entered the porch, was a boot box with a spigot and drain. The side of the boot box was granite-covered cement with a wood cover. The porch beams, joist, posts and ceiling were all cypress.

Figure 73. The large living room showing the exposed cypress beams. To the left is the edge of the fireplace. At the top is the entrance to the library. On the bottom is the entrance to the bedrooms and parlor. The weight of the Ludiwici tile caused the walls to bulge, warranting the additional support of metal braces installed in 1971. Picture taken in 2004.

Figure 74. The fireplace showing the mantle where C. M. Keys inscribed a poem.

Swimming Pool

The Keys built a swimming pool about 100 yards from the back porch of the "big" house overlooking Waldburg Creek (Figure 75). John describes it,

> It was a large concrete pool, 11 feet deep at the end with the diving board. At that time, water ran continuously into the pool from an old well that the Rauers had drilled to furnish water to their mansion and the old Waldburg house.[38] The water flowed into the pool to maintain the water level and out and out the scum gutters and into the marsh. Before Union Bag Paper Company in Savannah and other paper mills went into operation along the coast, the water from the artesian wells flowed (Figure 76).

Mary Williams Hartford visited the island with her family as a teenager. She described the pool as bitterly cold. While smiling and pantomiming a shiver, she said that it was cold enough for Aunt Gladys to store her milk.

Figure 75. The original swimming pool built by the Keys. They hired Fred Ginter, a contractor from Hinesville in 1931. The pool was fed by an artesian well located between the "big" house and the Rauers' house. There was a valve at the bottom of the deep end of the pool. The valve could be turned on above ground to drain the pool to the marsh and eventually into Waldburg Creek.

Figure 76. John's mother and her friend, Mrs. Marris Shaver, drinking at the well. The pipe to the left carries water to the two 5000-gallon tanks at the nearby power plant. Tabby blocks from the foundation of the Rauers house excess water and drained it to the creek above the bridge. Ca. 1940s.

The Keys also restored the first single-room slave cabin nearest to the "big" house[39] (Figure 77). The Rauers' black overseer lived in when John's grandfather bought fish from the black people on the island. The Key's built six more double-room cabins in the same style as the slave cabins still standing (Figure 78). They were built on a concrete slab with tile floors. They were framed and sheeted with wide boards, then covered with a sealing felt and nailed with plaster wire. Almost an inch of cement mixed with sand and oyster shells was plastered onto the outside walls. The cabins had Heatilater[40] fireplace inserts that circulated warmed air though them.

Figure 77. Toby Woods in front of restored slave cabin one. Photo by E. J. Noble in the 1950s.

Figure 78. Cabin number five, built in the style of a slave cabin. The road leading east to North Beach is in the foreground nestled between three crepe myrtles.

The Horse Barn

The renovation of the horse barn illustrates the care and expense that the Keys' invested in making St. Catherines meet their needs and in transforming it into one of the finest island estates on the Georgia coast (Figure 79). As John Woods tells it,

> The tabby horse barn that was built by the Waldburgs was in pretty good shape since the Rauers' family used it for their horses and mules, and it had a fence surrounding it (Figure 80). The Rauers probably had re-roofed the barn with sawed cypress shingles during their ownership, because when the Keys restored the barn, they didn't have to re-roof it.
>
> The door area was enlarged on the north end of the horse barn and large wooden doors with overhead tracks and rollers were installed on both ends. On the south half of the barn, the floor was laid with concrete and stalls for the horses had concrete walls about five feet high. On the wall there was side a feed trough and hayrack. The hay was dropped into the hayracks from the loft where it was stored. There was a wide area down the middle of the barn where the horses were led into their stalls with wooden bars lowered down behind them. On the northeast end of the barn was a rat proof

feed room where the grain for the horses was stored. Just past the middle
door (on the east side), steep stairs were built leading to the loft storage
area. On the south end of the loft was a window with a rope pulley extended
overhead to pull the hay into the loft.

**Figure 79. The view of the renovated barn from the
east. Two pecan trees are in foreground. The cotton
gin is to the left. Ca. late 1970s.**

**Figure 80. The horse barn before restoration by the
Keys. The Rauers' horses and mules were housed in
the barn. Ca. 1929**

Trouble in the Paradise

Keys and his co-owners purchased St. Catherines just as the Dow Jones Industrial
Average (DJIA) was reaching its peak. On September 3, 1929, five months after they acquired
the island, the stock market reached a high of 381.17. Unfortunately, the market peak lasted only
seven weeks before the famous market crash on October 24, 1929, known as Black Thursday.
The market lost nearly 20% of its value that day, closing at 299.5. The market appeared to
stabilize only to suffer severe losses again on October 29, Black Tuesday. The decline of the
market did not slow the renovations at the end of 1929 and during the early 1930s.

C. M. Keys and his colleagues were also riding the growth of the real estate market and
became major forces in the New York market before buying St. Catherines. In 1928, it was
announced that H. E. Coffin would head the Montauk Beach Development Company that was
taking over the development of Montauk Beach (NYT 1928:42), with C. M. Keys serving on the
board of directors of the corporation. The Montauk Beach Development Company rose out of the
ashes and dreams of Carl Graham Fisher.[41] Fisher made a fortune with the Prest-O-Lite
automobile headlight, which he later sold to Union Carbide (Fisher 1998; Foster 2000). In 1926,
after success with developing Miami Beach, he set his sights on Montauk Beach on the
easternmost tip of Long Island. Even Graham's net worth of an estimated $100 million was not
enough. The real estate bust in Florida and a hurricane that destroyed much of Miami Beach in
1926 forced Graham to seek outside funding.

The renovation activity on St. Catherines was paralleled by turmoil behind the scenes at Curtis-Wright and C. M. Keys, Inc. Keys resigned from Curtis-Wright early in December 1931. On front page of *The Wall Street Journal*, Keys announced his retirement from Curtis-Wright, chairman of the Board of Transcontinental & Western Air, Inc., and North American Aviation (WSJ 1932). He said (WSJ 1932:1), "On account of health, and also the pressures of other business, I am retiring from my aviation activities. I hope, in time, to resume some of these occupations, but I don't know when."

The untold story that was unfolding behind the scenes at the many companies headed by Keys was more complex. Keys had the excess cash from North American Aviation funneled through his company, C. M. Keys and Company, as a call loan. As of June 30th of 1929, the cash totaled $8.8 million and North American Aviation could "call in" the money as needed. Keys had unethically used these funds for his personal investments in aviation stocks, but during the boom in the aviation companies this was not a financial problem. When the stock market collapsed, however, Keys owed North American Aviation nearly $800,000 and could not cover this debt (Eltscher and Young 1998:61). The companies that he owed money to let him resign quietly, without any public announcement of the actions that led to his resignation. Van der Linden (2002:233) claims that the $800,000 was written off and that "Keys was wiped out."

Robert Van der Linden (2002:145) writes,

> His health was a concern. Keys' years of stress with business and Wall Street had left his nerves frayed. The collapse of the market in October had wiped out his personal reserves and had left him vulnerable. Unknown to most in the industry, including those in his own company, Keys had personally borrowed $14.5 million from North American in call loans. He used this money to invest in various other aviation and non-aviation stocks, as he had done successfully for years. But now the securities were virtually worthless. At some point the board would recall the loans, but Keys had no money to repay them. The resulting stress was understandably considerable. Increasingly, Keys spent time away from New York recovering from nervous collapse at his Saint Catherine's Island vacation home off the Georgia Coast.

To compound his financial worries, the Montauk Beach Development Company went into receivership in 1932 and operated under the bankruptcy statue through 1934. In 1938, C. M. Keys took control of the corporation since his company held the first mortgage (NYT 1938a:36). The company was modestly successful. In 1941, the *New York Times* announced that Keys' company had sold nine parcels of land (NYT 1941) – a far cry from earlier hopes of transforming Montauk to a must visit destination.

To add to their troubles, the news from St. Catherines was not very hopeful either. The Keys had realized that timbering might be necessary, and hoped that it could be done in a manner that would not destroy the island.[42] In April 13,1938, Keys informed Jack Rauers that an Ohio timber company had cruised the island and as ready to make a proposal (Keys 1938a):

> I think that this proposal will be more of a proposal to you than it will be to me, because I have been unable, during this business slump, even to get a rise

out of any of the offerings or inquiries that I have made. This property has
been offered to everybody whom I know who would be capable of buying it,
and I have not, of course, held to any price limit in the matter.

On May 31, 1938, Keys corresponded with J. J. Rauers (Keys 1938d) about the
possibility of selling the lumber and wrote,

In this part of the country all reorganization and, indeed, all organization of
business, appears to be almost at a standstill. Money is obtainable only with
the greatest difficulty. We are all trying to look forward and guess when a
turn can take place. A few optimists still talk of the early Fall as a likely time;
but people who are more realistic cannot see any great turn this year.

The realists in this case were correct. The fortune of the nation and of Clement Melville Keys did
not improve by the year's end. His only hope was for a quick sale of St. Catherines.[43] In August
1938, Keys informed Rauers that the property taxes had not been paid for 1936, 1937 or 1938
(Keys 1938b), and that he was having problems with paying the debt. He owed the Rauers
$615,000, but could not find a way to buy the island and clear the mortgage.

Keys wrote on August 30, 1938 that Blanchard & Calhoun had two prospective buyers
(Keys 1938c). J. J. "Jack" Rauers was impatient and told Keys, "I shall of course not hold back
on any plans already started for the Timber Cruiser, as prospects seem to be nearly dreams with
most of the brokers…(Rauers 1938). Rauers Cunningham quickly wired Mrs. Eugene Dupont
and Mr. Thomas McCabe[44] (Cunningham 1938a; Cunningham 1938b) with the following offer,

Have been advised you interested in acquiring St. Catherine's Island on the
Coast of Georgia Stop Am wiring as member of family having very large
interest in this property Stop Mortgage we hold long past due Stop Total
amounts involved six hundred fifteen thousand dollars Stop If interested in
acquiring will submit proposition five hundred fifty thousand dollars cash for
immediate acceptance Stop Now have proposition to timber property but
prefer selling outright Stop Necessary to make immediate decision on
timbering operation Stop Wire Western Union my expense.

On September 13, 1938, Rauers Cunningham received a response from Mrs. Eugene DuPont,
"Telegram received not interested in property returning booklet" (DuPont 1938). J. J. Rauers
appeared ready to begin a timbering operation. He received the report from L. B. Ackerman, on
September 10, 1938, saying that 13,363,000 board feet of lumber was potentially harvestable on
St. Catherines (Ackerman 1938).

C. M. Keys probably did not remember a poem that he had written in 1904 (Keys 1904),
entitled "Busted, B'Gosh":

'I'm the gent wat wus the miner from the North
    Pacific Coast' ---
Yas—that's me! An' it's true I had the million,
    Putty near, that is ---almost---
An' they said the 'game was easy' –so I confidently

came
An' o' course I didn't understand that I would be
    the "game"!

"They ketched me 'long o' copper, an they ketched
    me long o' steel;
They sez the fault is Morgan's —some talk a lot o'
    Weil---
An' I drifted from th' Waldorf t' places the gals
    Yells 'Hash'!

"I was long o' Steel at 40; 'averaged' it at 35
Puts some margins up at 30; buyed again at 25;
At 15 they teched me gently--- I was nearly busted
    then---
But they still kep' talkin' 'margins'---so they sol'
    me out at 10!

"I hev borrowed $20---an' I'm goin' back out West.
Where a feller buys his counters and then fares jest
    like the best;
I'm goin' to found a Stock Exchange, or p'r'aps a
    a gamblin' dive,
Er some other decent callin', with a chanst t' keep
    alive

John Toby assumed a more extensive role on St Catherines after the completion of the
renovations.

> After the Keys became the only owners of the island and after the
> construction was finished, Mr. Keys hired my daddy permanently and had
> him move up to one of the employee's houses. He was in charge of
> maintaining, taking care of, and general supervision and protection of the
> island along with the boats, and electric plant at a salary of $100.00 a
> month, which he didn't always get during the Depression. He was able to
> survive thanks to good hunting, fishing, and trapping. Mr. Keys also hired
> Lionel Tester and his wife, Mary, to be in charge of the "big" house, the
> seven cottages, lawn, and swimming pool. They were either from Maine or
> Rhode Island.[45]

Toby Woods Becomes Superintendent

After the renovation and revitalization of the buildings on St. Catherines, John Toby and
Lionel Tester oversaw the operations of the island. Eventually, John Toby was made
superintendent of the island. He and Gladys moved from the employees cabin and into the
servant's quarters of the "big" House.

The Testers moved to the mainland sometime in the late 1930s. They opened Knotty Knoll, a tourist court on Route 17 just south of Highway 84, after they left the island. The Testers took advantage of the opening of Route 17 over the Savannah River in 1924 (also known as the Atlantic Coastal Highway) (AC 1924a). In the summer of 1928, the southern portion of Highway 17 running between Brunswick and Jacksonville was completed. The Testers maintained the business for three or four years, but eventually moved to St. Simons where they returned to caring for the houses and grounds of residents. They did return a few times to visit John and Gladys while John was superintendent. John's folks would bring the Testers over for a weekend of fishing, since Mr. Tester was always interested in fishing.[46] He died in his 87th year on September 24, 1980[47] on St. Simons. Mary Tester had died at age 83 three and a half years earlier (February 1977).

After the major renovation projects, the financial situation became difficult. Toby, John's father, often had to wait for his paycheck. In 1939, the cost of the renovations and the Great Depression made it necessary for the Keys to return the island to the Rauers family. One of the last duties Keys performed as the owner of St. Catherines was writing a letter of recommendation for John Toby (Figure 81). The Rauers regained control of the island, eventually selling it to E. J. Noble in 1943.

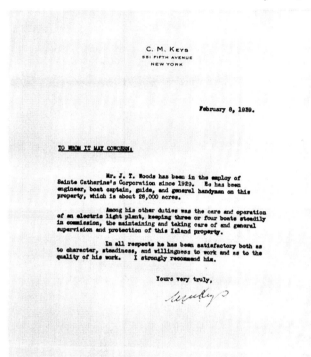

Figure 81. C. M. Key's last act on St. Catherines was to draft a letter of recommendation for Toby Woods in February 1939.

C. M. Keys suffered from a stroke and died on January 12, 1952 in his home at 24 West Fifty-Fifth Street in New York City. Indiola Keyes outlived her husband by almost a quarter of a century. She was 92 years old when she died in January of 1978[48] in Marion, Indiana.[49] John Woods appreciated the couple who, despite dealing with difficult times in their own lives, had show them such kindness. Over the mantle in the living room, C. M. Keyes carved a small poem that I am sure that he would have been pleased to be remembered by,

> Come to my forest in the circle of the sea,
> Come to my cottage and dwell awhile with me,
> Come to my garden where old timed blossoms grow,
> Smiles will come with you and sighs with you go.
> -C. M. K.

When St. Catherines was purchased by E. J. Noble, it was covered with a piece of plywood with wooden ducks attached to it (see Figure 74).

The Rauers Interlude: 1939-1943

The Keys, despite their financial difficulties, could have maintained ownership of the island for a while if they had been willing and able to develop a program to sell timber. But, Mr. and Mrs. Keys were principled about maintaining the island as a retreat, and only reluctantly tried to sell the timber.

St. Catherines reverted back to the Rauers family late in 1938. The cost of maintaining the island was a formidable task for the Rauers. To cope, they developed a plan to sell the timber and established sawmills on the north end of the island. Reynolds and Manley contracted the north end of the island, and authorized the Jack Thigpen Lumber Company to operate two sawmills at Sams Field (Figures 82 and 83). In 1939, W. E. Floyd drilled a 580-foot artesian well in the complex to provide water for the workers and to one of the sawmills.

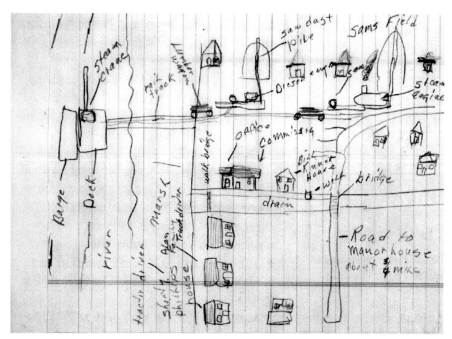

Figure 82. A map of the Thigpen Sawmill in Sams Field, created John Woods as he remembers it. Waldburg Creek is on the west side of the sawmill. A rail track was built for the four lumber wagons that carried the lumber from the two saw mills. Across the rail tracks were the office, commissary, and Bill Kinner's house. West of this was the well next to the drain that took excess water to Waldburg Creek. Yankee Bridge road crossed the drain with a wooden bridge spanning the drain. A small foot-bridge near the marsh led to the houses occupied by the white workers. Other shacks for black workers were located east of the road and north of the drain.

Figure 83. A Frick sawmill, the same kind used by the Thigpen Lumber Company on St. Catherines.

Mr. Harper[50] was the "timber cruiser," a key position in the timbering process. He could examine stands of forest and determine which should be harvested and how many board feet of lumber would be produced. Now, the United States Forest Service has software[51] that this job; but in 1939, the timber cruiser would do this with a pad, pencil and cruiser stick.[52] The cruiser would also determine the trees that should be harvested to most efficiently fill an order.

John said that Jack Thigpen brought over three international log trucks and a Diamond T lumber truck with wooden-spoked wheels and solid tires (Figure 84). In addition, they had three Farmall tractors and a smaller Caterpillar tractor (Figure 85). The hands, as John described them, would cut the trees and then cut them to length with cross cut (hand-pulled) saws. After cutting the tree to its desired lengths, the workers would drag the logs to the "rigging tree." The pulley system was used to load the log truck for transport to the mill. John describes it:

> The Farmall tractors had a tricycle type front wheel that was dangerous to drive. The front wheel would hit an obstacle, and that would spin the steering wheel. George Berryhill was working for the mill and was driving one of the Farmalls when it hit a stump and the spinning steering wheel broke his wrist. The Farmalls did not have hydraulic lifts, and when pulling a heavy log the front wheels would be off the ground and the driver would have to use the rear wheel brakes to steer it. The tractors would pull the logs to a rigging tree that had a pulley and cable tied to it where they would pull up the log and swing it onto the log truck to be carried to the sawmill.

Figure 84. Diamond T Lumber Truck with wooden spokes and solid rubber tires, similar to the one used by Thigpen.

Figure 85. A model M Farmall tractor, similar to those used by the Thigpen Lumber Company. The tricycle-like wheel on the front end created a problem for the drivers.

As a 19-year-old, Curtis Lee[53] (Figure 86) ran the steam dragline that loaded rough sawed lumber[54] onto the boats waiting at the dock at Waldburg Creek. It could take up to three days to load a boat or barge. Lee's father ran Knight's "junk yard"[55] and he taught his taught his son how to operate a drag line when he was only 16 years old. Curtis Lee, in John's words, was a "genius." He could repair anything, and if it was beyond repair and could not be buried,[56] he could demolish it. When the timber company ceased operations and the dragline was too heavy to be moved onto the aging dock, Curtis took an acetylene torch to it, cut it up into movable pieces, and took it to the junkyard to be sold as scrap.[57] John said that before the war, boats from as far away as Germany and Cuba would dock at the sawmill and pick up lumber. In addition to a boiler-driven mill, there was a diesel-powered mill.

There was also a commissary for the workers who traded in sawmill money, which Gee Little remembers were called "babbits" (Figure 87) The money was aluminum tokens originally manufactured for the Shearwood Lumber Company from Brooklet, Georgia.

The Rauers sold *The Nautilus* to the operators of the sawmill, but retained *The Guale* for their own use. *The Nautilus* made frequent trips to the mainland, and the workers and the Woods family could catch a ride anytime. Thigpen had Woodrow Rogers pick up a crew from Sapelo Island early each Monday morning and return them late each Friday afternoon. The sawyers lived in houses built near the mill. John described the set-up at the mill:

> They built four houses with regular doors, tongue and groove floors, and regular windows for the white workers. A number of shacks were built for the black workers from Sapelo Island (Figure 88).

Figure 87. A dollar babbit used for trade on St. Catherines.

Figure 86. Curtis Lee and Bill Riddle on St. Catherines. Bill Riddle was the bookkeeper for the Thigpen Lumber Company. He had an office next to the commissary and kept the records of the employees as well as the products produced by the mill.

Figure 88. Wooden shack used by the black lumber workers on St. Catherines. Later, it was moved to McQueens Inlet on Middle Beach and became Hoke Youmans' a watch house.

After Thigpen Company left Sams Field and removed the mills from the island, Younce Lumber Company began working the timber around Meeting House Field.[58] The dock at Sams Field was still used to load lumber onto the barges. John and his tractor were hired to transport the cut timber to the loading dock at Sams Field. John was paid 35 cents an hour[59] for his time and the use of his tractor.

In 1940, the Liberty County property tax assessment of St. Catherines was $85,000 (based on 40,000 acres), and it was reduced to $65,000 the following year. The change was due to a reduction in land assessed to the more realistic 20,000 acres. In a letter dated December 8, 1941, H. Wiley Johnson advised J. J. Rauers to pay $3266.30 in taxes[60] (Johnson 1941). In 1941, with the attack on Pearl Harbor, St. Catherines became vulnerable. The United States Army secured the island and was soon relieved by the Coast Guard. Each of the employees of the sawmill were issued a United States Coast Guard signed identification card by the Reynolds & Manley Lumber Company.

Conclusion:

The decade of the 1930s introduced the modern era to St. Catherines. The renovation of the "big" house and the complex associated with it was a monumental undertaking. The $1 million spent in 1930 would be equivalent to nearly $12 million in 2006. The demolition of the Rauers' mansion, renovation of the horse barn, reconstruction of slave cabin one, installation of the swimming pool, and the construction of the guest cabins constituted a big transformation for St. Catherines. The construction of the employee complex south of the bridge was also an essential feature of the transformation. Earlier, the Rauers were able to hire members of the local Black community to help with hunts and other activities.

The financial setback caused by the Depression in the mid 1930s forced Clement M. and Indiola Keys to revert ownership of St. Catherines back to the Rauers family. The foreclosure placed an additional burden on the estate and created a tax problem that took three years to resolve (Johnson and Corish 1942). The law firm of Johnson and Corish billed the estate for resolving taxes owed with the United States Revenue Service and the State of Georgia Department of Revenue for years 1938, 1939 and 1940 (Johnson and Corish 1943).

9

Uncle Aaron, Aunt Nancy and Eutherle Austin: The Last Black Family on St. Catherines, 1930-1941

Aaron and Nancy Austin[1] (Figure 89) and their adopted daughter Eutherle[2] made up the last black family to have lived permanently on St. Catherines. The family played a special role in young John Toby Woods' life. Eutherle was John's sole playmate on St. Catherines after his sisters were sent to the mainland to attend school in the early 1930s. The Woods and Austins had such a close relationship that in all our conversations, John referred to them as Uncle Aaron and Aunt Nancy. Uncle Aaron's house was on the south end of St Catherines.[3] He was the watchman and was often called on to assist John's father and the Keys during their major renovation of the buildings on the island.

Figure 89. Aunt Nancy and Uncle Aaron on the far right. Unknown individual and Mary Tester on the left. (Early 1930s)

According to John, the Austins' tabby house (Figure 90) was built during the Waldburg era to house enslaved populations. Their home was one of many tabby cabins that remained on the north and south ends of the island. John has extensively researched the origins of the tabby construction on the Island.[4] "According to history, practically all the tabby construction[5] dates from the Waldburg's ownership."

John remembers the house well,

The walls of Uncle Aaron's house were one foot thick. There were two rooms with a large fireplace on the connecting wall with one chimney between the rooms. The fireplace divides the house making it necessary to go outside to get from one room to the other. The floors were made of wide wooden planks. The roof originally was of wooden shingles but later covered with tin. The three windows in each room were covered with solid shutters. Each room had two wooden doors: a front and back door. Inside the walls were covered with newspaper applied by glue made from flour and water. There was no outlet for a stove pipe.[6] Inside the house was generally cool, easily heated when needed, but very dark.

Figure 90. Uncle Aaron's and Aunt Nancy's house on the south end of St. Catherines. Ca. 1980s.

Both John and Ben Chapman, his cousin, commented on a unique structure that they always associated with Uncle Aaron. John described that,

Outside the house you could find Uncle Aaron in the late afternoon resting on the board hammock nailed between two trees. We called it the Lazy Board. The location of the unusual hammock ensured shade throughout the day. Uncle Aaron had a mule to plow his garden. He also had a peach tree, a pear tree, and a grape vine.

John still remembers the setting, with the abundant vines surrounding the house and luscious grapes during the summer months.

Uncle Aaron, Aunt Nancy and Eutherle left St. Catherines in 1941 for Harris Neck. Uncle Aaron left a legacy. John describes,

when he left the island, Uncle Aaron left his mule behind. The mule soon joined up with the last feral marsh pony on the island. For a few years, the mule and a marsh pony ruled the island. They were always together and enjoyed the run of the whole island.

I asked John if Eutherle was living on the mainland. He reminded me about an EMC (Coastal Electric Membership Corporation) meeting in Hinesville, Georgia that I attended in the summer of 2000. The annual meeting was an enjoyable event for me. It was fun to see John – who I knew as a neighbor on his tractor a cutting a field of grass, fishing in his Cobbtown skiff, or riding his bicycle on his dock – moving effortlessly into a formal setting as the president of the electric co-op. Just before the meeting was to begin, one of the directors summoned John to meet someone in the audience of 300. A tall attractive black woman and John embraced warmly. After the meeting I asked John about the woman. He said that it was Eutherle, his sole play-mate on St. Catherines, whom he had not seen in 50 years. Six years later, we decided to see if we could find Eutherle and talk to her about her memories of St. Catherines.

In our search for Eutherle, John and I drove down to Harris Neck[7] to talk with Sonny Timmons; John used to run into him crabbing in the area

around St. Catherines. After only two inquiries at Harris Neck, we were able to locate him. Within a few minutes, Mr. Timmons remembered John and recalled an event 40 years earlier when John towed him from St. Catherines back to his dock on Harris Neck. I asked him how the he could remember the event after such a long time. He said that this gentleman, nodding to John, would not accept anything for the long tow from St. Catherines to Harris Neck.

John inquired about Albert Campbell,[8] who had captained one of his shrimp boats, and his brother Elliott, who worked as a striker. Albert's health was declining. Sonny said that he and Albert enjoyed, "Drinking mash and talking trash." John asked about Aaron Austin. Mr. Timmons said that Aaron Austin had passed,[9] but he still remembered Aaron fondly. He said that Aaron would proudly begin any sentence about his adopted daughter with: "My daughter Ucilea (Eutherle)…" We had taken enough of Mr. Timmons' time during our unannounced visit. It was a late Saturday afternoon, and he was cleaning his boat and preparing it for Monday crabbing as we talked. Mr. Timmons made it clear that Sunday was a day of rest.

Figure 91. Pop Durden's watch house.

About three weeks later, John and I called and made an appointment to visit Sonny Timmons and his wife at their home near Harris Neck. Sonny talked about the fishing and crabbing that occupied him for his entire adult life. He said that he had only worked one day in the "public." Soon after the Army had condemned the land on Harris Neck for an air base, he took a job preparing one of the runways. With a chuckle, he said one day of having someone telling him what to do was enough. Mr. Timmons' life is "in the creek," that is making a living harvesting the gifts of the creeks and rivers. Mr. Timmons' hands reflect his life of hard labor. His hands were so large and so rough, that shaking his hand was a memorable event. It was like grasping an inanimate object that came to life as he gripped on my hand.

In their reminiscing about Uncle Aaron, John said that one of his duties was to watch for poachers on the southern end of the island. Sonny said that if you had a "gift of libation," Aaron would allow you to hunt for a deer. John commented that Aaron was, in a sense, an equal opportunity watchman. Pop Durden, one of John's kin, who later held the same position in the 1950s (Figure 91), would also let you hunt if you provided a bottle of his favorite whiskey.

Before Aaron left the island, he bought a half-horse power Water-Witch outboard motor (Figure 92) that he would use to travel to and from St. Catherines and Harris Neck. Sonny described how he would frequently be able "out row" the Water-Witch powered boat. Sonny told us the tale of poaching a deer one night on St. Catherines. Sonny and his friend put their bateau on the south end[10] and proceeded to the woods where they knew that they would find deer. As they expected, within a few minutes they had sighted and brought down a deer. Just as they were getting ready to drag the animal to the boat, they heard a dog let out a few short barks. Assuming that the dogs were on their trail, Sonny said that he ran as fast as he ever had, jumped into his boat, and started rowing. He said he was running so fast that he did not know "if my skin would catch up with me."

Figure 92. Water Witch outboard motor.

John surmised that the bark he heard that night came from his dog Button, on a raccoon hunt. The single series of barks was Button's signature. John told Sonny that his father would never try to chase a hunter, but instead would go to the spot where they had likely left their boat.

Sonny described how you had to push the rules to make a living on the water. He was dragging in Mollclark River,[11] which was closed to shrimping, when the dreaded DNR (Department of Natural Resources) game warden came upon him and threatened to arrest him. They demanded that Mr. Timmons follow them to their office in Bryan County. He asked the wardens who was going to pay for the gas. They told Sonny that was his responsibility. Sonny had an answer for them. He didn't removing the top of his motor, knowing this would prevent his boat from starting. He commented to us that he was not interested in using his own fuel for the trip. The DNR towed him to their office and intended to lock him up for the night. He telephoned his wife and within minutes influential citizens were calling to free Sonny Timmons. When his wife arrived later, they were gladly to get Sonny off their hands and she took him home. The next day, Sonny returned to find his boat stripped of its contraband shrimp. Sonny jumped into the boat, flipped the hood of the motor up, and it started on the first try. As he drove off, he could see the DNR officers shaking their heads. But, as Sonny said, the officers did get a boatload of shrimp, making their capture of Sonny worth the effort.

Sonny Timmons did tell us that Eutherle is now Eutherle Mae Holmes. We did not find her on that trip. Gee Little, John's sister, had an extensive phone conversation with her. Eutherle told Gee that St. Catherines was not a happy time for her. She never understood why she was sent to live with her aunt, and why her brothers were not sent with her. Eutherle remembered playing with John as a child, and those were among the few pleasant memories she had of life on St. Catherines. She fondly talked about visiting Mrs. Keys in the Manor House, which she said was the most beautiful house that she had ever seen.[12] Eutherle said that Mrs. Keys was a caring person who would frequently give her beautiful clothes that she was never allowed to wear. She said that Nancy Austin, her stepmother, in one of her acts of "meanness," would hang the beautiful dresses on the wall of their cabin as decoration. She left them there until they no longer fit Eutherle, and then Nancy would pass them on to her own nieces. Eutherle never had a chance to wear any of the gifts given to her, and the dresses were a daily reminder of her unhappiness.

10

The Exodus from St. Catherines to Harris Neck and White Bluff

The tumultuous years leading up to the Civil War and its aftermath were turbulent times for the South and for the 'enslaved' populations on St. Catherines. As the threat of war escalated, Jacob Waldburg and many of those he enslaved moved from the island to the mainland. Waldburg had many problems with his enslaved individuals on the mainland. Some of them "escaped" to St. Catherines, forcing Waldburg to retrieve the "contraband," as the newspapers described them. As the Civil War intensified, more and more enslaved people sought refuge on the Sea Islands, which were abandoned by the planters once the Confederacy was no longer able to protect them.

After emancipation, Special Field Order 15 established the Freedmen State and led to an influx of freed Blacks on the Sea Islands. When Andrew Johnson rescinded Order 15, many owners, including the Waldburg reclaimed their land on the Sea Islands. Waldburg found that many of the freed Blacks on St. Catherines were not interested in working as contract laborers under conditions nearly equivalent to slavery. Harris Neck, White Bluff and Pin Point were principal areas of settlement after emancipation. White Bluff Road communities were a collection of villages, including Nicholsonboro, Rose Dhu, Twin Hill, and Cedar Grove (Georgia Writers' Project, Savannah Unit 1986; Georgia Writers' Program 1940). These villages were located on the Vernon River, about eight miles south of Savannah. White Bluff was the home of 400 former residents of St. Catherines, who left the island in 1868 upon Jacob Waldburg's return. To the east overlooking Shipyard Creek lies Pin Point. The town is famous for being the birthplace of Associate Supreme Court Justice Clarence Thomas, and was described in the 1940s as a bucolic community spread over a twenty to thirty acre site (Georgia Writers' Project, Savannah Unit 1986; GeorgiaWriters' Program 1940).

The Georgia Writers Project produced *Drums and Shadows; Survival Studies among the Georgia Coastal Negroes* (1940), which featured recorded interviews with many people living at White Bluff and Pin Point. In one interview, sixty-plus years-old Prince Sneed told a story in the Gullah Dialect (GeorgiaWriters'Program. 1940:73) that mentioned Jacob Waldburg:

> Muh gran say ole man Waldburg down on St. Catherine own some
> slabes wut wuzn climatize and he wuk um hahd and one day dey
> wuz hoein in duh fiel an duh dribuh come out an two ub um wuz
> unuh a tree in duh shade, an duh hoes wuz wukin by demsef. Duh
> dribuh say 'wut dis?' an dey say 'Kum buba yali kum buba tambe,
> Kum kunka yali kum kunka tambe,' quick like. Den dey rise off
> duh groun an fly away. Nobody ebuh see um no mo. Some say dey
> fly back to Africa. Muh gran see dat wid he own eye.

Nada Elia (2003:189-190) provides a translation and an interesting interpretation that suggests the origin of the folktale.

> [My grandfather said Old Man Waldburg down on St. Catherines
> owned some slaves that were not "climatized," and he worked

107

them hard, and one day they were hoeing in the field and the driver
came out and two of them were under a tree in the shade, and the
hoes were working by themselves.

The driver said "what's this?" and they said 'kum buba yali kum
buba tambe, kum kunka yali kum kunka tambe," fast. Then they
rose off the ground and flew away. Nobody ever saw them again.
Some say they flew back to Africa. My grandfather saw that with
his own eyes.]

Elia claims that the folktale originated among Muslim populations from Africa. She relies on two pieces of evidence to interpret this story. Hamilton (1985) discussed a similar folktale in her book *The People Could Fly*. Toni Morrison (1977) also uses the same folktale as the basis of her book *Songs of Solomon* . Elia makes a convincing argument that the names in the story are prominent in the *Koran*, and that the enslaved populations were likely Ibo from Africa. The Igbo (the preferred term for the Ibo), make up the largest ethnic group in Africa. Igbo are found in Nigeria (17% of the population), Cameron and Equatorial Guinea.

The ties between Harris Neck and St. Catherines made it a popular destination during the exodus from the island. The recent history of Harris Neck, however, includes another sad and difficult time for black Americans on the coast of Georgia.

Harris Neck

Holding back tears, Mrs. Timmons described to John and me how families were forced off their land on Harris Neck[1] at the beginning of the Second World War. The land was taken from them to build an air base, and they were paid as little as $10 an acre. Mary said that many families were forced to live in the woods until they had the resources to move into more acceptable housing. Harris Neck was a well-established community at the beginning of the Second World War until the United States Government condemned more than 1200 acres for an Air Force air base. The Air Force built a triangular landing strip for a training facility, and P-39s and P-40s (Kittyhawks) were the primary planes that were used to train pilots. The famous Flying Tigers were among the squadrons trained at Harris Neck.

The displaced Harris Neck community fully expected to have the land returned after World War II. Instead the Army transferred the land to McIntosh County for use as a municipal airport. Later, the FAA gave the property to the United States Bureau of Sport Fisheries and Wildlife, which established the area as a migratory bird refuge. There were a number of protests in 1979 organized by Edgar Timmons Jr. These led to arrests and jail time (Johnson 1979a; Johnson 1979b; Johnson 1979c; NYT 1979), but the land was never returned.

I asked Mrs. Timmons to tell me her maiden name. When she responded with Moran, John immediately recognized the name and asked if she was related to Mary Moran. Sixty-nine-year-old Mary Moran, the daughter of Amelia Dawley, was married to Mrs. Timmons' brother. I then realized the connection that John had made. In 1989, there were reports that a song sung by Amelia Dawley to Mary Moran as a lullaby contained the longest recorded American English text in an African language. Mary, who did not understand a word of the unknown language, just liked the melody. In 1932, Lorenzo Turner was researching Africanisms in the Gullah language (Turner 1949) and had recorded Mrs. Dawley singing the song.

In 1949, a graduate student from Sierra Leone, Solomon Caulker, identified words from the Mende language. But the story does not end there. In 1990, anthropologist Joseph Opala, ethnomusicologist Cynthia Schmidt, and Tazieff Koroma, from Sierra Leone, traveled to Sierra Leone to find someone who could identify the song. The documentary film *The Language You Cry In* (Toepke and Serrano 1998) tells the story of their journey to Sierra Leone to find the source of Amelia Dawley's lullaby. They eventually found Baindu, a young woman in a remote Senehum Ngola village, who recognized the lullaby as a funeral dirge that used to be part of an important burial ritual.[2] The film ends with a moving visit to the ancestral home of the song that eventually evolved into the lullaby sang by Mary. Mary witnesses the original song performed by Baindu Jabati. The performance brought tears to Mary's eyes. After the performance, Mary commented that if she had known that the song was a funeral dirge, she is not sure that she would have sung it to her daughter.

The improbable link between a mother's lullaby in Harris Neck, Georgia and a funeral hymn from a remote village in Sierra Leone defies all odds. The people from rice growing regions of Sierra Leone were forcibly brought to the rice growing areas of coastal Georgia. During slavery, it was policy to eradicate the cultural heritage of the human beings that were treated like chattel. The fact that the song survived both time and distance in Georgia, and was also preserved over many generations in Sierra Leone attests to the power of memory in maintaining the human spirit.

Every year 48,000, people visit the Harris Neck Wildlife Refuge. It's a popular sightseeing destination for visitors who come to our home on the coast, and I have contributed at least a dozen trips to the tally. In the dozens of times that I have visited Harris Neck Wildlife Refuge,[3] I never experienced the abundance of wildlife that attracts most of the visitors. I was more impressed with the miles of roads and runways remaining from the Harris Neck Army Air Field that still crisscross the area remained from the Harris Neck Army Air Field (Rippen 1977).

Although the remote field was deactivated 60 years ago, it is reverting back to nature very slowly. An aerial view of the field still reveals runways that form a nearly equilateral triangle (Figure 93). Tarmacs that bisect each of its angles provided access to the runways, and can still be seen on the photographs. Even after a decade of visiting the site of the Army Air Base at Harris Neck, I still didn't fully understand its role in the war effort, its impact on the community, or its relationship to St. Catherines. John gave me a short history of the area that helped to put the base in proper prospective.

Harris Neck and St. Catherines have been linked in many ways. To begin with, many of the black families who left St. Catherines

Figure 93. An aerial view of Harris Neck Army Air field. 1995.

moved to Harris Neck,[4] and many of them maintained relationships with friends and relatives that remained on the island. John's mother told him about going to the First African Church on the island with the black families from the mainland; many rowed the six miles from Harris Neck to the island for the Sunday service. Finally, the Woods family described the frequent flights over the island by planes from Harris Neck. They would frequently see planes pulling targets above the waters off the shores of St. Catherines.

It is not difficult to see what attracted Aaron, Nancy and Eutherle to Harris Neck. After the Civil War, the plantations were abandoned and the land was divided into small farms. The small farms were quite successful, and the rivers were a wonderful additional resource for the inhabitants. Harris Neck is so remote that many of the local residents believed it was a secret air base. In actuality, during the Second World War, the base was an important center for training pilots to fly P-39s (Airacobra) and P-40s (Kittyhawks)[5] for combat. The 13,738 P-40s built by Curtis were a major asset during the first half of the Second World War. The Flying Tiger, a P-40, was one of the most recognized planes flown in Second World War (Figure 94).

On December 7, 1941, after the attack on Pearl Harbor, a detachment from Hunter Air Force Base took over the runway on the airfield at Harris Neck (Rippen 1977). For two years it served as a gunnery training site. According to Rippen, in the fall of 1943 it became an auxiliary base of Dale Mabry Field in Tallahassee under the Third Fighter command. By 1944, the P-40 replaced the Airacobra at Harris Neck and 11 prefabricated buildings were completed. An Officer's club, barracks to house 125 men, and an NCO (Noncommissioned Officer) Club were also built.

USFWS

Figure 94. The P-40 E Warhawk Flying Tiger was used to train pilots on Harris Neck.

With the invasion of Europe in June 1944, there was increased activity at the base. The Fourth of July ceremony and celebration when Francis H. Hoye, a flight instructor, received the Four Bronze Oak Leaf Clusters to the Air Medal was a high point (Rippen 1977). There were 129 officers and 575 enlisted men on the base at that time. There was even a base historian, whose reports were the basis of the article by Charles Rippen.

The demise of the Air Base may have been begun with the preparation for a hurricane that hit Harris Neck on October 18, 1944. It was the eleventh hurricane of the season. It is now known as the Sanibel Hurricane of 1944 (this was the era before hurricanes were named), and it made landfall in Sarasota, Florida on the 19th of October. The hurricane moved over the southeast[6] and dissipated on the 21st. Equipment from the base had to be transferred inland.

By the end of October, there was a significant decline in personnel, with only 49 officers and 323 enlisted men staffing the base. By November, there were only 16 officers and 57 enlisted men. In December the base was deactivated, and was completely cleared by the last day of the year.

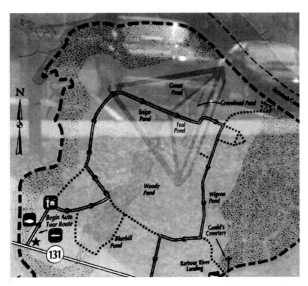

Figure 95. The Harris Neck Wildlife Refuge showing the footprint of the Army Air Force Base.

Rippen (1977:25) found reports of only one fatality in his research.[7] Gee Woods was well aware of these training missions and said that there were frequent crashes. The training practice frequently involved the water surrounding St. Catherines. John said that each year that the base was open he find hundreds of shell casings that washed ashore. The Aviation Archaeological Investigation and Research website reports that there were 24 accidents among the planes training at Harris Neck from 1942 to 1944.

The displaced Harris Neck families fully expected to have their land returned to them after World War II. Instead the Army transferred the land to McIntosh County for use as a municipal airport. McIntosh County mismanaged the land so badly that it was transferred to the FAA (Federal Aviation Agency). There was even a land grab by county officials. On May 25, 1962, the FAA gave the property to the United States Bureau of Sport Fisheries and Wildlife, which designated the area as a migratory bird refuge (Figure 95).

The Black populations who are still living in the area feel betrayed by the United States. They believed that after their sacrifice, they would be brought back to their land. This is a story of the loss of land has been told many times. In 1905, black Americans owned 15 million acres (Chini 1979). By 2004, ownership had declined to 7.7 million acres (Gilbert, et al. 2002).

11

War, The Coast Guard and Mr. Noble Come to St. Catherines

In March of 1943, Edward J. Noble had just purchased St. Catherines (NYT 1943b) intending to create a cattle ranch when the United States Coast Guard began establishing facilities to protect the island during the early stages of World War II. The United States Army secured the island and built a 25-foot lookout tower at the end of North Beach to watch for enemy ships that might try to land in America. Activity on St. Catherines foretold changes that would come about during Noble's ownership. When Mr. Noble first stepped onto St. Catherines Island it still housed the last of the lumbermen who were winding down the timber cutting operation.

At the end of 1939, C. M. Keys had returned St. Catherines to the Rauers family. They initiated an intensive lumbering operation to pay for the island's upkeep. The Jack Thigpen Lumber Company cleared large tracts of yellow pine,[1] found mostly on the north end of the island.[2] By 1943, the final stages of the cutting were undertaken by the Younce Lumber Company, which was harvesting the less desirable "black pine[3]" on the southern end of the island. Ed Younce, his wife, and their chief sawyer, Odell Powell, were living in the superintendent's house. Mr. Noble ceased the timbering operations, but in the early 1950s he had C. B. Jones Company thin some of the woods on the south end of the island and sold the timber for pulp wood.[4]

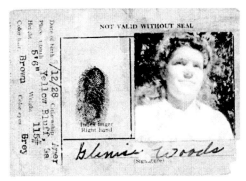

Figure 96. Gee (Glenise) Woods' identification card. The card was issued by Reynolds & Manley Lumber Company and signed by Ensign M. Bell of the United States Coast Guard.

Beginning in June 1942, all lumber employees and residents of St. Catherines had to carry identification cards issued by the United States Coast Guard (Figure 96). The Coast Guard established their presence on the island after the Army secured it in early in 1942. The Coast Guard replaced the Georgia National Guard, which was the first group called in to supplement the Army's security corps. The Georgia Guard, by all accounts, was not ready to be "prime time players." John said that they were ill-equipped, though many of the Georgia home guards were armed with issued shot guns to be used if it was necessary to defend the island.[5]

Young Ben Chapmen was puzzled by the endless marching in formation around the "big" house. He remembered his Aunt Gladys Woods commenting that she was not sure if they were marching around the house to protect her husband Toby, or if they were hoping that Toby Woods would protect them in the event of an invasion. Gee Little, who was 14 years old at the time, remembered being frightened by the soldiers when they would jump out from behind a tree with a rifle positioned to challenge whomever they saw. Gee said that they acted as if the enemy had already occupied St. Catherines. One night when they were returning to the dock, John, Gee and their parents were greeted with tracer bullets fired across the bow of the boat. While it was an impressive display, the Woods were concerned that the soldiers

Figure 98. Edward Wood, U.S. Army. The Army secured the island, built a watchtower on North Beach, before turning over their duties to the Coast Guard.

Figure 97. The jeep with a gang of Army-Navy" men with Ed and Lilly Younce on the St. Catherines Dock. The men are wearing "Daisy Mae" issue hats. This group was the first to secure the island before the Coast Guard arrived.

might mistake them for the enemy. Two Guardsmen, Ernest "Tex" Riedel (Figure 99) and Sid Mosby (Figure 100), were in charge of supervising the infrastructure to supporting the Coast Guardsmen on the island. Riedel and Mosby[6] trained at the Mounted Beach Patrol and Dog Training Center in Hilton Head, South Carolina and built the wooden barns and horse corral at that facility. They were to oversee the installation of the CCC (Civilian Conservation Corps) buildings that were shipped to St. Catherines[7] for a barracks on South Beach.

The crisis that created the need for a military presence on St. Catherines occurred early in 1942 when German Unterboots (U-boats) began sinking American ships along the coast of Georgia (Gannon 1990) as part of operation *Paukenschlag* (Drumbeat). On April 8, 1942, a U-123 operating near St. Simons Island torpedoed the tankers *Esso Baton Rouge* and *S.S. Oklahoma*, killing twenty-two sailors. Michael Gannon, eminent naval historian, friend and colleague from the University of Florida, has argued convincingly that these systematic attacks were a greater strategic setback than the attack at Pearl Harbor (Gannon 1990). Those living on the Sea Islands felt vulnerable and were always worried about another attack.

Two less dramatic but significant incidents increased the threat level for a possible German invasion. On June 13, 1942, a U-202 under the command of Lt. Commander Hans-Heinz Linder surfaced on a beach near Amagansett, Long Island, 105 miles east of New York City. Four men carrying $175,200[8] dollars in cash (equivalent to $2 million today) and four cases explosives[9] disembarked with a plan to sabotage aluminum factories in Tennessee, Illinois, and New York; locks on the Ohio River; the Horseshoe Bend railway complex west of Altoona, Pennsylvania (McILany 2007); and railroad terminals in New Jersey. Four days later, nearly 900 miles to the south of Long Island, a U-584 surfaced 50 yards off Ponte Vedra Beach near Jacksonville, Florida, depositing another team of four spies (Gordon 2007). Within 10 days of the initial drop, all of the spies were in custody.[10] While this immediate threat was quickly averted, the possibility of further aggression lurked in the minds of coastal Georgians. Just as post-9/11 America has been defined by a fear of "terrorist" threats, the period after these incidents was defined by fears of an incursion by German forces. The capture of the sabotage team did, however, provide some comfort to the eastern United States.

Figure 99. Tex Riedel and Button, the wonder dog.

Figure 100. Sid Mosby in his winter dress uniform.

The hero in the capture that eventually revealed the plot was a twenty-one-year-old unarmed Coast Guard "sandpounder,"[11] John C. Cullen, Seaman 2nd Class, who was walking his six-mile watch on Amagansett Beach. Walking through the night fog, he came upon a man emerging from the water of the Long Island Sound with three companions nearby. When Cullen asked what they were doing, the man, later revealed as George John Dasch, claimed that he and his friends had been "clamming" and had run aground. When one of the men, Ernest Peter Berger, spoke to another person lurking in the fog in German, Dasch became visibly upset. Cullen[12] was armed with only a flashlight knew that he had a problem. Dasch threatened him and then offered Cullen a $300 bribe to forget the matter. Cullen used the subterfuge of accepting the bribe and ran back to his superiors, Boatswain Mate Carl R. Jennette and Warrant Officer Warren Barnes, telling them about the surreal encounter that sounded like a plot from a "grade B" movie.

With the money as evidence,[13] the Coast Guard went into action and within 12 days all of the spies were apprehended.[14] Publications with titles such as "Spies who Came in from the Sea" (Nolan 1999; Swanberg 1970) and the "Keystone Kommandos" (Cohen 2002) still tell the story of the plan to sabotage America and how the plot was thwarted. The Military Commission[15] tried the eight, found them guilty and sentenced them to death. Dasch was spared the death penalty and his sentence was commuted to 30-years in prison because of his role in revealing the plot, and he has written his own account of the event (Dasch 1959).

Cullen's role in the spy saga made him a hero, and made the Coast Guard a vaunted branch of the Armed Services. The protection of America's coast became an immediate concern. On July 25, 1942, the coastal Naval Districts[16] were ordered to organize beach patrols that would be armed and provided with the best communication equipment. They initially thought that a volunteer civilian force would do the job (NYT 1942b). Newspaper accounts referred to these recruits as "horse marines" (NYT 1942c; NYT 1942d).[17] The Coast Guard soon realized that a volunteer force would not work, however, and they decided to do the job themselves. The Coast Guard's responsibility was never to provide armed military protection; they were to be the "eyes" and "ears" of the military, and their charge was to alert the Army so that it could marshal its "firepower" to repel any threat. The Coast Guard quickly established protocols for protecting the beaches. A manual for the Sixth District detailed all aspects of procedures and behaviors expected of the Guardsmen (Porter ND).

The Guardsmen were to patrol in pairs and were to be armed with rifles, sidearms or pistols. On St. Catherines, following regulations, phones were supposed to be placed at quarter mile intervals feeding back to the communication center in Employee Cabin 1. Not so on St. Catherines. John remembers the Guardsmen stringing heavily insulated phone line seven miles on the ground to the South Beach complex. On the beach, the line could be buried a few inches in the sand. When they placed the line above the ground it was strung from tree limb to tree limb. Even with its heavy insulation and its many splices, the phone line was in constant need of repair.

In 1942, the Guard introduced trained dogs[18] and horses to aid in the patrols. In 1943, dogs were part of the teams patrolling St. Catherines' north end. According to Gee, some of the dogs were trained as watchdogs, and others as attack dogs. John remembers that the seven dogs, German Shepherds and Doberman Pinschers, were housed in a kennel between the employee cabins. The kennels were strictly off-limits to him and his sister, John and Gee said that it wasn't a necessary restriction since the dogs were very aggressive. John describes how the dogs were always undergoing attack training with padded "aggravators[19]" who would challenge the dogs.

The Mounted Beach Patrol became the preferred mode of defense for the coastal islands[20] (Figures 101, 102, and 103). The Army Remount placed 3,222 horses on St. Catherines, and also provided all of the required saddles and bridles, cavalry boots, and Springfield rifles. The saddles issued to the Mounted Patrol on St. Catherines were surplus McClellan saddles[21] from the World War I, which John described as "instruments of torture" (Figure 104). The introduction of the horses and their riders caused, in John's words, "quite a commotion."

Figure 101. United States Coast Guard Beach Patrol, 1942-1944. From the left, Guardsman, winter dress, 1943; Petty Officer, summer dress, 1943; Mounted Patrol, 1942; Guardsman, summer dress, 1943; African-American Guardsman, foul winter dress, 1943.

Figure 102. Informal group picture of the Mounted Beach Patrol on St. Catherines. Ca 1943 or 1944.

Figure 103. Mounted Beach Patrol on the dock at St. Catherines. Taken the day that most of them were leaving the island for new assignments.

Figure 104. McClellan Saddle of the type used by the United States Coast Guard. Note the thick leather skirt and wooden stirrups. The McClellan saddle did not have padding and it was necessary use a saddle blanket.

Figure 105. George Glass was in charge of the South Beach patrol. He grew up on a ranch in New Mexico and was one of the few who experience with horses.

The Coast Guard history tells about the wonderful training facilities available to those assigned to be riders in the Mounted Patrol. "Tex" Riedel said that all those assigned to St. Catherines had undergone training at Hilton Head; but from what John describes, I am sure they would have liked a refresher course. George Glass (Figure 105), who was in charge of the South Beach Patrol, assigned horses and men randomly – not that it mattered. About half of the Mounted Patrol had been on a horse before their training at Hilton Head.[22] Only one ringer, Guardsman Foster, had been a rodeo rider and was able to give the others some tips. Ben Chapman, who was there to see the first meeting of man and beast, described one Guardsman who mounted his horse only to have it take off across the beach and throw him on the beach at the water's edge. After three weeks of intensive "on the job training," which involved a broken collarbone, a number of cracked ribs, a fractured arm, and many bruised egos, the men and horse became a functioning unit (Figure 106).

The Guard proudly described the training their men received to care for the horses, which included teaching some of them blacksmith and farrier skills (Bishop 1989:14). The plan was to send at least one person with these skills to care for the horses at each facility. On St. Catherines, a jeep, a truck and a weapons carrier provided additional transportation for the mounted patrol. The "liberty boat"[23] (Figure 107) would bring supplies from Savannah to the troops on the island and shuttled the Guardsmen who were reporting for duty or leaving for Savannah. By February 18, 1944, the Guard Headquarters announced that they it would be reducing the beach patrols in some areas by half. The Coast Guard contingent on St. Catherines was housed in two locations. Those in charge of the north end of the beach were in the employees cabins and their horses were sheltered in the barn that had been renovated a decade earlier by Mr. and Mrs. Keys. The south end group was housed in barracks converted from the CCC (Civilian Conservation Corps) buildings constructed in the 1930s

A corral with a horse barn and barracks were also built on South Beach (Figure 108). The Coast Guard's horses were supplied by the Army Remount Service that was authorized by Congress in 1908. The program was expanded in 1943 when the Coast Guard requisitioned 3000 horses for the beach patrol. When the danger of hostile submarine activity ceased, the horses were returned to the Remount Service.[24] Coast Guard activity was equally intense on and off the island. Local shrimpers were outfitted with two-way radios and local boat owners volunteered their time and vessels to the war effort. Many yacht owners even became members of The Coast Guard Auxiliary. Malcom Francis Willoughby (1980:86), in a history of the Coast Guard in World War II, described their contributions,[25]

An unusual flotilla at Thunderbolt, Georgia, was composed of fisherman and shrimpers, who served more than 30,000 man-hours each month. Their boats carried ship-to-shore radios, and they kept in constant touch with the navy, informing it of any suspicious objects or occurrences observed while carrying out their livelihood. These men operated their vessels at no expense to the Coast Guard and performed their share of rescues.

The Coast Guard and Mr. Noble had one battle that they did not anticipate. When Uncle Aaron left the island, he left a legacy. John describes the tale of Aaron's mule:

When he left the Island, Uncle Aaron left his mule behind. The mule soon joined up with the last feral marsh pony on the island. For a few years, the mule and a marsh pony ruled the island. They were always together and enjoyed the run of the whole island. Later, during World War II, the Coast Guard Mounted Beach Patrol, they tried to catch the pony and mule with no luck. The pony and mule knew the island well and they would hide in the thick underbrush.

Figure 106. Mounted Coast Guard Patrol posing with their horses on South Beach. The picture was taken on Cabbage Palm Garden on South Beach.

Finally the marsh pony died and was buried in Greenseed Field, which is located about a mile south of the "big" house if you take the State Road. I watched him being buried. The mule came in to live with the Coast Guard horses. Later, when Mr. Noble owned the island, he offered a twenty-dollar bill to anybody who could ride him. The Coast Guardsmen would rope him, but he was so bad and kicked so hard that they had no luck riding him. My sister Gee started feeding the mule and treating him good. The next thing we knew she was on his back and riding him. I don't remember if she got the $20.

John relates,

After the war was over and the Coast Guard was leaving the island, Mr. Noble bought two horses (Junior and Murray) from them. So the mule took up with them. It got to where you couldn't ride the horses if the mule didn't agree with them about where they were going or how fast they were

Figure 107. Coast Guard "Liberty Boat" loaded with sailors bound for Savannah. The vessel is a modified "picket boat."

Figure 108. Coast Guard Corral at South Beach.

traveling. The mule was clever enough to get between Junior and Murray and kick both of them at the same time. The mule could open a gate, if he had problems opening a gate, he would tear down the fence so that he could go along with the guardsmen and their horses. If he wanted a drink of water, the mule could turn on any spigot, which was a big problem since there were a number of spigots scattered about the "big" house and cottages. He never learned how to turn the spigots off, leaving the water running. Finally when Mr. Noble could no longer ride because of being harassed by the mule, he had us kill Uncle Aaron's mule. We buried him in Rock Field near the cow barn. We buried everything that died or stopped working on the island.[26]

There were constant reminders for most Americans that we were at war. I told John about how at seven years old I accompanied my older brothers while they collected milk pods for the floss that was used to fill "Mae West" life preservers. When kapok[27] was no longer available, milk pods were collected as a substitute (Witt and Knudsen. 1993).[28] I remember working in my father's store and pasting "food ration coupons" in sheets provided by the government. For Gee and John, the reminders of war were constant. There were the frequent flyovers of planes from the Harris Neck Air Base. The bombing range was to the east of St. Catherines. Planes were flown close enough to the island that they could hear the rapid fire of the P-39s and P-40's machine guns.[29]

Gee and John said that there were oil slicks and even "balls of crude rubber" that made it to the shores of St. Catherines. Frequently, bullet riddled bodies of dead turtles and dolphins would wash ashore. There was even an instance in which two one-person life rafts were found on North Beach (Figure 109). The life rafts became a popular attraction in the swimming pool where the family and even the Guardsmen enjoyed "mock combat" between the occupants of the boats. An Air Force observation plane saw the life rafts and dispatched a boat to retrieve them. John and Gee pleaded with the sea patrol to let them keep the rafts. The boat patrol

Figure 109. One of the two small single person survival rafts that drifted on to North Beach found by John and Gee as they rode their bikes in search of turtle eggs.

119

relented and let the Woods kids keep the contraband, only to return a few months later to take them away for good.

Gee said there was even an instance in which the target barge broke away from its anchor and floated down Waldburg Creek. Gee and Ben Chapman saw the break-away barge and one of them commented how cool it would be for the planes to swoop down on the barge. As if on command, the planes from Harris Neck spotted the "AWOL" barge, dove toward it, and strafed at it as it passed by the "big" house. Ben and Gee where stunned with disbelief as the plane flew south to begin another run. Even when the planes were shooting targets in their assigned area, spent shells were abundant. John found hundreds of shell casings from spent 50-caliber shells that washed ashore. Ever the pragmatist, he used some casings to make handles for knives that he gave to friends

Figure 110. George Chapman in the seat of the wreckage of a Grumman F4 (Wildcat) or F6 (Hellcat) that was found on the South Beach shore of St. Catherines. The plane was part of the Navy Air Force. Picture taken in early 1950s.

Ralph Chapman related an incident that indicated just how close the P39s and P40s were to the island. He was staying with his Aunt Annie and her husband George Berryhill during a heavy rainstorm when the roof of Employee Cabin 2 started leaking. George investigated the leak and found a hole in the galvanized tin roof and a 50-caliber bullet lodged in a beam.

When I talked to Gee about her memories of the island, she mentioned that there were a number of planes that crashed near St. Catherines (Figure 110). She had kept records and tallied about two dozen crashes[30] that she was aware of during the time the Guard was on the island. Since Jim Crawley, commander of the Crash Rescue Boat unit from Thunderbolt, was a frequent visitor to the island, there were updates about the crashes. John told me about one incident in which one plane flew into the tail end of another, sending both planes to the ground. This spectacular crash occurred on April 2, 1944, was one of five incidents in '43 and '44 that occurred in the vicinity of St. Catherines.[31] The planes landed on the sand bar near marker 124.

Charles Rippen's popular history of the Air Base at Harris Neck (1977:25) found only a report of only one fatality in his research.[32] The Aviation Archaeological Investigation and Research website (http://www.aviationarchaeology.com/) reports that from 1942 until the base close in 1944, there were 43 planes that crashed during training at Harris Neck.

Gladys and Toby Woods and Their Coast Guard Family

To focus only on the dramatic and often tragic events that transpired on St. Catherines would miss one of the untold stories of the island. The Coast Guard became part of the Woods' family. In a celebration honoring their 64th wedding anniversary at the Newington Baptist Church, John Toby and Gladys Woods related their memories of their life on St. Catherines Island (Lee 1988). They talked about having "had many experiences with many different kinds of people…some millionaires and some not so fortunate (Lee 1988:4)." While they talked proudly about entertaining Dwight D. Eisenhower and Richard Nixon, they fondly remembered the soldiers that arrived when war came to St. Catherines.

Toby said that during the war there were up to 42 servicemen stationed on the island. The Woods family and Mr. Noble made friends with them, and they have free access to the Woods' home in the superintendent's house. At night, it would not be unusual to have several of the men lying on their living room floor listening to live radio broadcasts (Lee 1988:4). The Woods' teenage daughters were also a major attraction; but, the friendly family was the main draw.

John remembers that on Saturday nights when the "Grand Ole Opry" was broadcasting from WSM in Nashville, Tennessee, there would be a floor full of Coast Guardsmen listing intently.[33] The "Grand Ole Opry" had become extremely popular in the early '40s. By 1944, the "Opry" began charging an admission fee of twenty-five cents in hopes of keeping the number of people attending live broadcasts to a manageable level. When the "quarter" admission did not discourage the crowds, the "Opry" moved to the Ryan Auditorium for their live performances. The popularity of the "Opry" was not restricted to Nashville. By 1943, NBC had 143 stations carrying the program. It is easy to understand why it was popular. John was not a big country music fan, but he did remember that artists such as Bill Monroe and His Bluegrass Boys were regulars on the show. In fact, bluegrass music was conceived when Earl Scruggs joined him on the "Opry."

The birth of bluegrass was less important than the songs that the lonely soldiers could relate to. Tex Ritter and the Texans had hits in 1944 that were especially relevant to servicemen away from home. "I'm Wasting My Tears on You" and "Jealous Heart" were favorites of the men. Both songs were featured on the "Opry" broadcasts.

Even at the Woods' home, space on the floor became a premium. One evening, John said that there was a floor full of Guardsmen and Uncle Woodrow (Woody, to the Guardsmen) was having trouble tending the fire because he could not reach the fireplace. The soldiers, who had learned to tease Woody as soon as they arrived on the island, playfully ignored him in his moves to get to the fireplace. Woodrow, undaunted, went out to the woodbin and collected a large armful of "fat-wood." Walking into the room and pushing himself to the fireplace, he put all the fat-wood into the fireplace. Within minutes, the fat-wood was engulfed in flames and drove the men away from the fire and out of the room. John still remembers the flames shooting out of the chimney. He thought that Woodrow had really done it that time, and that the house would catch on fire. The "Opry" was too good to miss and after a few minutes the men returned, more respectful of Woodrow and ready to listen again.

Figure 111. Johnny Martin in the jeep with Button and Tex Riedel.

In 2008, Ernest "Tex" Riedel (Figure 111) may be the last living man to have served on St. Catherines. He was in the United States Coast Guard stationed at Georgetown, South Carolina and was assigned to St. Catherines on March 15, 1943 to erect housing for the Coast Guard. He left the island four months later with the mission unaccomplished. He and Sid Mosby from Wellington, Kansas, were to erect barracks from buildings that the CCC (Civilian Conservation Corp) had used decades earlier. The CCC buildings arrived after they had already left for a similar assignment in Georgetown, South Carolina. "Tex"[34] was the leader of a 15-person detachment to the island that was housed in two of the employee cabins built by the Keys in the early '30s.[35] The Coast Guard arrived to take over for the Army once it had secured the island. The Army left a watchtower on the northeast side of the island. The Coast Guard abandoned the barracks on the South Beach after they left the island. It was disassembled by Toby Woods and his crew in order to make a cow barn on the north end of Rock Field, behind the superintendent's house.

Tex said that he remembers the hospitality of Toby and Gladys Woods. They were avid card players and taught him the intricacies of Cribbage. The Woods were living in the "big" house. Timber cutters, as Tex referred to them, were living in the superintendent's house. The "timber cutters"[36] were also part of the group that played cards. He was there when the timber cutting ceased and the Woods moved into the superintendent's house. The cribbage games continued in the new setting.

John fondly remembers the Coast Guardsmen who patrolled St. Catherines. As a thirteen-year-old boy, hanging out with the "big guys" had its advantages. The sailors would allow him to ride with them and he was even allowed to drive their Willis Jeep, that which John described as a "fine machine." Given the fact that he had been driving Mrs. Key's Model A convertible, the jeep was a marvelous change. John said that it didn't hurt that he had a couple of older sisters who everyone agreed were "beauties."

The coast guard men had an open invitation to visit the family at the house, and had use of the pool (when Mr. Noble was not on the island). In his daybook, Toby Woods only mentioned one special occasion (Saturday, April 22, 1943) when the Guardsmen were invited to a barbeque where a hog was prepared by Uncle Otis Edenfield. The Guard was such a part of the community that their frequent visits to the house were not mentioned in his daybook. The arrival of a new Coast Guard truck deserved mention (March 17, 1943), and when the weapon carrier "went overboard "[37] (September 21. 1943), it was duly noted. My favorite entry in Toby's daybook (April 5, 1943) was when he wrote, "Went across carried some Coast Guards & boat turned over & some of them got wet." John vividly remembers the discussion that followed that event. It was, as Toby noted, a "cold and windy" day on a return trip from Savannah when a gust of wind flipped that boat turning it on its side dumping some of Guardsmen as a gust of wind "righted" the boat. They had to rescue the men who were never in any great danger. Although the Coast Guard Mounted Patrol was the "guest" of E. J. Noble, they never really interacted with him. "Tex" Riedel remembers Mr. Noble as a figure that he would see in the distance.

There is one more story to tell. Romance did blossom on St. Catherines when Gee and Bill Waites began dating (Figure 112). He became part of the family. On March 26, 1943, John mentioned that Sam Powell and Bill Waites (Figure 113) were going to the mainland with him. After the Guard left the island, Gee and Bill soon lost contact with each other. A few years later, in the best tradition of a "love story," Ellis Little, a new beaux, came courting Gee. The challenge for Ellis, who never learned to swim, was to find a way to the island. He bought plans for a 12-foot boat,[38] purchased the lumber, and built the boat with his own hands. Learning to navigate the tricky rivers and creeks was another matter. Ellis was literally given a crash course in navigation. On one trip, Gee was in the boat but was committed to Ellis learning how to navigate on his own. He hit four sand bars and snapped four shear pins.[39] They made it the last few miles to the island with a bobby pin holding the motor in place. Years after they were discharged from service, a number of their "Coast Guard family" kept in touch with the Woods family. Sid wrote on Labor Day, 1956:

> Back in Kansas again and I must say I'm not too happy about it. Sure wish I
> could have stayed in the good old south-land for a little longer. I hope you
> people had as good a time as I did on vacation. I want to thank you for your

wonderful hospitality and all the trouble you took to get us on the island. I also want you to know it made me feel so good to see you again, it was wonderful, it seemed like coming home again. The trip to the island and seeing all you folks made my vacation a complete success! Don't work too hard out there now and take care of yourselves. I may come back again someday, who knows? Tell Woody to brush up on his cribbage!

Two decades later, St. Catherines remained in the dreams of many of the Guardsmen. Dwaine Rice (Figure 114) wrote to Gee Little on June 18, 1965 telling her about his dreams of the island:

I often kid my wife saying how nice it would be to have a small house in Sunbury and keep a boat so that we could fish, dig oysters until it came out of our ears. What a lasting impression St. Catherines has made on me. How nice it would be to wake up some day and have someone tell me it was mine. That would be quite a dream. There is no other place that I have been that I would and thought of visiting again like that island. All these years it has been a constant thought with me.

Figure 112. Gee Woods and Bill Waites on the South Beach dunes.

Figure 113. Bill Waites in his "dress blues."

Figure 114. Dwaine Rice, driver of the weapons carrier.

When war came to St. Catherines, the Woods' world changed dramatically. John said that Eutherle Austin was his only playmate as a child, but as a teenager, he suddenly has forty-three older brothers. The Guardsmen taught him to box and were always ready for a game of horseshoes or a swimming race in the pool or in the ocean. John says that none of the men could catch him while playing "gator" in the water. In the boxing ring, that was another story. Remembering riding horses with the "guard," or better yet, being at the wheel of the jeep, still bring a smile to John's face. Clel and Gee learned to deal with an island filled with admirers. Clel had many admirers, and for John and Gee that provided a dividend. When Odell Powell, the sawyer for Younce Lumber Company, wanted to take Clel to the movies, John and Gee were her chaperones. Gee said that as a 15-year-old, she had all these sailors and "no idea what to do with them," but as she matured in the three years they were on the island, she said, "I grew up to be someone who knows better."

Toby and Gladys Woods did what was natural for them to incorporate the lonely Guardsmen into their family. It was a role that they have had since the day they were married in 1924. For the men of the Mounted Patrol, they were placed in a unique social and physical environment whose images and relationships stayed with them for a lifetime.

The story of St. Catherines in 1943 and 1944 certainly features the Coast Guard and their presence on the St. Catherines. However, Mr. Noble had a cattle ranch that he had to get up and running. It was necessary to begin extensive refurbishing of the buildings on the island that had been neglected for years. John's memories of the work on the island in 1943 are all that remains. We have no letters or daybooks for the first year of ownership. John, as a thirteen-year-old, would visit the island on weekends and the summer of 1943. While his interactions with the guardsmen are part of his personal memories, he did observe much of what his father was involved with in that first year. He recalls that during much of that time, his father was involved in refurbishing the cabins near the big house. After Noble's purchase of the island in 1943, Toby and his team were involved, initially, in repairing cabins 1, 2 and 3 just north of the big house. Toward the end of the year, they did some repairs on the employee cabins that were being occupied by the Coast Guard and its employees. They also began repairs on the big house.

For a large portion of 1944, we do have Toby Woods' daybook (Woods 1944).[40] Toby notes that on the last week in 1943, they were completing the work on the small cottage[41] and beginning serious work on the big house. The first six weeks of 1944 were involved with bleaching the rafters and cleaning the living room in big house in preparation of painting it (Woods 1944: Day Book). In a time before scaffolding could be rented, Toby had to build them from scratch. John remembers his father and his workers straining to reach above them with hydroxyl chloride bleach to beams and paint the walls.

It took a little over two weeks to paint the living room and the trim on the windows. Much of March focused on preparing and sanding the floor of the big room. Sanding the floors was an enormous task. On one Saturday (March 11th) he spent 13 hours sanding and on the next day (Sunday 12th) he worked another 5 hours sanding. After finishing varnishing and waxing the floor (March 22nd), Toby then tackled the three day task of repainting of the pool. Finally, Toby and his crew repaired the roof on the big house. The flat parts of the roof covered with Ludowici tile were a problem since they were first built by the Keys in the early 1930s. Time increase the problems. Toby removed the tiles, repaired the rotted rafters, replaced the tarpaper and replaced the tile. As John reminded me, these repairs would never solve the problem since the Ludowici tiles were never designed for a flat roof. Eventually, Mr. Noble would remove the porch and John in 1971 would replace the tile on the flat roofs with copper sheets

As John reminded me, these repairs would never solve the problem since the Ludowici tiles were never designed for a flat roof. Eventually, Mr. Noble would remove the porch and John in 1971 would replace the tile on the flat roofs with copper sheets.

This work seemed insignificant when Toby received the news early in February 1944 that tragedy had struck the Noble family. Their daughter Sally, a sophomore at Sarah Lawrence College died unexpectedly on February 9th after a sudden illness (NYT 1944a). Alger Chapman and his family and the English family were on their way to the island for a visit when Mr. Chapman was informed of Sally's death. After notifying Toby about the death, he returned to Greenwich, Connecticut to be with the Noble family. At the end of the month (February 25th),

Mr. Noble returned to St. Catherines with the Myers family and Toby reports that he seemed pleased with the progress that they were making on the renovation.

Toby has to be a champion of multitasking before the concept became a part of the modern vocabulary. While he had to focus on making the cabins and big house livable, there were constant distractions that needed his attention. For example, on January 6th the float on the "big dock" sunk and had to be raised and on March 8th he had to spend the day cleaning out a septic line. On February 22nd he had to repair the pasture fence to "keep the hogs out." But to Toby, the work on the "boat without a name" was the most frustrating. In 1943, Mr. Noble on a trip to Savannah bought a boat while at the Thunderbolt marina. The boat with only its registration number 17A780 identifying it was not well designed for the needs of the island and poorly constructed. It had a cabin built so high that it made the boat unstable. The incident mentioned earlier when the boat flipped on its side throwing the Guardsmen into the water. Even the engine was problematic: On Toby's initial run of the boat with no name, he found that the engine was "running hot."

A more critical problem was that "the boat without a name" had to do with poor construction in which the caulking was ineffective in keeping the seams tight causing many leaks so the boat "took on water." On the January 10th, while the boat was docked it "filled with water to a level over the engine." It Toby two days for him to disassemble and dried out the engine and carburetor and get the motor running again. Toby still had to deal with the more serious problem of a leaking hull. While he could have used the Ambos marine railway at the Thunderbolt,[42] it was inconvenient given the constant need of repair.

On May 16th, Toby began the construction of his own ways, as the marine railways are known.[43] The ways was built south of the main loading dock below employees' cabin 3 where a small stream drains into the marsh. The ways was about sixty feet long and was constructed on the bank of Waldburg Creek, so the railway extended to the water at low tide. A cradle with iron wheels was built to hold the boat as it was pulled up.[44] At high tide the boat would be placed on the cradle. The ways was constructed so that the cradle could be pulled out of the water and then sliding blocks were placed under the boat to keep it upright as it was pulled up the slope of bluff to the bank where the bottom could be repaired. A tractor was used to pull the boat and cradle up the bank.

The ways required cross ties on which the rails would be attached. The ties were made from green wood that would not float out of the bank at high tide. It took Toby and his men 12 days to finish the ways and on June 14th he had the boat with no name on the cradle and pulled it up the bank. I asked John how long the ways was in use. He said that the ways was used only a few times after the boat with no name blew up in 1948 seriously injuring John. As usual, the drama of what was happening on the island was always behind the scenes. Irene Floyd,[45] the 15 year old daughter of well digger W. C. Floyd was a frequent visitor to the island and fondly immortalized 17A780 with a poem, The Boat without a Name, written in 1946. Toby Woods had successfully given his guests the impression that the boat without a name was ready to serve all those who visited the island. Toby did this quietly, without complaint and smiled when Irene read this stanza in her poem:

> *There's a blue and white boat without a name,*
> *But it will carry you where want to go just the same.*
> *It's home is St. Catherines Island by a pretty white dock.*
> *It's just as faithful as an old, old, clock.*

Toby again had done his job well.

12

Mr. Noble

His business associates called him "Ed" and his friends literally sang his praises as the "wonder boy," but on St. Catherines he was always "Mr. Noble" (Figure 115). In his letters, Mr. Noble always referred to John Toby Woods in the more formal J. Tobias Woods, even though it wasn't his name. He was John Toby Woods since birth, but he was known as Toby to his family and friends. While there was obviously a "class thing"[1] involved in how he transformed Toby into Tobias, it is interesting that Mr. Noble rarely stayed in the "big" house while on the island. Rather, he preferred to stay in cabin 1, the slave cabin from the Waldburg era that was "restored" and remodeled by the Keys in the early 1930s.

Although Mr. Noble stayed in a restored slave cabin on St. Catherines, the employees knew their place and there was no question about who was the boss. Many employees on the island helped serve at company parties hosted by Mr. Noble at the big house. They were in awe of him and wondered who else would have thought to put a hole in mint, the mythical story of how Mr. Noble transformed an ordinary mint into the LifeSaver candy. Mr. Noble was an effective charmer who had the standing of a millionaire giant of business, but to most of those who met him on St. Catherines[2] he was just an "all around good guy." Carmen Baughcom, who had lived on the island for many years and would often be called to work at Mr. Noble's parties, related an incident when Mr. Noble called her over to identify an insect in the grass that he did not recognize. She instantly recognized it, and told him it was a dung beetle struggling to push its prize back to its nest. Mr. Noble thanked her and commented, "Nature thinks of everything." A half a century later, she fondly related the story to me and used this interaction to show me how unassuming and how charming Mr. Noble was in his dealings with those working and living on the island. Mr. Noble was so well thought of that thirty-eight year old Annie and George W. Berryhill, who were working on the island at the time, named their son Eddie[3] after him. Eddie was born on June 21, 1951.

However, there is another facet to Mr. Noble's personality that belies the carefree image that he presented to most of the island's employees and to the world. Mr. Noble could show incredible kindness that brought a smile to your heart. For example, Mr. Noble paid to send Ben Chapman, Snooker Chapman's son and the cook at the big house, to the University of Georgia; and he paved the way for John Toby, Jr. to receive an athletic scholarship to attend St. Lawrence University in Canton, New York.[4] On the other hand, "behind the scenes" he displayed a "pettiness" that seemed out of place, yet recurred so often that I have accepted it as part of his character. He would constantly complain when Toby or one of his workers went to Savannah to get supplies for the island on a weekday rather than on Saturday. Mr. Noble monitored the time cards that the workers signed and that Toby approved.[5] Any trip taken during a weekday would result in a questioning letter. Saturday's schedule called for a half-day of work (four-and-a-half hours), but the round trip to Savannah took about five hours if you limited your shopping.

Mr. Noble attributed that the extra hour or two hours to the workers running errands for themselves. Shopping trips to Savannah during a weekday became an obsession for him. Somehow, he believed that the workers were pulling one over on him. To Noble, you were working when you were in the field cutting down trees, herding cattle, mowing the grass, or repairing a building. If employees went to Savannah to run a work-related errand on a weekday, Mr. Noble believed that it was not really "work," and consequently you were only working a four-and-a-half-hour day (Noble 1948a).[6] The relationship between Mr. Noble and those on the island is part of the untold history of St. Catherines Island. Mr. Noble's history on the island is revealed through his interaction with Toby Woods, which are documented in Toby's sparse notations in his day books, letters to and from Toby Woods and Mr. Noble, and John Toby Woods' and Gee Little's memories of their father and Mr. Noble.

Edward J. Noble purchased St. Catherines with the expressed intent to raise cattle.[7] He added timber cutting when he needed to thin out the dead trees and to make more pasture. I don't think that E. J. Noble ever imagined himself a cattle rancher or timber baron. In his best year, 1951, Mr. Noble had 200 cows, 250 hogs, five horses, 254 heifer calves, 200 hogs and 4 bulls on St. Catherines (Woods 1952a) that value between $45,720 and $59,162.[8]

Noble had letterhead with "St. Catherines Island, Dorchester, Georgia" printed boldly on top of the page, and "Beef Cattle" and "Southern Pine" touting its products in the left and right margins. Most of Mr. Noble's correspondences were on "American Broadcasting Company, Inc." letterhead with "Edward J. Noble, Chairman of the Board" embossed below on the left margin. Sometimes the letterhead was marked "private office" of the posh Thousand Island Club at Alexandria Bay in New York, which he also owned.

Figure 115. Edward J. Noble in the 1950s.

While raised cattle and hogs, cut timber, worked at preserving the deer population, and tried to revive the population of wild turkey,[9] Mr. Noble viewed the island as a place where he could get away from the city and bring his family and friends to recreate, and as a place where his Life Savers executives could come for their annual business meetings. Noble entertained some of the most powerful people in the United States on St. Catherines. Dwight D. Eisenhower, Richard M. Nixon (CDT 1958; Lambright 1958),[10] key state officials, and Liberty County's most important politicians were all visitors to the island. In April 1952, Mr. Noble added a P.S. to a letter he sent Toby (Noble 1952b: April 15, letter) informing him that his friend Mr. Thomas G. Corcoran was anxious to visit St. Catherines, and that Toby was to give him "every consideration." Corcoran, known affectionately as "Tommy, the Cork" (McKean 2004), was considered the ultimate insider who peddled influence within the Roosevelt administration through Reagan administrations. Corcoran was probably the first Washington lobbyist and was involved in many business ventures. They are still writing about how Corcoran's influence on both business and government.[11] Mr. Noble certainly ran with a fast crowd. Whatever business he conducted while on the island, it was not from some spacious office in the "big house"; Mr. Noble carried on his business from cabin 1.

Cabin 1 certainly represented a Spartan living situation for the owner of the Life Savers Company and soon-to-be owner of the ABC radio network (Figure 116). Its only source of heat in the winter was a fireplace, and there was no air-conditioning during the sweltering summer nights. Even the gnat-proof enclosed screen porches that were built by the Keys in the 1930s and afforded relief were removed rather than repaired or replaced. Mr. Noble felt that the expense was too great and that they were not needed. The only visible parts of the original slave cabin were the tile floor and exposed ceiling with hand-hewed beams. A part of the original tabby wall was incorporated[12] into the wall reconstructed by the Keys. The cabin, so near which was located close to the big house, had housed the "overseer" or "driver" for nearly a half-century.

Cabin 1 had a bathroom attached on the end near the fireplace. To the left of the brick

Figure 116. Cabin 1 on the Oyster Road.

fireplace was a door into the full bathroom, which had cold running water pumped from the two 5000-gallon water tanks adjacent to the powerhouse. On hot days, the temperature of the water might rise a few degrees after sitting in the tank for awhile. To the right of the fireplace was a walk-in closet with built-in shelves. While there may have been a suit or a few sport coats ready for a business meeting in New York, his wardrobe on the island was simple. In the summer, he had an array of t-shirts and shorts for lounging near the pool or walking the manicured lawns around the house. In the winter and for riding, he had light flannel shirts, slacks and sometimes boots.

In the main room, there was smaller dresser, a desk on the east side facing the wall, two chairs for guests, a lamp, a radio and a phone installed by Toby Woods that could be used to call the big house and the superintendent's house.[13] In the winter, the Heatilater installed by the Keys had a small water tank that would warm the water when there was a fire in the fireplace. A fire was started by the employees in the morning[14] and Mr. Noble would keep it going from the logs that were kept stacked on the porch.

Figure 117. Swimming pool with cabin 1.

Mr. Noble preferred to bathe in the near-by pool where he would "skinny dip" for his daily swim[15] (Figure 117). John said the water was bitterly cold, but the chilly water did not seem to bother Mr. Noble. Even during the coldest months of the year, he would stay true to form and not venture to the "big" house, as he called it, for the warmth of a shower with heated water. He would go to the house for meals and to entertain guests, but always returned to cabin 1 to retire after the festivities. However, friendly he may have been to the employees, Mr. Noble maintained an "air" that always reminded you that he was a "man of power." John related an incident that illustrates this aspect of Mr. Noble's persona:

Mr. Noble swam in his pool all year round. He also took his soap and bathed in the unheated pool. One morning in December[16] when I was on the island for the weekend, I was walking down the Shell Road across from the swimming pool when Mr. Noble saw me and waved me over. He said that he dropped his soap in the pool and couldn't dive in deep enough to get the soap. He asked me to pull off my clothes and dive in and get the bar of soap that was in the 11-foot end of the pool. I told him that somebody might see me, but he said that he would be my "lookout." Me, being young and stupid, I dove in and got the soap for him.

Figure 118. The "big house" during the Noble era, as seen from Waldburg Creek.

Cabin 1 was the center of activity when Mr. Noble brought guests from the Savannah area to St. Catherines. When the Thomas C. Myers or Morgan families visited the island, they would stay in cabins two and three. This provided them with privacy that would not have been available in the big house. They would go the big house for meals and for socializing (Figure 118), but they always returned to the three cabins that fronted Shell Road. His friends from Savannah were frequent visitors to the island. In 1945, Mr. Noble and his Savannah friends were on the island more than two dozen times. After Mr. Noble's death, the privacy of the cabins did attract other family members. Mr. Noble's daughter and her husband Frank Larkin stayed in cabin 2, which had more appeal after they were remodeled with mounted air conditioners.[17]

Mr. Noble Buys Himself an Island

The purchase of St. Catherines Island seemed almost a lark to his acquaintances on Colonels Island.[18] Mr. Noble was attending Bill Flynn's party at his Maxwelton Estate early in 1943 when he looked across the marshes and saw St. Catherines Island standing boldly on the horizon. Flynn told him that the island was owned by the Rauers family, who was interested in selling it after harvesting the most valuable timber. Since its timber had been cut and its uniqueness as a hunting preserve destroyed, it was rumored to be offered for sale at less than a half-a million dollars. In fact, E. J. Noble made an incredible deal. On February 13, 1943, he transmitted a $15,000 "earnest money" check[19] to secure the purchase of St. Catherines for the remarkable price of $150,000 (Noble 1943c).[20] Within months, Edward J. Noble had himself an island (NYT 1943b).

Those who knew E. J. Noble understood that he did not buy anything on a lark. St. Catherines was indeed a deal. The price was "right" and he immediately understood the possibility of transforming it into a cattle ranch that would translate into tax benefits with respect to Liberty County property taxes and business expenses. His frequent trips to entertain friends on the island were written off as business expenses. He was advised by Alger B. Chapman, one of the best tax lawyers in the United States, who certainly counseled him on how to leverage the island to his tax advantage. The owners of St. Catherines had leased the "oyster rights" to the island for many years. Noble continued this practice, and leased the rights to J. H. Morgan and later to the Ambos family[21] from Thunderbolt, and these revenues helped to pay the property taxes.[22]

Edward J. Noble was ready to enjoy St. Catherines. He was known for his ability to select excellent people to manage his businesses, and for taking time to enjoy his success. Once on the island, Mr. Noble showed a "firm hand" and managed its operations down to the minutest details. It was as if all the energy that would have once gone into running the Life Savers Company and ABC was focused on Toby Woods and his team of five employees.

St. Catherines would be added to a list of other retreats fitting a person of Mr. Noble's standing. In 1934, he purchased a 45-acre estate in Greenwich, Connecticut surrounding a 15-acre lake that was adjacent to 32 acres that he already owned (NYT 1934). This property was assessed four years later at $400,000 (NYT 1938b). His eighty-foot yacht, *The Monatoana*[23] was docked in Florida, and Noble owned and operated the Thousand Island Club[24] in Alexandra Bay, New York (Ingham 1983:1013). The Heart Island estate with the magnificent Boldt Castle[25] on the Thousand Island Club in New York that was "posh" enough that visitors in 1939 were charges 35 cents for a tour (Time 1939).[26] There was a summer home on the Canadian mainland, which was easily accessible by a plane that he piloted.[27] The last trip *The Monatoana* made to St. Catherines was a stop on the way to Miami where it was to be sold. It docked long enough for some of the yacht's furniture to be off-loaded and placed in the big house's living room.

E. J. Noble, the Business Man

C. M. Keys was a relatively obscure owner of St. Catherines. In contrast, Edward J. Noble was known to everyone. He was the epitome of the Horatio Alger story. Noble and his childhood friend, J. Roy Allen, bought the Life Savers Company in 1913 for $2900 and turned it into a mint (pun intended) that seemed to print money. As a 21-year-old advertising man, he discovered Life Savers, mints manufactured by Clarence A. Crane,[28] the owner of Mary Garden Chocolates who had been in business since 1891.

Crane, looking for a product that would not melt in heat of the summer months, invented Crane's Peppermint Life Savers using equipment that he saw in a pharmacy that produced round pills.[29] The machine was modified to pop out the center, giving the candy it its unique appearance.[30] Always an optimistic advertising salesman, Noble suggested that Crane could increase his business by launching an advertising campaign.[31] Crane, unhappy with his business prospects, offered Noble the trademark and stock of candy for $5000. When they could only raise $3900, Crane sold them the Life Savers for $2900 (Noble and Allen needed $1000 for the capital to run the business).

The business plan for Life Savers was to encourage repeat business for an inexpensive product. The mints would be displayed near cash registers as an impulsive purchase for waiting customers. Unfortunately, there were problems with the cardboard container used for the Life Savers. They not only zapped the flavor from the mints, but also imbued them with the taste of glue. Noble ingeniously thought of packing them in tinfoil to preserve the flavor. He believed that if a person received a nickel in change he would impulsively buy a five-cent pack of Life Savers displayed near the cash register.

There was even a myth reported in his obituary in the *Los Angeles Times* that Noble was the clever person who put the hole in the candy (LAT 1958). That honor belonged to Clarence Crane.[32] He put the hole in the peppermint, but Noble had the vision for how to market it. The Life Savers Company became immensely profitable. By 1920, the company was realizing a net profit of a million dollars per year. This average profit margin was maintained from 1925 to 1938. Although Edward Noble called Life Savers, "a happy whimsical business" (Time 1956), it was an incredible money machine. Just 25 years after its purchase, the company had a net worth of $22 million, an unprecedented 7586% increase in value.[33]

Life Savers visible ties to St. Catherines were reinforced soon after Mr. Noble purchased the Island. He sent down a 1940 Chevrolet quarter-ton panel truck emblazoned with pictures of Life Savers over the body.

The truck, designed to be noticed in the streets of American cities, had a three-foot-long Life Savers roll attached above the head of the driver to ensure that it would be noticed. A similarly painted 1941 Ford Panel truck was sent down later (Figure 119). On April 28, 1944, Otis Edenfield drove to Jacksonville, Florida to pick up the truck (Woods 1944:April 29).[34]

Figure 119. The concept cars that Ford was developing for the Life Saver Company. The '41 Ford "candy truck" sent to the St. Catherines was similar to model on the left. From http://www.sharonhollow.com/Life Savers37.htm

The '41 Ford rode the oyster and dirt roads of St. Catherines, while the Chevy rode the streets of Savannah. John said it was quite a sight. Wise Mr. Noble, an advertising man at heart, did not miss a chance to advertise his candy. It may have helped sales in the city, but on St. Catherines, boxes of Life Savers were frequent gifts from Mr. Noble, and the purchase of the treat was seldom needed. John said that they removed the Live Savers roll bolted to the top of the truck, but the painted Life Savers remained to the end.[35]

Soon after E. J. Noble bought St. Catherines in March of 1943 (NYT 1943b), he made big news at the end of July when he purchased the Blue Network from Radio Corporation of America (NBC) for $8 million in cash (NYT 1943c). He changed the name to the American Broadcasting Company (ABC),[36] invested in upgrading the network, and turned this business into a money maker. By the end of the year, Noble had sold a quarter interest to *Time Magazine* and Chester La Roche, who at one time was chairman of the board for Young and Rubicon, a major advertising company. A 1944 biography (Anon. 1944) described Mr. Noble:

> "Ed," as Noble is popularly called, is remarkably young-looking for his sixty-odd years. He is tall, athletic, and soft-spoken – a voluble and genial talker who displays fine teeth when he laughs, which is often and heartily. He has been described as "rich, happy and dollar-wise." His eyes are widely set and framed with heavy eyebrows.

Seven years later, Noble made page-one news again when ABC merged with United Theater Incorporated in what was reported as a $25 million dollar deal (Gould 1951). Edward Noble owned 1,689,017 shares of ABC stock, which after the merger, was worth over $12 million. He joined the board of directors of the new company. Since it was a forced sale, the deal was a tax free reorganization,[37] which meant there was no need to report capital gains. The merger had the imprint of Alger B. Chapman, who was appointed to the ABC board of directors in 1949 (NYT

1949b). But, E. J. Noble was not finished with his business dealings. In 1956, Life Savers merged with Beech-Nut Packing Company, which had been in business since 1891 (NYT 1956b). Noble assumed the role of board chairman and chief executive officer of the merged company (WSJ 1956). According to *Time Magazine*, Noble "bubbled", "this will be one last fling." (Time 1956). Noble also served on the boards of First National Bank & Trust Co. in Port Chester, N.Y (BM 1928), Commercial National Bank and Trust (NYT 1940a),and Union Bag and Paper (WP 1936). He retired from Union Bag's board in 1938 (WSJ 1938). Alexander "Sandy" Calder, Noble's friend, was then president of Union Bag. After the death of E. J. Noble, Chapman was appointed to the ABC-Paramount board (NYT 1959a). At that time, Chapman was chairman and chief executive officer of Beech-Nut Life Savers.

E. J. Noble, Public Servant

What is less known about Mr. Noble is his role as a public servant. In 1938, he headed the newly formed Civil Aeronautics Authority (CAA) (WP 1938b) created by President Franklin Delano Roosevelt. The Authority's task was to deal with safety, air mail rates (WP 1938a),[38] and other issues associated with regulating and encouraging the expansion of commercial aviation (Dorris 1938). Mr. Noble was considered the ideal person for the position since he was a "pioneer aviation enthusiast, [who]... travel[ed] in his own cabin plane and was one of the first persons to own an autogiro"[39] (WP 1938b:X1).

In 1939, Noble resigned from the CAA and became the first Undersecretary of Commerce, which was headed by famed politician Harry Hopkins (NYT 1939b). Noble was believed to be a force that could stimulate the economy. Noble (1940) showed that the Europeans were helping American trade even while fighting the war. Noble's philosophy appealed to businessmen. In a *Time Magazine* interview (Time 1939), Noble is quoted, "The way to do business is to do business—the more the better. As a businessman I have long known that volume is the cure for most business ills."

Noble was well-spoken for someone who had made his millions selling five-cent rolls of candy. He made headlines when he resigned from the Undersecretary post and announced that he would work for the campaign of Wendell Willkie (CSM 1940; NYT 1940b). Noble known for his candor commented:

> In resigning my government post, I told President Roosevelt that I felt that I could be really helpful in the field of national defense. My intension is to do all that I can to ensure the election of Mr. Willkie is a part of the program (NYT 1940b:7).[40]

> Mr. Willkie's election will give impetus to American business... In my opinion, it is the surest means of putting idle capital to work, stimulating industry and promoting reemployment. My support of Willkie is based upon confidence that his policies call for full speed ahead for business and a full speed forward for workers that will mean a larger share of national prosperity for everyone (CSM 1940:14).

In serving these two years, Noble said that he fulfilled his obligations and assistance to President Roosevelt and the nation (NYT 1940d).[41] His success resulted in politicians touting him for the

U.S. Senate (NYT 1940e), but he declined to run (NYT 1940c). He did continue to promote commerce by serving on the Advisory Board of the St. Lawrence Seaway Development Corporation (Ingham 1983), at the request of President Eisenhower. The corporation was a United States governmental agency that worked with Canada to encourage shipping through the locks that divided the countries.

Even though he was a graduate of Yale (1905), Noble promoted the small liberal arts college experience by promoting St. Lawrence University in Canton, New York. St. Lawrence University is located near Gouveneur, NY, his birthplace, and the Thousand Islands where he owned property. He was a member of the Board of Trustees for St. Lawrence University from 1941 to 1954 (Ingham 1983).[42] He retired as Chairmen of the Board in 1954 when he was named a "life member of the board" (NYT 1954b). In 1956, he donated $100,000 to build a library and $500,000 for a student center (NYT 1956a) that bears his name.

E. J. Noble, Philanthropist

Edward J. Noble was a supporter of the Community Chest and other charitable agencies which he called "Citadels of Democracy" (WP 1939). He believed that it was the German people's unwillingness to care for their own that led to those in need to accept Hitler's message. His work with the Community Chest, who history has been intertwined with that of the "United Way" organization, was an example of his own willingness to follow his beliefs.

E. J. Noble was presented with a seven-foot scroll with the names of 400 Salvation Army officers and workers for his role as national chairman of the 1947 and 1948 Annual Maintenance Appeal Drives (NYT 1947a). He was also involved in fundraising for the Greater New York Chapter of the National Foundation for Infantile Paralysis (poliomyelitis). However, his most outstanding contribution is the foundation that bears his name. In 1940, Edward J. Noble created the Edward J. Noble Foundation for educational, religious and charitable contributions (WP 1958). It became a major force in philanthropy in 1953 when he contributed $2 million to the fund (NYT 1953). Two years later, he contributed another $5 million (NYT 1954a). By 2002, its assets reached $122 million and the foundation had provided as much as $2.9 million in funding to environmental groups from 1973-2000. Ten years after his death, the Noble Foundation acquired the island and formed the St. Catherines Island Foundation, which still controls the island today.

Mr. Noble and Toby Woods

Mr. Noble's cattle and timber business did not require major changes in how St. Catherines functioned. Toby Woods already had a small herd of cattle that he had been keeping for income[43] since he was receiving his salary irregularly from the Keys during the last years of the 1930s. When Noble stepped on to the island, the timber operation had already been in place for nearly four years. For the cattle business it would be necessary to clear the stumps that remained from timbering and to prepare the soil for pasturage. There was tremendous secondary growth of many plants, and the acres of saw palmettos made clearing difficult. Dead trees, many of which had fallen, were not used as timber. Mr. Noble wanted a "clean island," and stumps and dead vegetation were an indication of poor ranch management in his eyes. Therefore, it was Toby's duty to clear the land, as quickly as possible.

There were other problems that demanded Toby's immediate attention. Many of buildings on the island had not been maintained for nearly a decade, and they too required work. Some of the walls needed to be repaired where plaster had fallen away, and all of the buildings needed to be repainted.

Toby would have to periodically interrupt some of his activities to focus on the annual business meeting of the key managers of the Life Saver Company. Each fall, Noble would bring the executives and regional sales managers to St. Catherines for their yearly "convention." The staff on St. Catherines referred to the convention as "the Life Savers party," reflecting the festive nature of the business meetings. The island was also used to entertain his Noble's longtime friends and family, and even state and local dignitaries.

I asked John about Mr. Noble's cattle and timber business. At the end of 1945, two-and-a-half years after he stepped on the island, Mr. Noble had 43 cows[44] (six were off color), 22 heifers, five bulls, 28 steers and 500 hogs[45] (Woods 1945). This was certainly a modest beginning. John recalls:

> When Mr. Noble bought St. Catherines Island in 1943, my father had a herd of about 50 mixed bred cattle. We always had two or three milk cows that provided us with all the milk we needed. There were about 300 hogs scattered around the island. The Keys and Rauers had let daddy stock the island during the years after the depression when they were not able to pay him.
>
> Mr. Noble bought the livestock from my father. He wanted to run the island as a farm. He was in the highest tax bracket and needed to be able to charge off the island expenses.

Figure 120. The Brahman bull that liked human company.

> My father started selling off the mix breed cattle and buying Black Angus cattle for Mr. Noble. The Black Angus were not full blooded registered cattle, but at the time daddy would buy a registered bull to help bring up their blood line.
>
> Later my father bought a registered Brahman bull, as Brahman cattle were supposed to be even better range cattle. This was a huge bull with a hump on his back.

As John describes it, the bull had very un-bull-like behavior. Instead of the threatening people, the bull took a "shine" to human companionship (Figure 120).

> He liked to stay on the lawn where family and guests would take their strolls frequently frightening them when he would try to saunter up to them. At night, when the guests were safely in the "big" house, he would wander up to the big window in the living room while they would be eating dinner.

> The look in his eye was like a puppy that wanted to have his master come
> out and play with him.

Whatever possessed the Brahman bull to seek the tranquil company of humans, it was not passed off to his offspring. Toby had a predicament:

> The only problem was that the Brahman bull's offspring would get wilder
> than the Angus would. We had to build a trap pen on the south end of the
> island just the south of Flag Pond to catch cows that had gone wild. The trap
> pen was built near an old artesian well that was still flowing. The pen would
> be baited with sweet feed[46] and after we had captured the cows, we would
> haul them back with a cow trailer that we had built. It was a difficult task to
> keep them in the trap pen since some of the Brahman cows were able to get
> over the 6-foot wooden fence that we had built.

John said that the cows were more of a problem. For the most part, they were an unfriendly bunch. It did not matter if they were Angus or Brahman cows, they would come after you if you tried to push them in a direction that they did not want to go.

> One difference I saw was that a Black Angus cow started chasing you and
> you jumped behind a tree, the Angus cow would sail by you. The Brahman
> cow would chase you around the tree. I saw one Brahman chase my daddy
> around the tree and caught him, knocked him down, butted him a couple of
> times while he was on the ground. My dad was not hurt. He was tougher
> than that cow. The cows would have been real dangerous if they had horns.

Mr. Noble was concerned about the unfriendly cows. In a letter to Toby (Noble 1952a: Letter, March 13) about a $92.00 feed bill from Chisholm Farm Service, Mr. Noble wanted assurance that the feed was used on the south end herds where Woodrow where he hoped, "… Woodrow has been working to make them more friendly."

In most of the fields that were cleared for timbering during the Rauers interlude,[47] thick impenetrable secondary growth underbrush made it difficult to provide pasture; saw palmettos blanketed the ground. It took Herculean effort to turn the underbrush into pasture, John relates:

> Mr. Noble had my father buy a HD-14 Allis Chalmers bulldozer (Figure
> 121)[48] from Morgan's Inc. in Savannah. The HD-14 was built before they
> had hydraulic lifts, and the bulldozer blade was lifted with a cable that ran
> over the top of the tractor to a winch on the back. The weight of the blade
> would hold it down.

Mr. Noble also bought a root rake with teeth instead of a blade to pile the stumps and underbrush for burning. He also bought a brush cutter that was being used in east Texas. The brush cutter had two large tanks fastened together so they could be pulled at an angle. There were blades all around the tanks that cut 10 inches into the dirt. When the tanks were filled with

Figure 121. The HD-14 Allis Chalmers bulldozer of the type they used on St. Catherines. The blade lacked a hydraulic lift system and the line above the driver's head operated the blade.

water the brush cutter weighed 22,000 pounds. It was all the HD 14 tractor could do to pull the cutter. My daddy faced another problem. When operating the brush cutter, leaves would be sucked into the radiator causing it to run hot. He installed a reversible fan blade on the engine to blow the leaves away rather than pulling them into the radiator.

The blade cutter did a terrific job. It cut and ground the trunks of a plant that were as big around as your arm. It would also destroy hornets or yellow jackets nest forcing the driver to run for cover.

A profit and loss statement for the first 10 months of 1947 (Noble 1947) listed the purchase of the HD-14 for $12,128.74.[49] That same year, they bought two lots at Half Moon landing[50] for $2750, a bull for $300, and a refrigerator for $379. Their expenditures for the year totaled $15,557.74. They had an income in 1947 of $7,913.69 from livestock sales ($1,483.69), oil lease ($5000)[51] and oyster lease ($400). In 1946, they had an income of $10,282.91 from the sale of livestock ($4882.91), oil lease ($5000) and oyster lease ($400). I was stunned by the willingness of someone to pay $5000 for an oil lease. I called my friend Bill Size, a geologist at Emory University, and he said that there was zero possibility of finding oil on St. Catherines. He said that there has been very little exploratory drilling in the area. He did mention that farther off the coast, in deeper water called the Blake Plateau, oil companies have leased plots for exploratory drilling. He said that they would not spend this kind of money unless they had sufficient data to justify drilling. Harold Rollins, a geologist that worked St. Catherines for thirty years, never heard rumors of oil leases. He suspects that these leases were the result of oil companies tying up as much coastal and near offshore land as possible. Rollins recounts that it was "a time when offshore development was just becoming a fashionable bandwagon." He goes on, "As far as I know, geologically speaking, St. Catherines Island has never been a serious target for development, nor is there any real potential there (again, as far as I know!)."

As the cattle business expanded, there was a need for more pasture. Mr. Noble decided that he would expand into the northeast part of the island where Thigpen had cut the virgin pine five years earlier. The area surrounding Sams Field[52] was high sandy soil full of stumps and overgrown with underbrush and saw palmettos. Toby and Mr. Noble decided to buy another bulldozer[53] to clear the land for pasture.

John described another task designed to increase the pasture on St. Catherines. There was a chain of natural fresh water ponds from just northeast of Sams Field to the Wamassee Pond area. They were shallow ponds and in the dry season, pine trees would thrive in the dried pond beds. Years later when there would be a wet season all of the pine trees in the pond area would die. John said that Mr. Noble had a passion for removing any dead trees that he saw on his rounds of the island. From 1954 to 1956, there was a concerted effort to dig a canal from Sams Field to Wamassee, a distance of about six miles (Figures 122 and 123). There were four side-canals cut into the main canal at right angles that diverted water into the marshes. After Mr. Noble's death, his daughter, June Larkin, had a more natural view of the environment and

Figure 123. The ditch through the pasture on St. Catherines near Savannah Woods.

Figure 122. County agent Joe Collins and Toby Woods examining a ditch that was being dug to drain series of ponds from Sams field to Wamassee pond. Note the dragline in the background

realized that dead trees provided a habitat for many species of plants and animals.

Based on Toby Woods' recommendation, Mr. Noble decided that the pond drainage would decrease the problem of dead pine trees in the low areas and would create cow pastures along the edges of the ditch. The resulting "dragline incident", as I will call it, illustrates the problem with trying to do things the cheapest way possible. Toby (and later John) were extremely frugal when it came to buying and repairing equipment. During the Keys era, Toby spent many years unable to buy or even repair the equipment necessary to keep the island functioning. So, he did what he had to do to keep the equipment running. In digging the draining ditches, they acquired a dragline from Richard Tuten, a National Guard pilot who frequently flew Mr. Noble to the island, against the advice of Curtis Lee. Lee, who knew draglines from running them on his dad's junkyard since he was sixteen, realized that Tuten's equipment was trouble. In a letter written to Toby, Mr. Noble said (Noble 1953:March 4 letter):

> I am very interested in Curtis' report on the drag line situation….While I
> want to be fair to him,[54] I am inclined to agree with Curtis' report to us, and
> it is quite probable that it would be an endless expense and loss of time to
> try and use this outfit.

Whatever the advice, Mr. Noble decided to use the dragline. Toby unloaded the dragline on February 14, 1954 at 5:00AM[55] (Woods 1954b: Day Book). Richard Tuten came over from the mainland and worked five nine-hour days early in March. They worked the dragline hard with nine-hour days for about 23 days and a total of 184 hours. Curtis Lee's predictions came true. Uncle Albert, who was in charge of the dragline, was an expert welder and cutter and spent many hours keeping the dragline functioning. On May 20, they spent the day repairing the dragline and about a month later they had to get a part repaired in Savannah. The dragline was used during 1954 and 1955. Later, Mr. Noble who seemed to have forgotten his doubts about the dragline, complained to Toby that he was using too much acetylene (Noble 1956b:Letter, January 18):

> Incidentally, the acetylene tank bills have run exceedingly high recently. I am wondering what is causing so many breakages that for correction need welding. Do you think that it is carelessness on the part of the people who handle the equipment or what is it?

John said that Mr. Noble was wrong in his thinking that the welding was due to misuse. Most of the welding was to repair gears that were so worn out that they could not mesh with other gears. Uncle Albert Rogers had to add metal to the teeth of the gears so they could engage the teeth of the other gears.

Less than a month later, Mr. Noble realized that the dragline was a liability but he seemed unable to let go of it. In a letter to Toby he wrote (Noble 1956a: Letter, February 16):

> I have had a talk with Richard about the drag-line matter and we left it that we will complete our discussions on my next trip down... And, of course, he won't move the drag-line until we solve our problem.

> I am in hopes that something can be worked out so that it will be left on the island but, of course, the final decision must be left to him, as I don't want to get in to any unpleasantness. It is just a question of fairness to both him and to me.

Given the problems with the dragline, it is not clear why he would want to have it remain on the island. The problem was never resolved. Less than two months after the death of Mr. Noble in 1958, Richard Tuten died tragically at age 39 on February 8, 1959. Children were playing with a carbine in another room in his house, and he was accidentally shot.[56] Four months later, a desperate Sarah Beth Tuten tried to get some resolution of the dragline's fate. She wrote to Toby Woods (Tuten 1959: Letter, May 31),

> Since Richard's recent death, I have not been able to give much thought as what disposition to make of his dragline, which I understand, is still on the Island. I do not know what would be the best to do; sell it where it is, or bring it to Savannah to sell or rent. I have also thought that you would know whether or not the present owners of the Island would like to purchase the machine and keep it on the Island.

Will the machine start, and if not, is it the battery? Are you now using the machine? If not, is it in working order? Do you have facilities to move it to the mainland and, if so, would you be interested in a contract to move it?

If you can help me with this in any way, Toby, it will mean a great to the boys and me.

The dragline sat 600 feet east of the power plant as a silent monument to inertia for another 12 years. While clearing land to extend an airstrip that was never completed, the HD-14 died in action after 21 years of loyal service and was left in the field. It was buried later when they were preparing the land for the New York Zoo's survival center. John Woods and crew decided to cut the dragline, which had become an "eyesore," into manageable pieces and inter it (Figures 122-124). At the time, there was little concern about the consequences of these practices. In 2007, research was undertaken to measure the possible contamination in two unlined dumps on the island (Gannaway and Knoll 2007). One dump was on the northwest corner, and a larger dump was to the south. The dumps were in Pleistocene sands containing an unconfirmed aquifer with a water table five to fifteen feet deep. The northwest dumps held diesel oil stored in drums that were previously used to burn trash. The more southern dump served more as a junkyard and had automobiles, oil drums and batteries. Gannaway and colleagues sunk 21 test wells to measure the contamination levels of 66 different chemicals. There was no evidence of hydrocarbons such as benzene, toluene and xylene, but there were two wells in the dump site with increased levels of copper, zinc and lead.

Figures 124-126. The death of the Allis Chalmers HD-14. In 1975, after the HD-14 was beyond repair, it was cut up and buried. The top photo shows the John Deere tractor pushing the HD-14 into the hole. The middle picture shows it being pushed into its final resting place. Note the acetylene torch in foreground. The bottom photo shows old HD-14 is ready for burial.

Given all the time and effort from 1953 to 1956 dedicated to increasing the pasture, one would expect an increase in the size of the herd. However, increasing pasture was more aesthetic than functional. In 1952, there were 250 cows, 50 calves, 12 bulls, 4 horses, 250 hogs and 100 pigs that were valued at $45,000 (Woods 1952a). By 1954, a year into the pasture project, they had 50 fewer cows, 50 more calves, 100 less hogs, and 5 more bulls (Woods 1954a). After the process had been completed in 1956, the inventory of cows had dropped to 175, hogs increased to 200, and there were four fewer bulls with a total value of $16,830, a 36% decrease compared to 1952 (Woods 1956). While there was an increase is the livestock in 1957 (Woods 1957), the herd reached its lowest level ever in 1958 with an inventory worth $13,800 (Woods 1958a). However, there was a significant increase of pasture, and that suited Mr. Noble's vision of a ranch.

After Noble's death, the trustees of the E. J. Noble Foundation began having second thoughts about the transformation of the island under his supervision. They commissioned a study to return St. Catherines to its natural state. William P. Baldwin, a land management consultant from Summerville, South Carolina, provided a reclamation analysis (Baldwin 1966). Baldwin suggested a three-year program for "habitat improvement for wildlife" that would cost $27,000 to $30,000 per year. Baldwin was aware that this transformation would result in a $39,500 loss[57] in annual revenues for St. Catherines. He suggested that the sale of winter hunting lease for $20,000 to $40,000 would help recover some of these loses.

The canal digging, land clearing, and other island activities were hard on the equipment. Edward J. Noble did not seem to understand that buying used equipment and working it for long periods took its toll. The cost of repairing equipment was a recurring theme in the Mr. Noble and Toby Woods' interactions. There were few things that missed his scrutiny. On January 22, 1948, Responding to Toby, Mr. Noble wrote a letter to complain about the cost of repairs on the eight-year-old candy truck and the purchase of a truck jack. Toby responded with impeccable logic (Woods 1948: Letter, February 6, 1948):

> …it seems me that I am always getting into dutch about some of my bills on overhauling jobs or whatever I have to buy. If I knew these things to happen ahead of time I could discuss it with you and maybe we could decide the best way and means to handle them. However, things always happen just when you least expect them and it looks like I do have to go ahead and have them fixed. We do try to take the best care we can of the Candy truck but as you know this truck is the only transportation we have from the garage to any place on the on the mainland other then the big truck….You made a little mistake in the mileage on the truck. The speedometer doesn't show but 72,000 miles, however the speedometer has been out of commission for about a couple of years.[58]

> About the Motor Supply charge of $21.90 for a 12 ton Jack; this is a very sensible thing to work with on St. Catherines Island. I will give you an example of how we have used it since we have had it. While we were hauling dirt with the army truck we bent the differential housing on it. Instead of taking the truck to Savannah to have it straightened, which would have cost a good sum of money, I bought this $21.90 jack and we straightened it ourselves. If we had had helper springs (bill for $27.75) on this truck the housing would never have bent. The above are the reasons for buying the helper springs and the jack.

All of this work, John notes, was accomplished with his dad leading a crew of 5 or 6 men. Six men, Toby, and unpaid Gladys Woods were running a 13,000-acre ranch that was hours from the main source of supply. In 1937, the *New York Times* (NYT 1937c) reported a jewelry heist at the Greenwich home of the Nobles. Neither the two maids nor cook living in the house, nor the butler sleeping 300 feet from the house, heard the commotion caused by the burglar.[59] The fact that the Nobles were accustomed to having extensive help on their 70-acre estate should have made him more realistic about the resources needed to run an enterprise as large as St. Catherines. In Greenwich, the grocery or hardware store was only a ten-minute ride away for the Nobles. On St. Catherines, it was at least a five hour round trip to go to Savannah for supplies or a critical part for a repair.

The time and efforts of the crew running the hog business also became an issue. Mr. Noble had second thoughts about the hog farming. He wrote to Toby on March 4, 1953 (Noble 1953),

> I am having some figures set up on the hog situation and I am not at all sure that the amount of time and expenses put on them justifies continuing this work. However by the time I get down there, I will know more about it.

An October 31, 1953, a livestock report to Mr. Noble listed the sale of 363 hogs and pigs weighing 24,510 pounds and valuing $2605.46.[60] The next year, the inventory showed that there were still 150 hogs on the island (Woods 1954a). In the last four years of Mr. Noble's life, there were an average of 143 hogs on the inventory (Woods 1955a; 1956; 1957; 1958a). Getting out of the hog business was easier said than done. The hogs that remained were prolific breeders and without capturing them for sale, the island would have been overrun by them. Up until 1958, hogs continued to be part of the Noble enterprise on St. Catherines.

Doc Brown, Mr. Noble, Toby and the Hog Business Adventure

The hog business created a need for a dog to herd the swine. Dr. Brown, a veterinarian who lived in Emanuel County near Swainsboro, gave Toby an English bulldog. According to John, the dog weighed about 100 pounds and was able to catch the wild hogs in the winter so they could be sold. The hogs were sold to hunting reserves to be turned out for hunters to shoot. The boars with large tusks were sought after for this use. Toby and his employees would trap hogs in a series of pens scattered about the island. John:

> Doc Brown would catch the hogs by the ears and hold them until his men could get to them. There was a problem. Doc. Brown wouldn't release the hog. You would have to beat him with a big stick and he still wouldn't release the hog –They finely learned that he was afraid of a switch, you could switch him and he would turn the hog loose. English bulldogs are the toughest animals that I know. The big boar hogs with their long tusks would back up in a thicket, where he would attack Doc Brown and cut him up. They would take a needle and thread with them to sew him back up. Sometimes they would stick Doc's head through part of a rubber inner tube to help protect him.

Doc Brown had a problem, he liked to catch and kill deer. Doc would see the hog trailer that was five feet above the ground and he would jump on it for the ride. If he sighted a deer, he would jump off the top of the hog trailer, run them down, grab them by the throat and kill them. So daddy was going to get rid of him. Doc had another problem. He would go out and hunt hogs on his own and since there was no one to make Doc release the hog, he would keep gnawing on the hog's ear until he had bitten it off. We had a bunch of hogs with just one ear and we were not able to sell them.

Figure 127. Doc Brown with Holly Woods.

I became intrigued by Doc Brown and asked John for a picture of the ferocious beast. John returned the next day with a picture of Doc Brown, the hundred-pound hunting machine, in all his glory acting as a sentinel for his two year old daughter Holly (Figure 127). So much for "dog profiling." When Mr. Noble brought his guests to the island, he drove them in his command car left over from World War II. As Mr. Noble drove by the house, Doc Brown would sail into the seat next to Mr. Noble, sitting there as if he were one of his guests. Mr. Noble fell in love with Doc Brown and took him back to New York by train. He kept Doc at the Thousand Island Club. Daddy received a letter[61] saying how much they cared for Doc and that he was living a life fit for a king.

Maintaining the Deer Population on St. Catherines.

Figure 128. Gee and Bum, Mr. Noble's pet deer, in 1948.

I was intrigued by a picture of Gee with a deer that looked like her pet. I asked John about it and he said that the State Fish and Game Commission had brought the buck to the island. The Game Commission had a program to restock deer in many counties in Georgia where they were plentiful at one time but had disappeared. Periodically, they would increase their efforts to capture deer from St. Catherines to restock deer on the mainland. In return, the Commission would bring bucks to St. Catherines in hopes of increasing the genetic diversity of the island's deer. In 1946, a young buck that was probably raised as a pet was brought to the island. The buck, named Bum, preferred the lawns of the residential areas of the big house and the superintendent's house where he would bum cigarettes from the employees (hence the name) (Figure 128). John said that nearly everyone.[62] Whenever Bum saw someone on the lawn at either residence, he would run up to them and nuzzle them for a cigarette, and they would oblige by giving him a cigarette.

While Bum was Mr. Nobles pet, he did have his share of problems with the young buck. There was an incident when Bum and Mr. Noble were showing off for some off his guests and Bum butted Mr. Noble into the pool. Mr. Noble while somewhat embarrassed, but saw the humor in the situation. As time went on, Bum spent more time with the wild deer and returned every two weeks or so. Eventually, he returned to the wild full time. Gee said that on one of his returns to the "big" house, Bum had shed the velvet from his antlers and, seeing Gee, raised up on his hind legs ready to attack her. Her father came out of nowhere to kick and knock Bum down. Bum made it to his feet, staggered and ran off to the woods, never to return again.[63]

On January 10, 1958, Mr. Noble and Toby met with Jack A. Crockford, the Commissions' Federal Aid Coordinator (Woods 1958b: January 10), to discuss a more systematic program to capture the island's deer. The work began on January 23, 1958 when Toby and Jack Crockford traveled to Blackbeard Island to retrieve the wooden crates[64] used to restrain the captured deer as they moved them off the island. The next day, Toby brought the "deer-catching jeep" over from Half Moon for the team. The jeep was outfitted with powerful lights to locate and stun the deer. However, much of the deer catchers' nocturnal activity was on foot. For two months there was a concerted effort to capture deer. The plan called for a three-man team of "deer catchers", as Toby referred to them, that had to stay for up to a week at a time[65] and capture the foraging deer at night by darting them. This was a difficult task, and some deer were fatally injured in the process. Toby recorded the capture of five bucks and 14 deer, and the release of a buck that was captured on another island during that time. The last visit in the spring was on March 20th and activity ceased during the summer months. The "catchers" returned on October 7th for a short visit to release five bucks from Ossabaw Island and to capture a deer on the St. Catherines. During the first week of December 1958, timed after the Sheriff's hunt that killed 19 deer on November 25th, 18 deer were captured and Toby transported them to the mainland for the deer catchers. On February 12, 1959, Toby (Woods 1959a: Day Book) reported that the deer catching had come to an end, and the Fish and Game Commission deer hunters returned to the mainland.

There were other issues between Mr. Noble and Toby Woods. One of the "thorns" in Toby's side was the electrical system that provided power to the island. From 1930 until 1946, a generator system provided the electricity for the island. John described the problems with the electrical system after Mr. Noble purchased two Hallett light plant engines:

> My father bought a set of glass Exide batteries in 1946 when the Fairbanks Morse diesel light plant engine was replaced by two Hallett light plant engines.[66] These two diesel engines were always trouble. The Fairbanks Morse was a single unit and never had a backup.
>
> Daddy always bought distilled water in 5-gallon glass jars in Savannah to add to the batteries to keep the top plates covered. He personally repaired and maintained the light plants all those years. Unfortunately the two Hallett diesel units that Mr. Frank Marx (the top engineer for the American Broadcasting Co) purchased in California for Mr. Noble put a lot of gray hair in my daddy's black hair. I don't think they were new when purchased.
>
> Mr. Charles Schaub, sales engineer for Hallett blamed my daddy for all the trouble that they were giving. The automatic switches that started the engine when the batteries need recharging were always giving trouble. The Hallett diesels were small high-speed motors that were too light to be used 7 day a week even with the spare engine. Broken crankshafts and dropped valves

were a frequent problem, and when he got one engine repaired the other one would break down.

He used these Exide glass batteries until about 1956, when he talked Mr. Noble into purchasing a new 2-cylinder 71 series 54-hp at 1800 rpm 2-cycle General Motors diesel engine with a 15 KW DC generator attached. The unit was bought from Morgan's Inc. I was a master mechanic working for Morgan's at that time. My father installed the unit in the light plant powerhouse on the Island and I made the initial start up inspection on it.

There was a modest lumber operation on St. Catherines. While Noble ceased the lease of lumber after he bought the island, they decided that they needed to thin some of the woods. There was also a problem recovering timber after fires killed a large number of trees. John described the activity after his father purchased a small saw mill. Although these small sawmills were designed to be moved from one part of the island to another, it stayed at Meeting House Field during Mr. Noble's time on St. Catherines.

The Coffee Pot or Pepper Pot Saw Mill

John told the story of his dad purchasing,

A used saw mill from Roger Youmans. Back then it was called a coffee pot sawmill, as it could be moved from one timber sight to another.

Mr. Noble and my father wanted the mill so that he could saw dead pine trees, and on the north end of the Island there was beach erosion that was destroying a good stand of Long Leaf pines. The lumber that was cut was green rough lumber that had to be stacked where it would dry out properly. That would make good lumber for bridges hog pens, gates, corrals, docks etc. The mill was powered with a 6-cylinder International diesel engine that was first started as a gasoline engine. After the engine has warmed up, it was then switched over to diesel.

To operate the mill, there had to be a sawyer, a log roller and turner, and an edger to size the boards by width so that could remove bark and provide a clean edge. The edger also caught the boards as they were sawed and put them on the rollers and pushed them down to the lumber catchers. The lumber that was sawed and edged was then rolled out and put on a track or wagon and later stacked in triangle or square pens where it would dry out.

During this time my father was the sawyer, Hubert Holmes was the log turner, George Berryhill was the edger, Woodrow Rogers and others would catch and load the lumber according to size.

On August 24, 1955, Mr. Noble wrote Toby about hiring Uncle Albert, and was concerned that they were cutting lumber. He wanted them only to cut the trees and wait for his arrival before processing them into lumber. He writes (Noble 1955),

> I will be down again around the middle of September so there ought to be sufficient logs at that time to saw (with a hand written note) for several days when I can help!!!

When I asked John about the letter, he said that when "Mr. Noble was on the island, it was one of his big pleasures to watch the saw mill operation. He would call himself working at the saw mill." It was wise of Mr. Noble to keep his distance as the workers cut the lumber. It was a task wrought with hazards. John described just how menacing it could be,

> Working at sawmills was a dangerous job. There were limited safety precautions. The replaceable saw bits would sometimes sling out of the big circular saw and go through the roof that was over the saw or anywhere else.

> One time a big log got stuck on the saw carriage with the circular saw protruding threw the log about an inch. Hubert[67] while helping daddy get the log unstuck and accidentally put his left hand on the rotating saw cutting his two middle finger almost off. He then reached over and caught his other hand in the saw too almost cutting those two other fingers off. He was lucky not to lose the fingers. He was off work for several weeks.

> The location of the sawmill was in Meeting House Field at the sight of another older saw mill. In fact they used the same sawdust pile. There was a saw dust chain that ran from under the circular saw to a pole and pulley on top of the saw dust pile and back. This chain pulled the sawdust up the saw dust pile.

> During the three summer months, when school was out, my three cousins George, Ben, and Ralph would sometimes work at the sawmill. Ben was working there when Hubert got his fingers cut.

> One summer lightning struck in the Savannah woods area burning about 50 acres of pine trees. Daddy and his crew sawed the trees into lumber and barged the lumber to the mainland and sold to the Savannah Planning mill. The sawmill was only used when there were trees that needed to be cut. The sawmill was made by Frick Machinery Co. Morgan's Inc. in Savannah sold Frick saw mills from the early 1930s to the early 1950s.

> The logs on the island were carried to the sawmill with a log cart pull using the Farmall "M" tractor that had tricycle type front (wheel) tires. The logs were pulled together using the 1953 Ford Jubilee truck and stacked in piles from three to five logs depending on the size.

The log cart was backed over the stack of logs and a cable ran under them and pulled the logs up off the ground. A drive shaft that ran from the tractor power take off to the log cart spool turned and pulled up the cable. Paul Robbins drove the Farmall tractor and also helped at the mill.

It was hardly ever four miles from the mill to where the trees were cut. The logs would be unloaded on the brow, which was four pine logs about two feet off the ground with one end that was leveled with the log carriage and the other end on a pile of dirt slightly higher.

Later, when I became superintendent of the island, we still used the sawmill. I was the sawyer, Hubert was log turner, George ran the edger and caught the boards as they were sawed then rolled the boards out to the lumber crew – Woodrow, Paul and later the college boys during the summer.

The lumber was then stacked according to size. Since some of the pine trees came off the beach with beach sand in the bark, we would have to sharpen the saw often.

One day I had to stop the mill to sharpen the dull blade. The main saw was stopped, but the edger was still turning. George, while attempting to oil the edger saws with his gloves on, got his glove caught in the edger saw and it snatched his right hand in and cut it off about half way to his elbow. The hand was too badly torn up to be saved. What a sad time this was. I also put a towel over his injured arm. I put a tourniquet on George's arm and took him to my house and gave him a bottle of liquor to drink. I would loosen the tourniquet every 20 minutes. While I was doing this, Hubert buried George's badly damaged hand into the sawdust pile. I put George in the Cobia, 22' inboard, outboard speedboat and took him to the Half Moon dock on the mainland. I then drove him to the emergency room at the Hinesville hospital where Dr. Whit Frasier was waiting for us. I told Dr. Fraser that I had given George whiskey to drink. Dr. Fraser didn't like that at all. He said that I should have let George bite on a nail. Dr. Fraser said that he would have to pump George's stomach out before he could repair the arm.

This accident ended George's employment on St. Catherines Island. Workman's compensation paid him until he was eligible for Social Security. After workman's compensation ran out, the Noble Foundation paid him a small retirement.

A Life Saver "Party"

Every fall, Edward J. Noble hosted the annual Life Savers Company convention on St. Catherines (Figure 129). The conventions were well-planned events; on July 29th 1952, Mr. Noble received a memo detailing the plans for the meeting that would not begin until October 24th. Nobel would then transmit the memo to Toby Woods who would note the dates. The pattern was for the eleven man executive group[68] to arrive Saturday morning, October 25th, on the Seaboard Air Lines Railroad at Dorchester (Noble 1952d: October 8, letter). Toby would then pick up the men[69] at Dorchester and transport them to the island where they would be met by Mr. Noble.[70] As soon as they arrived and before the group had even left the dock, the discussions began. John said that the executives were not afraid to have frank discussions with Mr. Noble. John and the people who worked on the island described this as "Yankee behavior." They had been raised to never argue with a guest in your house. The nine person District Sales Managers' group would arrive the following

Figure 129. A Life Savers Party preparing to leave the island. In the center are Annie Edenfield and Ruby Puolnot Easterland with Mr. Noble standing behind Annie. On the right, with his hand extended, is Gordon Young, a Life Savers executive. To the right of him is Tallie Easterland. Van Floyd, the well driller, is leaning over the dock. Picture taken in 1946.

Monday on the Silver Meteor at the same time. The executives and District Sales Managers would leave the island on the following Saturday.

Two of the executives flew into Savannah a day earlier and were picked up by Hoke Youmans, who took them to McQueens Inlet for a day of fishing. During the week of the Life Savers party on St. Catherines, Toby was also available to take a group hunting or fishing.

Mr. Noble would determine the menu and would order the essentials from grocery stores in Savannah, usually his favorite store. Hagans. The staff would pick up the supplies the day before the group arrived. Mr. Noble would usually instruct the cook to buy the ancillary supplies as she saw fit. Cornish game hens of a specific weight and size were always part of the menu. Steaks were ordered for the poolside barbeque prepared by Mr. Noble himself.[71] Any food that was leftover was returned to Hagans for a credit.

The loyalty of the St. Catherines' staff is evident from an incident that occurred at a Life Savers convention in 1950. Ruby Easterland was cooking for the group when her husband Tallie, who also worked on the island, died in his sleep.[72] Mr. Noble was informed, and in the dawn hours before the Life Savers group had awaken, Tallie's body was carried down the back stairs of the servant's quarters and taken to a funeral home in Savannah. Ruby

Figure 130. Toby Woods in a rare moment of relaxation.

continued cooking for the group for two more days before going to the funeral home to make arrangement for Tallie's burial.

Toby Woods was always a loyal employee who did more than expected of him (Figure 130). He "loved" the island and felt an obligation to give what he could to Mr. Noble and his family. His pay was modest by all standards, given his duties and how he fulfilled them. His salary from St. Catherines in 1950 was $5530 (Woods 1950), $5605 in1952 (Woods 1952b), $5333.32 in 1958 (Woods 1958c), and rose to $6166 in 1959 (Woods 1959b) . I was puzzled by the decrease in earnings in 1958. John Toby Woods was hospitalized or was in convalescence for 37 days during 1958. At the beginning of March, Toby wrote in in his Day Book (Woods 1958b) that he was sick and did not work from the 5th to the 7th and went to the hospital on March 8th. He was hospitalized for seven days for what turned out to be pneumonia. He returned to the island and for the next five days he could not leave the house, but he did have the workers on task. He missed work for 16 days. Less than two months later on June 16th, Toby was admitted to Memorial Hospital for an operation to repair an inguinal hernia. The operation was performed on the 17th and required eight days of post-operative care. He was released on the 24th and came home. As Gee Little remembers, within hours his temperature spiked and he returned to the hospital. He was diagnosed with pleurisy, likely induced by the pneumonia, and remained in bed until the 4th of July. He spent two weeks visiting friends in the Savannah area and returned to the island on July 17th. Toby was docked a month's pay for the work that he missed in 1958, and he had to pay for the operation.

Toby did not claim that the hernia was work-related, so it was not covered by Workmen's Compensation. Toby could not cite the specific work activity that "caused" the hernia, and was therefore unwilling to apply for Workmen's Compensation. On June 9th, a week before his accident, he loaded and unloaded five tons of nitrogen fertilizer.[73] This fertilizer was packaged in 100-pound sacks. He loaded all 100 sacks onto the boat at Half Moon by himself, but had help unloading it at the dock at St. Catherines because, as John joked, it was uphill there. On the next day, June 10th, he had George Berryhill and Paul Robbins help load and unload another five tons of 0-10-20 fertilizer, and on the following day they moved 81 cows and 4 bulls to North Pasture.

There is also the issue of whether Toby, superintendent of the island and a salaried employee, should have been given sick days. He worked five nine-hour weekdays[74] and a half-day on Saturday, for a total workweek of 49 hours. Yet, he was expected to fill out a time card. Workers were never allowed to put in the actual time they worked if it went over the nine hours during the week or the four hours on Saturday. There were days when Toby would put in a ten-hour day, and then spend six hours at night fixing the power plant. To Mr. Noble, that was a nine-hour day. In Mr. Noble's view (Noble 1948b: Letter November 29), Toby was in charge of the workers on the island:

> So after all, it is for you, as superintendent, to arrange the hours in a manner
> that can get the greatest amount of work accomplished for the number of
> hours spent.

Mr. Noble did have expectations for the workers on the island that led to a discussion with Toby. He reiterated his opinion that work on St. Catherines was farm work:

> Answering your question of how many hours a day I think your men should
> work and how many days a week—the latter question couldn't have the

tiniest bit of complaint if your men were putting in the number of hours
they worked a year ago, but you and I both know they are not, and it is to
try to get back to their endeavors in the earliest years that I am trying, in a
measure, to attain. Now this work is very similar to farm work. There are no
set hours a day for any farmers. A dairy farmer milks his cows at four
o'clock in the morning and doesn't get through with the night work until
sometimes between six and seven o'clock. In the busy season -- like haying,
harvesting, and the getting in of the crops – you will find farmers owning
their own farms working twelve to fifteen hours a day, but of course there
are many days when they do practically no work.

In 1958, Toby worked 28 hours on four Sundays, made 20 trips on Sundays to pick up
workers who needed transportation to the island, transported a jeep that the Fish and Game
Commission was to use on the island, and transported Mr. Davenport to work on the phone.
Toby's half-day Saturday work schedule was usually taken up by shopping trips to Savannah for
supplies for the Island. These trips took at least five hours of travel time, and shopping usually
took another four or five hours. When workers went to Half Moon to repair the dock, they
recorded only the hours worked and not the time getting to and from the island. When Toby
worked on the boat on the ways at Thunderbolt, the four hours of travel time was on his clock.
On St. Catherines, the notion of pay for overtime or compensatory time off did not exist.

In response to a letter sent by Toby Woods (November 26, 1948), Edward J. Noble
(Noble 1948b: Letter, November 29) offered a conciliatory message to him. He claimed that his
concern about spending is related to his concern about losing the tax write-off for the island:

…we are running awfully close to the end of the year, and I am very, very
worried about our income down there which must be of sufficient size to
justify the vastly increased expense we have gone to in the past year. There
is a certain formula that the tax people use on this in determining in what
manner tax levies will be made.

Noble reassured Toby of his position on the island. He said:

As far as anybody taking your place at any time as long as I live that is just
silly rot. On the other hand I do want you to worry just as much as I worry
about these problems for in thinking of the Island, as I said to you so many
times, I want you to think of it as your own,[75] just as though you were
running it and paying the bills, and to that extent be ME absolutely.

St. Catherines Hunts

When John described a typical St. Catherines hunt, I was immediately reminded of the
hunt described by Van Marter (1904) during the Rauers' era in 1904. The operation of the hunt
was similar, except for the earlier hunts used horses and there were drivers who specialized in
that activity. These drivers were so well known that when Perry Martin, the last black driver
from St. Catherines, died it was reported in the *New York Times* (NYT 1931). His obituary said:

For years Perry was known to financiers and professional and business men
of prominence who hunted deer on the island preserve…"

John also reminded me that although he used dogs to drive the deer, he found them to be a
distraction. The hunts had a pattern that would ensure their success. The sheriff's hunt would
begin at dawn when the Sheriff and his guests[76] were picked up at the dock at Half Moon at
dawn. In the dawn light the hunters were placed at their stands on the road along Sams Field
Woods. Once the hunters were in place, Toby would take the hunter's dogs and with couple of
his workers to start driving the deer toward the hunters. In 30 minutes, the first hunt would be
over and they would collect the deer (does and bucks) that were killed. The men would move
north to the next site, they would be placed in their stands, and the process would begin again.[77]

Pete Clark, who served as the administrator of the Liberty County Planning Commission,
described a "county hunt" that took place in 1959. Pete was 21 at the time and was working for a
family newspaper, *The Liberty County Herald*. When his dad, M. F. Clark, the Clerk of the
County Commission, could not make it to the hunt, he asked Pete if he would like to take his
place. It was a "big deal" to hunt on St. Catherines and to be asked to the County Hunt was a
"real big deal" and considered a prestigious honor (Figure 131).

Figure 131. Local
Dignitary Hunt on St.
Catherines Island (Circa
1956). Left to right
standing: Freeman
Smith, Adrian Long,
Fred Woods, Unknown,
Unknown, Clayton
Blount, Russell Smiley,
Joe Long, Paul Sikes, R.
V. Bobby Sikes, Dewitt
Branch, J. Toby Woods,
Sr., Ben Butler, Leroy
Coffer, Edward J.
Noble, Host, Unknown,
Marvin F. Clark, Jr.
Left to right seated:
Willie L. Hall, Mel
Price, Joe Smith, Roscoe
Denmark. The photo
was taken at the patio
on the side of the pool
built by Toby Woods.

Pete says that John's father picked up the group of thirty of Liberty County's most
important officials at St. Catherines dock on the Half Moon River at sunrise on a foggy day. He
said that visibility was less 20 feet, and Pete was not sure that they would make it to the island.
He asked Mr. Woods if they would be able to make it in the foggy darkness. It his usual talkative
manner, he replied "yup." Clark said that Toby started the engine, looked at his watch, the boat's
compass, and then the engine's RPMs as the boat moved away from the dock. He then sat down
on a stool, picked up the *Savannah Morning News,* and proceeded to read it. Clark said, "I wore

myself out running from bow to the stern sure that we would hit something." He said that after about twenty minutes on the water, they encountered a marsh. Toby backed off, looks at his watch, the RPMs, and the compass as if this ritual would magically take them to the island. It worked, and half an hour later as the fog was lifting, Toby arrived at Waldburg Creek and then to the dock at St. Catherines – just as he finished reading the *Morning News*[78].

The hunt was more that Pete could have anticipated. They were taken to Savannah Woods where he was given a "stand" behind a tree just behind a canal. As the deer squatted to jump the canal he would shoot them. That day he killed five deer. He took one of the dressed deer home. The other deer that he had killed were shared with those that were not so lucky. Pete said that the camaraderie was part of the hunt. The group that day included Ed Moody, Bill Martin, Joe Smith, Judge Durrance and Kermit NeSmith. At lunch while sitting on a log overlooking North Beach, Judge Durrance asked Bill Martin how much was two-tenths of an inch of rain. Bill Martin replied, "If you walked out into the ocean and peed, that's how much the water level would rise."

Pete Clark wrote a story about the hunt in the *Liberty County Herald*. He did not relate the question or Bill Martin's response to it. In the article, he mentions that one of the participants "had his shoe shined" an oblique reference to an "accident" in which one of the dogs relived themselves on the shoe of one of the dignitaries.

John told me about one of his favorite hunting escapades. I figured that he was going to tell me some fantastic story about one shot killing two deer. Instead, he told me about one of the hunts organized by John Underwood. John and Bobby Sikes were driving the deer and as they approached Wamassee Wood, Bobby grabbed a fifth of whiskey from the stash that he brought for celebrating the end of the hunt. John said that they drove the last of the deer and were walking out and came upon the large oak tree where they started drinking. They kept walking, taking a nip now and then, when they realized that they were back at the oak tree. Bobby and John decided to lighten the load by leaving the bottle by the oak tree since they figured that they would end up there again. The next trip they successfully reached "civilization." John smiled and said that if they could find the oak tree, the bottle would probably still be there.

Mr. Noble Remembered

John Woods is one of the few people still living who worked for Mr. Noble for an extended period. He still remembers his first interactions with him. John was always taught to respect his elders; yet Mr. Noble was special because not only was he older but, he also owned the island and was a powerful businessman. Initially, John worked at menial tasks:

> The first summer that I worked for Mr. Noble, he was probably sixty-one years old and I was thirteen. I worked for him every summer while I was going to school. My job was mostly cleaning and mowing the big lawn and cleaning the swimming pool. I actually was there to do anything that needed to be done. I enjoyed working on the island. Mr. Noble was always kind to me.
>
> I remember not long after he bought the island, he had two panel trucks sent down from New York. There was a 1940 Chevrolet truck to be used on the mainland and a 1942 Ford panel truck to be used on the island. These trucks

had all the different flavored Life Savers painted all over them. There was even a three-foot long roll on the cab of the trucks. We called them the candy trucks. We were happy to have them since before that all we had were the Model "A"s.

Mr. Noble was not interested in spending money unless it was absolutely necessary, and even then he would have to think about it. Usually, he had a practical solution to every problem. John told me about an incident when Paul Robbins and George Berryhill were raking leaves by the workshop. They had been pestering his dad to by the new lawn rake when,

Mr. Noble walked up and Paul held up the leaf rake that had three missing teeth. He asked Mr. Noble what he had to do to get a decent rake. Mr. Noble grabbed the rake from Paul's hands and a quick movement demonstrated that if you held it at an angle it would work fine.

As John said after relating the story to me, "Labor was cheep in those days." John surmised that he is probably the last living employee of Mr. Nobles.

Mr. Noble enjoyed horseback riding. Toby Woods found a five-gaited Tennessee walking horse for Mr. Noble. Tony was an excellent horse that his original owner had trained and outgrown (Figure 132). He had even been trained to kneel to aid in mounting him. John described Mr. Noble's interest in riding:

One of Mr. Noble's greatest pleasures was to ride horseback on the trails on St. Catherines (Figures 133 and 134). Anytime I was on the island, it was my job to catch Tony and the other horses and groom them. I would saddle them[79] (he used an English saddle) and ride them to be sure that they were okay and that the horse was not having any problems. I would meet Mr. Noble at number 1 cabin where we had a big cement block[80] for him to stand on to mount the horse. I would then open the gates on the trail that they would be taking. I would then be available to put them back in the pasture when they returned.

Mr. Noble was a good horseback rider, but in his later years, I don't think he could get on or off his horse without the use of the block.

One day I was driving the 1941 Ford panel truck down the shell road and crossed the bridge by the number 5 cabin going to the "big" house going about 50 miles an hour. Mr. Noble stepped out from behind one of the cabins and flagged me down. I should have realized that a truck adorned from front to back with the various flavors of Life Savers going 50 mph would have been an unusual sight. It took me a while to stop and back up to where he was. I thought that I was about to be fired. Mr. Noble smiled and asked to see my driver's license.

Mr. Noble loved John's stripped down Model A. The car had no doors, top, or fenders. The car was what was left of Mrs. Keyes fine convertible. It was John's pride and Mr. Noble coveted it. John remembered how

Daddy would help me fix up a Model A strip down, no doors, top, or fenders but with a flatbed on the back. Quite often during the summers, Mr. Noble would choose to drive my stripped down Model A Ford rather than the 1941 Ford Panel truck with the Life Savers advertisement on it. His two guests would be riding next to him on the front seat and I always rode in the flat bed in the rear. I was there in case there was a limb in the road that had to be removed or to crank the car if the battery ran down. I was there to hand crank it for him. There always places to go. There were about 50 miles of rutted roads on St. Catherines. His big pleasure was to run over a "cow pie"[81] in such a way (he knew how to cut the wheel) that cow dung would hit his passengers. Mr. Noble would make it look like an accident, apologize, and criticize his own driving. Mr. Noble was good at playing tricks on people.

Figure 132. Tony being ridden by Mary William's friend on North Beach

Figure 133. The Coast guard barracks lives as a barn built for the cattle and horses. Toby and visitor are in the picture.

Figure 134. Kate, the horse, in front of the cattle chute.

Mr. Noble Dies

Figure 135. Vice President Richard Milhous Nixon and Mrs. Maye Cooper. Nixon and his family spent a week at St. Catherines in June 1958 (Lambright 1958). Mrs. Cooper would help Snooker cook during at special events such as the Life Saver parties.

Edward J. Noble died on December 28, 1958. His obituary in the *New York Times* (NYT 1958) did not mention St. Catherines, where he spent a large part of the last decade and a half of his life. In his last year, he visited St. Catherines three times. In early January, he entertained friends from Savannah, and in March he and Mr. Lange came to work on the phone. On May 22, Mr. Noble, his wife, and the Chapmans arrived for an extended stay that would eventually include a visit from Richard Nixon and family (Figure 135). Vice President Nixon, Patricia Nixon, their daughters, and Nixon's secretary Rose Mary Woods[82] arrived on the 31st of May. They were joined by Noble's son-in-law, Assistant Secretary of the Air Force David Smith, and Jane Noble Smith[83] (Woods 1958b:May 22 to June 7). The Nixons stayed on St. Catherines for a week. During that time, Toby Woods spent 62 hours attending their needs. A thin Mr. Noble is pictured with Nixon in a Savannah newspaper; it would be his last visit to the Island.

On that last visit to the island, Mr. Noble and Toby drove to South Beach. Mr. Noble thanked Toby for all that he had done for him and for St. Catherines. He told Toby that he planned to leave him $10,000 in his will.[84] Toby thanked him and suggested that he remember Woodrow Rogers and George Berryhill who were valuable members of the team. In the end, Toby received a bequest of $5000, while Woodrow and George received $2500 each. Toby used his bequest to help purchase the farm in Newington. Woodrow, after all those years, bought himself a new green four-door six-cylinder standard shift Chevrolet with the money, and George bought a marsh lot near Yellow Bluff.

I asked John what his father reaction was to having his promised bequest be the source of the gifts to George and Woodrow. According to John, he never said a word about it and never revealed to George and Woodrow that he pleading on their behalf to Mr. Noble. I was somewhat taken aback by the action and had assumed that Toby would have been bitter about it. At the time, this bequest from Mr. Noble was in lieu of any retirement, which was not included in his employment benefits. After the death of Mr. Noble, the estate under the administration of Alger B. Chapman did provide him with a modest retirement.

John said that in retirement, his dad often made more from his ten-acre pecan orchard than he did from being superintendent of St. Catherines. In a good year, he harvested 20,000 pounds of pecans that he sold at up to $1 a pound.

Mr. Noble left the island as he had envisioned it. When he purchased St. Catherines, it was claimed to be ideally suited for a cattle ranch. In actuality, it took extraordinary effort to transform it into what Mr. Noble thought a cattle ranch should be. When he rode his command car from one end of the island to the other, he wanted to see "order." Toby and his staff gave him what he wanted. A dead tree or a fallen branch did not remain there for long. The extensive draining of the island with the ditches that transverse it not only to increase the pastures, but also to ensure that the flooding of the low lying areas that frequently killed the trees would no longer be a problem.[85]

Toby was vigilant in keeping the grounds around "the big house" impeccably manicured, as Mr. Noble liked to see them. Even the removal of the moss in the tree surrounding the "big" house brought order to Mr. Noble's life.

To his last days, Edward J. Noble was directing Toby in how he wanted things. Marion Hawley, Noble's secretary, wrote to Toby (Hawley 1958a) and told him that the past week "has not been at all good" but, "He told me to write to you and tell you to go ahead with the fertilizer and buy what is required. Also the Range Check for the cattle." She then told him "to do nothing" until he heard directly from Mr. Noble about a couple that Toby considered hiring. Mr. Noble died a week later.[86]

Toby Woods in his day book wrote for Monday, December 29, 1958:

> Cloudy and cool
> Catching hog for market 5[87]
> To HM[88] and Midway to send telegram to Mrs. Noble 4
> Mr. Noble died last night

The next day, Mr. Noble would have been pleased with Toby. He worked four hours catching hogs and five hours working with the cattle.

The picture that emerged from my analysis of the relationship between Mr. Noble and the staff demonstrated that he had high expectations of them. Universally, the women who worked for him spoke of his charm, wit and humor. There was a way in which Mr. Noble and St. Catherines had a lasting impact on those that were touched by the island and him. The children also told me that when he would arrive on the island for a visit, he would take them for a ride in his command car as he inspected the island. Telling me about these trips, one of the men smiled and said that Mr. Noble used these journeys to gather information about what was happening on the island while he was in New York or Connecticut. He said that Mr. Noble spotted a deer, stopped the command car and looked down at him and asked, "I bet it is easy for someone to shoot a deer." He remarked that even as children, they all knew that he was "fishing" to see if anyone on the island was poaching deer.

Curtis Lee, who had worked on the island as a nineteen-year-old dragline operator involved with the timber operations, was remarkably loyal. Lee was asked to inspect the dragline that Mr. Noble was interested in purchasing from Richard Tuten. Mr. Noble sent him a check for his services, and Curtis Lee (1953:Letter, March 28) replied in a hand written letter:

> I received your check today and it was just like finding that much money. I
> told Mr. Woods, that I didn't charge anything for what I done, because the
> pleasure I spend on the island is more than the money that I have can buy
> for me. And I'm always glad to help anytime. As for being homesick for the
> island, I stay that way. Many thanks for the nice things you said about me
> and (for) the check.

Most of the workers were not aware of Toby's difficult interactions with Mr. Noble. To them Toby was always a friendly soul who did not complain or criticize any one. Toby was their rock, and he buffered them from any unpleasant encounters. And he set an example with his work ethic. Toby's commitment to work is reflected in a letter written to Mr. Noble on November 26, 1948, "I don't know just how the rest of the men feel about it, but I know that I would love to get every bit of work done that I possibly can."

John Woods says that he could not think of a time when Mr. Noble was unpleasant to him. John is emphatic that Mr. Noble was unduly harsh on his father, and he did resent that aspect of his behavior. When I read the correspondence between Mr. Noble and Toby Woods, I found Mr. Noble to be an intense "micromanager" who would question even a 38-cent purchase. Toby Woods was able to handle it for the most part. However, John says that he would reach his limits and Toby would say, "Mr. Noble I think that its time for you to get someone else to run this island." Mr. Noble would come back the next day and say, "Toby, how would you like to have a new television set?" Things would then cool off until the next crisis. Sometimes it did get expensive. Mr. Noble bought Toby Woods a car in 1952 after one such episode. It was a stripped down Chevrolet gray standard two door model without a radio or heater. Mr. Noble was sure to make a deal on anything he purchased. When he realized that this would be considered compensation, he remitted the tax to the IRS, a wonderful gesture on his part[89] (Noble 1952a). Toby did have to pay Woodrow's fare to New York to pick up the car. John said that the car did double duty. It served the Woods' family, and transported Mr. Noble's visitors to and from the McIntosh and Savannah railway stations. John recalls that Mr. Noble bought his dad a refrigerator and a television. To the end, Toby was a loyal worker who always did more than expected of him. And for all his criticism, Mr. Noble (Noble 1948b: Letter, November 29) reaffirmed what an important employee he had in Toby Woods:

> Now don't make any mistake. You do please me immensely. I like your
> frankness of your letters and the way you put things. There is not the
> slightest tendency to alibi or unreasonable arguing. I expect you to tell me
> when I am wrong, as I want the privilege of telling you when I think you
> are. Never once have I felt inside of me that I was being and, on the other
> hand, I have never read (even between the lines!) in your letters that you
> were so to me, frank, honest, discussion never hurts anybody; it really
> cements friendships and confidence.

13

Wonder Boy and Nineteen Old Bums:
The Anatomy of a Hunting Trip on St. Catherines

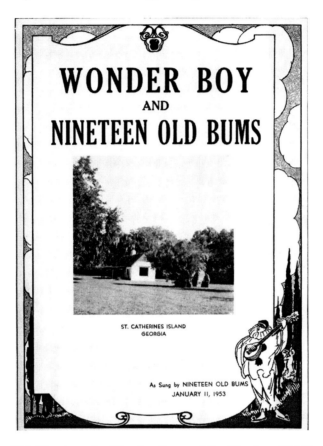

Figure 136. Sheet music: Wonder Boy and the Nineteen Old Bums.

John handed me a piece of sheet music with a view of St. Catherines on its cover (Figure 136). The ruins of a slave cabin obscured by a tree lie in the foreground. A cabin built in the style of slave quarters is in the center of the picture. The sheet has the words and music for two songs "Wonder Boy" and "Nineteen Old Bums," with the notation: "as sung by NINETEEN OLD BUMS on January 11, 1953."What is the story behind this sheet music, who are the nineteen old bums, and what happened at their rendezvous on St. Catherines Island?

John was as puzzled as I was about the group and the songs. Neither "Wonder Boy" nor "Nineteen Old Bums" made the top songs of 1953. The top ten hits that year included: "Vaya Con Dios" (Les Paul & Mary Ford), "Moulin Rouge" (Percy Faith), "Rags to Riches" (Tony Bennett), "You, You, You" (Ames Bros), "Doggie in the Window" (Patti Page), "I'm Walking Behind You" (Eddie Fisher), "Till I Waltz Again" (Teresa Brewer), "Don't Let the Stars Get in Your Eyes" (Perry Como), "St George & Dragonet" (Stan Freberg), and "No Other Love" (Perry Como).

While the songs may not been winners at the jukebox, they certainly showed respect for the host. The song "Wonder Boy" was a tribute to Ed Noble. "Wonder Boy" echoes what the business community had been saying about Edward J. Noble after he purchased the Life Saver Company and transformed it into a money maker. He showed his magic once more when he purchased the "Blue" network from the National Broadcasting Company (NBC)[1] and it became the successful American Broadcast System (ABC).

As I became more familiar with Mr. Noble and his group, I was intrigued about the context of the songs and what transpired on St. Catherines on January 11, 1953. As I discussed the occasion with John, it became apparent that events such as this were fairly common happenings on the Island. A history of St. Catherines would not be complete without a discussion of the interaction between Mr. Noble and his friends and John Toby Woods Sr. and his team as they prepared for a gathering on the island. The song lyrics are below:

Wonder Boy

> *Gazing down on Ed Noble*
> *As he rides or strides into view,*
> *Let us drink, every man,*
> *Let us drink while we can,*
> *To the joy of our dreams come true.*
>
> *Wonder Boy, Wonder Boy!*
> *What a perfect sight for joy,*
> *There he is, here are we,*
> *Why, it's even wunder bar!*
>
> *Does he sing well?*
> *Very badly.*
> *Does he shoot well?*
> *Not a miss.*
> *Does he ride well?*
> *Rather madly,*
> *But he's true blue*
> *If he likes you.*
>
> *Wonder Boy, Wonder Boy!*
> *He's our favorite star of all,*
> *What a bright shining star,*
> *Very tall and wunder bar!*

Nineteen Old Bums

> *To the mosses of St. Catherines,*
> *T o the place where Edward dwells,*
> *To the live oaks of the Isle that cast their spell,*

Sing the wanderers assembled,
With their glasses raised on high,
Though the singing doesn't sound so very well.

Francis, Earl and Arthur Carter,
Al and Austin, Jim and John,
Ted and Bob and Len and Alva
And some more;
Phil and Amos, Bill and Larry,
Warren, Medley, Bill and Ed,
They will sing, then be forgotten
As of Yore.

We're nineteen old bums who have gone astray,
Bum! Bum! Bum!
Yes, aging old men in a hul-ov-a-way;
Bum! Bum! Bum!
Nineteen Old Bums who stretch for a mile,
Settled down here to remain a while,
Lord have mercy on Ed Noble's Isle
Bum! Bum! Bum!

The second song is of greater interest, not because it has any redeeming value musically, but because of the lyrics of the second verse.[2] In the second verse, one of "Nineteen Old Bums" is identified by his first and last name, the rest are identified only by their first names:

Francis, Earl and Arthur Carter,
Al and Austin, Jim and John,
Ted and Bob and Len and Alva
And some more;
Phil and Amos, Bill and Larry,
Warren, Medley, Bill and Ed,
They will sing, then be forgotten
As of Yore.

I asked John if he remembered the "nineteen bums" from his time as superintendent of the island; he didn't. John said that excursions were common events on St. Catherine, and meetings of the Life Saver Corporation leadership happened every fall. After Mr. Noble's death, groups involved in wildlife conservation would visit the island. Although John couldn't recall the "nineteen old bums," he had documents that solved the puzzle. John has a knack for finding the answer to any question that I ask him. "Better than a memory," John said as he handed me two documents that identified the troubadours who introduced the two songs to the world and St. Catherines Island that day in 1953.

John had found a letter on ABC letterhead from Mr. Noble to Toby, John's father, detailing the logistics of the visit. The second document was his father's daybook for 1953 that cryptically detailed the accomplishments of the day. John describes his dad as a man of few

161

words, and if his dad's daybooks are any indication, it is an apt description. For example, in his day book for January 6, 1953 when he was preparing for the visit, he wrote, "Mr. Noble called. He is coming tomorrow."[3]

In the letter dated December 3, 1952, Mr. Noble instructs Toby about the arrangements for the visit on January 11, 1953 (Noble 1952e). As if he were responding specifically to my question about the identity of the nineteen bums. He wrote, "There are nineteen of us: Francis Allen, Earl Anderson, Arthur Carter, Al Chapman, Austin Igleheart, Jim Johansen, John Lovejoy, Ted Montague, Bob Noble, Amos Peaslee, Len Quackenbush, Alva See, Larry Sharples, Philip Sharples, Bill Taylor, Warren Snow, Medley Whelpley, Bill Wilson and myself."

Never leaving anything to chance, Mr. Noble wrote to Toby five days later (Noble 1952c: December 8, Letter) telling him,

> ...all of these men are important people, and I would like to have everything looking as nice as possible around the big house and cottages and also along the roads throughout the island.

> It might be a good idea for you to talk with Hoke about a fishing party on Sunday, the eleventh. Also, if there is any way to entice a few more ducks over there at this time by wading in advance,[4] but if this is done of course every effort should be made not to let anyone do any shooting prior to the men's coming down.

Mr. Noble's excursion for his friends included a day of hunting (January 9th) at Palmetto Bluff, a 20,000 acre island owned by Union Bag (Union Camp). Palmetto Bluff[5] is located between Hilton Head and Savannah. It was a 20,000-acre tract of pine forest that was once the home of Richard T. Wilson, an industrialist who was also the brother-in-law of Cornelius Vanderbilt (Riddle 2001). The tract bounded by the May, New and Cooper Rivers is described as an undisturbed pine forest with majestic live oak teeming with deer, feral pigs, duck and fox. Wilson built Palmetto Lodge, a Greek Revival considered the most palatial house in the Low Country South Carolina (Riddle 2001). The house was destroyed by fire in 1926 and was never rebuilt.[6]

I asked John about the names, but he could not recall the particular individuals except for Al Chapman (Alger B. Chapman) and Mr. Noble's brother Bob (Robert P. Noble). In the true deductive approach of a detective, I became (in John's view) "possessed" with identifying the people behind the names.[7] In some instances, the search was relatively simple, since names such as Austin Igleheart, Amos Peaslee, Larry and Philip Sharples, and Medley Whelpley were so unusual that I could put a person to the name. To be confident that I had correctly identified the individual, I had to establish some relationship between the person and Edward Noble. For example, Noble and Anderson were colleagues at the Life Saver Company. I found the Greenwich city directories useful in providing full names, which made the search more manageable.

Social news about Noble and his friends' activity at the Round Hill Club in Greenwich, Connecticut revealed friendships that dated back nearly two decades. *The New York Times* reported on events such as the "Hungarian Ball" (NYT 1935) and the "Hollywood Party" (NYT 1937a) that were part of the New Year's revelry at the Round Hill Club. As many as seven family members from the nineteen bums were active in organizing these events that attracted such luminaries as Prescott Bush, father of George H. W. Bush and grandfather of George W. Bush. The Hungarian Ball featured a wedding scene with Mrs. Edward Noble as the bride, Colonel Arthur Carter as the groom, Mr. Noble as the priest, and Mrs. Francis Allen, Mrs. Austin Igleheart, and Mrs. William S. Wilson as bridesmaids. Mrs. Alva See headed the committee that planned the event.[8]

The "nineteen bums" and their reunion represent one set of characters, while John Toby Woods, Sr. and his crew on St. Catherines were the other. Hosting such a large group was a complex undertaking that required planning. The "nineteen bums" included:

Francis Allen (Francis J. Allen)

> Francis Allen was a friend of the Nobles and a longstanding member of Round Hill Club. There is a *New York Times* article that reported his purchase of six acres of land on Round Hill Road overlooking the Long Island Sound in Greenwich for his home (NYT 1927). In 1965 (Bender 1965:34), his home was part of a tour of Greenwich houses to support the American Shakespeare Festival in Stratford. Mrs. Francis J. Allen described her house, "Nothing was thought out in this house. I just built it and lived in it." Mrs. Allen described herself as a widow whose husband "was in his own business, nothing you'd write down."

Earl Anderson (Earl E. Anderson)

> Earl E. Anderson joined the Noble brothers at Life Savers Corporation in 1933, and was elected to the board of directors in 1938. Until 1956, he managed Life Savers investments. He was also president of WMCA, a radio station that E. J. Noble bought and was the center of a lawsuit that took nearly a decade to resolve. He was elected a board member of St. Lawrence University in 1954 and later became chairman of the board. He served on the boards of Rexall Drug and Chemical Company (1941-1961), Drilling and Exploration Company, and ABC. He died on January 8, 1971 in Montclair, New Jersey. He was 84 (NYT 1971).

Arthur Carter (Arthur Hazelton Carter)

> Arthur H. Carter was a major figure in accounting and was a proponent of independent audits for corporations. In 1933 he testified before the Senate Committee on Banking and Currency, arguing that security firms should be audited by independent CPAs.[9] He reached the rank of Major General in the U.S. Army (he received the Distinguished Service Medal with an Oak Leaf Cluster), and left his mark by instituting fiscal reform. In 2004, Carter was inducted into New York State Society of Certified Public Accountants Hall of Fame. They noted that he was Executive Accountant for the U.S. Department of War from 1941 to 1946. He recommended improvements in the auditing, organization, and procedures of the War Department. After completing his service, he was still referred to as Col. Arthur Carter. He was a day away from his 81st birthday at the time of his death (NYT 1965). He lived in Greenwich, Connecticut and Delray, Florida.

Al Chapman (Alger B. Chapman)[10]

> Alger B. Chapman was a longtime associate of Edward J. Noble at Life Saver and the American Broadcasting Company. He became executive director of the Edward J. Noble

Foundation in 1958. Chapman was a major force in the Republican Party and managed the New York phase of Governor Thomas Dewey's unsuccessful presidential bid in 1948. Chapman served as director of the Noble Foundation and had extensive interaction John Toby, Jr. Chapman died on November 3, 1983 in his 79th year (Saxon 1983b).

Austin Igleheart (Austin S. Igleheart)

At the time of this reunion, Austin S. Igleheart was president of General Food. Two years later he was named board chairman of General Foods, held that position for two years, and then retired. After his retirement, he served as director and member of the executive committee of General Foods until 1961. Igleheart was then named director emeritus. He was also on the board of directors of the Chase Manhattan Bank, and served as a director and executive committee member of the Commercial Solvent Corporation and Mead Johnson & Company. He died at age 90 on October 24, 1979 in Greenwich, Connecticut (Clark 1979).

Jim Johaneson

According to June Noble Larkin, Jim Johaneson was a friend from Thousand Islands, New York.

John Lovejoy (John Meston Lovejoy)

John Lovejoy and Everette L. DeGolyer were the co-founders of the Amerada Petroleum Company. Lovejoy became president in 1930, chairman of the board in 1953, and then retired in 1954. He was also president of the Inland Exploration Company that won a 75 year concession to explore for oil in Afghanistan (NYT 1936). This concession involved the possibility of constructing a pipeline from Afghanistan across Iran. He received the Egleston Medal (for distinguished alumni) from Columbia University. He died November 10, 1968 at 79 (NYT 1968a).

Ted Montague (Theodore Giles Montague)

Ted Montague was appointed president of the Borden Corporation when he was 39 years old. He retired as chairman of the board of directors in 1964, but continued as director of the board's finance committee. Montague introduced Elsie the Cow, which became a successful symbol that gave the Borden Company a warmer image. He was 69 at the time of his death in 1967 (NYT 1967).

Bob Noble (Robert P. Noble)

Robert P. Noble, Edward J. Noble's brother, was one of the founders of the Life Saver Company in 1916, and was elected as its president in 1949. In 1955, when Life Saver and Beechnut merged, he was vice chairman of the board. He retired in 1964, and died on March 4, 1973 at the age of 92.

Amos Peaslee (Amos J. Peaslee)

Amos J. Peaslee has been called an Ambassador Extraordinary and Plenipotentiary.[11] He published extensively on international affairs and was a major figure in formation of the United Nations (Peaslee 1942; Peaslee 1943; Peaslee 1945; Peaslee 1956; Peaslee and

Xydis 1961). He was Ambassador to Australia from August 12, 1953 until Feb 16, 1956. He died August 29, 1969 at 82 years old.

Len Quackenbush (Leonard Charles Quackenbush)
Len Quackenbush was a resident of Greenwich Connecticut. He was an oil broker who was at one time associated with Tidewater Oil. He died on September 30, 1959.

Alva See (Alva Benjamin See)
Alva Benjamin See was the son of the founder of A. B. See Elevator Company. Alva See served as its president. The company was a major supplier of elevators, and merged in 1938 with Westinghouse. See also served as a trustee for the Harlem Bank in NYC. His father, Alonzo, became instantly famous in 1928 when he replied to a request for a contribution to Adelphi College with "all women colleges should be burned." His views were later published in a book, *Schools* (See 1928). Alonzo See eventually made peace with the notion of women's colleges. Alva See Lived in Greenwich Connecticut. He died February 10, 1975.

Larry Sharples (Lawrence P. Sharples)
Lawrence Sharples held several patents for centrifugation processes and was vice of the Sharples Corporation from 1932 to 1962. He retired from the Sharples Centrifuge Division of the Pennwalt Chemical Corporation in 1962. The Sharples were among the five founders of the AOPA (Aircraft Owners and Pilots Association) in 1939, and Larry Sharples was chairman from 1940 to 1974. The Laurence[12] P. Sharples Perpetual Award is given annually to the private citizen who does the most to advance aviation. He was a major benefactor to Widener College in West Chester Pennsylvania, where he grew up. Sharples Hall, originally a freshmen women's dormitory, was dedicated in his honor for his service to the college, and for his work on the admission of women. The tribute mentions that he took his first parachute jump at the age of 71. He died on August 27, 1976 at the age of 85.

Philip Sharples (Philip T. Sharples)
Philip T. Sharples was a founder of the Sharples Corporation, Sharples Chemical Inc. and the Sharples Oil Corporation. These companies were industrial leaders in decanter centrifuge application. The Sharples Corporation and Sharples Chemical merged into Pennwalt Chemical Company in 1940s. Sharples was a member of the boards of directors of Pennwalt, the Philadelphia Federal Reserve Bank, and Fidelity Bank of Philadelphia. He collaborated with Joseph Pew in directing the Pew Charitable Trust to focus on cancer research and the founding of the Institute for Cancer Research (ICR). Philip Sharples was a major benefactor to Swarthmore College, and was a board emeritus trustee at the time of his death. He contributed $1.2 million to build the Sharples Dining Hall at the college. He died on January 19, 1982 at the age of 92.

Warren Snow (Warren H. Snow, Sr.)
In 1950, the *New York Times* reported on the formation of the Blair, Rollins and Company investment banking company (NYT 1950b). Warren T. Snow was its president, and he held the position for twenty years. The company specialized in underwriting

government, municipal, and public utilities and was one of the oldest investment banking companies in America. At the time of his death, he was president of Snow-Sweeny in New York. Snow died on May 7, 1973 in Greenwich, Connecticut at the age of 76 (NYT 1973).

Bill Taylor (William T. Taylor)

William Taylor was likely the source of the sheet music that features the Nineteen Bums. His obituary states that he worked his way through Columbia University and the Columbia Law School as an oratorio baritone soloist singing in the finest churches in New York City. In 1920, Taylor had the lead in Columbia University's first all-male review, "Fly with Me." Richard Rogers composed the music for the review, and Lorenz Hart wrote the lyrics. Taylor was an officer of Bankers Trust and was a former president of the New York State Bankers Association. In 1964, Columbia University awarded him the Alexander Hamilton Medal for "distinguished service and accomplishment." He died in Greenwich, Connecticut on March 15, 1976 at the age of 75 (NYT 1976).

Medley Whelpley (Medley G. B. Whelpley)

Medley G. B. Medley was a partner in the Guggenheim Brothers, financiers. He played a major role extricating the Guggenheims from ventures in the Chilean nitrate industry (Glaser-Schmidt 1995). From 1930-1931, he organized and was the first president of American Express Bank and Trust Company. He joined Guggenheim Brothers in 1932 and retired at the end of 1944. During the Second World War, he served on the Advisory Committee on Commerce and Industry of the War Finance Committee for New York He was a trustee of the John Simon Guggenheim Memorial Foundation and the Solomon R. Guggenheim Foundation, and a director of the Philharmonic Symphony Society. Whelpley was also a trustee of the John Simon Guggenheim Foundation, which is a major contributor to the arts and education. He was a trustee from 1939 until 1965, and then served as vice president from 1959-1965. He died on March 23, 1968 at the age of 75 (NYT 1968b).

Bill Wilson (William S. Wilson)

William S. Wilson was a broker who lived in Greenwich, Connecticut. He was president of the Greenwich Boys Club. He died at age 88 on March 3, 1982.

The ties that bind this group are quite interesting. There are bonds of kinship between the Noble brothers and Sharples brothers. The link between Edward Noble and the Sharples was likely the result of a shared interest in aviation. Noble was chair of the Civil Aeronautic Authority from August 1938 to June 1939, when he became Undersecretary of Commerce in the Roosevelt administration. The Sharples were founders of The Aircraft Owners and Pilots Association in 1939.

In the real estate business, they say the three most important factors in selling land or a house is location, location, location. While there is more to friendship than location, the physical proximity of the men obviously aided in the formation of ties between them. Twelve of the nineteen lived in Greenwich, Connecticut. In 1953, the Noble brothers, Igleheart, Lovejoy, and Quackenbush all lived on Round Hill Road. The others lived nearby: See on Old Church Road, Snow on Mayfair Lane, Carter on Doubling Road, Montague on Old Mill Road, Taylor on

Glenville Road, Wilson on Horseneck Lane, and Francis Allen on Siwanoya Road near Khakum Wood Roads. Most of the group members were active in the Round Hill Club.

Edward and Robert Noble, Al Chapman, and Earl Anderson were longtime business associates at Life Saver or ABC. Igleheart and Montague were also involved in the food industry. At least seven shared significant roles in banking and investment: Snow (Blair, Rollins and Company, Snow-Sweeny & Company), Whelpley (American Express Bank and Trust Company), Philip Sharples (the Philadelphia Federal Reserve Bank and Fidelity Bank of Philadelphia), Igleheart (Chase Manhattan Bank), See (Harlem Bank), and Montague (Bank of New York, National Bank of Fairfield County).

Edward Noble, Amos Peaslee and Al Chapmen headed major presidential campaigns. Noble quit the Roosevelt administration to help the presidential campaign of Wendell Willkie in 1940 (CSM 1940). Al Chapman ran the New York campaign for Thomas Dewey in the election when Harry Truman was elected president (Egan 1948; NYT 1950a; Peason 1948), and Amos Peaslee was a supporter of Harold Stassen, a perennial presidential candidate in 1948 (NYT 1969; Phillips 1951).

The last refrain in the Nineteen Bums is, "They will sing, then be forgotten, as of yore" could not be further from the truth. The impact of these "nineteen bums" on the business community is well documented. A number of them served as college trustees, including Philip Sharples at Swarthmore, Noble and Anderson at St. Lawrence, and Chapman at Adelphi. Edward J. Noble's foundation, Whelpley's work with the Guggenheim Foundation, and Philip Sharples' influence with the Pew Charitable Trust have also left their mark. The self-proclaimed nineteen bums have not been forgotten.

John and his crew spent weeks preparing for the arrival of the "nineteen bums" to St. Catherines. The preparations for a visit were well established, and it was a drill that the island's staff engaged at least a dozen times a year. While the nineteen bums were well known to the world, John Toby and his team are interesting in their own right.

From Toby's Day Book (in bold):

January 6, 1953, Tuesday
Weather fair and Cool
Finished cleaning up lawn and roof of main house
Geo. & Jim plastered in Main house
Woodrow prepared boat from Sea Side.
Mr. Noble called. He is coming down tomorrow

The notes in Toby's day book were used to prepare him for his frequent briefing with the boss by phone, and for the detailed monthly report that he had to prepare. Despite the brevity of these notes, they spoke volumes to John Toby who had a quarter of a century experience with the process. For example, the weather was an important part of every communication to Mr. Noble. As Mr. Noble monitored the work on the island, he wanted to be assured that when the weather made outside work difficult, that Toby and his men focused their attention on interior work. As John commented, there was always something to do. If Toby had workers attending to the lawns "too early," Mr. Noble would suggest that they wait until it closer to the time of his arrival. John said that Mr. Noble would have been pleased that his father had waited until the day before his arrival to finish cleaning the lawn and roof of the main house.

John mentioned that plastering and painting the main house and the cottages were an ongoing project. Since the roof frequently sprang leaks, repairing the damage to the ceilings was an essential undertaking before a visit. The roof would then be patched with tar, but there would soon be another spot that needed repairs.

Boats and equipment were also constantly in need of repair. John pointed out that the cable that brought electricity to St. Catherines was not laid until 1961. His father frequently had to work in the "light House" on the generators that provided electricity (direct current) to the island. Boats were an essential mode of transportation on the island, were constantly being maintained. The frequent trips to Savannah, Yellow Bluff and Half Moon, as well as travel around St. Catherines, put many hours of use on the boat's engines.

The Toby Wood's Team

George Washington Berryhill (Figure 137) was part American Indian and, as John remembers, he had a very distinctive feature: one brown eye and one blue eye. He came to St. Catherines from Yellow Bluff, where he ran a party boat for Roger Youmans. He married John's Aunt Annie Hall who was previously married to Otis Edenfield. Otis left the island and went into the trucking business after a serious disagreement with Annie Hall, whom he eventually divorced.

George's tenure on St. Catherines had a sad ending. John Toby was working the saw mill and stopped the saw to sharpen the blade. Even though the saw had been shut down, one of the trimmers was still rotating. George's glove caught in the blade and his arm was severed just above the wrist. John applied a tourniquet, gave him a pint of liquor to drink, carried him by boat to Half Moon, and drove him to Hinesville to be treated. George received disability payments from Workman's Compensation until he reached retirement age.

Jim Crawley, as John remembers, was in charge of the crash boat for the army and was stationed at Thunderbolt. The crash boats were quite active since the

Figure 137. John Toby Woods and George Berryhill on the dock at St. Catherines. Gee Little said that they are outfitted in typical island work clothes.

area around Ossabaw and St. Catherines Islands was an area for training pilots of P-39s and P-40s from Harris Neck Army Air Force Base. After the end of World War II, Jim got into some trouble and needed a job. Toby Woods, John's father, knew that he was an excellent worker and hired him even though he was overqualified for work on the island. He initially came to the island with Carmen Lee, but they eventually divorced. After Jim and his second wife, Mildred, divorced, she married Woodrow Rogers.

In a rogue's gallery of lovable characters, Woodrow Rogers would stand out (Figure 138). With a twinkle in his eye, John describes Uncle Woodrow as a "wirey" man who was four feet and eleven inches tall, "and if he were carrying a 10-pound sack of sugar would have weighed about 100 pounds." Uncle Woodrow had two loves: cars and women. He was encyclopedic knowledge of the horsepower and top speed of any car that had been built. He could cite "rhyme and verse" of all of the special features of John Toby Woods' 1937 Hudson

Figure 138. Uncle Woodrow Rogers and an unidentified friend.

Terraplane. John said that he never saw uncle Woodrow read a book or magazine. He enjoyed just sitting and smoking a cigarette. But when a woman walked into the room, he would become an attentive charmer.

Woodrow like the other workers on the island was a "jack of all trades." He would help the family in the main house when they visited. For a group like the "nineteen bums," he would become the bartender. John added that after serving drinks, he would become the waiter, and after dinner he would become the dishwasher. At St. Catherines you did what had to be done.

Woodrow was one of Mr. Noble's favorites and he frequently asked about him when calling or in letters that he sent to Toby. In a letter to Toby dated March 4, 1953, Mr. Noble discussed the purchase of a drag line from Richard B. Tuten, expressed his concerns about how workers were spending their time, was upset by the fact that J. M. Wilder, engineer at WFRP, was seeking employment elsewhere, confirmed his plans for an upcoming visit to the island, discussed the possibility of getting out of the hog business, and ended the letter with:

> I am terribly sorry to hear about Woodrow and hope I will get a letter in a day or two saying he is better. If there is anything that ought to be done, be sure to do it for he is one grand little man in my opinion. You know how much I think of him.

Gee Little, John's older sister, said that part of the special relationship was that Woodrow would "stand up to Mr. Noble." There was what an anthropologist would call "a joking relationship"[13] between the two men. John described an incident in which Mr. Noble had Woodrow go to the library to fetch an 18-pound cannon ball. Mr. Noble proceeded to tell a long story about the cannon ball, well aware of Woodrow's discomfort. Woodrow, however, would not be intimidated; he set the cannon ball on the floor and went about his work. Woodrow paid attention to Mr. Noble's likes and dislikes. He knew how Mr. Noble wanted his steaks grilled, and his drinks mixed, and when to refill them.

John described when Woodrow took the speedboat built by Curtis Lee on a trial run. The 14-foot plywood speedboat was powered by a 20-horsepower motor. Near the bottom of the boat, there was a wooden strip to reinforce its plywood body that went the length of the boat. Curtis and his friends had returned from marsh hen hunting and the gear, shotguns, shells and fishing rods were stored on the boat. Woodrow took it out for a test run with Curtis and the gang standing on the dock, and with Mr. Noble by the pool watching from a distance. Woodrow had it at full throttle and attempted to make a sharp turn, but the wooded strip caught a wave and flipped the boat, tossing Woodrow into the water and submerging the engine. Ellis Little, Gee's husband, went to the rescue. Gee described the difficulty that Ellis had in convincing Woodrow to climb on to the stern of his boat. Woodrow kept trying to climb into the boat on the side. When they finally got to the dock, Woodrow's only comment was, "How did I get into the boat?" After they had rescued Woodrow, Mr. Noble, hearing the commotion, came down to the dock to see what had happened. Chuckling, he told Curtis to send him the bill for repairing the boat. John doubts that Curtis sent him the bill. Mr. Noble also knew that Curtis would not accept his offer.

Mr. Noble had an intense interest in speedboats. John mentioned that a model of a boat named "Miss Behave" was prominently displayed on a bookcase shelf[14] in the main house. Since 1926, Mr. Noble was a familiar figure speeding on the St. Lawrence River piloting his 33-foot Baby Gar, Snail. The Baby Gars were the invention of Gar Wood, a Detroit industrialist and friend of Ed Noble, and they were extremely popular.[15] The Baby Gars were designed after the boat that Gar Wood used when he won the Harnsworth race in England and the Gold Cup Race in Detroit. In 1934, Wood introduced a 16-foot split cockpit runabout that caught Mr. Noble's eye. Noble asked him to design a small sporty boat that would ride in the waters as rapidly as the European sport cars that could be seen cruising the highways of the continent.

Gar Wood responded to Noble's request with a 16-foot high performance boat that had two seats aft of the six-cylinder "spitfire" engine. The "Speedster," as it was christened by Wood, was similar to the cut-down Miss America racer that had won so many races.[16] Noble became so enamored with the "Speedster" that he ordered the first dozen that were produced and had them sent to his estate on the Thousand Islands for use by him and his friends on the St. Lawrence River. Noble named his boats "Miss Behave," "Miss Adventure," "Miss Chief," and "Miss Conduct." Speedster racing became a regular summer event until the start of World War II. The original "Miss Behave" is in the Thousand Islands Shipyard Museum. Mr. Noble would be pleased to know that in 2005 "Miss Chief," in original mint condition, was offered for sale at $112,000.

I asked John about his most vivid memory of Uncle Woodrow. "He was a fighter. All his life he had to deal with teasing. They would call him 'runt,' 'shorty' and other names such as Pedrow. But he was tough. He was as tough as a mean dog that after he is dead will still growl and bite you. And he did save my life."

January 7, 1953, Wednesday
Partly Cloudy and Warm
Mr. Noble came down with Richard and a few men
Geo. & Jim painted Boat No. 1
JTW worked on Bateaux[17] & Boat 1
Wilder & Mr. King the GE man came over

Richard B. Tuten was a National Guard pilot that frequently ferried Mr. Noble from Savannah to the island on a Guard plane. While this was against regulations, Tuten and his plane were frequent visitors to the island's cleared cow pasture. Tuten was fearless and would even land at night. John said that he rode once, and only once with Richard. Tuten asked John if he wanted to fly to Atlanta with him. The trip to Atlanta was stormy and rather uncomfortable. The ride back, according to John, was another story. As they were flying back, Richard and John were in conversation when all of a sudden Richard shouted to John that he couldn't see the light. They had flown past Savannah and he didn't know if they had enough gas to get back. Tuten finally got his bearings and landed safely with some gasoline still in the tank.

I asked John if he flew with him again. John said that Tuten had his wings clipped by the commander of the Guard. Tuten was rolling the plane back to the hanger and it slipped of its guide and he bent the prop. The Commander called John and wanted to verify that Tuten had flown an emergency mission to St. Catherines to bring medicine to Ann's sick child, Carlann, who had hydrocephalus. John lied, something that he still feels was wrong, and Tuten was not written up. I asked John if Tuten was still living, and he related a sad story. In 1959, children playing with a carbine in another room accidentally fired a bullet through the wall, killing Tuten.

Mr. Wilder and Mr. King were General Electric technicians from Savannah who regularly maintained and repaired the wireless radiophone that was the communication link from St. Catherines to the outside world. While wireless phones bring up images of an instrument thinner than a deck of cards that can capture and transmit pictures, send and receive text messages, track the scores of your favorite team or the quotes of your favorite stocks, download games, and even be used as a phone, this was not GE wireless radiophone. It had one and only one function: to keep in touch with Mr. Noble; and it did not do that well. Toby was in a constant battle with the experimental radiophone that Mr. Noble had procured on an experimental basis from the General Electric Company. Years ago, when John told me about the "trials and tribulations" of the radiophone, I pictured a contraption that would look like a walky-talky from World War II. This was a gross misconception. The guts of the machine were so large that it filled a credenza the size of a four-foot tall and four-foot wide bookcase (Figure 139). As John describes it, there were dozens of vacuum tubes that would burn out or malfunction.

The radiophone required considerable infrastructure. A "light house" to generate alternating current was required since all of the electricity generated on the island was direct current. The generator could be started from within the house, but it to be fueled frequently. The signal from the house was linked to an antenna perched on the top of a hickory tree just outside of the house. In addition, it had to have a tower atop the General Oglethorpe Hotel on Wilmington Island, nine miles from Savannah, Georgia. From the tower, the operators in Savannah would patch the call into the phone system on the mainland. At times, Mr. Noble would become brusque and the operators would take their time in responding to him. Mr. Noble, well aware of just how far he could push the operators, would ask, "How would you ladies like some silk stockings?" Service immediately got better.

Figure 139. John Toby in the Superintendent's house with the radiophone on the left. Above it is the license for its use. The Lamp in the background was given to Gladys Woods when the Keys left the island.

January 8, 1953, Thursday
Partly Cloudy Cool
All worked on house and grounds

While all hands at St. Catherines were preparing for the arrival of the "nineteen bums," nine[18] of them were departing from New York at 3:40 p.m. on the Atlantic Coastline West Coast Champion for Hardeeville, the disembarking point for Palmetto Bluff.

January 9, 1953, Friday
Partly cloudy
To Savn'h for supplies
Anne and Baby, Flynn, Becky & Marie & other lady
Also Carlann came.
Crawley went to Sav'h with me

While many of the workers on the island could leave for the weekend, for a special event such as this, they would stay. Extra help (Annie, Flynn, Becky, Marie and the "other lady") would be brought over to prepare food and rooms for the guests. They would then make the beds and clean the rooms and cabins for the guests.

January 10, 1953, Saturday
Cloudy with rain
Open oysters for Mr. Noble
Went to Halfmoon for luggage for the party
Mr. Noble came down on Union Bag boat

The Union Bag boat was Sandy Calder's new 55-foot yacht. Mr. Noble arranged for the Union Bag to pick up the "nineteen bums" at Palmetto Bluff, South Carolina at 10:00 AM and bring them to St. Catherines in the early afternoon on Saturday (Noble 1952e). The plan: "Sunday morning there will be a guided fishing party, marsh henning, duck and turkey for those who got none at Palmetto Bluff" (Noble 1952e). Sandy Calder was president of Union Camp, a company that processed the pine forest into paper. He was a graduate of St. Lawrence University, which gave him a special relationship to Ed Noble. In his letters to the invitees, Calder requested that the luggage be carried separately to give them more room on the yacht; it was transported over land.

January 11, 1953, Sunday
Cloudy, cold and windy
Went to McIntosh for Mr. Peasly[19]
Went duck hunting with Mr. Noble's party.

McIntosh is the railroad station that was closest to place to disembark from the train. The Atlantic Coastline East Coast Champion (ECC) and West Coast Champion (WCC) were the preferred mode of overland travel. These were state of the art trains that featured coach and Pullman service to the east and west coasts of Florida. The ECC that left New York City at 1:45 p. m. would have arrived at McIntosh[20] around 6 a.m. Those who arrived earlier would have gone on the duck hunt.

January 12, 1953, Monday
Fair and cold
Went fishing Mr. Noble party

Carried Mr. Noble party to McIntosh & Mr. Lovejoy to Savh. Jim & Myself

For the return trip on Monday, Mr. Noble arranged for a special car to be put on the Atlantic Coastline East Coast Champion that would stop at McIntosh around 6:00 p.m. for those going to New York arriving at 10:15 a.m. the next day (Noble 1952e). Lovejoy was most likely flying out of the Savannah Airport. Before leaving, Toby took them out for one last fishing trip.

January 13, 1953
Fair and cool
Mr. Calder party came from St. Simon & had lunch with Mr. Noble
Woodrow carried Mr. Alford Jones[21] (Alfred W. Jones) to Half Moon
Carried Mr. and Mrs. Cowart & Mrs. Pat to HM

This party, not related to the "nineteen bums," consisted of sixteen individuals[22] in addition to Sandy Calder. The lunch with Mr. Noble was the prelude to an outing at Palmetto Bluffs in Bluffton, S.C. Calder's invitation (Calder 1952) was for "a combination wild turkey hunt, fishing party, and golf party." They were to depart Olsen's Dock on St. Simons Island at 8 AM on Tuesday the 13th, arriving on St. Catherines about noon for lunch. Calder described the lunch in more detail, "Mr. Ed Noble, Chairman of ABC Broadcasting Company, will provide us with lunch at his home on St. Catherines. Incidentally, he will be there in person to greet us and to make sure that everybody is happy." He warned them, "There will be nothing on the boat to drink, except bourbon, scotch, martinis, brandy, and various other cordials, to say nothing of champagne, so watch your step, you might fall overboard."
After lunch, they went on to "Palmetto Bluffs for dinner and a good night's sleep." Tuesday and Wednesday they were to hunt wild turkeys, fish and golf on the "materially improved" approach and putting golf course. Friday on their return trip they planned to stop for lunch again with Mr. Noble on St. Catherines at 1:00 PM.

January 14, 1953, Wednesday
Partly cloudy and warm
Went to help Geo. And Jim get tractor off stump
Mr. Pin Hoster came and Mr. Beddenfield
I went fishing and caught about 35 trout

Dr. John Pinholster was the family doctor and was John Toby Jr.'s physician when he was seriously burned when a boat exploded on St. Catherines.
The one constant in Toby's life was his love of the outdoors. John said that if there was any tension in his life, an outing to fish or hunt would be a way for him to relax. This personal recreation would have to be done after the workday. Finding time was often a problem, since the nine hour day[23] would often lengthen to ten, eleven or even twelve hours. If there was a problem, Toby had to deal with it. For example, when the tractor got stuck on a stump, it was Toby who had to respond to solve the problem.

January 15, 1953, Thursday
Rain in the afternoon
Went coon hunting last night killed 11

Repaired wheel on Mr. Noble car
This morning opened oysters
Worked on jeep this afternoon
For Mr. Noble Party Wick is coming tomorrow at 2:00 P.M.
Mr. Noble called and gave me H. for using telephone so long

John smiled when he read me the line from Toby's day book that said the "Mr. Noble gave me H." He said that he never heard his father utter a swear word. I was surprised that Mr. Noble would expect the phone to be free. He just had Sandy Calder and his group over for lunch on the 13th, and was having them return of the 16th for lunch. Even with this schedule, Toby was expected to keep the phone free for Mr. Noble.

Reading her father's day book entry recording his successful raccoon hunt reminded Gee Little of hunts that she had witnessed.[24] The hunters carried headlights powered by batteries that were used to spot the 'coon eyes[25] when the light hit them. The "eye shine" from the raccoon treed by Button, the dog, would be the target. Gee told me that sometimes shine from stars (star shine) would be mistaken for shine of the 'coon's eyes, leading to a missed shot. John laughed and said that you couldn't blame Button for the hunter's inability to distinguish "eye shine" from "star shine." Button, the wonder dog that he was, had done as much as he could.

Raccoon hunting had the added advantage of taking place at night, so it did not interfere with daytime activity on the island. Toby and other workers would frequently get a dog and go out on a hunt.

January 16, 1953, Friday
Fixed hog pen
Partly Cloudy & Warm
Went out in boat to look for boat that broke down.
Found it in shape to run
Mr. Caulder (Calder) party was over carried them to ride
Woodrow carried them to Yellow Bluff

The reference to the hog pens is the first in a series of notes in Toby's day book. There were a number of pens that would have to be built and maintained. They were feral hogs that had to be corralled for eventual sale. For most of the rest of the month, this was a focus of some of the workers. Toby was the official guide, and special visitors such as Mr. Calder and guests would be given a tour of the island. Woodrow's trip to Yellow Bluff was to take someone who was to return by land rather than with the yacht.

January 17, 1953, Saturday
J. T. W & Jim to hog pens taken down
Farmall M. Stearing (steering) gear

The hog pens would be taken down when the animals in that area were corralled, and then be rebuilt in another area,
The Farmall tractor is the classic tractor with the two small wheels in front. The tractors were difficult to maneuver on rough terrain. If the two front wheels hit an obstacle, the steering

wheel would whip around with enough force to potentially fracture the driver's arm. This was also hard on the steering apparatus, which would often be in need of repair.

January 18, 1953, Sunday
Rain in the Afternoon
Geo. Berryhill to Sav.
Ellis, Gee, John, Curtis[26], Maggie and Buster came over on Sat & went back today
Glayds & myself went to Savh with Jeep motor

John said that in 1957 Mr. Noble bought a new jeep that was only to be driven by him. Toby and John said that on any trip to Savannah, you went to the junkyard for materials if you had any extra time. Toby was rebuilding a jeep that had been picked up as junk. Toby spent nine days during the month working on the jeep that would have been used on the island.

January 19, 1953, Monday
Cloudy
Worked on Jeep motor at Motor Supply

January 20, 1953, Tuesday
Cloudy
Worked on jeep motor till noon
Picked up feed for hogs & came back to island at night

The hogs and the hog pens represented a major project during the remainder of the month. There were many hog pens that were built, rebuilt and moved. The activity suggests that they were getting ready to sell the hogs. Looking ahead to the February 23 entry in the day book, Toby and George did take the hogs to market in Jessup.

January 21, 1953 Wednesday
Went other hog (pen)
Worked on Farmall
Worked on H-D 7 tractor and Jeep motor

The H-D 7 tractor is really a bulldozer with tank-like treads to move on unstable ground. Toby had the ability to work on all kinds of equipment and vehicles. This was essential since the equipment was in constant need of repair.

January 22, 1953, Thursday
Fair and cool
Went to the Hog pens
Worked on Jeep panting motor
Geo. & Jim picked up in pasture
Woodrow pulled moss out of tree

Mr. Noble expected any limbs, moss and any other materials to be removed from the pastures and from the grazing areas. If a tree has been uprooted, he expected it to be cut up, removed, and then burned. When Mrs. Larkin became head of the Foundation, she did not have these materials removed. Instead she allowed them to rot in place, thus providing food and shelter for animals and insects. This was an ecologically sound principle that allowed for a more natural setting for the wildlife.

Woodrow was assigned the task of removing the moss from the trees near the pool. I had assumed that this would involve just removing the lowest hanging segments that could fall into the pool. John said that all the moss was to be removed. Woodrow would climb the trees with a long pole and try to extricate the moss from all the branches. It was a time consuming and dangerous activity. John said that Mrs. Keys had been even more obsessed with removing the moss. She wanted all of the trees surrounding the main house denuded of moss.

January 23, 1953, Friday
(No entry)

January 24, 1953, Saturday
Cool windy with some rain
JTW & Mildred to Savh for supply
Mr. Durden and friend came over

January 25, 1953, Sunday
Fair and Windy
Geo. to Half Moon to take Annie & babies to Collins.
Cecil Durden went over

January 26, 1953 Monday
Fair & cool
Jim and myself worked on body of jeep
Woodrow & George worked at hogs

January 27, 1953, Tuesday
Fair and cool
Worked on Jeep
Burned Savh Woods
4 hrs

After clearing the pasture and other areas, the debris would be burned. There was also controlled burning to keep underbrush from accumulating and creating the potential for a major forest fire. Toby and crew spent the last days of January clearing and burning trees and branches that had fallen.

January 28, Wednesday
Cloudy with Rain at late afternoon
Cleaning up dead logs & trees on Savannah road

January 29, Thursday
Fair and Cold

Went to Halfmoon to get Joe Collins & returned
Also went to Dorchester to get express package
Cleaned up dead trees On Savh Road in afternoon

Joe Collins was the Liberty County agricultural agent who was supervising the canal to drain the ponds to increase the pasture.

January 30, Friday
Partly Cloudy & cold
Cleaned up dead logs & trees on Savh Road
5 hrs
Burned woods in afternoon
4 hrs

January 31, Saturday
Fair and warm
I & Crawleys to Savh.
The Crawleys To Metter
Curtis and family & John came over
Marvin Cowert

Conclusion

The first three weeks of January were, as usual, a busy time. The visit of the "nineteen bums" and the two lunches for the Calder party added to the burden of the St. Catherines staff. In addition all of the normal activities, the staff prepared 36 breakfasts, 60 lunches, and 36 dinners; and guided hunts, fishing trips, and tours of the island over a five day period. January included 21 trips to and from the mainland, 54 man-hours of lawn care, 48 man-hours of house repairs, 40 man-hours of boat repair and maintenance, 112 man-hours clearing the fields, 56 man-hours tending the hogs,[27] part of 10 days repairing cars, and 6 days repairing tractors. They still found time to shuck oysters for Mr. Noble and his friends.

Toby had little spare time, but when he was free he engaged in his own enjoyment of the island. In addition to guiding fishing and hunting trips, which he enjoyed, Toby had time to hunt and fish on his own. The 35 trout he caught and eleven raccoons he killed attest to his ability. There was another dimension to his stewardship of the island. During the month of January, he had 21 friends and family visit St. Catherines on the five weekends. I would often tease John that although the Keys and Noble bought the island, Toby and his family "owned it."

14

John Woods' Battle for Life:
The Boat Accident in His Own Words

On the morning of July 8, 1948, I was on the island while mother and daddy were on vacation in Alabama. Daddy left me a list of chores to do while he was gone. I had to go to the mainland and get a load of fertilizer.[1] Daddy always considered it to be a one-man job because it was downhill from the truck to the boat, so I did the chore alone.

I gassed up the freight boat (Figure 140), which was a converted shrimp boat that had been fitted with two 55-gallon oil drums to serve as gas tanks. Mr. Noble purchased the boat in Savannah. The boat, as it is pictured, was a remodeled version of the earlier cabin that was built on the shrimp boat and made it top heavy.[2] I climbed into the boat, touched the starter button, and then the boat blew up.[3] I somehow had time to put my hands over my face. The blast[4] blew the floor off of the boat with me standing on it. Fortunately, I wasn't blown overboard. I was able to climb up on the dock. Lucky for me, it was still early and I had on my shirt,[5] or else I would have been dead. From the waist up I had 1st and 2nd degree burns. My arms up to my shirtsleeves were covered with 3rd degree burns,[6] with the skin all burned off and hanging down.[7] My shirt was scorched and I had blisters all over my upper body and face. I didn't have socks on, and the skin around my ankles was hanging down over my shoes.

Figure 140. The freight boat with no name.

My little uncle[8] was working nearby and heard the explosion. He ran to the dock in time to pull the rope off the piling and get the burning boat away from the dock so that it wouldn't catch the boathouse on fire and burn up the other boat, "Sea Beaver"[9] that was hanging up in it.[10] The flames were 15 or 20 feet high. Having done that, we both went up the dock to the superintendent's house, which was about 100 yards away from where we were both living. Uncle Woodrow used the radiophone to call Uncle Hoke Youmans. Luckily, Uncle Hoke was late in leaving his house and agreed to have his plane ready when we got there. Uncle Hoke had his own plane, a four passenger Cessna, and his own airfield and hanger.[11]

I went to the bathroom mirror and looked at myself; I was not a pretty sight. My hair was almost completely singed off. I was almost all black. Marie, the wife of one of the employees, heard the explosion from her house and came running. When she saw me she burst into tears and got a sheet and put it over me. I couldn't stand it, so I threw the sheet off of me.

Uncle Woodrow and I went back down to the dock. He lowered *The Sea Beaver* into the water. It[12] was picked up by a two-hand pulled-chain hoist, so he had to lower the boat by going back and forth between the two handles.[13] He ran up the dock and got a can of gasoline and as

179

he was pouring it in, I backed out and headed to Uncle Hoke's dock on Bluff Creek, about 30 minutes away. We said only a few words. I asked him if he thought that I was going to die. Uncle Woodrow said, "I don't know." Nothing else was said on the ride to Uncle Hoke's.

I stepped off the boat at Uncle Hoke's dock and he saw me. I'll never forget the look on his face. We walked about a little more than 100 yards to the plane. When I got into the plane, I took the last steps that I would take for a year. It was my first plane ride. Uncle Hoke and Uncle Woodrow saved my life that day. The ambulance was waiting for us at the airport,[14] and they put me on a stretcher and carried me to the Warren Candler Hospital in Savannah.[15]

A nurse supervisor, Ruth Ray, met me in the emergency room. At the time, my eyes had swollen shut. She took scissors and cut off my pants and the loose skin hanging of my body. I believe that they covered my burns in an ointment and wrapped me up. Since I didn't have anyone with me, I had to give them all the information that they needed before they could do that.

They put me in a private room and hooked me up to a glucose drip. The only veins available were in my neck or feet. For seven months, they gave me a crystalline[16] shot every morning and pain shots every four hours. I had three private nurses for those seven months. The hospital room had no air conditioning back then. Blowflies[17] would find a way to get into the room and the nurses would have to swat them.

Every few days, Dr. Pinholster, our family doctor, assisted by Dr. Upton, would remove the bandages to put on a new dressing. Removing the bandages would pull off all the new skin. Later what Dr. Pinholster called "proud flesh"[18] started growing on the burned area where there was no skin. He would have to take scissors and trim it off. Finally, Dr. Pinholster decided that he needed to do skin grafts,[19] so he put me to sleep in the operating room with gas for approximately four hours. He and his assistant took sheets of skin off my upper legs and sewed it on my arms. The problem was where the skin was removed there was no skin left and "proud flesh" would grow up there.

Dr. Pinholster told me they had a new device[20] and they were going to cut skin off of the skin on my stomach and sew it on my ankles (back to the operating room). I was given blood before and after these operations. That operation was a success. I think that that they took off a layer thin enough so that it worked both ways.

So after about seven months, my arms were healed enough for me to feed myself. I still couldn't straighten my arms out. They started weaning me off the pain shots that I had become addicted to. I gave nurses a hard time during that time. Finally, I was well enough that they let the nurses go.

Dr. Pinholster sent me home for short times of two or three weeks, but some areas on my leg were still raw and my arms and legs were still stiff. I wasn't able to walk. I went back to the hospital and Dr. Pinholster put me back in the operating room and did a pinch graft operation – 100s of pinches of skin were planted on the raw area. Drs. Pinholster and Upton each took a leg. I still have the different sized scars on my thighs from where they took the skin.

I was eventually well enough to start moving around. So again, Dr. Pinholster put me back in the operating room and broke my joints loose. He had a masseur[21] work on my joints daily. Finally, I got out of the hospital after a year and one week. I could hardly move on crutches, I went back to the island and started getting stronger every day.

I believe that if Dr. Pinholster had been able to use the same device on my thighs that he used on my stomach, I would have gotten out of the hospital at least two months earlier.

I was glad that I was working for Mr. Noble when I had the accident. Workman's compensation paid my hospital bill. Mr. Noble visited me one time that I remember, and that was not long before I got out of the hospital. He said when he got to New York that he was going to send down two 410-gauge pump model 42 Winchester shotguns for daddy and me, with the understanding that we would have to let the guests use them, too, whenever we took them mash hen hunting. By the time I retired, we had both of the shotguns rebuilt and restored.

Epilogue from George J. Armelagos

I had known John Woods for a decade before he told me about the accident. John was talking about Uncle Hoke's plane, and I asked him if he ever went flying with Uncle Hoke. He mentioned the accident and said that it was the first and only time he flew with Uncle Hoke. It was the first time that he mentioned the accident to me. This account is the first time that he has told the story to anyone. As he became more comfortable with the events of those days, he realized that important events during that year were a blur. As John shared his story, he became more aware of the support that family and friends had given him.

John shared his account of the accident with Dorothy Williams. He realized that either Dorothy, her daughter Mary, or her husband Clarence had visited him nearly every day. The Williams hosted John during his first excursion out of the hospital after nearly six months. The Williams brought John to their home on Christmas Day of 1948 for dinner and festivities. He also remembered Ben, the black orderly that was a constant source of support for him during that year. He recalls that Ben helped him into the wheel chair and lifted him into the car that day.

Dorothy Williams and John were discussing that year when she reminded him that she had seen him being transported to the hospital. The ambulance with its long, narrow windows passed 37th Street and Abercorn on its way to the hospital. Dorothy and Mary Williams were walking to the Bible School that was a part of their summer activity. Hearing the siren, Dorothy looked up to see a "black" man a "white" ambulance. She commented to their daughter that it must have been a serious accident for a "white" ambulance to be transporting a black person to the "white" hospital. In 1948, Savannah was a segregated city with "colored" and "white" hospitals and "colored" and "white" ambulances. Dorothy was well aware of the segregated medical system. Her husband great grandfather, Thomas F. Williams, a Savannah merchant and minister, founded the Georgia Infirmary[22] in 1832. It was the first African American hospital in the United States. By the time they arrived at their home on 37th Street, they received a call and were told that John had suffered severe burns and was at Candler Hospital. They then realized that the "black" man was John, whose face had been blackened by the explosion.

John said that while he was in the hospital there was concern that he would not walk again. In this account he described that the doctors "broke his joints loose." Before the accident, Mr. Noble had arranged an athletic scholarship for John to St. Lawrence University in Canton, New York. Mr. Noble, who was Chairmen of the Board of Trustees of St. Lawrence from 1941 to 1954 (NYT 1956a), was impressed with John's athletic ability. Even though he was not a competitive swimmer or boxer, Mr. Noble was convinced that John would be a worthy student. In the tenth grade, John was enrolled at Georgia Military College, at Milledgeville, and boxed as a welterweight (maximum of 147 pound) on the team. After the accident, Mr. Noble never mentioned St. Lawrence to him. Perhaps he was in such poor physical condition that it may not have occurred to Mr. Noble that he was still interested in going on to college.

John said that he soon discarded his crutches for a walking stick that he used for a short time. It sounded as if this was a quick recovery. As I learned more about his life after the accident, I realized just how debilitating the injuries were. He was telling me about his friend George Ginter[23] who came to St. Catherines to stay a few days and reestablish their friendship. John said that George would lift him up and put him in the 1931 Model "A" Ford that Curtis Lee had brought down from Cedartown as a gift for Gladys Woods. It became her personal car as she cruised the island. John said that it wasn't much of a problem, since he only weighed about 100 pounds; he had lost over 60 pounds while in the hospital.

The Korean Conflict started in June 1950, and by August that year Camp Stewart was reactivated as the Third Army Anti-Aircraft training center.[24] John comments about that time,

> Not being able to do much physical work, I leased a car and drove it as a taxi. In Hinesville and Camp Stewart, a lot of my school buddies were in the Guard and were called to serve in the Third Army. They were living in large tents at Camp Stewart and I enjoyed hanging out with them. I got my draft notice and thought that I would be soon joining my friends. I went to Jacksonville, Florida for my physical exam. They checked me out and told me that I was no condition to serve. I was 4-F.

> Since I could not serve in the army, I decide to run a filling station in Midway, Georgia. Uncle Albert and I leased a filling station and I ran it for a year.

> I was still looking for something that would keep my interests. I decided to go to a vocational trade school in Americus, Georgia and started a course in diesel engineering. I received my certificate for the 18-month program in just a year.

> On December 31, 1955, I married Katherine Oetgen, who was a public health nurse. She graduated from St. Josephs Hospital School of Nursing and later graduated from Vanderbilt University with a B.S. in Nursing and a major in Public Health.

> We rented a house in Savannah and then bought one of Katherine's father's[25] rental houses in East Savannah.

> I was working at Morgan's Inc. in Savannah when I met Katherine. Morgan's was a General Motors Marine Diesel Engine Distributors. Shrimping was in its heyday. Morgan's sold engines and marine equipment, often financing the sale. Morgan's sent me to the G.M. Diesel Engine School at the Factory Service School in Detroit. I was soon promoted to Master Mechanic. As a Master Mechanic, I started inspecting the shrimp boats that Morgan's sold and financed with our installed engines and equipment.

> Morehead City Ship Building Corporation in North Carolina was building at least a shrimp boat a week, and I inspected many of them that had installed our engines. I would fly to New Bern, North Carolina, rent a car, and drive to Morehead City Ship Building Corporation facilities where I would inspect the

engine installation and take the boat on its first trial run to ensure that it was performing properly. I was performing the same services for Diesel Engine Sales in St. Augustine, Florida. The company was also producing a shrimp boat a week. There were smaller companies that would call me to inspect the equipment on the boats that they were building.

When I left Morgan's in 1958, I bought a small shrimp boat, put a crew on it, and went to work for J. H. Morgan and Sons, who had a shrimping business at Sunbury, Georgia and Key West, Florida. I worked summers at Sunbury and winters at Key West.

15

The Mico[1] of St. Catherines:
John Woods Becomes Superintendent of St. Catherines

After the death of E. J. Noble in December 1958, Toby Woods thought about his future on St. Catherines. He had been on the island for three decades and wanted to go back to the farm. His father decided to retire after buying a 150-acre farm in Newington, Georgia.[2] While he was pleased to see his father realize his dream of going back to farming, John grasped the implication of his dad's decision to leave St. Catherines.[3] He understood that, for the first time in his life, his family ties to the island would soon be severed (Figure 141). This realization forced John to make a decision. He recalled,

> In December 1958, Mr. Noble died, and by 1960 my daddy, having worked
> on St. Catherines for 31 years, wanted to retire. So, the Noble Foundation
> set up a retirement for him. I decided that since St. Catherines had always
> been my home and I was about to lose it, I would apply for the job of
> superintendent to replace my father.

**Figure 141. The three generations of the Wood's family: John
Toby Woods, I, Johnny Woods and John Woods**

Down of the Farm with Toby

After leaving St. Catherines, Toby Woods was a successful farmer by all accounts (Figure 142). John said that friends and neighbors could not visit his dad without leaving with a trunk full of fruits and vegetables. Toby and his farm were frequently a topic of discussion in

Figure 142. John Toby Woods in his 90s.

Figure 143. Gladys Woods dressed for the 50th wedding anniversary of Fred and Saddie Waters

Newington. Runnette Davis, in her column "At Home in Screven County" (Davis 1982:18), wrote about "Mr. Woods' Garden." Ms. Davis wanted to know why people were fussing about "the most talked about gardener is Screven County." Neighbors of Mr. Woods had been calling her to brag about his bumper crop of fruits and vegetables and she, as the Screven County agricultural agent, had to check out the reasons for his success. While talking to Ms. Davis, Mr. Woods was, as usual, modest to a fault. To him, it was just the simple matter that he planted more than the others. He said, "The difference in me and a lot of people is I make a lot of stuff." In actuality, eighty-one year Toby Woods had time tested practices that led to his super farm. He prepared the soil well, used hybrid seeds, and "planted by the change of a full moon, especially (when planting) ground crops." Toby Woods did not leave anything to chance.[4] I am sure that the 20 truckloads of pecan leaves and the truck load of soy bean hulls that he worked into the soil were more important than the phase of the moon at planting time. Toby Woods was into heirloom tomatoes at a time when genetically altered plants were gaining popularity (Whiteside 1977).[5] Mr. Woods did plant the popular Super Beefsteak and Big Boy hybrids, but came to the conclusion that the "old time varieties" of tomatoes were tastier and would grow as big as the new genetically engineered tomato plants if given proper attention. During his conversation with Ms. Davis, Toby Woods failed to mention one of his proudest agricultural triumphs. He was pleased that his restored ten-acre pecan orchard could, in a good year, produce up to 20,000 pounds of the finest nuts in this part of Georgia.

Abundance was survival in the Woods' world. John Toby and Gladys Woods were also proud of their garden's ability to provide the necessities of life. The fruits and vegetables were an essential part of their larder, and well-stocked pantry, which always had a year's supply of food stored in case of an emergency. There were always at least two freezers that were filled to the brim. The Woods had, in their lifetimes, experienced "hard times" and even in a time of plenty they were prepared for the worst. Gladys Woods' pantry was like a supermarket, and she was prepared to make dinner for a single visitor or a dozen visitors. Her years on the island taught her to be ready for anything (Figure 143).

I was not surprised at what Toby Woods has able to produce on the old Tucker-Evans Place that he bought from the R. L. Fruittichgers. Knowing how well he had maintained a 23,000-acre island, a 150-acre farm would be "a piece of cake." Free from the need to remove moss from the trees, keep the fleet boats in the water, and clear the fields for the cattle, or prepare for one of Mr. Noble's hunts, Toby Woods was in his element. It was an easy task to keep his tractor and truck running. Not having to fix the power plant or the Farmall, he instead built his own garden cart with bicycle tires that rivaled anything sold at the local Western Auto or Ace Hardware store in Savannah. The cart was similar to the popular Vermont garden cart that was designed to haul heavy loads. Toby said that his cart war so efficient that it would "roll by itself."

In 1961 when he moved to the farm on Olive Street in Newington, he was ready to transform it. He quickly renovated the dilapidated house that stood on the land (Figure 144). The Woods cleared the 150-acres farm of underbrush. According to John, he bulldozed all the fences and redid them the way that he wanted. He has his pasture, forest, orchards, vineyards, and gardens fenced separately. For a few years, he even had a herd of up to 25 brood cows on the farm. But he found that cattle tied him to the farm and restricted his opportunities to travel.

At the time of their 64th wedding anniversary in 1988, Gladys Woods told the *Sylvania Telephone* (Lee 1988: 4) that they "wanted to get away from the salt water." After 32 ½ years on the St. Catherines, I could understand their desire for change. Martha Lee (1988:4) described their life on the island: "There were no schools, churches, or stores on the island and trips to the mainland were eleven miles by water. Twice a month they traveled by boat for the mail and once a month for supplies."

Figure 144. John Toby Woods' farmhouse in Newington, soon after its renovation in 1961.

Toby planted fruit orchards, and built two fish ponds that he connected to the water supply of the house. Toby used a quarter of a mile of 1.5" PVC pipe to supply water to the ponds. He even stocked the pond with fish for "his older friends" to use. Given a choice, he preferred to fish in the Savannah River. Toby was proud of the crops that he planted in rows as straight as if they had been laid out with a surveyor's transit.

One thing that Toby Woods' did not leave on St. Catherines was his ability to multitask. He did all of this work on the farm while constructing a house for John in Sunbury.

Apply for the superintendent position was a tough decision in some ways. John owned a shrimp boat and had a well-paying job inspecting and repairing engines in Key West for J. H. Morgan, who had a fleet of 15 shrimp boats docked there.[6] John told me that, "It was easy to make money in Key West. When I wasn't keeping the engines repaired for J. H. Morgan,[7] I could work on other engines or on my own, and in Key West I sold marine batteries and other marine supplies on the side. I also had income coming from my shrimp boat."

Alger B. Chapman, Executive Director of the E. J. Noble Foundation, soon hired John to be superintendent. Mr. Chapman, as John always addressed and referred to him, was an extremely busy executive. John appreciated that, given his many responsibilities, Mr. Chapman always had time to talk with him about family and other matters not related to the functioning of the iIsland (Figure 145).

187

If there is a theme to this untold history of St. Catherines, it is the role of "giants" like Musgrove, Bosomworth, Waldburg, Rauers, Keys, and Noble that shaped the island's development. Add to that list Alger B. Chapman, who was often the man "behind the scenes" and an important figure in E. J. Noble's successful career. Chapman was a successful tax attorney when Governor Thomas E. Dewey met him and was so impressed that he appointed him chief tax and financial officer for the State of New York. Chapman's appointment came with a salary of $12,000, which was considered hefty at that time.[8] Dewey often bragged about his well paid aides (Ryan 1948). While Dewey was proud that the New York State government salaries were higher than those being paid for similar

Figure 145. Alger B. Chapman and John Toby Woods on Colonels Island. Picture taken just after John retired and left the island in September 1982.

positions in the federal government, they were well below what Chapman had earned in the private sector. Chapman had paid taxes on an income of $150,000 the year before he accepted Dewey's $12,000 offer to join the state government.[9]

In 1943, Chapman and Brady Bryson (1943), who would later become partners, wrote an influential article on excess profits. In that same year, Bryson wrote the contact for the National Broadcasting Company's sale of the Blue Network to E. J. Noble (Rasmussen 2006). Bryson later had an illustrious career serving as a lawyer during the Nuremberg trials.

In 1946, Dewey entrusted Chapman to run his successful campaign for reelection as New York State Governor. Chapman chaired Dewey's successful bid for governor again in 1950 (NYT 1950a). It was Chapman who was able to "deliver" New York during Dewey's unsuccessful run for president in 1948,[10] and during Dwight D. Eisenhower's successful bids in 1952 and 1956 (Saxon 1983a). Even the famed John Foster Dulles called on Chapman to run his campaign for the United States Senate (NYT 1949c). Long after his active role in politics, John remembers Chapman receiving phone calls from presidential candidates seeking advice and counsel on a speech they had just made.

In 1949, Chapman was elected to the board of directors of ABC (American Broadcasting Company) (NYT 1949b). He had been in practicing law as a senior partner in the Chapman and Bryson law firm. After Paramount acquired ABC (American Broadcasting Company), Chapman was elected to its board of directors in 1959 (NYT 1959a).

In 1956, Life Saver merged with the Beech-Nut Company, and E. J. Noble was named as Chairman of the Board (WSJ 1956). At that time Mr. Chapman was not listed as a board member, but in 1958 he became chairman of the board of directors of Beech-Nut Life Saver (NYT 1959b).[11] He is recognized as the force behind Beech-Nut Life Saver Company's expansion into the food service industry and beyond with the merger of Dobbs Houses[12] (WSJ 1966), and later with the acquisition of cosmetic and toiletry companies (WSJ 1964). After the company merged with E.R. Squibb in 1967[13] (WSJ 1967), Chapman became the chairman of the Squibb Beech-Nut Corporation.[14] He retired from Squibb in 1974 to become finance chairman of Governor Malcolm Wilson's election campaign[15] (WSJ 1974).

When John and I talked about Mr. Chapman's accomplishments, he was not surprised. John described Mr. Chapman as the smartest person he has ever known. He relished the idea of working with someone who was so smart and so down to earth, and he was ready for the challenge. He recalls,

I was glad to get the job, even if it was lot less money, so I sold my shrimp boat to a shrimper in Port Royal, South Carolina for more than I paid for it. I bought a lot at Sunbury and moved my mobile home from Key West to Sunbury. I moved my family (Katherine, Holly and Johnny) (Figure 146) to my mobile home in Sunbury. I moved our furniture out of my house in Savannah to the superintendent's house and rented my house in Savannah.

Figure 146. Johnny Woods on the tractor that he would drive after it was started by his father and put into gear. Johnny learned to stop it by turning off the key. Ca 1963.

When John returned to St. Catherines as superintendent, he inherited many familiar faces as employees.

When I went to work on St. Catherines, the employees that lived on the island and worked for my father were Aunt Snooker and Uncle Hubert Holmes.[16] They lived in the "big" house. Snooker was the housekeeper (Figure 147). Uncle Woodrow Roger lived with my mother and father in the superintendent's house. Paul Robbins and his wife Peggy lived in No. 1 employee cottage.[17] Uncle George Berryhill and Aunt Annie and their three children[18] lived in Cottage No. 2. Jack and Carmen Baughcom lived in No 3.

Figure 147. Snooker Chapman was in charge of main house.

My daddy continued to live with us on the island for awhile, as he wanted to help with the construction of the new R.E.A. electric cable[19] on St. Catherines in 1961. The island furnished the boat and barge used to put the cable in. Mr. J.B. Bargenon was the manager of Coastal EMC and a friend of Daddy's.

When John took over as superintendent, St. Catherines and the Foundation was still in the cattle business. E. J. Noble eventually had up to 300 head of Black Angus as brood cows. John said that the cattle business had not changed from his father's time on the island.

We sold the cows and yearlings that we didn't want to keep in the fall of the year so that we didn't have to feed them through the winter. The cattle were considered range cattle, as they ranged the whole island to eat. In the winter they also fed on the hard marsh flats and the spartinia marsh around the edges of the island. We sold the yearlings as feeders. My Daddy always used the Swainsboro stockyard owned by Forrest Lewis. I chose to use the Baxley Stockyard owned by Mr. H G Miles since they were bigger and had more buyers. Farmers would bid on the cattle and turn them out on their corn fields to fatten them for slaughter. I enjoyed going the stockyard to see the cows being auctioned off. You had to pay attention at the auction. In case that they didn't bid high enough, you could cancel the sale.

Although the cattle were free ranging, there was still a great deal of work involved in maintaining them. In the summer, they had college students help harvest the hay for the winter. While the cows would graze on the hard marsh flats, their feeding had to be supplemented. We put away 10,000 bales every winter. There was also the problem of transporting them to the stockyards. The cows were taken on a barge to Half Moon where we would drive them off of the barge through chutes that would take them to trucks from the stockyards. As John describes it, it was not always an easy chore:

> One time when we were pushing a barge load of semi-wild cattle to the mainland to sell, about halfway there, the barge started sinking. I pushed the barge up on a sand bar that was about three feet under the water. The cattle stood neck deep in water until we could get extra pumps and pump out the barge and stop the leaks. They could have escaped, but they didn't. They had nowhere to go.

Dr. Willis Hollingsworth was hired as the island's veterinarian.[20] Hollingsworth was frequently called to vaccinate the cattle to prevent diseases such as brucellosis. Hollingsworth was also called in to castrate the bulls. After a couple of the bulls died from hemorrhaging after the operation, John told me that he (John) became the chief castrator. He had developed a method of castrating hogs that was more effective and safer for the animal.

> We also trapped and sold wild hogs to the Baxley stock market. They brought a good price, as most of them went to hunting preserves. We also had a small international Diesel powered saw mill that we used to cut long leaf heart pine trees and used the lumber for docks, bridges, hog pens, and cattle chute's, etc.

> When Mr. Noble was living, he used Judge Joe Oliver as the island's attorney. After Mr. Noble died and Judge Joe Oliver was no longer used, daddy recommended that Mr. Chapman hire Judge John Underwood from Hinesville to legally represent the island. I had known him when I was in high school and also when working at Sunbury. We used the county agent for advice on planting and other agricultural activities. Jones People and Joe Collins were frequent visitors to the island. Joe Collin supervised the ditching of the island when daddy was in charge.

Ten years after the death of Mr. Noble (1968) and the transfer of St. Catherines to the Edward J. Noble Foundation, many options were considered for the island.

> During this time, St. Catherines was part of the Noble Estate. The Noble Estate would consider a buyer for the island. Charles Fraser from Hilton S.C. came over to talk with Mr. Chapman about buying the island to develop, but didn't come up with enough money to be interesting.

Charles E. Fraser was a member of a legendary family that lived in Liberty County. General Joseph P. Fraser, Charles father, served in World Wars I and II, the Korean War, and commanded the South Carolina National Guard (Martin 2002). He was also deeply involved in the timber business. In 1949, the General and Fred C. Hack were "timber magnets." Through their corporation, the Hilton Head Company, they bought 8,000 acres on the southern end of Hilton Island so that they could harvest the sea pines that densely populated the island. The following year, Hack, Fraser and a new investor, Olin T. McIntosh, formed the Honey Horn Plantation Company and purchased an additional 12,000 acres. Charles E. Fraser, General Fraser's son and a Yale trained lawyer, convinced his father that Hilton Head would be a better investment as a planned resort. It was this concept that led the *New York Times* (Riddle 1996) to call Charles Fraser "the visionary pioneer of Hilton Head Island." Fraser had learned the tool of creating covenants in law school and believed that could control the ecological impact of development on the island. While Fraser is often thought of as an environmentalist, his concern for ecology was based on a motive to increase profits. He believed that the land would be worth more for development if it were in a pleasant setting. This model was so successful that Fraser's protégés became significant figures in the Disney Company and many other residential development companies.

While Charles Fraser may have been interested in St. Catherines, he was never willing to buy it outright. He sought to partner with the Noble Foundation in the development of the island. Mr. Chapman was not interested in having the Noble Foundation involved in such an endeavor. There was another obstacle preventing its sale. It would be necessary to build a bridge to provide easy access for its inhabitants. At Hilton Head, the state built the bridge to the island and it was doubtful that the State of Georgia would be as generous.

John told me that there were always people coming to St. Catherines and investigating the possibility of purchasing the island. John, who knew the island best, would spend the day showing them all of the "nooks and crannies" of the island. John remembers a Texan who flew in and was given the tour of the island. At the end of the trip, the Texan looked at John and commented, "Hell, son, if we can't put oil wells on it, we don't need it; I don't have much use for land without oil. I have all the land that I need."

It was at this time that that NASA considered St. Catherines as the site for a launch facility. Cumberland Island was rejected since it would have created "unacceptable interference with the Intracoastal Waterway" and suffered from a lack of infrastructure. St. Catherines shared both of these shortcomings and therefore never made it to the "short list" of possible flights. Ultimately, NASA acquired Merritt Island land and the rest is history.

Just when you thought that you had heard it all, John would relate an event that surprised even me. He said that at one time St. Catherines was considered as the "moon launching site" before NASA decided on Cape Canaveral. He was not sure how seriously they were considering St. Catherines, but they did have diagrams showing a proposed bridge from Harris Neck to St.

Catherines. It turns out that in the early 1960s, NASA was considering as many as 100 Saturn-type launches per year that would require a mobile launch concept (Lethbridge 2006). According to Cliff Lethbridge, Cape Canaveral could accommodate only a small percentage of the launches and therefore many other sites would be needed so that rockets from a central facility could be transported by train or barge. This concept of multiple launch sites was scrapped after President John F. Kennedy announced on May 25, 1961 that the United States would send a man to the moon and return him to earth by the end of the decade. NASA was forced to quickly settle on a location to meet the President's goal. NASA wanted to acquire Merritt Island, which is just west of the Cape, but the Air Force had already claimed it as the area where they would develop their own space program. Lethbridge reports that NASA considered Merritt Island, man-made facilities offshore of Cape Canaveral, Mayaguana Island in the Bahamas, Mainland Site near Brownsville, Texas, White Sands Missile Range in New Mexico, Christmas Island in the South Pacific, South Point Island in Hawaii, and Cumberland Island off the coast of Georgia.

Alger B. Chapman Remembered

John had a special affection for Mr. Chapman. Chapman was the executive director of the Edward J. Noble Foundation when John was hired in November 1960.

> Mr. Chapman would spend a week's vacation on St. Catherines most every year. He would usually bring Mr. and Mrs. English, and his wife and two sons, Bill and Duke with him. By the time I went to work on St. Catherines, his wife had died. Later he would bring his secretary Catherine Hubbard, who he later married.

> Mr. Chapman would tell me about when he managed Governor Dewey's presidential campaign, or when Mr. Noble bought the Blue Network, later the American Broadcasting Company, and wrote out a check for $8,000,000.00 to pay for it. In the early 40s that was big money, and according to Mr. Chapman, Wall Street was impressed.

> I remember one time, I had just bought a new International 4-wheel-drive Scout for the island. Mr. Chapman, his wife, and another couple drove to the north end of North Beach. Mr. Chapman was showing off for his guests attempted to drive across the sand bars to Bird Island. The Scout drowned out and they had to walk home through the Engineers Road over 3 miles.

> We took the World War II army truck. When we got to the Scout just the windshield was showing. We took a long rope and pulled it out and back to the shop. I had it running by the next morning, but it soon rusted out. Mr. Chapman was really embarrassed. I felt sorry for him.

Skipper Chapman Duffy remembered the event well. She was a couple of months pregnant and walked the three miles back to get help. She said that Chapman, as she called her stepfather, would not accept a ride back in the army truck that rescued them. After dinner that night, she said that all that Chapman could talk about was how he walked the three miles back on Engineers Road. His role in the fiasco had conveniently passed from his "steel trap" memory.

When Aunt Snooker retired in the early 70s, we needed somebody to replace her as caretaker of the "big" house. The Sierra Club came over for their annual camping trip. With them was Virginia Blackwood (Figure 148). When I gave them a tour of the "big" house and told them that we needed a housekeeper, Virginia immediately held up her hand and said that she would like to apply for the job. I discussed with her what she would be getting into. Being impressed with her attitude and personality, I decided to call Mrs. Larkin, Mr. Noble's daughter on the board of the E.J. Noble Foundation. She gave me permission to hire Virginia. I found out later that she couldn't cook. I thought that all middle-aged women could cook. I was really mad, but she told me that she would buy some cookbooks and learn. She was the daughter of a wealthy medical doctor from Atlanta and had been the wife of a big time lawyer.

Returning to Mr. Chapman:

Mr. and Mrs. Chapman would often visit the island. Virginia, with her personality, would get invited into the big living room to talk to them. They were talking one night when Mrs. Chapman said that they were ready to eat. (Virginia had forgotten to cook dinner).

That didn't matter too much; for a while they had trouble eating it [the food] anyway. Mr. Chapman would brag on the food and Mrs. Chapman would turn blue, she would be so mad.

Figure 148. Virginia Blackwood cooking.

One morning, I went to the "big" house to pick up Mr. and Mrs. Chapman to take them to the airport. They were in the kitchen telling Virginia good bye. Mr. Chapman was dressed to travel with his suit on and fine New York hat. He was flipping his hat and trying to catch it on his head. Each time he was missing and Mrs. Chapman was getting madder and madder. She said, "Alger, don't do that again." Mr. Chapman asked her, "What are was going to do about it?" Mrs. Chapman said "Do it again, and I will show you." So he flipped it again and missed. She lifted her foot with her high-heeled shoe and stomped the hat flat. Alger said, "Catherine, that is the worst thing that you have ever done to me." Then he thought for a minute and said, "almost."

Virginian later told me one reason Mrs. Chapman was so mad. Alger always gave her a $100.00 tip when they left, and she would laugh at his jokes.

We thought the world of Mr. Chapman. Although he did have a drinking problem, especially when he was on the island.

One time, not long after we had hired Virginia, I picked up Mr. and Mrs.
Chapman at the airport and brought them to the island and to the "big"
house. Virginia did not have Mr. Chapman's liquor set out for him (like
Aunt Snooker always did). We kept it locked up in the gun room cabinet
and Virginia couldn't find the key. I thought that he was going to fire both
of us before I could pull the pins out of the cabinet hinges and get the
liquor.

"Skipper" Chapman[21] remembers visiting St. Catherines with her stepfather, who she
affectionately called "Chapman." She made her first trip to the island in 1959 when she was 14
years old, and it became an annual event. She learned to drive on the island in the jeep that had
no brakes. Skipper said that Snooker Chapman, the cook in the big house (no relation to them),
became such a maternal figure that she and her mother called Snooker "mom." She became
friends with Snooker's son Ben and his wife Louise, and they remain friends to this day. She
said that Snooker was the "perfect mother" and was "kind hearted" to all the children. She said
that in addition to all her gifts as a human being, she was also an exceptional cook. Skipper said
that Snooker would always have a chocolate meringue pie ready when she arrived to St.
Catherines. Snooker's chicken pot pies were a special treat. She was on the island when Charles
Mayo and his wife spent a month there. Skipper said that they raved every day about the meals
that Snooker prepared for them.

Mr. Chapman was always concerned about the health of the staff on St. Catherines. When
Aunt Snooker was having some circulation problems with the arteries supplying blood to her
brain, Mr. Chapman was worried. John remembers,

> When Aunt Snooker was our housekeeper, she had been going to the
> doctors in Savannah. Her arteries going to her head were partially clogged
> and the doctors wanted to operate on them. Mr. Chapman paid her way to
> New York and had his personal physician examine her. His Doctor
> recommended that they not to operate. Aunt Snooker outlived her two
> former husbands by well over 25 years. She died in 2006 at ninety years
> old.

> Once when Uncle Woodrow was sick and not able to work, Mr. Chapman,
> at the expense of the Foundation, sent him to the Mayo Clinic in Minnesota.
> They examined him and decided that there was not much that they could do.

John and the staff quickly developed a rapport with the island's visitors. Charles Mayo, the
iconoclastic son of one of the founders of the Mayo Clinic, spent a month there writing his
memoirs. John said that he would frequently take Dr. Mayo and his wife on afternoon tours of
the island. John and Dr. Mayo were talking about Woodrow and John asked about his prognosis.

> Later, when Dr. Charles Mayo and his wife spent a month on St. Catherines
> when he was writing his memoirs (Mayo 1968), he told me that the only
> thing that he knew to do for Woodrow, would be to take him to the end of
> the dock and push him overboard.

John Saves Mr. Chapman's Life.

Mr. Chapman, (during the time the "big" house was being rebuilt) called and said that he and Catherine, his wife, were coming to St. Catherines for the weekend and that they would do their own cooking. I bought the food for them and brought them to the island.

The next afternoon, a Saturday, I was driving my jeep down the Oyster Shell road (Figure 149) when Mrs. Chapman who was by the swimming pool saw me and started waving and yelling for me to come. She was in a panic. Mr. Chapman was floating face down in the swimming pool.

Mrs. Chapman said that Alger was playing tricks on her. I told her that if she didn't mind that I pulled off my pants, I would dive in and pull him out. Of course, I had on my underwear.

I dove in and towed him down to the shallow end of the pool and pulled him out, which was quite a job since he weighed well over 200 lbs. That was before the pool was remodeled, and the sides were about a foot and half above the water.

I laid him down on his stomach and so that the water could drain while I was trying to resuscitate him. Mr. Chapman had turned dark blue. Having no luck, I turn him over on his back, removed his false teeth, pinched his nose closed and started blowing air into his lungs.

I told Mrs. Chapman to go to my house and get my wife, who was a public health nurse.

To my surprise in a short time he started taking short breaths and started breathing better. He finally came to. The first thing he said to me was, "What round is this?"

By that time Mrs. Chapman was back with my wife Katherine. Mr. Chapman motioned for his wife to come to him and whispered, "Where are my teeth?"

What had happened was both of them had had several drinks. Mr. Chapman had taken off his pants and told Mrs. Chapman that he was going to dive in. She said no, and he sailed in belly first, knocking the air out of him.

By that time, two of the college boys had come up, and we put him in a lawn chair and rolled him to their cabin. I sent my 12-year-old son Johnny to the mainland to call for an ambulance. He came back to the island but

Mr. Chapman would not go to the emergency room. I had to send Johnny back to let them know that we were not coming. He traveled 44 miles during those trips. At the time, we only had a 2-way radio at the house at Sunbury, and Katherine was on the Island. I wanted to take him to the hospital but he wouldn't go. We had to stay with him most of the night. He was freezing one minute and burning up the next. The next day (Sunday) he was well enough for me to take them to the airport. He said that he had never been so sore in all his life.

On their next visit to the Island, they brought me a nice gold watch. Since it was not waterproof, I gave it to Katherine. It would not have lasted me very long back then. That happened in 1971 and he died in 1983, so I guess he could thank me for those last twelve years. And I also thank him for all that he did for me in those 12 years.

Alger B. Chapman died on November 3, 1983 (Saxon 1983a). On May 7th at the grand Marble Collegiate Church on Fifth Avenue, preacher Norman Vincent Peale gave the eulogy at his funeral. It was a fitting tribute to a life well lived.

Figure 149. Oyster Shell Road connecting the bridge to the "big" house. Four cabins on the left were facing the road. Cabins 5, 6, and 7 on the other side were facing Waldburg creek and were staggered so that they would have a view of the water.

16

Salvaging the *Pinta* and the Decline of the Shrimping Industry

John was showing me some slides of St. Catherines' landmarks when a picture of a beached ship flashed on the screen. The vessel's name, *Pinta*, was barely visible under the ropes draped over it, and it was deeply mired in the sand of North Beach (Figure 150). An oil barrel under its bow seemed to keep it from tipping further on its side. In reading the history of St. Catherines, the drama of ships being driven on its beaches is a recurring story. In 1893, Jacob Rauers refused to allow the owners of the *Beatrice McLean* to recover their boat after it was blown onto the island. The *Atlanta Constitution* (AC 1893a:3) headline reported "Can't Get His Vessel, Captain Rauers

Wants $500 Because a Schooner Went Up on His Island." The schooner was driven onto the island by the 1893 hurricane that devastated the Sea Islands (AC 1893f:1). Rauers demanded compensation for the damage to his island. Matthew Balmer, the ship's master, took Rauers to Superior Court to seek relief. But that's another story. I was brought back to the image, and asked John why the oil barrel was holding up the boat.

John began to tell me the story,

Figure 150. The Pinta aground on St. Catherines's North Beach (1962). Katherine Woods by the Pilot House.

> On July of 1962, the shrimp boat *Pinta*, dragging in Glory Hole on the north end of St. Catherines, went aground when a Northeaster pushed it up on to the beach. Lawrence Jacobs of Valona, Georgia was buying the *Pinta* from Mr. Hugh Burrows, who had the boat built at St. Augustine, Florida in 1957. The *Pinta* was 55 feet long, 17 feet 3 inches wide and had a draft of 6 feet 7 inches and a net weight of 24 tons. Mr. Burrows, with another one of his shrimp boats, tried to get the *Pinta* off of the beach for several weeks. As the Northeasters kept pushing the boat higher up on the beach, they gave up. They removed the engine and all the rigging then left the *Pinta* on the beach. I knew the boat well. In 1957, I was working for Morgan's Inc., which was the source of machinery for the *Pinta*. They had sent me to St. Augustine to inspect the *Pinta* and I took it out on its first trial run.

As he told me the story, many questions emerged. I wasn't familiar with the spot where the *Pinta* had gone aground. John said that it "went aground on sand bars out from North Beach." He pointed out that North Beach has changed dramatically in the last half of the century. Bird Island sanctuary was just a sand bar out from the beach at that time. I asked John why he would be sent to inspect the *Pinta*. Morgan's[1] required an inspection before every boat was put into service. As John told me, they would not even let the shrimp boat owner connect the electrical system. As the master mechanic for the company, Morgan's sent John up and down the east coast for inspections.

John knew Hugh Burrows, and this provided an opportunity to ask him for the salvage rights. Lawrence Jacobs was buying the *Pinta* from Burrows, who had purchased the salvage rights.

> I had worked for Mr. Burrows before and he knew my father, who was superintendent of St. Catherines at that time. By then it began filling up with sand and Mr. Burrows had bought the rights of salvage from the insurance company. He also had little success since the boat was rapidly filling with sand. After the *Pinta* had been abandoned I asked Mr. Burrows if he would sign a deed giving me the abandoned hull. He was glad to, as they had taken everything of value off.

I asked John what his friends thought of his plans to get the *Pinta* off the beach. In the decade that I have known John, I have been in awe of his ability to solve problems that seem intractable. Even with his reputation as a wizard, I was sure that his friends thought that he had taken on an impossible task. He replied:

> Everybody that I brought to see the shrimp boat high on the beach filling with beach sand said that it couldn't be saved. I asked Mr. Chapman if I could try to salvage the hull on my own time in the late afternoons, nights, and on the weekends. He said sure, but he thought that I was wasting my time. He did like the idea of me giving a try.

John had a team that was willing to help him. Jack Baughcom was an expert in boat repair. He had the ability to work with wood in ways that were ultimately important in making the *Pinta* seaworthy.

> I did have help with my friends that were working on the island. Jack Baughcom and Hubert Holmes were willing to help me. John Underwood's two sons, Johnny and Joe, helped me when they could. Johnny hauled two truckloads of second hand oil drums from Fort Stewart for me.

I was still puzzled by how John planned to get the *Pinta* off the beach, given the previous failures of Jacobs and Burrows. John responded:

> I rented a 4-inch mud hog pump from Morgan's, Inc. and on high tides started pumping sand out of the hull. We took the oil drums along with two 500-gallon fuel tanks and would fasten them in the bottom. After pumping the sand out, we would then wait for a spring tide. Fortunately, most spring tides are either early in the morning or late in the afternoon.[2]

I purchased a 600 feet of ¾-inch nylon rope, and when the spring tide was at its highest point, we would take the island freight boat. The St. Catherine was 40 feet long with a 3½-foot draft. It had a 225-hp Gray marine diesel engine with a 1½ to 1 reduction gear. I also had my 16-foot outboard to take the rope from the *Pinta* out to the freight boat. We would then pull the rope tight with the freight boat and wait until we saw a big wave going toward the *Pinta*. I would then pull full throttle. The ¾-inch nylon rope would stretch about 50 feet and the freight boat would stall and slingshot back about 100 feet. It was a strange to feel the freight boat "slingshotting" back at about 30 miles per hour. On one of our tries, we hit the end of the rope full throttle, the rope broke and we shot forward. Uncle Woodrow was watching on the beach, and he told me later that the rope snapped and it sounded like a cannon had been fired.

In retrospect, John told me just how dangerous this tactic was since the backward catapult could have easily resulted in the boat flipping over. While John was and is an extremely competent pilot, he still considers himself lucky. By then, he had become discouraged and considered letting the *Pinta* rot on the beach.

The spring tides would take loose the tanks and drums and put more sand in the bilge. We would have to start over again. I was just about ready to give upon getting the *Pinta* off the beach, giving it a last try, full throttle stall and shooting backward, when the *Pinta* started moving. We kept up the process and finally pulled the *Pinta* off the beach. It was just before dark as we pulled the *Pinta* down Waldburg Creek, floating deck deep in the water. There were a number of shrimp boats anchored in Waldburg Creek. They waved and cheered as we passed them.

Some of the shrimpers had been watching the process from the ocean and I found out later that they had been making bets that we would not be able to recover the hull. We pulled the *Pinta* up to the Cattle Dock and tied it off. Everybody said that it would just rot there, but with Jack's expert help we fitted new boards in the hull at low tide, when the boat was aground. The boat didn't leak too much. I was able to keep it floating by pumping it out. A short time later, I had a shrimp boat tow the *Pinta* to a railway in McIntosh County. I believe it was J. W. Brannon's railway at Bellville.

While John had a hull, he still needed to outfit the boat. Again, John relied on his knowledge as a master marine mechanic to bring the *Pinta* back to life (Figure 151).

Mr. Hugh Burrows had the 6.71 Series Detroit Diesel engine with the 4 ½ reduction gear rebuilt at Morgan's Inc. in Savannah. I borrowed the money from the bank and bought back the engine and rigging. I had the boat rebuilt and had the engine and rigging installed along with a new 3-inch brass shaft and a new 36 x 46 propeller. I got a 5-year loan at 6%, and brought the *Pinta* to J.H. Morgan's dock at Sunbury, GA (summer 1963).

I hired Albert Campbell as captain and his brother Elliot as striker. They were from Harris Neck. Their mother told me that, as a child, they would row over to St. Catherines to go to church. She was the older sister of Sonny Timmons, the famous oyster man and crabber. People from all around this area of coastal Georgia still buy oysters from him in the winter.[3]

John was pleased with the success of the *Pinta*. He sent the boat to Key West.

In the fall of the year, I sent the *Pinta* to J.H. Morgan and Son's shrimp dock in Key West. My Uncle Albert Rogers was bookkeeper there and he also had a couple shrimp boats of his own (Figure 152). My boat stayed there fishing in the gulf at night for over two years that I didn't see it. I was happy since they were sending me a check every couple of weeks.

When they finally came back, I had to send it to Thunderbolt to get the bottom re-nailed with stainless steel nails after all the punishment it had taken on the beach and Key West fishing. Financially, I think that I would have been better off had I just bought a boat. Anyway I paid off the 5-year loan in 3 ½ years. I never missed a payment, and many months I doubled up on a payment.

His success was had an impact on his friends. He said that,

> My friend Curtis Lee saw some of the checks that I was getting and decided he wanted to build fiberglass shrimp boats. In 1968, he built the first fiberglass shrimp boat that I know of on the east coast, and I was stupid enough to buy it.

I had heard that marijuana was being smuggled into Colonels Island and the surrounding area by using shrimp boats. John described those times,

Figure 151. Jack Waters and Everett Dix on the restored *Pinta*

During the time I owned the *Pinta* and later the *Laura Lee*, marijuana was being brought into this country by shrimp boat and unloaded along the coast. Some was unloaded at Laura View and any remote place that they could fine. Several friends of mine served time that was involved.

One friend of mine tried to get me to send the *Pinta* to the Bahamas to pick up a load of "chicken feed" (marijuana), bring it off shore from St.

Catherines Sound. He would pick up the marijuana with speedboats and bring it in.

I was not interested in the so-called easy money. I always lived within my means and really didn't need the money. This friend that wanted me to have the *Pinta* bring in chicken feed for him later got caught flying drugs across the Mexican border also had to serve time.[4]

I asked John how long was he in the shrimping business. He replied:

Albert and Elliot Campbell continued to shrimp the *Pinta* until 1968. I then sold the *Pinta* to my friend, who wanted me to go the Bahamas for a load of chicken feed. As far as I known, he did not use it to smuggle marijuana. He made money fishing for shrimp. After selling the *Pinta*, I bought the *Laura Lee* from Curtis Lee (the boat was named after his granddaughter). I put Albert and Elliot on the *Laura Lee* and fished out at Sunbury late summer. My payment plus insurance was $1,000 per month.

Mr. Tommy Thompson, one of Mr. Noble's top men at the Life Saver Company, met Della Armstrong (she helped serve meals) and fell in love with her while on a annual Life Saver meeting on St. Catherines.,...Years later, after his wife had died and Della's husband had died, he moved to Savannah to be with her. He got me to help him pick out a boat for him and Della from Fountain Marine at Thunderbolt. He chose a 24-foot inboard-outboard cabin boat with a 150 horse V-6 Buick engine and an OMC out drive. I had to teach him how to run it since he had never owned a boat before. We also brought the boat to my dock at Sunbury where he and Della could take it out on practice runs.

I told Mr. Tommy that I was going to have to borrow money to pay for the *Laura Lee*. He said that he would be glad to lend me the money at 6% interest. The *Laura Lee* did real well fishing out of Sunbury. By the time I got ready to send it to Key West in December, I was well ahead on boat payments and had over $10,000 in the boat account. I paid Mr. Tommy Thompson back in full ahead of time. Never missed or was late on a payment.

John said that there were times when he was sorry that he became a shrimper, but as he said, things worked out for him. He gave me an example.

On the way to Key West the *Laura Lee* ran into rough seas and bent the out riggers (which was not strong enough to start with). Albert and Elliot had to take the boat into Fort Pierce to have the out riggers rebuilt. When they started fishing out of Key West, everything seemed to go wrong. The hydraulics wench oil lines were busting, creating the problem of having to get the nets in by hand turning the wench. The hydraulic steering was too slow (you have to be able to spin the wheel to dock the boat). Finally Etherige Morgan called and said that he was sending the boat back to Sunbury. That he couldn't keep it working.

I had to have all the hydraulics removed and replaced with mechanical steering and wench. Having done this, I put the boat back to work and it did fine, and I was glad to have a fiberglass boat with a lot less maintenance problems. I could go two years without going to the railway; worms didn't cause problems like they would on a wooden boat.

When we were talking with Sonny Timmons and his wife, they said that Albert Campbell was not doing well. They said that they thank God that he had social security. John was proud that he had paid social security for his shrimpers. As he said, it was the right thing to do.

During the time I had the *Laura Lee*, Elliott Campbell was called into the service and was in the Vietnam conflict. When he got out of the service two years later, he came back to be on the boat with his brother Albert. Finally in September 1974, I sold the *Laura Lee* to the St. Catherines Island Foundation for use as a freight boat. The Foundation needed it to replace the island boat and barge, which were worn out. I got Albert and Elliot a job fishing for my Uncle Albert Rogers' fine shrimp boat built by Diesel Engine Sales in St. Augustine, and they took it back to Key West that winter. I always paid Social Security on Albert and Elliot; most boat owners didn't as they were considered self-employed.

Old Time Shrimp Boats

John talked about what he called "old time shrimp boats." He remembers his daddy talking about the shrimp boats coming to St. Catherines.

Back in the early '30s, when the Keys owned the island and everybody was broke, daddy let some of the shrimp boats tie up at the main dock. They mostly worked for Mr. Ambos out of Thunderbolt. He owned a fleet of shrimp and oyster boats that he built on the shore at Thunderbolt. They were small boats anywhere from 30 to 50 feet long with wooden masts and booms. The one net that they pulled was brought in with a rope rig (double block and tackle). A 10-quart bucket was used to wash the shrimp and deck

The double block and tackle, though more efficient that a single block and tackle, is still quite limiting in bringing in the shrimp. The shrimper is limited to a single net. Even the steering mechanisms were limited. John describes:

The steering system was a rope spool attached to the steering wheel. The rope went back to the rudder through a series of pulleys. A hand pump was used to pump out the boat

There were wooden water tanks built on the sides of the pilot's house. The tanks were built about a foot higher than the deck so they could turn on a spigot to fill a pot with water. They used mostly kerosene stoves. The only navigational aid they had was a compass. They talked from one boat to another with hand signals. If the boats leaked bad, they have to sleep with one foot in the bilge to let them know when to pump out the water. Down in the ice hold, there would be 300-pound blocks of ice. They would shave off the ice to spread on the shrimp.

The shrimp boats began to see improvements in the boats and the nets. They started outfitting the boats with caterpillar engines and better drag nets. He describes the changes:

Later the boats had a caterpillar diesel engine. They didn't have electric starters. They had a small gas engine that they would hand crank with a rope that acted as a starter to get the diesel going.

I remember Mert Young, C. M. Briggs, and others that were friends of daddy. They would tie up overnight, get fresh water, head their shrimp, repair nets and other things that had to be done. After dark, some of them would come up to the house to play cards with daddy and mama. They were always ready for a game of Setback[5] or cribbage. They kept us in shrimp and sometimes, I would get a bag of candy. And we would keep them supplied with milk and vegetables.

I remember one time when strange shrimp boats tied up to the dock (I think that they were from Darien). Daddy told me to get a bucket and get a mess of shrimp for dinner. I went to their boats to get the shrimp. They were not very friendly and didn't speak much English. They threw a few shrimp in the bottom of the bucket. I showed daddy what they had given me. That was one of the few times I ever saw my daddy mad. He went down to dock and threw their ropes back on the boats. When they finally got their boat started and they circled back and said that they left their dog on the island. Daddy pulled out a single shot shotgun that kept in the oil house and told them to get going. Latter Daddy let another shrimp boat take them their dog.

A couple of the shrimper friends of daddy's had earlier been rum runners and had delivered rum to Uncle Luke.

Shrimp boats today are mostly made of fiberglass, steel, and wood. Most of the wooden boat bottoms have been covered with fiberglass. My son Johnny has a 65-foot long, 17 ½-foot' beam, 5 ½-foot draft fiberglass shrimp boat (the *Papa T*, see Figure 153). It has a 3406 turbo six-cylinder Caterpillar engine that produces 450 hp. There is a three-cylinder diesel generator that serves as a light plant and powers the air conditioner, hot water shower, toilet, radar, GPS plotter, color depth finder, automatic pilot, and compass that you hardly need any more because the plotter shows you where you to go. The plotter tells you how fast, how far, and where and how to get there. *The Papa T* has two radios—VHF and CB – and a heavy-duty cellular phone and color T.V., and gas stove and microwave oven.

Johnny pulls up to four nets or two 60-foot nets with 8 foot X 40 inch doors with stainless steel cables and stainless steel tickler chains that you pull in front of the nets to stir up the bottom so the shrimp will into the nets. He still has to use the 12-foot tri net (test net) that is used to find and to "stay on the shrimp." Each net has a turtle and fish excluder. Given all the expenses, the shrimpers are faced with a market in which the price for shrimp in now is lower that it was 20 years ago.

Figure 152. Uncle Albert's Two Shrimp Boats, *The Kathey Dean* and *Miss Sandra Dean*, Featured on the cover of *Coastal Georgia* magazine

Early in our discussion about the shrimping in the 1960s, John said that as business "got bad," many of the shrimpers "sold their boats to the Yankees." I replied to John that I found it hard to believe that a northerner would get into the declining shrimp business. John gave me an incredulous look that let me know that I had missed his point. "George", he replied, "the shrimpers burned their boats and collected the insurance money; that's selling it to the Yankees."

Shrimping as a business on the Georgia Coast is in decline. In the United States, 1.3 billion pounds of shrimp are eaten ever year, suggesting that business for the shrimpers should be excellent. However, when you realize that only 200 million pounds come from this country, you realize that shrimping is in a crisis (Lynn 2006). Most patrons (94%) of coastal Georgia restaurants assume that they are consuming locally harvested shrimp, but 80% are imported farm-raised critters (Lynn 2006).

Following the lead of the Vidalia Onion Cooperative, twenty eight Georgia shrimpers raised $500,000 and organized the Georgia Shrimp Association (GSA)[6] based in Darien (Chapman 2003a). The Georgia shrimpers have organized the "Wild Georgia Shrimp" campaign to help them stay afloat. John Wallace, president of the GSA, described the golden days of shrimping when there was an armada of 1500 trawlers, and days when he had catches that brought in $18,000 (Chapman 2003b).

At one time, there were 18 shrimp boats docked at Sunbury; now, there may be one or two. Danny Goodman from Sunbury built *The Amazing Grace* in 1987.[7] The trawler was truly amazing. The 101-foot fiberglass boat was powered by twin 500-horse powered Cumming diesel engines and had a speed of 10 knots. The trawler had a seven-foot draft with a 354,000 displacement. It could drag four 85-foot nets. *The Amazing Grace* could carry 9500 gallons of fuel and 2000 gallons of fresh water. The cost of fueling up *The Amazing Grace* was over $28,000 dollars. After outfitting the trawler with a freezing unit, Danny Goodman took the boat out a few times, but the coast of fuel made it an unprofitable endeavor. Smaller shrimp boats, such as *The Papa T*, have the same issues of fuel cost and the deflated price for shrimp. They do, however, have the advantage of flexibility.

Figure 153. The Papa T, Captain Johnny Woods, with Nets Ready to Drag. Note Sea Gulls on Out Rigger and Cables ready for a meal.

17

Life on the Mainland: The Excavation of Billy Joe Harris

In *Rich Man; Poor Men*, David Hurst Thomas and colleagues (Thomas, et al. 1977) tell the story about the excavation of W. J. L. Harris' burial, located between a live oak and palm tree next to the house that John Toby Woods was building on Billy Joe Point. The burial overlooks Sunbury Creek and the Medway River and is about 75 feet from the border of the salt marsh that extends about 600 feet to the bank of the creek. When I read the account, I was puzzled. I live about 800 feet from John's property, and I have always known it as Billy Harris Point. When I asked John about this discrepancy, he gave a simple answer: the point has always been "known" as Billy Joe Point, but was "written" as Billy Harris Point. I later found out that that the enslaved black populations and freed Blacks referred to it as Billy Joe Point as well.

Figure 154. The Grave before Restoration.

A report published by The American Museum of Natural History (AMNH) (Thomas, et al. 1977) described the excavation of the burial of the late Billy Joe Harris. He was born on May 1, 1841 and died on December 21, 1859. After a century of neglect (Figure 154), the grave adjacent to John's house was in ruins. John wanted to restore the grave and asked David Hurst Thomas to excavate the burial and study the remains. John would rebuild the vault and Billy Joe would be reinterred at a later date. The grave goods and material remains consisted of a few bones and 17 teeth of the late W. J. L. "Billy Joe" Harris. There is abundant evidence that great care was taken in preparing him for burial. The mahogany casket and buttons that were part of burial clothing were imported from England. These material remains are an indication that the family cared for Billy Joe as they laid him to rest.

In the century since his death and burial, natural processes have destroyed most of the coffin, and the weight of the dirt has crushed many of the bones. His burial below the natural ground level of the water assured some preservation of the mahogany casket. Unfortunately, fluctuations in the water level led to periodic soaking and drying of the wood, thus weakening the structural integrity of the casket. When the top of the casket collapsed, the damage was done. The remaining teeth show evidence of an enamel defect, suggesting that Billy Joe Harris suffered from childhood illnesses that caused his tooth enamel to mineralize improperly, leaving a visible line across the teeth. Since Billy Joe's two front teeth (the incisors) had completed development by age six, we know the illness occurred between birth and sixth years of life (Goodman and Armelagos 1985). Our research (Goodman and Armelagos 1988) on archeological populations has shown that the stress, such as an infection or high fever, that produces these defects in the tooth enamel of the teeth during the childhood can shorten one's life.

The story yet to be told about the excavation is revealed in the picture above showing all the actors in the drama posed at the side of the excavation (Figure 155). John Toby Woods, Clark

Spencer Larsen, Dennis O'Brien and David Hurst Thomas surround a women sitting in a lawn chair and an elderly man sitting on a wooden carpenter's horse. I asked John about the picture, and he said that when he told Uncle Ernest and Aunt Bessie (Figure 156) about the excavations, they immediately became sentinels and watched every move from their seat and sawhorse.

Figure 155. John T Woods, Aunt Bessie Youmans, Dennis O'Brien, Uncle Ernest Youmans, Clark S. Larsen, David Hurst Thomas at the excavation of Billy Joe Harris. May 26, 1976

They were likely responding to rumors that great wealth was interred with the remains of W. J. L. Harris, better known as Billy Joe. Thomas and coworkers recounted the slave's tale of a casket that was so laden with an unknown bounty that the oxen strained to pull the wagon, and the slaves that lowered the body into the ground did so with great difficulty. The legend claimed that it was filled with gold. This was a time before the impending Civil War, when people were concerned about saving their wealth in the case of invasion. Burial of gold and other precious valuables was one way to ensure that it was hidden and safe from the enemy.

The rumors that great wealth was buried in the grave were enough to lure intruders who were intent on robbing the grave. Some say that the relatives of Uncle Ernest were concerned that if the land were sold, then all would be lost. Attempts at clandestine excavation were unsuccessful. When excavation was initiated by David Hurst Thomas and Clark Larsen in May 24, 1976, there was still the possibility that wealth remained in the grave, not from the Harris family but from the Blacks who remained on Colonel's Island long after emancipation

Figure 156. When Aunt Bessie Youmans spoke you listened. She was an impressive person. She is showing the buck that she shot with an automatic twelve gauge shot gun that is in the foreground. School bus is to the left was driven by her husband Ernest.

Aunt Bessie, Uncle Ernest, and others watched intensely as each shovel full of dirt was removed during the two-day excavation. At exactly six feet below the ground, when the archeologists reached the burial and removed the remains of the mahogany coffin, the crushed bones and teeth of Billy Joe, and the few grave goods, they announced that they were finished. Not so for a disappointed Aunt Bessie, who commanded loudly, "keep digging."

John provided another chapter to the story. After the bones were returned a year later by Clark Larsen and David Hurst Thomas and were to be reburied in a reconstructed grave, John

Figure 157.Billy Joe Harris' grave after restoration

asked that the box containing the bones be opened. He had a bicentennial coin that he wanted to place in the coffin. John described how Dave Thomas seemed reluctant to open the box. He eventually opened the box, revealing a hand of cards tacked to the lid: aces and eights - the dead man's hand.[1] With a wry smile John placed his centennial coin in the box.

The final interment later that day was attended by about 40 people, including archeologists working with David Hurst Thomas and Clark Larsen on other excavations on St. Catherines (Figure 157). It was a celebratory event made even more joyous with the aid of a couple cases of beer. Walter Meeks, a friend of John's, gave the eulogy. Meeks is described by John as an imposing figure whose six-feet-plus stature was made more daunting by the black suit and hat that he wore for the occasion. Meeks led the procession from the house to the grave, with an open Bible at his side, and recited from memory a passage from *Ecclesiastes 12*:

And the doors shall be shut in the streets, when the sound of the grinding is low, and he shall rise up at the voice of the bird, and all the daughters of musick shall be brought low;

Also when they shall be afraid of that which is high, and fears shall be in the way, and the almond tree shall flourish, and the grasshopper shall be a burden, and desire shall fail: because man goeth to his long home, and the mourners go about the streets:

Or ever the silver cord be loosed, or the golden bowl be broken, or the pitcher be broken at the fountain, or the wheel broken at the cistern.

Then shall the dust return to the earth as it was: and the spirit shall return unto God who gave it.

Meeks took his task seriously and began a sermon-like eulogy that soon captured the attention of his audience. As he ended the eulogy, he reached over and plucked a camellia blossom from his wife's coat and carefully dropped the white petals on the earthly remains of Billy Joe Harris. John recalled turning to look at the mesmerized group and realizing that not a single can of beer was in sight. The revelers had found religion and were hiding the beers from Walter Meeks and the eyes of God. Back at Walter's house, however, beer again became an important part of Billy Joe Harris' wake, which was over 100 years coming.

Thirty years later, I interviewed Walter Meeks, who remembers the incident as if it happened last week. He said that as an eight-year-old boy, he had memorized passages from the Bible. His uncle, a church elder who viewed the task as more educational than religious, gave Walter anywhere from a nickel to a quarter for each verse he memorized. Walter said that not only did he enjoy learning the verses, but that they also came in handy during special occasions, such as the sermon for Billy Joe.

Billy Joe Harris is better known to the world now than he was during his lifetime. Why was Billy Joe buried on the family's land and not in the consecrated cemetery with the rest of his family? The point of land that holds the burial site has one of the most impressive views on Colonel's Island. Some say that Billy Joe drowned, hence the burial overlooking the Medway River. But John Toby finds that theory unconvincing. He points out that Billy Joe was anonymous in his lifetime. He is not mentioned in the *Children of Pride* (Myers and Jones 1972), the most significant history of Liberty County. Even a search of 4000 unpublished letters by Dr. Jones, described as a "compulsive correspondent," did not reveal even a passing reference to Billy Joe in his letters to Dr. Harris.

John Toby believes that Billy Joe was mentally challenged and was "hidden from view" by the family. The epitaph, to John, reveals a great deal: "What I do thou knowest not now but thou shalt know hereafter" (Figure 158). In the passage from the Gospel According to John 13:7, Jesus humbles himself by washing the feet of his disciples, and when questioned, responds that the mystery of his being will soon be revealed to them.

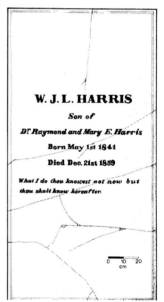

Even in death, Billy Joe was denied by his family. Raymond Harris, Billy Joe's father, was buried near his two wives at Walthourville Cemetery when he died in 1888. Billy Joe's brothers, Stephen Nathan Harris and Raymond Benjamin Harris, died in 1854 and 1910, respectively, and were also interred in the Walthourville Cemetery. Billy Joe alone remains on Billy Joe Point, named is his honor.

Figure 158. The stone that covers Billy Joe Harris's grave. From Thomas, South and Larsen (1977).

I was tagging along with John as he was delivering shrimp to the co-op in Darien. It is an ideal time for discussing politics, events of the day, and whatever else crosses our minds. As usual, I kept coming back to some topic that we had thought had long been settled. I mentioned to John that I was struck by the contrast between the way that the Harris family dealt with their son and the way that the Rogers family had treated Jimpsey "Jimp" Rogers, who was similarly challenged. "Jimp," who is described by John as being "mentally challenged," was born about 70 years after Billy Joe's death (Figure 159). But the way that Jimp was treated could not have been more different. John said that, "Jimp could swim, ride a bicycle, dress himself, carry on a limited conversation, but his biggest pleasure was cutting and splitting wood for the stove. He loved his axe and kept it under his bed at night." Grandma was pleased with Jimp and his sharing of the family chores. The wood stove and the fireplace were the sole source of heat on cool winter days, and Jimp helped keep the fires burning. Grandma kept Jimp's axe blade sharpened, and she was also in charge of repairing the broken handles. John remembers a number of times when Grandma would scrape the oversized handle with a broken piece of glass (ensuring its sharpness) so that it could be hafted into the head of the axe. Jimp would patiently wait for his precious tool to be sharpened and repaired so it could be used or placed under the bed for safekeeping.

I asked John if there were any difficulties with Jimp. He remembers, "I wasn't allowed to have my second-hand bicycle at grandmother's house, as he might ride off too far and get lost." Jimp was fascinated by the bike, and when he would see John without it he would inquire, "Where's your wheel?" John said that they were never able to teach him how to tie his shoes; but that was never a problem. Jimp had slip-ons that became part of his persona. He goes on, "It was grandmother's greatest wish that she would outlive her son." Jimpsey died in 1982 at the age of 62. She nurtured for him for those 62 years and even at age 92 she still had the energy to care for him. Grandma received her wish, outliving him by three years. She died in 1985, at the age of 96. "Her work was done." I was surprised that Jimpsey had lived such a long life. John told me that soon after his birth, the doctors said that he would be lucky to make it to his second birthday. At age two, they gave him five more years to live. Making it to his sixth decade was a testament to their care for him.[2]

I was talking to John's sister Glenise, or Gee (Ghee), about Jimp. I have always enjoyed my visits to her house; it reminds me of a hands-on museum where there is a perpetual science project in progress. We would sit in her vast sunroom, which was teaming with plants and birds. On one of my first visits to her house, Gee was nursing a seahorse that was caught in her nephew Johnny Woods' shrimp nets. She made a makeshift salt water aquarium and kept it alive for weeks.

I never asked her how she got the name, but one afternoon she inadvertently revealed the story of how the name Gee was born. She was proudly describing how they taught Jimp to dress himself, how to cut wood, and how to recite his ABCs, a task that he could never quite master. One afternoon, they were teaching him their names and he was having trouble saying Glenise, but Jimp recognized the letter G and shouted "Gee!," and from then on Glenise became Gee.

Everyone had a story about Jimp. Ben Chapman, who spent a great deal of time with him, said that Jimp had many endearing qualities. He loved babies and would hold Ben's younger brother Ralph for hours. The infant was in good hands and always seemed to be comforted by Jimp's warm grasp.

In a conversation with Ben, Jimp every so often would give Ben a big smile and wink with both eyes as if to say, "I understand everything you are saying, I understand it all, keep talking." There was a way in which Grandma and the rest of the family taught Jimp "people skills" that made his 62 years on earth a pleasant time for him and those came in contact with him.

Jimp's one vice was a pipe that he smoked constantly. That is, if he had tobacco. His mother would dole out his supply for the day each morning. He knew how to clean his pipe using small pen knives that were gifts from John. John said that they would frequently break or lose them. While grandmother might be the keeper of the tobacco, Jimp was the source of the funds to purchase it. Jimp carried a small change purse and family members would give him loose change. Friends, neighbors and fishermen moving in and out of the docks at Bluff Creek knew about Jimp's love for his pipe, and would frequently ask him, "Need some change?" Jimp's only reply was, "That wouldn't hurt." John said that in all the years that he knew Jimp, he never remembered him asking anyone for change.

Figure 159. Grandmother Rogers and Jimpsey. Jimp with his ever present pipe and slip-on shoes.

I never thought to ask John about Jimp's death. One afternoon, he told me the story. He said that Jimp died doing what he enjoyed most. He was splitting wood and suffered a massive heart attack with his axe in his hand. His mother came out to discover his lifeless body. In 1982, still without a phone, grandmother went to her hand-powered siren to signal for help. Uncle Hoke and Uncle Ernest were not at home, and only later did help arrive. Arthur Goodman, a mile away at Yellow Bluff, heard the siren, but was not aware that it was a call for help.

John's mother Gladys was in charge of the funeral, and told John that at least one family friend refused to act as a pallbearer. Somehow, it was thought that to participate in the funeral of a mentally challenged man would diminish one's status.

John, Gee and Ben were proud of Jimpsey, and even though there were trying times, they talked about how much pleasure he brought the family. "George, we could have done so much more. He wanted to learn. We tried to enroll him in school, but the teachers said the students would be afraid of him." It is a pity that Jimp was never was allowed to go to school. His classmates could have learned much from this special person. I was still bothered by the contrast between Billy Joe's life and that of Jimpsey. John, ever the pragmatist, put it into perspective: "That was then, this is now." I asked John if he had any more thoughts about Billy Joe Harris. He surprised me with a discussion of the other burials mentioned in *Rich Man, Poor Men*. John, putting on his anthropologist hat, said that he was impressed by what we had learned about Billy Joe that would have been lost to the world without the excavation of his grave. He provided another insight on a matter that I had missed. I was so focused on Billy Joe's burial, that I missed the significance of the two burials on St. Catherines that were also reported in *Rich Man, Poor Men*. Just as the context and location of Billy Joe's burial revealed how his family treated him, the burials of two enslaved individuals on St. Catherines reflect how these individuals were ostracized from their spiritual community.

The bones of the two enslaved individuals reveal much about how they lived and died. Both of the men had robust bones and well defined muscles attachments that indicated heavy use, suggesting a life of intense physical labor (Capasso, et al. 1999; Kennedy 1998). Both men also died of trauma. One of the individuals (burial 3) suffered from arthritis, as evidenced by changes in his joints, and, had a broken leg that became infected and likely led to his death. The other individual (burial 5) died from a gunshot wound from a military type weapon.

John pointed out the significance of the two men not having been buried with their kin in the community cemetery. Thomas (1977) cites Combes (1974:56) regarding the burial practices of coastal Blacks. "The most important aspect of the burial area, or for that matter the whole burial phenomenon, is the importance attributed to the final resting place of the deceased spirit. It is imperative that the deceased be buried with the spirits of the other members of the family." Combes goes on to say that, "The penalty for not being buried with one's family is, indeed, serious and results in a wandering spirit. There is not one other more important to one's life than to insure one's place in the family cemetery."

Billy Joe and the two enslaved individuals, now only known to God, would have final resting places away from their family and friends. The social facts are the same, but the spiritual implications are quite different.

18

A Fish Story:
The Yellow Bluff Shark, Bass and Trout Tournament

In a room stocked with evidence of an outdoor lifestyle, there is one particular trophy that dominates John Wood's study. Its two and half foot double brass columned base is topped with a bronze fish in all its glory jumping out the water. I asked him about the trophy, and he gave me article from *Update*, a newsletter of the Coastal Electric Member Cooperative (Pate 1992) (Figure 160). John Toby, Wayne Collins, and Wayne's son Will were teamed in the Fourth Annual Yellow Bluff Shark, Bass and Trout Tournament & July Fest.[1] John and his team decided that the winner was waiting for them at his favorite fishing spot on Grass Island. The night before the contest began, John climbed into his Grady-White, traveled the few miles to his cherished spot, anchored, and waited by taking a long nap. Wayne and Will Collins were to join him in the morning. As he recounted the event, I asked if his early start was a chance to fish before daylight. He looked at me incredulously. That I would even think that he would break the rules was beyond belief. In my defense, most of my fishing had taken place at the Atlanta Fish Market, where the rules about fishing are hardly ever discussed.

Woods, Collins and son win at Yellow Bluff Shark Tournament

It was just moments after midnight as John T. Woods, Jr. walked quietly across the long boardwalk over the tall marsh grass toward the floating dock on Jones Creek behind his Colonel's Island home. A brisk southwest breeze blew as he pushed the throttle forward on his Grady-White and turned into the Midway River headed toward St. Catherines Sound.

At nearby Yellow Bluff Fish Camp, other boaters would wait until daybreak before heading out to their can sometimes be spoiled by motor trouble.

By now, the tide was just beginning to turn and for the next hour or so this fishing drop (a closely guarded location don't you know) would produce more than one fine specimen for the weigh in board.

But a fishing tale would not be complete without mention of the one that got away. "Actually the biggest trout broke my line," Toby said. "He probably weighed more than four pounds."

Figure 160. From Update, A coastal EMC Bi-Weekly News Letter, edited by Suzanne Pate, August 7, 1992

In John's short journey to Grass Island, he encountered about twenty white anchor lights from the boats of other fisherman who were also getting an early start. John's target was much different. He was going to his favorite spot on Grass Island in pursuit of the elusive trout. His "brothers" on the water that night were in search of the more plentiful shark that smell their prey and will take bait during the day or night. Trout see their prey and bite in daylight, a not so subtle difference that I had never known until John pointed it out to me.

Within minutes of the first light of day, when the contest officially began, John had hooked himself a trout that he thought would be a winner. Olin Frazier's son, fishing 20 yards away, thought so too and remarked, "Captain John, looks like you got yourself a winner." John confidently replied, "I think so too, I'm going in." He claimed, and I would never doubt his word, that his first strike that day was a bigger trout that got away. I realized that John hadn't mentioned his teammates. I ask about their reaction to his early success. "They never made it to Grass Island," he said. Wayne had boat trouble and they were "dead" in the water. John, confident that he had a winner, returned soon after 6:30 that morning and came upon his stranded teammates, his second catch of the day. He threw them a line and towed them back to Yellow

Bluff. At 8:00 AM, before most others had gotten into the water, John, Wayne and Will officially entered their trout, which weighed in at three pounds and two ounces.

The *Update* story described them waiting around for the rest of the day until the official end of the contest at 5:00 PM. I couldn't imagine that John would spend the day waiting at Yellow Bluff. In fact, John confirmed that after dropping Wayne and Will off at Yellow Bluff, he went back to Billy Harris Point to begin his daily chores. Their trout was indeed the $1000 winner. John shared the prize with his team members, but kept the trophy. "I did catch the fish," he explained. The article ends with Wayne asking John Toby, "Are you going to enter again next year?" and John answering "Enter...heck, I'm going to win." This did not sound like John, and he confirmed that he never uttered those words. I asked if he ever entered again. "I never entered again; I didn't need to," he answered. It was the response that I had expected. It was the last and only fishing contest that John ever entered.

During the first five years that I lived on Colonels Island, I checked the progress of the annual fishing contests religiously, and I have never seen anything that approached the crowd of 2,000 fishing contest fans mentioned in the *Update* story. Yellow Bluff hasn't had a contest in nearly five years, but they still sell a T-shirt every year with a different logo. My friend Will Darsey and I went to Yellow Bluff last summer, not to fish but to buy the T-shirts that memorialize the event that no longer exists. Raburn Goodman, one of the owners of Yellow Bluff, was visibly upset. The Annual Yellow Bluff Shark, Bass and Trout Tournament & July Fest T-shirts were lost in delivery. It is one thing not to be able to catch a fish, but it is a sad day on Colonels Island when you can't even buy the fish T-shirt.

The decline of the fishing contest is just the first sign of change at Yellow Bluff and Colonels Island. The fishing camp with a century-old tradition is metamorphosing into a gated community. I still preserve Yellow Bluff in my mind as I remember it from just a few years ago. I recall my first trip to Yellow Bluff. It was a ten-mile drive on Island Highway (GA38/US84) from I-95 that ends at a dirt road with the entrance to the fishing camp on your right. It is an idyllic setting. As you enter the camp, as you are surrounded by tall loblolly pines[2] that give way to stately live oaks draped with Spanish moss.

As you approach the hoist, you pass the five houses of the permanent residents on your left. The trailers and cabins on the right break the idyllic spell. The rustic cabins have been a part of the cam since its inception. The trailers sit on land rented by fishermen whose wheeled homes are as varied as they are. The brick house of Arthur Goodman, Raburn father, is located just before you reach the appropriately colored Yellow Bluff Company store. As you park in front of the store, you have a commanding view of Ashley Creek and the vast salt marsh that it winds through. To the left of the hoist and just east of the store is a large non-descript wooden building with a painted sign so weathered that it could hardly be read. In its former glory, the sign proudly identified the Yellow Bluff Tea Room.

The Yellow Bluff Company store still sells refreshments and essential supplies, such as bait and tackle. There is a gasoline pump to the right of the hoist with a long hose that services the boats on the floating docks below. John proudly told me that he has never had to buy bait (he catches his own bait) and that he has never gassed up at Yellow Bluff.[3] Real fishermen, in John's world, catch their own bait. John and many others carry gas in portable tanks, saving the 50-cent premium that is tacked on to the prices at the closest local gasoline stations, which are about ten miles away.[4] For my wife and I, the gas pump at Yellow Bluff is a frequent destination, since we are always in need of a refill.

In the center of the complex is a dry boat storage building that can house at least 100 boats. The basic structure of the building is post and beam. Poles that once carried the electric co-op wires bring in power to Colonels Island have been recycled for the posts. A tin roof and galvanized doors protect the boats from the weather. This was a utilitarian building and, as such, it served its purpose with little concern for style. Surrounding the boat storage are more cabins and trailers on rented space that serve as weekend homes for the fisherman interested in getting on the water and not sitting on a patio. Herman Wheeler's[5] house is on Oyster Point, the farthest point to the north of the camp that has one of the most commanding views at Yellow Bluff.

For me, the charm of Yellow Bluff has been its utilitarian nature as a fish camp. The proposed row of town houses and the five styles of cottages (coastal, saltbox, four gabled house, bungalow and low country) that are being built will also be very functional, just as at home in a suburb of Atlanta, Macon or Augusta as they are on Ashley Creek. They don't reflect the uniqueness of Yellow Bluff. It will become another gated community featuring a boat hoist that will serve the members who share the combination to the gate. John told me about a conversation that he had with a friend he worked for at Sunbury. At the height of the Cold War, his friend was building a bomb shelter at his home at Sunbury. As he was completing the underground bunker, he told John not to expect to be invited into the bunker after the nuclear attack; it was for family only. Gated communities don't protect you from nuclear attack, but they are constant reminders that they if you don't have the combination, you don't belong. I know many people that live in gated communities in Atlanta because of the security it gives them. They would be surprised to know how many pizza delivery people and taxi drivers know the secret code that they believe is only shared with their neighbors.

The popularity of Yellow Bluff has always been the abundance of fish that can be caught in the waters adjacent to it. In addition to the trout (spotted seatrout), spot tail bass, and shark that were featured in the Annual Yellow Bluff Shark, Bass and Trout Tournament & July Fest contest, the fishermen sought whiting (southern kingfish), sheepshead, black drum, Atlanta croaker and southern flounder. From Ashley Creek it is just a short trip to St. Catherines Sound, where there is an abundance of shark and even tarpon.

Yellow Bluff is also the jumping off point for deep-sea fisherman. Gray's Reef, a National Marine Sanctuary, is a 17 square nautical mile area that is about an hour from Yellow Bluff's shores. The sanctuary features both sandy flat areas and coral ledges that can reach 6-8 feet and are submerged 60 to 70 feet below the sea. The coral ledges feature complex nooks and crannies where invertebrates attach themselves or hide from their predators. In some places, the sea life is so dense that the rough sea floor is obscured, producing what has been described as a "live bottom." Fishing is allowed in the Gray's Reef sanctuary as long as you do not disturb the bottom by dragging a net or dropping an anchor.

Sunday afternoons are typically the busiest time at Yellow Bluff. In the last year, I have never seen more 25 cars with their empty trailers, or Raburn Goodman having more than a couple of boats waiting to be hoisted to or from the water. In 2006, on the 4th of July, John and I drove over to see what was happening at Yellow Bluff. There was no fishing contest again this year, but more important changes were apparent. The 30 acres that was Yellow Bluff had been sold for $5.25 million (Burke 2004) to Ron Keel, Allen Brown, Jobie White and Fred Shore, the developers who are transforming it into an 85-lot gated community. They have been so successful that even before the first new resident moved in they purchased an additional 40 acres across Youmans Road for $2.2 million. The land lacks water access or a marsh view, but will the the site of future expansion. The potential development, with permission to share the amenities of Yellow Bluff, makes the potential profit at today's prices $8 million.[6] The advertisements proclaim that you that you can live at Yellow Bluff, "for a weekend or a LIFETIME." It will feature a clubhouse, common park area, dry boat barn (each selling for a mere $60,000, up from $50,000 just a year ago), boat hoist and dock master. That image brings a smile to my face. Calling Arthur Goodman or his son Raburn the "boss" is easily acceptable, but to call them the "dock master" seems as out of place. Arthur and Raburn seem happy as the bosses sitting on the ever present white plastic chair or golf cart at the hoist, waiting for the next boat and ready to chat with anyone interested in exchanging niceties with them. Yellow Bluff promises that you are only eight minutes from Hinesville, which is about 25 miles away, and 30 minutes from a "bustling" night life. I have never made the drive to Hinesville in less than forty minutes, and never seen "night life" – teeming or otherwise – within a half-hour's drive from the Bluff. Those in search of a bustling night life are not likely to find it in coastal Georgia.

The Yellow Bluff Store, which is featured in the promotional material for the new development, will remain as a symbol of the past. Plans show an elaborate new store to be built near the proposed clubhouse. John will not need this symbol to remind him of the place that was a significant part of his upbringing. There are many images from Yellow Bluff that play in his mind. There are pleasant memories of visiting Jean Youmans,[7] the daughter of his cousin Roger Youmans and owner of Yellow Bluff, to swim in the pool that was just across the dirt road from the store. The swimming pool and the fishing were an attraction for groups that would come from as far as Atlanta. He recalls bus loads of church groups that would come to Yellow Bluff for their yearly summer outing. The Tea Room served meals for the day-trippers and the fishermen. The pool was filled in when the Goodman's bought Yellow Bluff.

John remembers many of the mile-long trips on the path[8] from his grandmother's house through the woods to the Yellow Bluff Store. The supply of flour, sugar or salt was exhausted before it could be replenished by his father's monthly trips to grandmother's house to refill their larder. Ice, which we now see as an indispensable addition to cool our cocktails, was a necessity to preserve their food. Electricity came to Colonels Island in 1940, but a refrigerator for grandmother was still years away. One trip stirred up a particularly vivid memory of his grandmother that he related to me.

> Once, when I was six or seven, she sent me to Yellow Bluff store to get 10 pounds of ice. I forgot what she wanted and brought back sugar. She sent me back again to get the ten-pound block of ice. Dark caught me and I got scared because there are Indian shell mounds along the dirt road to Yellow Bluff. I was so scared that I ran the mile with the 10 pound block of ice on my shoulder.

The website accurately claims that Yellow Bluff has been a recreational area for a century and a fishing camp since 1923 when "Doc" Youmans[9] bought it. His son, Roger, ran Yellow Bluff from 1938 until 1951. In its early years, the day-tripper church groups were almost an afterthought to fishing, the main activity on Yellow Bluff. Arthur and Mildred Goodman purchased the 39 acres of highland and 1395 acres of marsh (Fishman 1999) from Roger Youmans, on October 14, 1951.

Arthur joked that the only fish that he knew then was the gefilte fish, a traditional Jewish food.[10] Gefilte fish has not become part of the low country cuisine of coastal Georgia. Mildred Goodman,[11] who was Roger Youman's niece by marriage, grew up on the Bluff (Groover 1987) and met Arthur when he was stationed at Fort Stewart as an infantry instructor and she was working in a military shop in Hinesville. Goodman claims to be the twelfth owner a Kings Grant Property[12] that originated in 1759. Three of the twelve cabins are as they were when they bought Yellow Bluff. The deal came with 25[13] boats. At the time, they charged a $1 a night for a cabin and $3 a day for meals in the Tea Room. The Atlanta Hunting Club would book the place twice a year for excursions to the coast (Fishman 1999). The Goodmans also sold oysters harvested from the marsh adjacent to Yellow Bluff for a short time. John remembers oysters being opened between the store and where Arthur built his house. The shells would then be scattered about the area to provide footing for the workers maneuvering boats into and out of the water before the floating dock was built. As you look to the south east, a midden is clearly visible on the bank of Ashley Creek. It attests to the success of Doc Youmans' enterprise when he owned Yellow Bluff during the heyday of oystering.[14]

In the modern era, fishermen would bring their boats with 300-horsepower engines and have Arthur or Raburn put their boats in the water with the electric lift. This is a recent phenomenon. Earlier, the fisherman would rent boats from Yellow Bluff and hire someone to take them fishing. Small twelve-foot to fourteen-foot flat bottom boats (bateaux) were available.[15] Some fishermen would bring a small 5-horsepower motor to propel them; others would row their own boat or hire a local guide for this arduous task. Local guides, who were predominately black, could be hired for the day.

In 1999, a satisfied Arthur Goodman was quoted saying, "Isn't that remarkable?" … "Everybody's developing, but I'm not doing nothing. My wife and I have our son[16] living here and our daughter. I've got the salt air, fresh shrimp and crabs, and some of the finest people in the world passing through. Why would I want to change anything?" (Fishman 1999). But an aging Arthur Goodman, who was terminally ill at the time, could not pass up an offer that was beyond his dreams. Arthur died on January 27, 2005 soon after Yellow Bluff was sold. He was 87 years old.

After Yellow Bluff's rebirth, there will be cottages and townhouses for sale "for a weekend or a lifetime." As we drove around Yellow Bluff, we could see that five cottages in different styles and a row of townhouses were nearing completion. We were comfortable driving in John's white Volvo, which was getting a patina of dust from dirt roads that would soon become Marina drive, Ashley River Drive, Oyster Point Drive, Yellow Bluff Drive and Marsh Drive. The concrete curbs suggested that the paving will begin shortly.

The objective our trip was to take a last look at the Tea Room that John described as playing such an important role in the social life of Colonels Island families.[17] He said that there would be a dozen or two families having a square dance on a Friday or Saturday night. As the evening progressed, the men would surreptitiously slip out the door for some "air," eventually reaching their cars for a quick nip from a stashed bottle. The women were well aware of the subterfuge, but tolerated it as long as it was discreet and the men kept dancing. The dancing became livelier as number of trips for air became more frequent.

Uncle Hoke would frequently call the dance, and he and his friends would hire local black musicians to play the fiddle. Even before they were interested in the activities on the inside of the Tea Room, John said that the youngsters were brought along and played hide and seek under the Tea Room while their parents frolicked above them. The back end of the Tea Room was built over the edge of the bluff, providing an excellent place to play and to observe the goings on as the men congregated around their cars getting their "breaths of air." As the children grew older, they moved into the Tea Room and become part of the social scene. In Savannah, the elites had their coming out parties and debutante balls to signal the coming of age. At Colonels

Island, your coming of age was signaled by your move from under the bluff of the Tea Room to the adult world of the square dance.

We were one day too late to see the Tea Room. As we drove up, we could see that it was now just a pile of timber. The demolition of the Tea Room was expected. It sat on a prime piece of real estate on Ashley Creek, which the corporation magically transformed into Ashley River. The developers believe that if you live in a gated community, it should over look a river and a not lowly creek. For my coastal friends, a creek is a perfectly acceptable term and generates wonderful images of marsh shorelines teaming with crab, fish and oysters. For city folks like me, a creek conjures up other images. I grew up in Lincoln Park, Michigan, where a creek was hardly a pristine waterway. When my friends and I would go skinny dipping in the Ecorse Creek, we would often notice thankfully indescribable waste floating by. Years later, I read that the creek had made the list of Michigan's most polluted waters.

While searching for how they were marketing Yellow Bluff, I came across the website for Dolphin Island Preservation. I asked John where Dolphin Island Preservation was located, and he responded with a puzzled look. "Dolphin Island Preservation? Never heard of it." He thought a minute and said, "I do remember that there is something being developed on the Jericho River." In retrospect, this was not surprising since the Dolphin Island Preservation concept was developed out of "whole cloth." The land along a bend where I-95 crosses over the Jericho River was transformed during the construction of the interstate that passes within 600 feet of it. The Interstate construction required a solid base and mud had to be dredged from the construction site to the marsh that is now Dolphin Island. Joe Parker, who supervised construction for the contractor in the early 1970s, described the difficulties in building the interstate in that area. He had to bring in oxen to drag trees away from the swamp that was in the path of the soon to be highway (Figure 161).[18] The subcontractor built a dirt retaining wall and the mud was pumped from as far away as a mile in each direction. The subcontactor called for the sludge to be a certain distance above high tide. Because the sludge settled, it never reached that height. The developers of Dolphin Island had to haul fill dirt in for a year to bring it to its present level. Having piqued John's interest, we made an excursion to the site. John's immediate reaction was, "I wouldn't want to live here, but there are probably a lot of 'Yankees' that would like this place." John enjoys reminding me of my heritage.

The promotional material available for Dolphin Island is substantial. There is one 56-page booklet of covenants and 78 pages of architectural suggestions that will guide builders in formulating their blue prints and construction plans in what they describe as "coastal vernacular architecture." Every aspect for the development, from the home site and home to the style of the fence posts and slats, door and window frame, porch, dock, and roofs are provided in the covenants and in the *Dolphin Island Architectural Guidelines.*

Figure 161. Oxen were used to remove logs during the Construction of I-95 in early 1970s. Courtesy of J. Parker

As of June 2006, there were 62 "home sites" that were selling from as low as $265,000 to as high as $645,000. Theses lots seem expensive for an "island" created from fill dirt during the construction of Interstate I-95, which is the most prominent feature of Dolphin Island Preservation. The promotional materials take this negative aspect and make it one of the amenities. They say that it has easy access to I-95. While the interstate is just over 600 feet from the Interstate, John and I measured nearly a nine-mile drive from the Dolphin Island Preservation gate to where the Jericho River crosses under I-95.

John is much more tolerant of Dolphin Island than I am. It may be a matter of semantics. I am skeptical of claims of environmental preservation, when the site was creating using fill dirt to build up land whose natural level is barely above the high tide. Though I am critical of their attempts to create "coastal vernacular architecture" with 134 pages of guidelines, it does ensure that you will not have a McMansion built next to a bungalow. They should be applauded for that. John is more practical. He is concerned that those who choose Dolphin Island Preservation are building their homes on fill site; but even that problem can be solved. There is a more serious issue about location. "George, they are 30 minutes away from the water. When I remind him that all the lots are on rivers or lagoons, he quickly revealed a prejudice shared by many coastal residences. To them, "the water" is the St. Catherine Sound or ocean. In a sense, they are correct. The nearer you are to the ocean, the more varied the ecology, giving you more ways to exploit it recreationally.

To John, change on the coast is something that everyone expected. Even I had no illusions that Colonels Island would remain as a place lost in time. However, the change is more rapid than any of us had imagined. Our 4th of July trip to Yellow Bluff and the development at Dolphin Island Preservation provided evidence the changes are coming more rapidly. Waterfront property is a valuable commodity. As Yellow Bluff becomes a gated community, there will be fewer places to put in larger boats. Half Moon Marina on the South Newport River, which is open to the public, was almost sold to the developers of Hampton Island. Half Moon has a particular problem for its future. They built condominiums years ago, near the boat hoist. John pointed out to me that the site of the hoist and condos are in a river bend that is particularly susceptible to erosion. If the erosion continues, the river will encroach on the infrastructure of the dock and hoist. The possibility of moving the dock back is limited by the condos that were built so near the hoist.

The accessibility of boats to the water will become more of an issue as development proceeds. After the completion of the Yellow Bluff development, the Half Moon Marina will be the only boat hoist in the area. Sunbury has a public boat ramp, and there is an additional ramp at the public park at the Isle of Wight. John has lobbied Liberty County Commissioners to include purchasing land for water access from the county as part of the plans for development.

The story of development on Colonels Island has another dimension that is similar to gentrification in urban areas. Those who once opted for the simple life on the coast with a small cottage and a simple dock are being driven away by increasing property taxes. Many property owners are not interested in selling homes that they purchased for less than $100,000 for the $1,000,000 going rate for prime waterfront property, but they are forced to sell because taxes have climbed beyond their means. Many are coastal inhabitants living on fixed incomes who never expected the demand for waterfront property would eventually force them out of their homes.

Few coastal residents anticipated the pace of change that Colonels Island is experiencing. In 2000, the *Savannah Daily News*, described Colonels Island as one of the least developed areas on the Georgia Coast – a "hidden treasure" that "boast[s] wildlife and solitude" (Lowrey 2000). In the newspaper account, Raburn Goodman said that Colonels Island is composed of three communities. "Most of the population is at Half Moon, maybe 200 to 300 homes. Then there is Camp Viking with a couple of dozen houses.[19] Yellow Bluff is the smallest. There are maybe 10 houses here, but not all the owners are full-time residents." Goodman and others interviewed for the article claim that, while there has been increase in population, there has been no increase in the number of homes.[20] Growth was limited by the availability of land. Four families owned the majority of the land and did not make it available for development. The descendants of John Stevens still hold 10,000 acres of land extending to I-95 and Sunbury, with about 3,000 acres on Colonels Island in limited use as natural protected area.

Lori Parks, a staff member on the Liberty County Joint Planning Commission, stated, "We've issued permits for a few single-family homes during the past few years, but really nothing significant. I've lived down there before and visited there all my life....I'm glad it is staying the same as it always has been" (Lowrey 2000). In six years, Colonels Island has seen the development at Bluff Creek, Yellow Bluff, and the condominiums at Half Moon. Developments east of I-95 will also surely impact Colonels Island. In addition to Dolphin Island Preservation, The Village at Sunbury is another residential development. It is a socially engineered town (Ross 1999) modeled after Disney World's Celebration[21] (Donahue 2004). The Tire Rack distribution center and the Target Corporation distribution center are also nearby, located just off of Island Highway (GA 38/US 84) a few miles east of the I-95 interchange (Exit 76). The Target building is 1,500,000 square feet under a single roof. There will likely be others availing themselves of the space in this industrial park, increasing pressure for further development.

Roger Youmans was one of the founding forces of the Coastal Electrical Cooperative that brought power to Colonels Island in the early 1940s. He served as its first president. John Woods has served as president of the Coastal Electric Cooperative for the last 22 years.[22] He has seen the growth on Colonels Island from the perspective of a lifelong resident, and as head of the cooperative that supplies the energy to area. This growth is just the tip of the iceberg. By 2020, John comments, they expect that 40% of Georgia's population will be living east of I-95. John is pleased with his role in the development of Colonels Island, but he is sad that the new residents will never have experienced the scene of fisherman putting in at Yellow Bluff or watch a fishing contest unfold. The T-shirts sold for the now defunct event are a poor substitute.

Authors' Biography

George J. Armelagos is Goodrich C. White Professor of Anthropology and former Chair of the Department of Anthropology at Emory University in Atlanta, Georgia. His research has focused on diet and disease in human adaptation. He has coauthored *Demographic Anthropology* with Alan Swedlund and *Consuming Passions: The Anthropology of Eating* with Peter Farb. He has also co-edited *Paleopathology at the Origins of Agriculture* with Mark Cohen and *Disease in Populations in Transition: Anthropological and Epidemiological Perspectives* with Alan Swedlund. Armelagos has written extensively on how race has been misapplied in the history of anthropology. He has published over 225 articles, and in 2005 he was awarded Wenner-Gren Foundation's Viking Fund Medal, which is considered one of anthropology's highest honors.

John Toby Woods was superintendent of St. Catherines Island from 1960 until 1982. John's reputation as a naturalist and sportsman is legendary in the Low Country. He was a frequent guest on the Southern Sportsman, and was featured on Merlin Perkin's Wild Kingdom and the Today Show with Robert Dotson. He is a public servant that served 40 years a board member of Coastal Electric Member Cooperative (EMC), and never missed or arrived late to a meeting during that time.

Notes

Chapter 2. John's Story
[1] The Coastal Electric Membership Cooperative.

[2] The Cobbtown Skiff was manufactured by Vernon Sikes in Cobbtown, Georgia, which lies on Georgia State Highway 23 about six miles south of where it intersects with I-16. Sikes manufactured the Cobbtown Skiff from a mold that John and Jack Baughcom designed, and that Jack built. The boats are one piece of six-inch thick foam encased fiberglass that, in Lynn Sibley's terms, is "solid and safe." For a hydrophobe like me, this is reassuring. I talked to Vernon Sikes on May 25, 2007 and he has built over 100 Cobbtown Skiffs since he made the first one for John in 1997. In addition to the foam construction, the flat bottom draws only six inches of water and can easily navigate the creeks on Colonels Island at low tide and make the trip to McQueens Inlet on the Ocean side of St. Catherines. In addition, there is a bulk head that divides the boat into two parts. The boat is piloted from the stern that remains dry when fish are dumped in the front compartment. The compartments have four one-inch drains with plugs to keep them dry or to hold water in them. Without asking, Sikes reassured me that while changes have been made, the design has not changed since Jack built the first one in the early 1970s. The boat was Sikes' introduction into the saltwater craft business.

[3] The collection is known as the St. Catherines Island Foundation and Edward John Noble Collection.

[4] Jones collected most of his artifacts on Colonels Island, where he was a major planter. Fernbank Museum said that he visited St. Catherines and engaged in some unscientific collecting.

[5] The documentary says that the mission was found after a four year search. John pointed out that within a 100 yards of where the mission was found there is a concentration of Indian potsherds and sparsely scattered Spanish pottery around the watering hole, tell-tale clues. A few Spanish beads in the bottom of the stream leading to the water hole were important evidence of Spanish activity in the area.

Chapter 3. On the Trail of Button Gwinnett
[1] Ernest "Tex" Riedel, who headed a Coast Guard unit on St. Catherines in 1943, told me that on one afternoon on the South Beach, Button chased a raccoon into the ocean. Tex thought that he saw the last of the raccoon and the dog. Button returned triumphantly from the surf. The raccoon was nowhere to be seen.

[2] Gwinnett paid for his passage with money that was supposed to pay off a debt in England. As we will see, this pattern of behavior continued on this side of the ocean.

[3] It is not clear how much time he was able to spend on the island since he was involve with projects on the mainland. In addition, he spent considerable time dealing with political matters that would have required him to be away from St. Catherines.

[4] *The Atlanta Constitution* (AC 1929c) "English Woman Visits Savannah Home of Gwinnett" reports that a distant relative of Gwinnett said that the story of the duel didn't surprise her since there is a "hot headed streak in the Gwinnett family." Gertrude Gwinnett visited Charles F. Jenkins before her visit to St. Catherines (AC 1929b), which may explain her search for the home of Button Gwinnett.

[5] This would have been a problem since Lyman Hall's wife is buried next to him in the spot that was slated for Gwinnett.

[6] The mural is duplicated on the back of the two dollar bill. In the original, John Adams is standing on Thomas Jefferson's foot. But they redid the engraving and moved Adam's foot off of Jefferson's foot.

[7] Marshall T. Newman is described by Williams as an archeologist. Newman, who I knew quite well, was a biological anthropologist specializing in the study of living populations.

[8] In fact, Funk pointed out the problem with this description based on Hugh McCall's questionable description in Sanderson's book. Obviously, the issue of height would not be relevant if the femur was in fact that of a female.

[9] "Swash" in this context means a small creek. John said that they may have dammed a small stream to make a slough there.

[10] Uncle Hoke is John Toby Wood's cousin. Because of his age and the closeness of the relationship, he was given the honorific avuncular title that was used by most of the family that knew him. John and Hoke, later in his life, had a close relationship.

[11] John says that Uncle Hoke inherited the boat's name when he bought the boat.

[12] On Wednesday June 8, 1955, Toby wrote that he spent 4 hours traveling to the Ambos Marina and put the boat on the way to repair and paint the *St. Catherines*. He worked on the boat for twelve hours on the 8th, 9 hours on the 9th, and after another 9 hours on the 10th, he returned to St. Catherines after a 3 hour and 45 minute trip.

[13] Mr. Noble had a wireless phone and the Woods were to monitor it two hours a day in case of a call from him. John said that the phone was notoriously unreliable. Nonetheless, it was to be manned at the appointed hours.

[14] Noble, writing to Jenkins (Noble 1943b: March 31, 1943), commented on a facsimile of Gwinnett's signature: "The signature looks as though he didn't use it very often. Perhaps that is why the few known signatures brought so high a price!"

[15] "Brief but brilliant was the career of Button Gwinnett," observed Charles C. Jones, Jr., author of an early meager sketch of the Signers. "Rising like a meteor, he shot athwart the zenith of the young commonwealth, concentrating the gaze of all, and, in a short moment, was seen no more." An appropriate and truthful epitaph." From Robertson (1946:307).

[16] The Library of Congress has an 1876 portrait by Ole Erekson in its Prints and Photographic Division (Digital ID 07837). There is another portrait painted between 1757 to 1760 that I had not seen before that is in the Charles F. Jenkins Papers (Anon ND). The pamphlet uses information from his book (Jenkins 1926). The pamphlet was transmitted by antique dealer G. W. Michelmore (1932).

[17] John has evidence that the Musgrove house was near the Waldburg house.

[18] These supports attach to both sides of the house, span its length, and maintain the stability of the structure.

[19] June 19, 1991.

[20] Misspelled on the web site.

[21] The Atlanta Constitution, July 7, 1929, pE4 (Georgia's Signers of Declaration).

[22] According to Robertson, C. F. Jenkins traced these "suppositive portraits" to Dr. Thomas Addis Emmett, who wanted portraits of all the signers to go with his autograph collection. In 1869, Emmett commissioned H. B. Hall to do a portrait of Gwinnett even though no description of his likeness was or is known. I am reminded of the story about the teacher who asked the young student what he was doing. The student answered, "I'm drawing a picture of God." The teacher responded with "No one knows what God looks like," and the child answered, "They will in a minute." So it was with H. B. Hall and the Button Gwinnett portrait.

Chapter 4. Mary Musgrove and the Reverend Bosomworth

[1] In the last decade, a Gwinnett autograph is worth 20 times the value of Ludwig Van Beethoven's signature, which is valued at $7800 (Saffro, et al. 1994).

[2] Muskogee is the official name of the Creek. On their official site, the "tribe" is called the Muskogee (Creek) nation.

[3] She always referred to herself as Coosaponakeesa.

[4] Also written Ponpone.

[5] Culture brokers act as liaisons between two groups. Musgrove's knowledge of Creek Indian and English culture allowed her to move comfortably between both groups. Her role is illustrated in "Malatchi's Speech to Heron," C.R.G. XXXVI, 315-325. 1747. In Juricek (1989:152), when Malatchi says, "There is Mary our Sister, in whom the whole Nation confides, because She is of our own Blood, a friend to us as well as the English. And whatever she says we shall be determined by, because She has more Sense, and knows what is for our good…".

[6] In "Mary Bosomsworth's Memorial to Heron" (C.R.G. XXXVI, 256-273 See Juricek 1989: 140), she writes (in the third person) "That She is by Decent on the Mothers Side (who was sister to the Old Emperor) of the Same Blood of the Present Mico's and Chief's now in that Nation, and by their Laws, and Voice of the Whole Nation is esteemed their Rightful and Natural Princess."

[7] The Creek are a matrilineal society with descent and power passing through the mother's line.

[8] Lower Creek Recognition Of Mary Bosomworth As Princess With Authority To Negotiate Over Lands. CRG, XXVII, 207-209. 1749. In Juricek (1989:209).

[9] It has been assumed that she was a member of the Wind Clan, since it was the most powerful clan among the Creek.

[10] This meeting is immortalized in William Verelt's, "Trustees of Georgia," oil painting in The Winterthur Museum in Delaware. Eight Indians met with the Trustees of Georgia at the Palace Court, Westminster, summer 1734.

[11] An early "Map of the County of Savannah," based on original drawings from Oglethorpe, shows the Yamacraw Tract as "Indian Lands" on the banks the Savannah River immediately north of Savannah.

[12] Before cotton became king in Georgia, deer-skin trade was one of the most important products in the colony. The Musgrove's trading post was extremely successful and had revenues equal to one-sixth of Charles Town's annual intake (Fisher 1990:53).

[13] The rule was eventually changed.

[14] They made this move at the request of Oglethorpe, who wanted a presence on the southern border to counter Spanish interest in the area.

[15] Mary blamed her financial problems on her years of service to the colony. In any difficult dispute between the Creek and English, she was called to duty.

[16] William Stephens' Report on Tomochichi's Land Grant to the Mathews. CRG, IV, 49-50. See Juricek 1989:86.

[17] Mary was also providing beef for the colonists, and was the unofficial hostess for Indians visiting Savannah and English visitors to the colony (Fisher 1990). She bore the expense of hosting these visitors.

[18] See George Galphin's Report to Horton on Mary Bosomworth's Denuciation of Oglrthorpe. CRG, VI, 356-357. 1746. In Juricek (1989:130-131), he states, "… the Generall was a Roge and would had his heed Cut of when he went home for Ingreris."

[19] Richard Y. Irby's popular web site http://ngeorgia.com/people/musgrove.html.

[20] The most likely location for the village would have been the Persimmon Point area and south near Wamassee Creek, where a source of fresh water is always available. John Woods says that in 1981 you could still see the logs that the Indians used to create a dam for a fresh water pond.

[21] William Horton, in a letter to Thomas Bosomworth (C. R. G. XXXVI, 289, 1746. See Juricek 1989:132), states that they always considered St. Catherines Indian land that they were free to use as they wished.

[22] Fisher (1990:194) states that the transaction was recorded in the Carolina records. The land was part of the 1739 treaty signed by Oglethorpe. Malatchi received 30 head of cattle and trade goods.

[23] Des Barres, J.F.W. (publisher). The Coast, Rivers and Inlets of the Province of Georgia, Surveyed by Joseph Avery and others. 1780.

[24] Lawton B. Evans, First Lessons in Georgia History (New York: American Book Company, 1913) pg.78. See the John Duncan Collection, Armstrong University. www.sip.armstrong.edu/Indians/catalog2.html.

[25] There is a wood engraving, "Mary Bosomworth Inciting the Indians to Violence," that reinforces the notion of force and fear that the Bosomworths created. See Hezekiah Butterworth, Zigzag Journeys in the Occident. The Atlantic to the Pacific. A Summer Trip of the Zigzag Club from Boston to the Golden Gate (Boston: Estes and Lauriat, 1885), pg. 79. See the John Duncan Collection, Armstrong University. www.sip.armstrong.edu/Indians/catalog2.html.

[26] The sale to Levy began part of the confusion. The Bosomworths did not have the rights to sell the land and the sale could not be registered. Mary and Thomas Bosomworth were in need of funds and lived off these funds.

[27] Poaching was also a problem since St. Catherines had abundant game and people felt that they were free to hunt and fish there.

[28] Mary Bosomworth's Memorial to Heron (C.R.G. XXXVI, 256-273. 1747.) See Juricek 1989: 140.

[29] Deed From Malatchi To The Bosomworths For Three Coastal Islands. S.C.S.M.R. Book I-I, pp 426-428. 1748. (See Juricek, 1989:157), and Deed From Malatchi To The Bosomworths For Three Coastal Islands (Revised Version). S.C.S.M.R. Book I-I, pp 520-523. 1748. (See Juricek, 1989:159).

[30] Confirmation Deed From Malatchi and other Creek Headmen to the Bosomworths for Three Coastal Islands (S.C.S.M.R. Book I- I, pp.428-430). In Jericek 1989; 208-210.

[31] Upper Creek Repudiation of Graham Deed and Confirmation of Bosomworth Deed. S. C. S. M. R. Book I-I, pp. 433-434. In Jericek (1989:225-226). The document was signed by 17 Creek dignitaries.

[32] Malatchi's Speeches to Govenor Glean: Extracts of the Land Controversy in Georgia. McDowell, *Indian Affairs*, 1750-1754, pp. 396-397, 404-405. In Juricek (1989: 226-227).

[33] Fisher (1990:518) surmises that Mary died sometime in the summer of 1765.

[34] McQueen purchased Sapelo, Little Sapelo, Blackbeard, and Cabretta Islands in 1784. According to *A Sapelo Island Handbook* (http://www.uga.edu/ugami/esapelo_handbook.html), he was "living beyond his means" and was forced to sell the Island for £10,000 to Frances Marie Demoussay Delavauxe in 1789.

[35] Nathan Brownson was a physician who lived in Riceboro. He was a member of the Continental Congress in 1777 and elected Governor of Georgia in 1881. He was also a founder of the University of Georgia. A historic marker on US-17 near the Midway Church commemorates his contributions to Georgia.

Chapter 5. The Plantation Years

[1] Reference to Gaius Gracchus (159-121 BCE), an agrarian and a flamboyant and powerful speaker who was a major political force in changing the Latin political system by providing more power to citizens who were not land holders.

[2] While there was no physical confrontation, Jackson was relentless in his written attacks and continued even when Waldburger was in his last months of life.

[3] This source report is from The Georgia Gazette (8/5/1790, 3:2). "Jacob Waldburge, Esq., to Miss Kitty Millen, daughter of Stephen Millen, Esq., deceased." The report of marriage was important, since without a "prenuptial agreement" all of the property became the property of the husband. The marriage was recorded in the Deed Records of Chatham County (H379-385) on July 31, 1790 and October 19, 1970. The agreement was recorded before and after the marriage.

[4] Was the son of prominent businessman who inherited the lower part of Ossabaw Island from his father, John Morel. The senior John Morel was a friend of the senior Waldburg from the time they were associated with James Jackson.

[5] One of Georgia's leading statesmen and a colleague of James Jackson who filled his seat in the United States Senate. Milledge was a revolutionary war hero and Governor of Georgia from 1802 to 1806. In 1803, Milledgeville, the state capital, was named in his honor.

[6] Jones was another colleague of James Jackson. He was the U. S. Representative from the 2nd district of Georgia from 1792-1793.

[7] Compiled from Columbian Museum and Savannah Advertiser (6/15/1803, 3:5).

[8] An earlier name for tuberculosis. This was the same illness that took the life of her first husband, Jacob Waldburger, who died in 1797.

[9] Recorded in the Deed Records of Chatham County (2E 47-49) on November 20, 1812.

[10] It is not clear where she was buried or if she was interred at the St. Bonaventure Cemetery with her children. A stone fragment with "Millen" inscribed was found at the cemetery at the burial site. There is no written record that Catharine was buried in the cemetery.

[11] U.S. Code (1807): "that the captain...of any ship or vessel of the burthen of forty tons or more, from and after the first day of January, one thousand eight hundred and eight sailing coastwise, from any port in the United States, to any port or place within the jurisdiction of the same, having on board any Negro, mulatto, or person of color, for the purpose of transporting them to be sold or disposed of as slaves, or to be held to service or labour, shall, previous to the departure of ship or vessel, make out and subscribe duplicate manifests."

[12] Secretary of Treasury William H. Crawford and political patron of the Colonization Society (American Society for the Colonizing the Free People of Color of the United States). The purpose was to establish an American colony in Africa inhabited by American free blacks.

[13] Richard Wylly Habersham, District Attorney of Georgia, ordered Marshall Morel to house the Africans in Savannah. Habersham corresponded with Secretary of State John Quincy Adams about the situation. Adams informed President James Monroe, who ordered Habersham to defend the Africans who were being claimed as captives.

[14] Judge John Macpherson Berrien was the attorney for John Jackson, the Captain of *The Dallas* who claimed salvage rights to the captives.

[15] John Marshall, Chief Justice of the Supreme Court, wrote the majority opinion.

[16] It is not clear if any of the captives spent time on St. Catherines with the Waldburgs.

[17] Gout now refers to a disease where uric acid crystals inflame the joint. In the 1800s, any disease that also produced joint pain was called gout. In Morel's case it was likely kidney disease and hypertension that caused his death.

[18] His physician was Dr. Habersham. He died at his home on Perry and Jackson Street.

[19] The Great Ogeechee Church was established in 1803. It was the second church to be established by the First African Baptist Church, the oldest black church in North America. The First African Baptist Church on St. Catherines was still holding services in the late 1920s. Gladys Woods attended services held in the old plantation house on the south end of St. Catherines in the 1930s when she was living in the Oemler house. Many of the members would row their boats the six miles from Harris Neck to attend the church.

[20] There is no other information about any marriage of his father.

[21] We are not sure where the "pasture fence" was located.

[22] A Thomas Oden was listed as an Overseer of the Butler Plantation by Franny Kemble. See John A. Scott (ed.), *Journal of a Residence on a Georgian Plantation in 1838-1839 by Frances Anne Kemble* (Athens: University of Georgia Press, 1984), pp. 210-211.

[23] The estates of James Wilson (9 enslaved individuals), John Winn (26), William Ward (57) are all listed as having slaves on St. Catherines. Doctor Paul H. Wilkins, Jr. had 22 slaves on the Island.

[24] Original data: United States of America, Bureau of the Census. *Fifth Census of the United States, 1830.* Washington, D.C.: National Archives and Records Administration, 1830. M19, 201 rolls. From Ancestry.com. *1830 United States Federal Census* [database on-line]. Provo, UT, USA: MyFamily.com, Inc., 2004.

[25] The census is at odds with the report on absentee slave owners.

[26] John Woods has pointed out to me that the evidence for Button Gwinnett building the house in question is suspect. To claim that many of the old tabby buildings come from this period is difficult to support. We know that the Waldburgs used slaves to construct many of the tabby buildings such as the cotton gin. According to Mandrake Floyd (1937), the most authoritative voice on tabby construction, the buildings are of similar construction and date to the Waldburg era.

[27] "Congestive chills" was a term used for malaria or malaria with diarrhea.

[28] George M. Waldburg's will Number 244. Probate Court of Chatham County, Savannah, Georgia.

[29] The reference to the "big" house as the Button Gwinnett house began in the 1930s with C. M. Keys and his wife Indiola.

[30] The chimney still stands and can be seen from Waldburg Creek.

[31] The Union and Southern Rights party grew out of the 1850 Compromise crafted by Henry Clay. The compromise was a way to deal with the slavery issue as the country expanded westward. California was admitted as a free state. New Mexico, Nevada, Arizona and Utah would decide later by a vote of their citizens when they applied for statehood. The most controversial aspect of the compromise was the Fugitive Slave Act, which required American citizens to return escaped slaves to their owners. There were those in the Southern Rights Party that wanted to remain in the Union, and they formed the short lived "Union and Southern Rights Party."

[32] Yellow Fever devastated Savannah that year (see George Miller Sternberg, *Report on the Etiology and Prevention of Yellow Fever*) (Washington, DC: Government Printing Office).

[33] We have not found indication of the marriage of George Sr., or details about the birth of George Jr.

[34] Dropsy describes an accumulation of water in the tissue of an individual usually suffering from congestive heart failure.

[35] The headstone lists 26 Jul 1822 as the date of birth and date of death as 28 Jul 1847.

[36] In 1870, they were living on the Refuge Plantation. According to the census they had land worth $10,000 and personal property valued at $50,000. Source Citation: Year: 1870; Census Place: Not Stated, Camden, Georgia; Roll: M593_139; Page: 671; Image: 88. Ancestry.com. 1870 United States Federal Census [database on-line]. Provo, UT, USA: MyFamily.com, Inc., 2003. Original data: 1870.

[37] This organization was not ordered by General Saxton.

[38] The Atlanta Constitution reported that the Rauers "bought it from a Cuban named Rodriquez, who, six years before, had purchased it from the estate of Jacob Waldburg." The Cuban referred to in the article is Anna Rodriguez, who was listed on the property transfer documents.

[39] Elizabeth Waldburg is listed in the census as Mrs. Jacob Walburgetter (age 80). J. H. M. Clinch, planter, and E.S. W. Clinch are also listed. There were two servants and their child living in the house. See Source Citation: Year: *1880*; Census Place: *Savannah, Chatham, Georgia*; Roll: *T9_138*; Family History Film: *1254138*; Page: *381.1000*; Enumeration District: *19*; Image: *0325*. Source Information:Ancestry.com and The Church of Jesus Christ of Latter-day Saints. *1880 United States Federal Census* [database on-line]. Provo, UT, USA: The Generations Network, Inc., 2005. 1880 U.S. Census Index provided by The Church of Jesus Christ of Latter-day Saints.

[40] She is buried in lot 125E.

[41] The 1900 Census (Year: *1900*; Census Place: *Savannah, Chatham, Georgia*; Roll: *T623 186*; Page: *7A*; Enumeration District: *56*.) lists Elizabeth age 68 and John H. M. Clinch age 78 living on Oglethorpe Avenue. John's occupation is listed as capitalist.

[42] She was buried on March 19, 1903 and is buried in section C-16.

[43] John Houston McIntosh Clinch was buried on March 16, 1904.

Chapter 6. The Forgotten Century

[1] Eutherle, who was two years old at that time, was not listed in the census. She was Nancy's niece and joined them after the census. Eutherle was adopted after 1930.

[2] In this account, James C. Willson is incorrectly identified as James C. Wilson.

[3] The house that he occupied was called the "Wilson House." It was assumed that it referred to the house of one of the new owners of the island. It is more likely that it was used to refer to the house being occupied by the superintendent.

[4] Clelma was listed as Clettus in the 1930 census records.

[5] Glenise was listed as Gerrnesse on the 1930 census records.

[6] Incorrectly referred to in the *New York Times* account as Jacob Paners.

[7] Slavery was prohibited by law in 1735 and became legal in 1751.

[8] The Creek practiced enslavement of captives from other Native American groups. Enslaved women and children were frequently incorporated into the Creek social system. The Creek were also familiar with enslavement of blacks. Most traders had at least one slave.

[9] The purchase was a long term lease.

[10] Since his wife and child were not with Gwinnett, the grant was not finalized. Two years later, with the return of his family, he re-petitioned the Council and the land was again awarded to him.

[11] Gwinnett used Quamina, Sam, Cuff, Qua, Cleo, and Doll as security for the loan from Noble Jones (Jenkins 1926:46).

[12] Darnie, Boston, Jacob, Mary, Doll and her children Judith and Flora were sold to James Read of Savannah (Jenkins 1926:49).

[13] Waldburg civil records can be found under Waldburger.

[14] On February 17,1786, the court ordered the island be divided with half going to John McQueen, a fourth to Nathan Brownson, and a fourth to Henry Putnam.

[15] We have not been able to determine where the pasture fence was located.

[16] Of the 100 plantations on the coast (15th Militia District), only six had at least 1000 acres and 100 slaves. In addition to those listed, Moses L. Jones and Joseph H. Jones, Sr. also had 1000 acres and 100 slaves.

[17] Original data: United States of America, Bureau of the Census. *Seventh Census of the United States, 1850.* Washington, D.C.: National Archives and Records Administration, 1850. M432. 1,009 rolls. Available from Ancestry.com. *1850 U.S. Federal Census -Slave Schedules* [database on-line]. Provo, UT, USA: MyFamily.com, Inc., 2004.

[18] Glover (1987:146) claims that Waldburg had 120 "slaves."

[19] Original data: United States of America, Bureau of the Census. *Seventh Census of the United States, 1850.* Washington. D.C.: National Archives and Records Administration, 1850. M432. 1,009 rolls. From: Ancestry.com. *1850* U.S. Federal Census Slave Schedules (database online). Provo, UT, USA: MyFamily.com, Inc., 2004.

[20] George M. Waldburg Will #244. Probate Court of Chatham County, Savannah, Georgia.

[21] Original data: United States of America, Bureau of the Census. *Eighth Census of the United States, 1860.* Washington, D.C.: National Archives and Records Administration, 1860. Rolls. Available from Ancestry.com. *1860 Federal Census – Slave Schedules* [database on-line]. Provo, UT, USA: MyFamily.com, Inc., 2004.

[22] E.P.B., correspondent for the *New York Times* was on the U. S. Steamer Madgie in St. Simons Sound. The report was filed on October 31,1862.

[23] *The Liberator* was published by William Lloyd Garrison in Boston from 1831-1865. He was considered a careful reporter of events in the South.

[24] Order 15 states that 40 acres would be provided for each emancipated slave. There is no mention of a mule.

[25] Cimbala (1989:600) reported that 40,000 ex-slaves were settled on 400,000 acres of land set asides by Sherman's Order 15.

[26] Hamilton Delagall   May 1   5 family members, 30 acres

Richard Buffett	May 1	6 family members, 30 acres
John Pier	May 1	2 family members, 10 acres
Cesar Bristow	May 1	4 family members, 40 acres
Geo. Delagall	May 1	2 family members, 20 acres
Chas. Dolly[26]	May 2	1 family members, 10 acres
Theodore Mitchell	May 2	4 family members, 40 acres
Bill Tice	May 2	2 family members, 25 acres
Prince McIntosh	May 2	3 family members, 25 acres
?Truin Low	May 12	2 family members, 20 acres
Andrew Neal[26]	May 15	5 family members, 40 acres
Sandy Milledge	May 17	2 family members, 15 acres
Horace Hamm	May 17	4 family members, 20 acres
Remus Elliot	Aug. 11	4 family members, 40 acres
Farmer Jones	Aug. 11	10 family members, 30 acres
Robert Monroe	Sept. 6	3 family members, 40 acres
Peter Lloyd[26]	Oct. 6	9 family members, 40 acres
John B. Savage	Aug. 4	3 family members, 40 acres
Isaac Jones	Oct. 6	3 family members, 40 acres

[27] Tunis Campbell clearly over stepped his authority. He assigned land to himself, his sons, and even Blacks that were born free.

[28] The cotton production after the Civil War was too much like slavery for many of the Freedmen.

[29] *The Radical Abolition Press* claimed that southern whites would be hostile to northern whites.

[30] John was 40 years old at the time and living with his wife Sarah B. Winchester, who was ten years younger than him. There were two children Sarah (8 years old) and Henry W. (6 years old). Date Source: Ancestry.com. *1860 United States Federal Census* [database on-line]. Provo, UT, USA: The Generations Network, Inc., 2004. Original data: United States of America, Bureau of the Census. *Eighth Census of the United States, 1860.* Washington, D.C.: National Archives and Records Administration, 1860. M653, 1,438 rolls. Census Place: *Lynn Ward 1, Essex, Massachusetts*; Roll: *M653_495*; Page: *507*; Image: *6*.

[31] The story of the *Alligator*'s beginnings is as fascinating as its tragic end. The *Alligator* was the "brainchild" of Brutus De Villeroi, whose occupation in the 1880 United States Census was listed as "natural genius." Smith (2006) tells the how the green cigar shaped vessel resembling its namesake was tested in the water near Philadelphia, and it created such a commotion (the *Philadelphia Inquirer* page 1 story described it as an "infernal machine") that it was confiscated and those involved in the test arrested. Subsequently, De Villeroi was contracted to build a submarine for $14,000 and deliver it within 40 days.

[32] There is an effort by the Navy & Marine Living History Association (NMLHA), National Oceanic & Atmospheric Administration (NOAA) and Office of Naval Research (ONR) to recover the Alligator. See http://www.navyandmarine.org/alligator/.

[33] The Freedmen's Bureau grew out of the Port Royal Experiment. Given the *U.S.S. Sumpter*'s use of Port Royal, Winchester may have been aware of the possibility of St. Catherines a site for his ideas about farming cotton.

[34] Tunis Campbell had advised them not to accept employment from Winchester and Schuyler.

[35] According to Cimbala (1983:277), Winchester died in "considerable" debt and Schuyler returned to the North "utterly" bankrupt.

[36] The *New York Times* (January 4, 1868, Pg 8.) reports that H. Winchester, Mrs. J. F. Winchester, Miss Sarah Winchester and servant arrived in New York on the steamship Huntsville from Savannah.

[37] On the original census record, Jacob occupation was listed as merchant planter. The planter designation was crossed out.

[38] Source Citation: Year: *1880;* Census Place: *Saint Catherines Island. Liberty, Georgia*; Roll: *T9_155;* Family History Film: *1254155;* Page: *21.1000;* Enumeration District: 66; Image: *0395*.

[39] Their racial identification is relevant given the topic of this chapter.

[40] The term "productive segment of a population" is a technical demographic term indicating the percentage of individuals between 15 and 65 years of age.

[41] Given the Rauers' goal to make the island a game preserve, these farms were small family plots.

[42] The correct term is hostler, which means stableman.

[43] In the most complete later history of the island (Durham and Thomas 1978:237), the name is spelled Umbler. This reflects how much of what we know about the later occupation of the island is dependent on oral histories.

[44] The statement that the Oemler house was built on the foundation needs further study. When Thomas was on the island, part of it had been removed because of damage that occurred while it was unoccupied after Oemler left the island. There was a chimney that remained, located away from the renovated building.

[45] The 1920 Census used the term "colored" as the racial identifier.

[46] There has been extensive interest in the role that Tunis Campbell played in the history of the island. There has been little interest in understanding the demographic changes on the island.

Chapter 7. How St. Catherines Got Her Groove Back

[1] Given all that was revealed of the hunt, it is surprising that some newspaper accounts claimed that the hunters were reluctant informants. They were hunting out of season and feared that the Liberty County game wardens would pursue them. The Chicago Daily Tribune (1902b:9) said that, since the hunt was on private land, the game laws did not apply. This is certainly a misunderstanding of the law.

[2] As part of the sales price, Rauers paid Anna M Rodriguez's $5000 mortgage at 10% interest held by O. H. Schreiner of New York. In addition, he signed a promissory note for $17,250 (Rauers 1876b) paid on September 1,

1876. Rodriguez and Mrs. Schreiner shared the "big" house on St. Catherines. Jacob Rauers bought the personal property for $5000 (Rauers 1876a). There is an inventory that lists the furnishings for the house by room.

[3] The newspaper account had the caveats "it was said" and "traditions have it," leaving the veracity of this story open to interpretation. John Woods and I have not found any sources that support the Cuban angle reported in this story. The Spanish-American War began and ended in 1898. The war's end brought Cuba into the American sphere of influence, ending its ties with Spain. One of the heroes of the Spanish-American War was Admiral Winifred S. Schley, who was mentioned in accounts of hunting deer on St. Catherines. The Cuban twist to St. Catherines may have the result of playing to Schley's reputation and emphasizing the importance of St. Catherines in that phase of American history.

[4] An infant died in childbirth.

[5] The 1880 census reported Frieda's name as Fredericka.

[6] Van Mater (1904) reiterated the point that Rauers only allowed limited agricultural activity, and is quoted as saying (1904: 442), "My host further told me that he allows no cultivation of the soil, excepting small garden patches, for fear of disturbing the deer..." He also claims that Rauers "found that it was injudicious to encourage the settlement of more negroes on the island than were actually necessary for the work, for in the African there is, deep rooted, the making of a poacher." The statement about Africans having a "deep rooted" propensity for poaching" is suspect. In the article, there are numerous racial references, suggesting Van Mater's bias. In portraying the head beater, Van Mater (1904:444) described him "with a mouth and teeth which would make the fortune of a minstrel singer..." Van Mater further states that 10,000 to 20,000 deer inhabit the island, making the issue of poaching by black residents a non-issue. John suggests that the island could carry 1,000 deer maximum on the available land.

[7] He was known as Wayne Cunningham.

[8] When he resigned shortly before his death, he was conferred the Order of the Crown.

[9] The town of Pilsen, Germany claims that the pilsner style of beer for which they are famous dates back to 1307. In actuality, in 1840 there was a movement by the burghers to raise the standard of the beer. Soon after the 1840s, many breweries in the United States began using the same process and standards.

[10] Rauers was intent on ensuring that he was protected by purchasing the marsh around St. Catherines. On January 27, 1893, he purchased Moss Island from Lancaster King for $150 as recorded by the Clerk of Court (Liberty County 1893). Moss Island was composed of several hammocks between South New Port River and Moll Clark Creek.

[11] The party consisted of Jacob Rauers, Harry Daniels, James Dent, Florance Minis, Charles Shearson, Mayhew Cunningham, and Dr. William Duncan from Savannah. J. W. Schley from Atlanta was also present.

[12] The island is twelve miles long and three miles wide.

[13] Venery in this context refers to the chase or hunt.

[14] It is six miles from the mainland and thirty miles south of Savannah.

[15] Schley commanded the "Flying Squadron" during the blockade of Cuba. William T. Sampson, who was officially in command, was not in a position to participate in the battle when the trapped Spanish Admiral Pascual Cervera y Tolete tried to "run" the blockade. Even though Schley was following the battle plan of William T. Sampson, he was considered the hero, with Sampson, to his chagrin, all but forgotten. The bitterness of Sampson led to a dispute that went to an official hearing. Teddy Roosevelt, in his infinite wisdom, called it a "Captain's battle" with Samson "technically in command."

[16] The *McCauley* was outfitted with a whistle that was a steam siren taken from *Almirante Oquendo*, a ship that Schley crew sunk at the battle in Santiago.

[17] In addition to Schley, Gordon and Rauers, General Gordon's son, W. W. Gordon Jr., W. W Williamson (partner in business), J. L. Dent, P. W. Meldrim, and Jimmy Schley were present.

[18] This pejorative term was common in the early 1900s, and was not considered as offensive as other terms. It is interesting that during this sojourn, Schley was well received in his visits to the black colleges in Savannah.

[19] Most of the descriptions of the hunts mention staying at the mansion, which was used as the base of operation.

[20] John Wood explained full choke was used to shoot deer and modified choke for birds and other small animals. John said that with his shotgun, he would have one barrel with a full choke and another with a modified choke.

[21] *Outing* began publication in 1882 and ceased publication in 1923.

[22] One picture shows eight hounds and three horses.

[23] John surmises that they had stopped at Mary's Mound.

[24] A footnote from the editors of *Outing*: "The shotgun is always unsportsmanly on deer, no matter what the conditions, and its use cannot be excused on any ground. Our southern friends are far behind in the ethics of the game. – Editor."

[25] Alexander McDonald and his brother and James McHenry used their middle names in tribute to their Scottish heritage on their mother's side of the family. McDonald was host of the hunt. His father had died in 1904 and John Jacob, his older brother, was involved in the family businesses. McHenry was in his sophomore year at Yale.

[26] The steamer belonged to Major and Mrs. W. A. Wilkins of Waynesboro.

[27] William F. Tempkin was in the United States Engineers Office in Savannah. Tempkin said that Albert W. Jones from Sapelo Island gave him a copy of the act. He (Tempkin 1927) wrote that "I enjoyed every minute of the stay at St. Catherines," and said, "Please call on me anytime if I can deliver packages, messages, etc., when en route south."

[28] A. Pratt Adams was Samuel Adam's nephew, and was his partner in the law office of Adams, Adams and Douglas in Savannah.

[29] The newspaper account says Ossabaw Sound. It was most likely St. Catherines Sound.

[30] One of the appraisers for Liberty County thought that it was worth eight times the $60,000 appraisal.

[31] The same account said that the revenue ship *Boutwell* brought the Rauers family safely to Savannah from St. Catherines, which suffered "much damage."

[32] After the yellow fever epidemic of 1876, which killed over a 1,000 people in Savannah alone, the U. S. Marine Hospital Service established the South Atlantic Quarantine Station on Blackbeard Island. The quarantine station was designed have the capability to disinfect ships and, if necessary, quarantine them on Blackbeard Island. The *Hygeia*, a launch, would meet and disinfect ships, their ballasts, and if necessary transport people to the island. The objective was to inspect all ships coming from the Caribbean to the ports of Savannah, Darien, and Brunswick, Georgia (Sullivan 2003). The remains of the crematory built in 1904 can still be seen from Sapelo Sound. John and I have seen the remains of the building many times on our trips around the islands. The crematory is all that remains of the quarantine center in the South that served the same purpose as Ellis Island in the North.

[33] In subsequent deposition it was determined that the *Beatrice McLean* was blown onto the marsh on the west side of the Island.

[34] In an earlier case, Judge Gamble of the Middle Circuit placed an injunction prohibiting interference with the removal of the *Beatrice McLean* from the marsh. Rauers appeal argued that Gamble and the Middle Circuit did not have jurisdiction over St. Catherines Island.

[35] Interestingly, the newspaper account reported that Oemler took the corpse and his assailant to the Chatham County authorities, and was informed that St. Catherines was part of Liberty County. John Woods suggested that, at that time, most contact was with Savannah and it would have "made sense" to take the body there. In 1906 (AC 1906b), there was a report on the recovery of Lieutenant Henry Morgan, who drowned in the 1898 hurricane that hit Tybee Island. Gus Oemler (the paper spelled it Emler) helped exhume the body from a shallow grave.

[36] As I mentioned earlier in the chapter, the agreement was filed in Liberty County Superior Court in 1918 when the issue of fishing rights on private estates became an issue. It was filed again in when the Rauers leased oyster rights to C. Philip Maggioni and Joseph P. Maggioni, recorded on January 23, 1928 (Liberty County 1929b).

[37] At the end of the lease, he was to remove all of these structures.

[38] In the most complete later history of the island (Durham and Thomas 1978:237), the name is spelled Umbler. This difference in spelling reflects how much of what we know about the later occupation of island is dependent on oral historiesy. The family is divided on the pronunciation. Most pronounce it "Ahmler," and others "Emler."

[39] John's mother always referred to the car as Mrs. Oemler's convertible. She also pointed out that it was the first automobile on the island.

[40] His biography attributed his death to apoplexy, which in modern medicine would be called a stroke.

[41] Acts of The General Assembly, 1918, page 256.

[42] In the *Atlanta Constitution* report, his name is given incorrectly as R. F. Bashan. Dr. Peter F. Behnsen moved to Americus, Georgia in 1900 and was appointed Georgia's First Veterinarian in 1907 and held the position for 20 years. He died in 1961.

[43] Incorrectly identified as Samuel E. Adams in the *Atlanta Constitution's* account.

[44] Adams was certainly not an impartial legal observer. He was a friend of the family and was an executor of Jacob Rauers' will, which that had been filed on June 6, 1904.

[45] These inflated numbers were from the *Atlanta Constitution* report, "Cattle Dipping May Not Extend to Coast Islands."

[46] The tabby blocks are different from the tabby used in constructing the tabby dwellings of enslaved populations. The tabby was poured in forms and then left to harden. The forms were removed and placed on the newly hardened layer to form another layer.

Chapter 8. St. Catherines' Resurrection and Fall from Grace.

[1] This was C. M. Keys' second marriage. His first marriage ended in divorce.

[2] The honor was presented by TJRF, a journalism trade magazine, and Master Card International. See http://www.newsbios.com/newslum/notables.htm#k.

[3] The first transcontinental flight was a combination railroad and plane travel. Since airplane travel was restricted to daylight hour, you traveled by train during the night, See Arthur D. Dubin. 2003. Coast to Coast by Rail and Air in *Classic Trains*, Winter Issue, page 20. As Dubin describes it, "The route used the PRR between New York and Port Columbus,Ohio, a brand-new air-rail terminal seven miles east of Columbus, where 5,000 people waited in the rain on the morning of July 8 to watch the passengers as they transferred to two nearby TAT Tri-Motors. The planes would take the adventurers to 'Airport,' Okla., a new landing field 4½ miles from Waynoka, on the Santa Fe's southerly main line. At Waynoka, they found waiting for them another Pullman for an overnight trip to Clovis, New Mexico. At Clovis on the morning of the third day, the passengers again boarded Tri-Motors to fly to Los Angeles, where they landed in the late afternoon, amid cheers from another waiting crowd."

[4] Transcontinental & Western Air Transport eventually became TWA.

[5] Each transcontinental passenger received a solid gold fountain pen made by Tiffany, the exclusive New York jeweler.

[6] In one interview, Gee alluded to the fact that Mrs. Keys was the one "with the money." She described Mr. Keys as somewhat "morbid." Keys had suffered financial reversals and was said to have suffered a "nervous breakdown."

[7] On January 21, 1903, the show opened on Broadway at the Majestic Theatre in New York. The production was extremely popular, and with over 290 performances, it was one of the longest running shows of the decade. I have not seen any reference to her participation in the New York Production. In the *Los Angeles Times* story that announced the wedding, which took place in Providence (Los Angeles Times 1904), it was said that she had been playing the Fairy Queen for several months.

[8] Internet Broadway Database http://www.ibdb.com/person.asp?id=30149.

[9] The term "the real McCoy" has been attributed as a description of "Kid McCoy." According to the story, a man at a bar challenged the dapperly dressed McCoy to fight, even though his friends warned him that McCoy was a boxing champ. Not believing them, he engaged in the fight and was knocked out with a single punch. When he came to his senses, he uttered the words, "Oh my God, that the real McCoy" For other possibilities, see http://en.wikipedia.org/wiki/Real_McCoy.

[10] He married nine times; Indiola was his sixth wife. Wife three, four and five was the actress Julia E. Woodruff. They were married in1897 and divorced on November 28, 1900; remarried on January 7, 1901 and divorced on January 11, 1902; and remarried yet again on April 11, 1902 and divorced again on January 9, 1903. After a manslaughter conviction in 1924 for the death of a fiancée, Ms. Theresa Mors, Selby served eight years in San Quentin. He was later hired by Henry Ford. In 1940, he committed suicide in a Detroit hotel room, leaving a note signed Norman Selby and addressed "To whom it may concern." He explained, "I can't stand the world's madness any longer." In another note addressed to the "youth of America," he advised, "keep your bodies clean" and "be always in condition for any emergency."

[11] Source Citation: Year: *1920*; Census Place: *Glen Ridge, Essex, New Jersey*; Roll: *T625_1029*; Page: *5B*; Enumeration District: *55*; Image: *1158*. Source Information: Ancestry.com. *1920 United States Federal Census* [database on-line]. Provo, UT, USA: MyFamily.com, Inc., 2005. Note: Enumeration Districts 819-839 on roll 323 (Chicago City. Original data: United States of America, Bureau of the Census. *Fourteenth Census of the United States, 1920*. Washington, D.C.: National Archives and Records Administration, 1920. T625, 2,076 rolls.

[12] The children never visited St. Catherines Island.

[13] Indiola Reilly is listed on several passenger lists traveling to and from Cuba with Hugh J. Reilly, Jr. Reilly and his father, a New York politician and railroad contractor, were involved in a long lawsuit in Cuba over a contact dispute. In 1910, she traveled alone from Havana, Cuba to New York on the *S. S. Havana* (Source Year: *1910*; Microfilm serial: *T715*; Microfilm roll: *T715_1486*; Line: *5*; Ancestry.com. *New York Passenger Lists, 1820-1957* [database on-line]. Provo, UT, USA: The Generations Network, Inc., 2006. In 1912, she was with her husband. Source: Year: *1912*; Microfilm serial: *T715*; Microfilm roll: *T715_1908*; Line: *30*; . Ancestry.com. *New York Passenger Lists, 1820-1957* [database on-line]. Provo, UT, USA: The Generations Network, Inc., 2006.

[14] Willson is the correct spelling.

[15] Fred W. Jones was the local Associate of Wayne Cunningham, a broker and the Rauers's son-in-law. *Christian Science Monitor* (CSM 1929) also mentions the sale for $1 million.

[16] The influential online Sherpa Guide book states that Coffin owned St. Catherines and that he enlarged and restored Gwinnett's Old House.

(http://www.sherpaguides.com/georgia/coast/central_coast/st_catherines_island.html). St. Catherines is rife with misinformation.

[17] Willson's name in the document was spelled Wilson.

[18] Only a single slave cabin (cabin 1) was renovated. The other tabby cabins were built in the style of slave cabins, with the addition of screened porches.

[19] In the late 1960s, Tom Watson of IBM fame had his chief pilot develop a plan for an airstrip that would accommodate small jets. When they made plans for the animal survival center, the plans were scrapped.

[20] It was assumed that the Wilson house that served as the superintendent's house was built for James C. Willson. As we pointed out earlier, describing it as the Wilson house is likely a reference to Arthur Wilson, who was living in the house at the time of the major renovation.

[21] The New York Supreme Court denied her petition for separation, claiming that they lacked jurisdiction. They believed that their legal residence was in Kentucky.

[22] In an interview (Lee 1988), he said his first position on the island was as a carpenter's assistant.

[23] *Egg Island* was sold after the renovation was completed.

[24] From John: Daddy met my mother, Gladys Rogers, who was raised on Colonels' Island (Liberty County), while she was visiting relatives in Lexsy, Georgia. Later they married on December 19, 1924 (Dad was 24 years old and. Mom was16 years old). They farmed the Durden property at Covina, Georgia, near Swansboro, for about two years. They moved to the coast near Colonels Island. Daddy sold fish trapped and sold wild animals, 'coons and mink one winter on Ossabaw Island.

[25] The restored "slave" cabin was Cabin 1 which is nearest the "big" house.

[26] Later, when Mr. Noble began the cattle business, Rock Field was enclosed with a fence.

[27] John said that the recycling of the materials from the Rauers mansion included a process in which key elements, such as mantles and mirrors, were protected in the barn until ready for installation and then the materials were placed in a save pile or a discard pile, All the cement tabby like blocks from the foundation were saved and were used for the at least a half a century. When Mr. Noble needed a block to aid in mounting his horse, a Rauers foundation block was retrieved. Toby Woods, always the recycler, used foundation blocks for building his fish fry area, to catch water from the artesian well, and for many other projects through the years.

[28] "The big Swede" was another nickname that was used for Wilson.

[29] These buildings were built in the area where the slave cabins were originally constructed. These building were offset so that four cabins facing Waldburg Creek would have an unobstructed view of the creek.

[30] John said that years later, Johnny told him that he was trying to remove a limb that had fallen on the hand rail when he slipped off and fell into the water that was shoulder deep. He couldn't climb out since the sides were too steep.

[31] The glass jar batteries were made by the Willard Battery Company and Exide Battery Company. Deacon Tire and Battery on Whittaker Street, Savannah were later distributors.

[32] In 1946, E. J. Noble modernized the system with Hallett motors, which created additional problems for his father.

[33] The converter may have had a number of appliances attached to them. By turning off the converter, the electricity stored would last throughout the night.

[34] John suspects that the Hallet engines were used, and were not designed for long hours of use that occurred on the island.

[35] In 1971 another renovation undertaken by the Noble Foundation provided the need to determine how the earlier renovation was undertaken.

[36] This is what Ben Chapman called the oyster laden cement that simulated tabby.

[37] The weight of the roof was a problem, and the stress showed on the walls of the house.

[38] The "big" house that the Keys referred to as the Button Gwinnett House.

[39] Restored is somewhat of an overstatement since all that remained of the original cabin 1 were the exposed beams and one wall. A tile floor, metal windows, a full bathroom, and porch were all added features that made the cabin livable in the summer heat.

[40] Heatilator was invented in 1927. The Keys spared no expense in providing the latest technology in constructing the "slave" cabins for their guests.

[41] Carl Graham Fisher was to the highways what C. M. Keys was to aviation. Graham was a major force in building roads that link key parts of our nation. He conceived of the Lincoln Highway and the Dixie Highway. He was instrumental in beginning the Indianapolis Motor Speedway in 1909. His most ambitious project was turning a bug infested mangrove swamp into Miami Beach.His success in Florida led to his efforts to make Montauk the Miami Beach of the North.

[42] In the original deed to Willson and the St. Catherines Corporation, timbering was prohibited.

[43] For some reason, in the May 31st letter, Keys seems to think the problem in getting out of his dilemma was a impending Wage and Hour Bill. The Fair Labor Standard Act of 1938 was passed by Congress and signed by President Roosevelt on June 23, 1938.Keys feared that the bill was holding up the recovery of the South because it banned child labor, made the minimum wage 25 cents an hour, and made the maximum work week 44 hours.

[44] Thomas Bayard McCabe was President of Scott Paper Company from 1927 to 1967 and turned it into a $2 billion enterprise.

[45] The 1930 census has them living in Branchburg, New Jersey.

[46] By all accounts, Mr. Tester was not much of a fisherman. John surmises that he was on the dock and had his picture taken with the fish. John said that Mr. Tester and his dad would go casting together and share the money from the fish that were sold. Eventually, Toby convinced Mr. Tester to stay home. He would go casting by himself, but he would still share the profits with Mr. Tester.

[47] Certificate number: *031231*. Ancestry.com. *Georgia Deaths, 1919-98* [database on-line]. Provo, UT, USA: MyFamily.com, Inc., 2001. Original data: State of Georgia. *Indexes of Vital Records for Georgia: Deaths, 1919-1998.* Georgia, USA: Georgia Health Department, Office of Vital Records, 1998.

[48] Number: 555-21-3974; Issue State: California; Issue Date: 1973. Ancestry.com. Social Security Death Index [database on-line]. Provo, UT, USA: MyFamily.com, Inc., 2006. Original data: Social Security Administration. Social Security Death Index, Master File. Social Security Administration.

[49] Indiola Arnold Keys was born on the 23rd of October, 1885.

[50] Mr. Harper was Dorothy William's father. Dorothy and Clarence Williams were good friends of Toby and Gladys.

[51] Website: http://www.fs.fed.us/fmsc/measure/cruising/index.shtml.

[52] The Biltmore cruiser stick is an ingenious device. It was a ruler that had a 25-inch reach (the cruiser would hold the stick 25 inches from their eye to measure). It would measure diameters from 6 inches to 74 inches in 2-inch increments. It could measure tree heights to up to 144 feet by 16-foot log lengths.It could even determine the board foot values of the 16-foot logs that were being measured. The Biltmore cruiser sticks are still available from forest supply houses for $55.95.

[53] Curtis did not use his given name Daniel. Daniel Curtis Lee died on May 14, 1986 in his 66th year.

[54] It was then taken to Reynolds and Manley to be processed into finished lumber.

[55] The original salvage yard was on East Broad Street, south of Liberty Street in Savannah. The city of Savannah forced Curtis to move the "junk yard" to Louisville Road near the railroad complex in West Savannah. The Lee's "junk yard" was shrine-like for the Woods. There was always something that needed repair, and the budget was always tight when it came to repairing equipment.

[56] The practice on the island was to bury animals that died or any equipment that was beyond repair.

[57] When Curtis left St. Catherines, he bought a junkyard in Cedartown, Georgia. His letterhead for Lee Iron & Metal Company said it was the "Buyer of Scrap Iron, Metal, Paper and Rags." Curtis bought the junkyard from Knight and was operating it when he was forced to move it to West Savannah.

[58] They eventually moved down to Yamassee Field to harvest the timber surrounding it. Yamassee Field is approximately two miles south of Meeting House Field.

[59] The Black lumber stackers loading the lumber were paid 30 cents an hour.

[60] The bill for 1941 was $2516.70. The additional must have been from another year.

Chapter 9. Uncle Aaron and Aunt Nancy

[1] The 1930 Federal Census, taken in April of that year, lists Aaron's age as 45 and Nancy's age as 35. Eutherle is not listed in the census. Susanna Jones, age 48, was listed as living in the Austin house as a boarder. Her occupation was servant for a private family. The only other inhabitants listed in the census were Arthur Wilson and his wife Anna, their three daughters (Josephine, Mary, Margaret) and son John. George Wilson, a boarder, is also listed.

[2] When John and his family knew her, she was called Ucilee.

[3] Just before leaving the island, Aaron, Nancy and Eutherle moved to the north end of the island, where Uncle Austin was the watchman at the sawmill. A key duty of the watchman was to maintain the fire for the steam boiler that drove the sawmill.

[4] The issue of who built the tabby manor house has been a focus of John's research. He challenges the claim that Button Gwinnett built the manor house.

[5] Tabby was made of lime-burnt oyster shells and sand.

[6] They cooked outside or in the fireplace.

[7] Harris Neck is in McIntosh County, Georgia, about fifty miles south of Savannah "as the crow flies." To reach Harris Neck, you exit I-95 at Exit 67 and travel south on U.S.-17 for approximately one mile, then east on Harris Neck Road for nine miles to the general area.

[8] The Campbell name was likely taken as a tribute to Tunis Campbell, who was the leader of the freed Blacks on St. Catherines following emancipation. He established the Freedmen State on the island.

[9] The Social Security Death Index (2006 Ancestry.com, Provo, Utah: MyFamily.com, Inc) recorded the death of Aaron Austin, who was born 2 May 1886 and died in June 1953.

[10] John said that Persimmon Point was the most likely place they beached their boat.

[11] Mollcreek River connects the North Newport and South Newport Rivers between St. Catherines and Harris Neck.

[12] We sent her a picture of the manor house, a picture of her family, and a table that her father had made for her when he was the watchman for the sawmill on the north end.

Chapter 10. Exodus from St. Catherines.

[1] Harris Neck was part of Peru Plantation, which became land for the freed Blacks after Sherman's Field Order 15.

[2] The song was rarely sung after World War II, since returning soldiers had converted to Christianity or Islam. Baindu Jabati was taught the song by her grandmother, who wanted to be sure that she was properly buried. Baindu was not only taught the words, but also all of the associated rituals and even the gestures that she must use to ensure that her grandmother could "cross the river."

[3] To drive to the Harris Neck, you take Route 131 off of Highway 17.

[4] Pin Point was another major destination of families that left St. Catherines.

[5] There were a number of modifications in the series of P-40s. The P-40E, nicknamed the Warhawk, was the best known. The P-40Q (only one was built) was last in the series. The P-40s were superseded by the P-47 Thunderbolts and P-51 Mustangs.

[6] The hurricane caused the loss of 300 lives and $100 million (1944 dollars).

[7] Rippen said that he found the report of a crash by James E. Beard. I could not verify this accident.

Chapter 11. War, The Coast Guard and Mr. Noble

[1] Yellow pine was the most desired wood and was comprised of long leaf and slash pine. They cut much of the timber from the high lands of St. Catherines. They cleared much of Sams Field Woods, East Road to King New Ground, and Green Seed Field.

[2] In John Toby's 1944 day book, he notes that a 580-foot deep well with a 3 inch casing to 160 feet was drilled by W. E. Floyd in 1939 at Jack Thigpen's Mills. This was the beginning of the Rauers' exploitation of the timber. A covenant in their purchase agreement prevented the Keys from selling the timber, even though it might have allowed them to maintain their ownership a bit longer.

[3] The Younce Company sawmill was at Meeting House Field and later moved down to the Yamassee Creek area during their final days on the island.

[4] The timbering during 1950s was to "thin" the woods. Charles M. Jones, who became a prominent attorney, boarded with the Woods family while working for C. B. Jones, which was also cutting timber at that time. Charley Jones, who died at the age of 77 on May 2, 2007, was the majority whip of the Georgia House of Representatives from 1967-1970. In 1998, he was in the national news during the Bank of Credit and Commerce International (BCCI) scandal. Jones was the go-between for Georgia politicians and Ghaith Pharaon, who bought and sold the Ford Plantation in Richmond Hill, Georgia. Pharaon was indicted by the FBI for his part in the financial dealings of BCCI.

[5] The shotguns were issued for riot control and would not have been effective if St. Catherines were invaded by German forces.

[6] Mosby was a carpenter before joining the Coast Guard. Riedel was a railroad man, but had worked for a carpenter.

[7] Riedel said that he knew that the barracks were scheduled to arrive on St. Catherines, but had no clue where they originated from.

[8] There is some discrepancy about the amount of money that they were carrying. An FBI memo (German Espionage and Sabotage against the U.S. in World War II: George John Dasch and the Nazi Saboteurs) gives the amount used here. It also confirms the $300 bribe was actually $260.

[9] Some of the explosives were cleverly designed as lumps of coal to be thrown onto coal cars carrying fuel to the factory.

[10] Their capture was due to the action of Cullen, who told his authorities about the spies, and Dasch having second thoughts. He called the FBI on June 14, 1942, giving his name as "Pastorious" (the name of the first German

immigrant during colonial times) and wanting to set up a meeting with J. Edgar Hoover. Five days later, he went to Washington DC, called the FBI, and was taken into custody.

[11] The term used to describe the beach patrol that would walk or ride their designated observation routes on the sandy beaches.

[12] Cullen was also suspicious, since this was an area in which clams were not found.

[13] One account claims that Cullen was shortchanged. There was only $260 when it was counted at the headquarters.

[14] Dasch almost immediately had concerns and contacted the FBI. He had illusions that he would be hailed as a hero and would receive personal thanks from President Franklin Delano Roosevelt.

[15] This action was similar to The United States Military Commissions Act of 2006, Pub. L. No. 109-366, 120 Stat. 2600 (Oct. 17, 2006) that was used to deal with non-combatants following the 9/11 attacks.

[16] St. Catherines was in the sixth Naval District, with headquarters at Charleston Navy Yard in Charleston, South Carolina.

[17] Horse marines were made famous in a 1901 play that made the actress Ethel Barrymore an instant success (Fitch 1902). The play featured a song sung first during the Civil War.

I'm Captain Jinks of the Horse Marines
I feed my horse on corn and beans,
And sport young ladies in their teens
Tho' a Captain in the Army.
I teach the ladies how to dance
How to dance, how to dance
I teach the ladies how to dance
For I'm the pet of the Army

chorus: I'm Captain Jinks of the Horse Marines
I feed my horse on corn and beans,
And often live beyond my means
Tho' a Captain in the Army.

[18] The Coast Guard eventually enlisted 2,000 dogs for patrol duties. Some of the dogs were trained at Hilton Head, S.C. As part of the beach patrol, the dogs were placed on duty in all the districts. On St. Catherines, once the Mounted Patrols were in place, the dogs ceased to be used on the island.

[19] The aggravators were other dog handlers.

[20] Willoughby (1980:50) said that a mounted patrol could cover twice the distance of a foot patrol, and thus cut human resources in half.

[21] This description is from Armed Forces History, Division of History of Technology, National Museum of American History. Catalog #: 273382 Accession #: 54537. According to the Smithsonian Museum (National Museum of American History), Captain George B. McClellan was assigned a tour of Europe to search for ways to update the tactics of the military. He returned in 1859 with modifications to the calvary saddle that was adopted by the United States War Department. It remained the standard issue during the history of the cavalry. The saddle was simple, less expensive, sturdy, and provided support for the rider.

[22] Harold Wilson King, the cook, received his training at the Coast Guard, Manhattan Beach Training Camp in 1942. Walter Winchell, the famous radio news commentator factiously described Manhattan Beach Training Center as the only legal "Concentration Camp" in the world.

[23] It was called the liberty boat since it shuttled Guardsmen to and from Savannah during leave. It was a modified "Picketboat."

[24] Website:
http://www.quartermaster.army.mil/OQMG/Professional_Bulletin/2001/Spring01/quartermaster_remount_service.htm

[25] Willoughby reports that the USCG considered a volunteer mounted beach patrol in which individuals would provide mounts, feed, and stable at their own expense. There was not much interest in the program and it was scrapped on September 18, 1942.

[26] There is a picture of a tractor beyond repair being buried.

[27] The Kapok tree (*Ceiba pentandra*) produces a seed that is light, buoyant, and resistant to water and it was used to fill the safety vests.

[28] According to (Witt and Knudsen 1993), the floss was such a good substitute that eleven million kg of pods were collected to fill 1.2 million "Mae West" life jackets.

[29] The planes flown from Harris Neck Army Air Base were the famous P-39Q "AirCobra" that had a 37 MM cannon firing through the hub of the propeller, two 50-caliber machine-guns in the nose, two 50-caliber machine-guns on the wings, and 500 lbs. of bombs carried externally. The P39Q was replaced with the P40N "Warhawk" that had six 50-caliber machine guns and could carry 700 lbs. of bombs externally. The Warhawk was made famous by the "Flying Tiger Squadron."

[30] There were 43 crashes of planes attached to Harris Neck Army Air Force Base from 1943 to 1944, according to the Aviation Archaeological Investigation and Research (AAIR) group that has provided the most accurate record of plane crashes.

[31]

Date	Plane	Pilot	Location
10/17/43	P-39Q	William F. Hanes Jr.	8 Miles N Harris Neck AAF
03/23/44	P-40N	Edward R. Wheler, Jr	5 Miles East, Harris Neck AAF
04/02/44	P-40N	Robert R. Bean	4 Miles Off Shore E. Harris Neck
04/02/44	P-40N	William J. Ladwig	4 Miles Off Shore E. Harris Neck
04/07/44	P-40N	Edwin C. Beethoven	3 Miles E Harris Neck

[32] According to Rippen, the plane piloted by James E. Beard was the only crash that he was able to uncover in his research.

[33] The Guardsmen's taste in music varied. Gee said that on the Saturdays that Ed Glover was not on duty, he would come to the house to listen to The Metropolitan Opera narrated by Milton Cross and sponsored by the Texaco Company. Texaco sponsored the opera as an act of atonement for their president who was a fan of Adolf Hitler and housed a German spy at Texaco headquarters in New York City in the 1940s. After 63 years, Texaco figured that they has atoned enough and dropped their sponsorship.

[34] "Tex" was a nickname that he received as a member of the United States Coast Guard. After he left the service, he was never referred to as "Tex." Ernest says that the nickname was resurrected when he would reunite with those who served with him, or when he was talking with the Woods family. The 88-year-old veteran lives in Carmine, Texas. He spends three afternoons a week playing dominoes.

[35] Tex and Gee remember that a Guardsman named Bedenbaugh took over the assignment to build the barracks.

[36] The Younce family was cutting timber on St. Catherines.

[37] The weapon carrier was parked on the dock and left out of gear. It rolled down the dock, hit the Coast Guard boat, and sank into Waldburg Creek. Jim Crawley and his crash boat crew came over and retrieved the boat from the water. The date shows that there were still Guardsmen on the island, even after the announced cutbacks in the Mounted Patrol.

[38] John said that the boat was powered by a 7.2 (60) Martin outboard motor. Martin Outboard Motors Company was a division of the National Pressure Cooker Company. The engine was engineered by George Martin and used a poppet-valve induction system. This valve controls the intake of gas and the flow of exhaust. With that tidbit, I have exhausted my knowledge of outboard mechanics.

[39] The shear pin snaps so that the propeller and engine are not damaged when hitting an object in the water

[40] The 1944 day book has entries from January 1-10 and from February 3 to December 31 of that year. For reasons unknown, from January 1 to February 2, the 1944 day book has entries for April 20 to June 7 1945.

[41] Toby Woods called cabin 1 the "small" cottage.

[42] 17A780 had a speed of 10 knots and the trip to Thunderbolt would take about five hours.

[43] I asked why his father had not built a ways earlier. His response solved a mystery. In one of the few letters that remain, Mrs. C. M. Keys (1932:June 28, Letter) wrote to Toby, "In regard to the rope to haul up the *Nautilus*, I would suggest getting a little larger rope though according to Mr. Fisher the boat only weighs 3 tons." John explained to me that his father had rigged a system in which the *Nautilus* would be brought to the boathouse at high tide and tied to the joist, and as the tide went out, the boat would be tied above and his father could work on the bottom of the boat. In the same letter, Mrs. Keys asked about the stability of the dock and thought, "it looked wobbly." John said that his dad had substantially stabilized it for its use as a hoist.

[44] The cradle of the carriage was weighed down by two 200-pound metal ballasts that were salvaged from buoys that had washed ashore. The metal ballast was attached to the bottom buoys with metal chains designed to keep them upright as they bobbed in the water. The buoy was cut in half, and the bottom half had many uses. Toby used one of the bottoms filled with water to test the outboard motors and another to scald hogs as they were processed for food.

[45] Irene Floyd Dykes now lives in Florida.

Chapter 12. Mr. Noble

[1] There was a condescending manner belying class and regional bias in how Mr. Noble treated Toby when he reported an accident. In a letter, Noble responded (Noble 1948a: November 19, letter), "I would hate to think that you are not able to drive an automobile carefully enough to avoid accident regardless of the number of cars on the highway. We have the same situation up here all through the week and I haven't had an accident myself for the past twenty-five years and my chauffeur has never had one to my knowledge."

[2] There were many people hired to help with the special occasions such as family visits and the Life Saver parties.

[3] Edward Berryhill was killed in March 1982 when he was shot confronting someone stealing hubcaps outside of a Hinesville tavern.

[4] After John was injured in an accident and spent a year in the hospital, Mr. Noble never mentioned the offer again.

[5] Mr. Noble wrote (Noble 1948b: November 29, letter), "Incidentally, I am wondering if you go over the timesheets before you send them up here so that you know, even on the days when you are not there, just what is going on? I assume, however, that you must do this. As far as making up the timesheets is concerned, it would take the men just a moment or two longer to write them up in more detail and this would save a lot of questioning on our part."

[6] In the letter, Mr. Noble wrote, "With reference to shopping on Saturday—I have been looking over a great number of timesheets and find that we lose a lot of the men's time because throughout the past months they have been going over on Friday or some other day, and the average work per man down there has not run anything like five-and-a-half days. With Friday taken off it leaves us only four-and-a-half days a week…" As John pointed out, Mr. Noble seemed to imply that all of the workers were only four and a half days when any single worker went to town on a week day. In the same letter, Mr. Noble complained that the workers had taken off Armistice Day. He told Toby, "I noticed that the men took off Armistice Day. This day is not observed as a working holiday anywhere I know. It is a holiday for banks and Wall Street but all the offices and factories in this area, and I believe you will find also in Georgia, worked just the same as ever."

[7] In the "The Once Over" column in *The Washington Post* (March 12, 1943, Pg10), H. I. Phillips wrote the following: Mr. E. J. Noble, a New York man, has bought the 23,000-acre St. Catherines Island in Georgia, and says he will raise Black Angus cattle.

> Lives there a man who hasn't said
> Against inflation's battle
> I'll buy a ranch and get ahead
> By raising Angus cattle?

[8] John pointed out that these were estimates made by his father. He said that there were likely 1000 hogs on the island during this time. The comparison of the best year is based on the estimated value of animals. For example, in 1952 there were more cows (250 compared to 200) but fewer calves (50 compared to 264). This resulted in more tonnage of animals for that year, and hence a higher inventory.

[9] The wild turkeys disappeared when the lumbering activity began on St. Catherines. The cleared land made the turkey chicks vulnerable to attacks from red tailed hawks. In 1946, the last inventory to include wild turkeys listed 14 (Woods 1946). Domesticated turkeys, listed as "tame turkeys," did not did not do much better. In his day book, Toby Woods described trips to Collins to pick up an incubator that was built by his brother Rowey. In 1945, there were 18 domesticated turkeys listed in the inventory (Woods 1945) and five in 1946 (Woods 1946). After 1946, Mr. Noble was out of the turkey business.

[10] During the Keys era, President Herbert Hoover visited the island in 1932 (NYT 1932).

[11] President Harry S. Truman had FBI director J. Edgar Hoover tap Corcoran's home and office phones (Lichtman 1987). Corcoran was so powerful that he talked with impunity about deals that could be ethically and legally challenged, knowing that the phone lines were tapped.

[12] The restoration of a tabby structure is a complex undertaking. The restoration of three tabby slave cabins on Ossabaw Island will cost a million dollars (Shelton 2006).

[13] This phone system established during the Keys era had an underground line to the big house, the superintendent's house and to the mainland. It was a hand cranked system. When Mr. Noble bought the island he decided not to maintain the link to the island, but a line connected cabin 1 to the local system. The underground wires finally deteriorated and the system was abandoned.

[14] If a guest were staying in any of the other cabins, the same procedure was followed.

[15] I asked John if Mr. Noble ever used that heated water from the Heatilater for his shower. He wasn't sure and said that on a cold rainy day in January, he might have showered in the cabin. But, Mr. Noble wanted you to believe that he preferred the pool to the creature comfort of a warm shower.

[16] John was 14 and was working on the island during the summer.

[17] When the archeology program was initiated, the archeologists stayed in the cabins.

[18] Uncle Albert Rogers was at the party and briefly met Mr. Noble. He was surprised when he heard that someone at the party had bought St. Catherines.

[19] The check was sent with a letter written on WMCA station letterhead. WMCA was purchased by E. J. Noble, and a dispute over the sale was in court for almost a decade. In 1941 he bought the station from Donald Flamm, who later claimed that he was forced to sell it to E. J. Noble (NYT 1943a). The controversy eventually led to a congressional hearing (NYT 1944b) that found no evidence of coercion (NYT 1944c). After a trial (NYT 1946a), Flamm was awarded $350,000 (NYT 1946b), and on appeal he was awarded an additional $107,508 as interest (NYT 1947b). After the threat of an appeal by Noble in 1949, an out-of-court settlement was reached, finally ending eight years of litigation (NYT 1949a).

[20] This is equivalent to $1.7 million dollars today. C. M. and Indiola Keys spent over a million dollars on renovation and construction of a number of buildings. In addition to the renovation of the big house, the horse barn, and cabin 1, they built a swimming pool, six additional guest cabins, the superintendent's house, the power plant and three employee cabins. There was a provision in the sales agreement that the Rauers estate could repurchase the island within a year for $165,000. A bill from the H. Wiley Johnson and Julian F. Corish law firm (Johnson and Corish 1943), dated January 1, 1943, described St. Catherines legal situation, "... regarding compromise settlement of deficiencies tax claim by the collectors of Internal Revenue and the State Department of Revenue covering the years 1938, 1939, and 1940." This suggests that the Rauers were having financial difficulties with the island and this was a "distress sale."

[21] The Ambos family was an important family in Thunderbolt, near Savannah. Louis G. Ambos was a Thunderbolt City official for 40 years. The family owned Ambos Sea Food, the Trade Winds Shrimp Company, and Ambos Marine Service, which had a marine railway that Toby used.

[22] While this may have been the plan, the oyster rights were sold in 1946 and 1947 for only $400 a year (Woods 1947).

[23] The First Nations name for the Thousand Islands means "Garden of the Great Spirit." The boat captained by Zay Power was docked in Miami.

[24] Noble sold the "palatial fifty room" club, eighteen hole course, and cottages on 175 acres fronting the St. Lawrence River to the Canada Steamship Company in 1944 and purchased it back in 1950 when it was valued at $500,000 (NYT 1950c).

[25] Construction of the castle began in the late 1890s. George C. Boldt intended it to be a Valentines Day gift for his wife. During its construction as many as 300 workers (stonemasons, carpenters, and artists) fashioned the six-story, 120-room castle. The castle had tunnels, a powerhouse, Italian gardens, a drawbridge, and even a dove cote (a place where pigeons and doves were kept). When his wife Louise died in 1904, Boldt stopped construction and never returned to the island. E. J. Noble bought it 1925 when it was valued at $5 million dollars (NYT 1925). In 1939 a tower was destroyed by a fire started by sparks from a fireworks display (NYT 1939a). The decorative iron and the heating system were scrapped for the war effort (NYT 1942a). In 1977, the E. J. Noble Foundation transferred ownership to the Thousand Islands Bridge Authority.

[26] Jack Baughcom, Toby Woods, and their wives visited Mr. Noble on the Thousand Islands and had lunch with him in a cabin with a painted white line in the middle of the floor marking the border between the United States and Canada.

[27] *Time Magazine* states that he hired a pilot to fly his plane (Time 1939). Other accounts said that he flew his own plane. In articles about his accession to the CAA, they mentioned a "cabin" plane that would have been flown by a hired pilot.

[28] Clarence Crane's other claim to fame is that he fathered Hart Crane (Crane 2006), one of America's most famous poets (Fisher 2002; Gabriel 2007; Reed 2006). Once asked the source of his creativity, Hart Crane replied it was a gift from his father who had invented the Life Savers.

[29] Crane hit on the novelty of producing a mint that was a different from the pillow shaped mints of Europe. The hole in the middle of the round mint gave it immediate recognition.

[30] There are a number of myths related to the Life Savers story. One claims that he designed the hole in the candy because he had a daughter that choked on a piece of candy. Another claimed that Noble used his grandmother's recipe for the Pep-O-Mint candy. Gee Little said that Mr. Noble told her that he and his brother Robert developed

the Life Saver recipe from their grandmother's recipe. He also told her that his first job was selling salt door to door. It appears that Mr. Noble enjoyed projecting the image of him and his brother toiling in the kitchen developing Pep-O-Mint Life Savers.

[31] Crane's promotion of his mints certainly needed help. His advertisement showed an old seaman throwing a Life Saver to a woman swimming with the slogan, "For that stormy breath."

[32] A NASA internet site on the chronology of inventions lists Crane's Life Savers invention between the 1903 invention of the engine powered airplane (1903) and the discovery of Penicillin in 1928. http://scifiles.larc.nasa.gov/text/kids/Problem_Board/problems/invention/timeline.html. While I am a fan of Life Savers, I find it difficult to equate it with the discovery of penicillin or the engine powered airplane. It also says something about his genius. Crane made the invention, but without E. J. Noble's ingenuity the Life Savers might be a mere memory in Cleveland.

[33] Life Savers are now produced in Canada because of a lower price for sugar. The candy comes in 12 different rolls of 25 flavors. Life Savers are sold at 1,000,000 locations in the United States. Each year, 46 billion Life Savers are produced, weighing a total of 57.5 million pounds. If all the Life Savers produced in a single day were lined up end to end, they would form a line 54 miles long.

[34] Even this was not a simple task. To get gas rationing coupons, Toby had to go to the Rationing Board in Hinesville (Woods 1944:April 24). Later, he had to take Otis to Midway where he would board the Greyhound Bus to Jacksonville.

[35] The candy truck from the island was traded to Uncle Albert Rogers for a surplus army truck that he bought after the Second World War.

[36] It was originally named the American Broadcasting System, and E. J. Noble shrewdly renamed it so that it would be easily recognized as ABC.

[37] Tax certificates issued with the purchase of the Blue Network were the first issued and made it unnecessary for "General Sarnoff" to pay capital gains on the profits.

[38] It was an issue that C. M. Keys dealt with when he was trying to develop a profitable airline. Another link is that Pitcairn Airline, which helped develop the autogiro, was once owned by Keys.

[39] The autogiro looked like a combination between a helicopter and a fixed wing plane. It had rotor blades and a propeller. The rotor could be engaged to lift the plane off the ground, and the propeller would thrust it forward.

[40] The front runners in the Republican Convention in Philadelphia were Robert Taft and Thomas Dewey. Willkie emerged as a "dark horse" candidate and won the nomination. Willkie was soundly defeated by FDR. Roosevelt received 27 million popular votes and 449 electoral votes compared to Willkie's 22 million popular votes and 82 electoral votes.

[41] The new report said that while he was on friendly terms with Harry Hopkins, he met with difficulties within the Department of Commerce. Hulen (1940) reported that Noble resigned, saying his methods were ineffective under Hopkins' leadership. Hopkins resigned ten days later, citing ill health (Hulen 1940). He remained a confidant of FDR and undertook many missions for him. Hopkins died in 1946 after a long battle with cancer.

[42] In 1948, Mr. Noble arranged an athletic scholarship for John Toby, Jr. to attend St. Lawrence. John was severely burned in a boat accident on the island in 1948, and was forced to spend a year in the hospital. Mr. Noble never mentioned the scholarship again. After he recovered from his burns, Mr. Noble presented John with a shotgun that he prized.

[43] John said that the income from his dad's fifty-head herd of cattle and the hogs was used to send John's sister Clel to Georgia Southern University in Statesboro, Georgia.

[44] The Black Angus were not registered cattle. He was concerned that the cattle were not entirely black.

[45] The hogs were harvested rather than farmed. They were allowed to range free and had to be captured when they were sold.

[46] Sweet feed was grain was spiked with molasses. Many feed companies sell sweet feed in pellet form, which used beet pulp with molasses to make it more palatable.

[47] Even a decade later, John said that his mother and father would talk about the virgin pine forest that made St. Catherines such a beautiful island. They still remember walking through the pines with the Keys and understood why they were reluctant to cut down such a beautiful stand of trees. The Keys did consider timbering as a last resort, but it was too late. The Rauers realized that even with the timbering, it would not have been enough to pay what was owed them.

[48] As always, John provided the specifics for the HD-14. The tractor was powered with a General Motors 6-cylinder, Series 71 diesel engine that could develop 165 horsepower.

[49] The tractor was $11,000. Towing it to the island ($90), and purchasing a mowing unit ($163.74) and grubber for the tractor ($875) brought the total to $12,128.74.

[50] The lots were used to build a dock and eventually a garage to store vehicles. This facility was St. Catherines' link to the mainland.

[51] We have not found any other indication of the oil leases.

[52] Sams Field was cleared and had been used as a staging ground for cutting the timber that surrounded it.

[53] They bought an Allis Chalmers HD-7 tractor with a GM 3-cylinder 71 diesel engine that developed 82 horsepower. It was furnished with a root rake blade. It was later traded for an HD-9 with a GM 4-cylinder engine that had 110 horsepower.

[54] Richard Tuten.

[55] The 5:00 AM off-load was required because they needed a high tide to unload the dragline. The evening of the 14th showed a waxing moon, two days from a full moon.

[56] State of Georgia, Indexes of Vital Records for Georgia, 1919-1998. Georgia. USA. Georgia Health Department, Office of Vital Records. 1998.

[57] There would be a $30,000 loss from timber, $2,000 loss from hog sales, and $7,500 loss from cattle sales.

[58] When Mr. Noble sent the candy truck to St. Catherines, it had over 30,000 miles of city driving.

[59] Mr. Noble was at the Thousand Islands Club at the time, and his wife Ethel said that she was too frightened to scream.

[60] The 1952 Livestock Inventory listed the 350 hogs and pigs with an estimated weight of 31,500 pounds and worth of $3700.

[61] Marion Hawley reported (Hawley 1958b: Letter, July 28, 1958) that, "Doc Brown is quite a dog – he has at least learned to stay away from skunks after his first catch. He looks fine – think the ring-worm is just about gone." She wrote (Hawley 1959: Letter, June 11,1959) about six months after Mr. Noble's death saying that, "I saw Doc Brown when I was in Greenwich with Mrs. Noble and he is living the life of a king. Chasing everything that moved all day long. She sure does like him and so did I."

[62] When John said that nearly everybody smoked, he laughed and said that not everybody carried cigarettes with them. Mr. Noble never carried "smokes," but would bum one to share with you. Carmen Baughcom and Ruby Easterland told John that Mr. Noble smoked only one brand of cigarettes – OP. When I told Carmen that I had never heard of the OP brand, she laughed and said that Other People's cigarettes was the full name of the brand.

[63] Gee fantasized that a hunter would sit on a log to smoke and Bum would lean over his shoulder and take the cigarette out of his mouth.

[64] These were plywood crates with air holes punched in them. The crate let in as little light as possible. The darkness would calm the animals. They were never kept in the crate for more than a day.

[65] The "deer catchers" paid three dollars a night for room and board.

[66] John suspects that the Hallett engines were not designed for the many hours of use that occurred on the island.

[67] Hubert Holmes.

[68] The executive group at the 1952 Convention included William A. Goebel, G. W. Posthill, R. P. Noble, H. A. Thompson, M. B. Bates, E. E. Anderson, G. C. Young, R. G. Cornelius, J. E. Grimm, E. J. Jordan and M. L. Benford (Goebel 1952: July 29, 1952).

[69] In the October 8th letter, Mr. Noble left no detail untouched and told Toby to bring two passenger automobiles plus the Dodge pickup truck. He was concerned that Pop Durden had been on working on cottages for the help rather than for the guests. He wrote (Noble 1952d), " Also notice on his work cards he (Durden) has done considerable work on cottages. Are these cottages the guest cottages or the help's cottages? If you remember, there was a lot of work to be done on the guest cottages before the men came down—touching up inside where the plaster is falling down, painting the window frames, roller shades, etc., and easing up the apparatus that opens and closes the windows. ... Please make sure that all the cottages are in good shape in this respect before the 25th."

[70] The pattern each year was the same. We use the 1952 conference (Goebel 1952) as an example.

[71] John chuckled when he talked about Mr. Nobles as chef. While he loved to grill steaks, the Life Saver group was not above teasing him about their steaks being overdone.

[72] In a letter to Mr. Noble about boat engine parts, Toby Woods (Woods 1949:October 5, letter) commented, "Tallie is in the hospital. The Dr. says he has angina and wants him to stay in bed 2 weeks. I went to see him and he is feeling much better." He did not work the convention that year.

[73] Ammonium nitrate.

[74] Mr. Noble insisted that the work on the island was agricultural work, and that farmers worked a nine-hour day.

[75] In this letter to Mr. Noble, Toby pointed out that he often did not report island expenses when he was off the island. John relates one instance in which his dad bought a mule that died the first day on the island. Toby paid for it out of his own pocket rather than report its death to Mr. Noble.

[76] The sheriff would set the date of the hunt with Toby and Paul Sikes, and he would invite the participants. Sikes was careful to invite the Liberty County politicians who were his supporters and those that were his political foes. On the hunt, political rivalries were forgotten on the surface.

[77] By the second stand, the dogs were of little help. There were so many deer moving in different directions that the dogs were on their own.

[78] When John and I talked about his father's trip, he said that his dad was a practical man. "If it was dark and foggy, what could he do? If you can't see, you may as well read the paper. Daddy knew that he would get busy and may not have time to read the paper later."

[79] In addition to Tony, I would do the same for Junior and Murray. Junior and Murray would be for his guests.

[80] The block was from the remnants of the foundation of the demolished Rauers house.

[81] The cows liked to sleep in the road, and left many piles of cow manure.

[82] The inclusion of his secretary did not signal that this would be a working vacation. Rose Mary Woods had worked for Nixon since 1951, and in 1973 she erased a critical 18½ minutes from a Watergate tape. She was like a family member. Trish (aged 12 at the time) and Julie (age 9) Nixon called her "Aunt Rose." Pat Nixon and Rose Mary Woods often exchanged outfits. In his memoir (Nixon 1978), Nixon said that he had Rose Mary Woods tell Pat Nixon and the children that he was resigning the presidency (Sullivan 2005).

[83] The Smiths left for home on June 3rd.

[84] There were no plans for a retirement. Toby was eligible for social security benefits.

[85] In retrospect, the drainage and removal of dead trees were factors that changed the island environment. Even though the County Agent supported these changes, in interfered with the natural environmental processes of the island's ecology.

[86] The death of Mr. Noble marked over 30 years of service on St. Catherines for John Toby Woods. He was tired of the "salt water" and wanted to return to the mainland and his life as a farmer.

[87] He spent five hours catching hogs, and four hours sending the telegram to Mrs. Noble.

[88] Half Moon.

[89] Mr. Noble paid $1380.14 for the car that, when fully equipped, sold for about $2000, and the withholding tax was $345.00 (Noble 1952a). The car is a collectable and now sells for $14,000.

Chapter 13. Wonder Boy and the Nineteen Old Bums

[1] The business community was particularly interested, since the $8 million purchase price was the first transaction to establish the worth of a radio network.

[2] Katherine Woods, John's wife, pointed out something that should have been so obvious to me. The music and lyrics of Nineteen Bums is derived from the Whippenpoff song. The first stanza:

> To the tables down at Mory's
> To the place where Louie dwells
> To the dear old Temple bar we love so well
> Sing the Whiffenpoofs assembled with their glasses raised on high
> And the magic of their singing casts its spell

[3] The line that says, "picked up Nixons in Sav'h," refers to Richard Nixon's visit to St. Catherines in 1958.

[4] It is not clear what Mr. Noble had in mind when he mentioned trying to entice more ducks. John said that he could have baited the pond. Wading in the water would not have increased the ducks for the hunters.

[5] To get to Palmetto Bluff (the Inn) today, you take I-95 to exit 8 and proceed east on Highway 278. Take the SR-170 exit and make a right turn onto Highway 170. At the stop sign, take a left onto SR-46 toward Bluffton. The Palmetto Bluff entrance will be on the right side of the road.

[6] The Union Bag Company, now the Union Camp Corporation, bought that property in 1937 to protect the wildlife, preserves the scenic areas, and to grow pine trees for pulp. Union Camp executives and clients used the 14 bedroom lodge for hunting and fishing. Sandy Calder, who died October 22, 1962 at the age of 76, and his wife are buried overlooking the May River (Riddle 2001). Union Camp sold the land for $100 million. It is now being developed for 5,000 house sites. 5,000 acres will remain as a nature preserve.

[7] It took over a month of research to identify 18 of the 19 old bums.

[8] Mr. and Mrs. Alva See were involved in many projects, but never as a couple.

[9] In the hearings, he was asked "Who would audit you?"(the CPAs). Carter answered "our conscience." It is interesting that it was a failure of conscience that led to the Enron fiasco.

[10] After E. J. Noble's death, Al Chapman would later be involved with the Noble Foundation's operation of St. Catherines. We will discuss his accomplishments and relationship to John Toby Woods, Jr. at that time.

[11] The title implies that he was an ambassador that could make decisions in the name of the Government.

[12] This appears to be a misspelling.

[13] A joking relationship is formalized set of social interactions between two people who are permitted tease or make fun of the other. Those in a joking relationship cannot take offence at what is said or done.

[14] Jack Baughcom made the model for Mr. Noble. He, Carmen, Toby and Gladys Woods had taken a vacation ending at the Thousand Island Club, where they were the guests of Mr. Noble. The model was made from memory, reflecting one of Jack's talents.

[15] One of his colleagues, Christopher Columbus Smith, left Gar Wood's team and founded Chris-Craft, one of the most famous wooden boat producers.

[16] These boats were known as "gentleman runabouts." To reinforce this image, Gar Wood was photographed piloting one in a tuxedo.

[17] A bateaux is a flat bottomed boat that was used for fishing at McQueens.

[18] Anderson, Chapman, Johaneson, Lovejoy, Montague, Snowie (as he is referred to in the letter), Taylor, Whelpley and Wilson would depart from New York. At the stop in Philadelphia at 5:32 p.m., Larry Sharples would join the group. Francis Allen, Arthur Carter, Philip Sharples and Austin Igleheart were to arrive separately from Florida, where they were hunting. Quackenbush and See were "shooting" north of Palmetto Bluff and were to arrive on their own.

[19] Amos Peaslee.

[20] McIntosh was not a regular stop and provisions would have been made to depart from that station. Mr. Noble arranged for a special car to be put on the ECC arriving at McIntosh at 6:00 p.m. The train schedule has an official stop at Richmond at 3:25 a.m. I have assumed that it is a nine and a half hour ride to Richmond.

[21] Alfred W. (Bill) Jones.

[22] The invitations went to Francis L. Abreu (Cottage 79), William Whitcomb (Cottage 54), Ralph Cutler (Cottage 28), Boyd Donaldson (Cottage 127), Bud Gasque (Cottage 89), James L. Garard (Cottage 59), Col. J. T. Houk (Cottage 93), Alfred W. Jones (Cottage 78), Daniel E. Pomeroy (Cottage 92), I. A. Harned (Cottage 9), Harold C. Strong (Cottage 22), Norman B. Tooker (Cottage 56), DeForest P. Willard (Cottage 85), Alan Tappan (Cottage 111), James C. Chilcott (Cottage 126), and Jack Lawless (St. Simons Island).

[23] Since this was farm work, Mr. Noble considered nine hour as the work day.

[24] Hunts that took place in the 1940s.

[25] "Eye shine" is caused by a special lining in the retina of some mammals, the tapetum lucidum, that captures "lost light" and increases the eye's ability to absorb light.

[26] Curtis Lee, Gee remembers, had worked on the island before Mr. Noble bought it when timber was being cut. He operated a crane that transferred lumber from the island dock to waiting boats. Some of the boats were Cuban and German schooners. Curtis began work on the island as a teenager. He learned to operate a crane at his father's junk yard when he was 16.

[27] Mr. Noble eventually realized the porcine department of the cattle ranch was not profitable, and he got out of the hog business.

Chapter 14. John Wood's Battle for Life.

[1] The usual load would be 10,000 pounds of fertilizer. The boat (17A789) was the freight boat used to haul supplies. John described that they would tie a forty-foot barge to the bow side of the boat and push it to the dock on the Half Moon River where it would be loaded with the fertilizer.

[2] John: "The way the boat had been changed with the cabins above the deck made it top heavy. Uncle Otis said he was with my daddy when they were crossing the sound with some Coast Guard men aboard. They hit a big wave and with a strong wind. It turned the boat on its side and threw two of the men overboard that they had to rescue. In daddy's notes (day book) he wrote 'two Coast Guard men got wet.' Daddy rebuilt the cabin by lowering it, making it more stable and low enough that it would fit in the boat house."

[3] John: "One of the 55-gallon drums must have rusted and leaked gas under the bilge under the engines."

[4] John said it was the heat of the explosion that caused his burns. The flames never touched his body.

[5] Since childhood, John would go shirtless from the first signs of spring until the first frost.

[6] Skin 101: Skin is the largest human organ. About 15% of a person's body weight is comprised of the skin which has a thickness of between 2 to 3 mm and a surface area of nearly two square meters (25.5 square feet). The skin is comprised of three layers: the outer epidermis, the dermis and the hypodermis. A 1st degree burn involves the outer layer, the epidermis. A sun burn is a 1st degree burn. A 2nd degree burn involves the epidermis and dermis. These are painful and dangerous since the dermis has 1000 nerve endings per square inch. This area has 20 blood vessels and 650 sweat glands. A 3rd degree burn also involves the hypodermis, making them slow to heal.

[7] The pain comes from the 1st and 2nd degree burns. The 1000 nerve endings in every square inch transmit the pain. 3rd degree burns have destroyed most of the nerves, as it destroys the flesh that makes up the hypodermis.

[8] Uncle Woodrow Rogers.

[9] Since *The Sea Beaver* was Mr. Noble's private boat and was to be used only by him, it was always stored in this manner when he was away from the island.

[10] Uncle Woodrow showed incredible judgment. *The Sea Beaver* was the only other transportation to the mainland at that time.

[11] On old topographical maps of Colonels Island, the air strip was evident. The Bluff Creek subdivision pasture covers the location of the landing strip.

[12] *The Sea Beaver.*

[13] He had to lower it a couple of feet on the stern end and go the length of the boat to the bow to level it and lower it.

[14] They landed at Travis Field Airport, which is now Savannah International Airport.

[15] In the 1930, The Georgia Hospital Board of the Methodist Episcopal South Church purchased the Savannah Hospital and renamed it Warren Candler Hospital. In the 1960s it combined forces with the Telfair Hospital for women. In the 1980s it moved to its present location on Reynolds Street. In 1997, Candler and St. Joseph's Hospital signed a joint operating agreement and is now known as the St. Joseph's/Candler Hospital.

[16] This is an early form of penicillin that was stable in the crystalline form. From United States Patent 20020193587: "The crystal of the invention is the crystal of diphenylmethyl 2-methyl-2-triazolylmethylpenam-3-carboxylate 1,1-dioxide which is stable substantially without decomposition or degradation of properties even when left to stand at a temperature of 5 to 35 degree C. for a period of 1 year."

[17] This is quite disconcerting, since blowflies (genus Diptera), identified by their iridescent metallic color, seek decaying flesh to deposit their larvae. The larvae known then as "maggots" feed on the rotting flesh. They are the first insects that make their home on decaying flesh. The term "to blow" means the laying of eggs by insects.

[18] Proud flesh refers to the welting that causes unsightly scarring. The term that is now used is hyperthrophic scarring.

[19] They now have artificial skin that can quicken the healing process. One product, Dermagraph –TC uses foreskins to manufacture its product. It sold for about $3600 per square foot in 1997.

[20] Initially, Dr. Pinholster was using a scalpel to remove a thin layer of skin. The instrument he mentioned was a dermatome, which removes a 1-mm thick patch of skin. The dermatome works on the same principle as a cheese shaver in that the thickness of the skin removed (usually 1 mm) is consistent. There are robot dematomes that allow a physician who is not adept at using a scalpel to harvest skin successfully.

[21] Candler did not have a physical therapist at this time, and a masseur was hired to provide the daily therapy.

[22] The Georgia Infirmary that served freed Blacks and slaves in the 1800s was recently reopened by St. Josephs/Candler Hospital as a center for stroke victims.

[23] Ginter's father was hired by the Keys to build their swimming pool.

[24] John and I live 24 miles east of Fort Stewart, and some evenings you can hear the shells that are shot as part of their training.

[25] Katherine's family owned a 700-acre cattle ranch. Mr. Oetgen retired from the Sea Board Railroad shop after 50 years of working for them.

Chapter 15. The Mico of St. Catherines.

[1] There was a sign that the New York Zoological team placed in front of the superintendent's house announcing "Superintendent and Mico." Mico, the Guale word for chief, was an affectionate term used by his staff when referring to him. William Conway, director of the New York Zoological Society's Park (Bronx Zoo) from 1962-1999, supervised the Wildlife Survival Center on St. Catherines and presented the sign to John. The sign is now at the driveway entrance to his house on Billy Harris Point. Many of his friends also refer to him as "Captain John."

[2] The farm in Newington, known as the Tucker-Evens Place, was a little over 40 miles northwest of Savannah. A newspaper account in 1982 described it: "... the greenhouse in the pecan grove just out of Newington on the Oliver

Road" (Davis 1982:18). It was father's home for 30 years, and it was so well run that it could have served as a model to be featured in *Small Farm Digest.*

[3] Originally, Toby Woods' retirement was a $5000 bequest from Mr. Noble. Mr. Chapman, according to John, set up a retirement plan for his father. He was to receive $300 a month. There was no cost of living clause in the retirement plan. Although inflation quickly decreased the buying power of the dollar and hence the retire income, John said that his dad was appreciative of the efforts of Mr. Chapman in securing it for him. As John relates, his father was doing very well in his efforts at farming.

[4] There are websites devoted to planting by the phases of the moon. The rationale is that the moons gravitational force affects the water levels in the soils and makes it easier for root crops to send up their shoots.

[5] In 1971, Dr. H. H. Bryan and R. B. Volin at the University of Florida genetically engineered a tomato, MH-1, that was designed be mechanically harvested. To say that it had a tough skin was an understatement.MH-1 could withstand being dropped from a height of six feet to a tile floor without sustaining any damage. Whiteside (1971) asked Dr. William Haddon, Jr., who was the president of the Insurance Institute for Highway safety at the time, to compute speed at impact. The tomato was calculated to reach a speed of 13.4 miles per hour as it hit the ground. Bumpers on American cars at that time were mandated for required to be able to withstand an impact of five miles.

[6] John was paid a salary by J. H. Morgan and was on-call to repair the fleet as needed. This frequently required work on weekends and holidays. When there was no work to do on Morgan's boats, he was free to work on his own projects.

[7] John was in demand since he was a certified master mechanic that had been trained by General Motors.

[8] U.S. Congressional salaries were $12,500 plus a tax free expense allowance of $2,500.

[9] In 1942, Dewey's income from his law practice was $100,000 (Ryan 1948:3).

[10] This was the famous election that Dewey was supposed to have won easily. In fact, on September 12, 1948, the New York Times (The Practical Men around Thomas E. Dewey by Leo Egan) speculated on who would make up his presidential team. Chapman was listed as a "pinch hitter," who was called upon for his special expertise.

[11] Alger B. "Duke" Chapman, Jr. told me that in 1958, as an incentive to leave his lucrative law practice, E. J. Noble gave his father a "contract for life" to head the Beech-Nut Life Saver company and become Chief Executive Officer of the Edward J. Noble Foundation.

[12] Dobbs Houses operated airline catering services, restaurants and snack bars.

[13] Chapman's expertise was used to make sure that Beech-Nut and Olin (Squibb parent company) would not have any tax liability.

[14] In 1971, it became the Squibb Corporation. Alger "Duke" Chapman said that the merger was a tax spin off.

[15] Wilson was lieutenant governor when Governor Nelson Rockefeller resigned in December 1973. Wilson lost to Hugh M. Carey.

[16] Hubert Holmes was Snooker's second husband. Holmes originally owned a farm and had Snooker's children (Ben, George, and Ralph Chapman) working there for long hours. The children did not have much good to say about their step-father. Eventually, Hubert moved out of the "big" house and lived in an employees' cabin until Snooker decided that she had had enough and told him to leave the island.

[17] I asked John if the Robbins were related to the Woods. They were not relatives. John's dad hired him because he desperately needed a job.

[18] Carla Ann, their daughter, was seriously disabled with hydrocephalus and required intensive care by the family. She frequently required medical treatment. They would have to support her head with pillows when she sat up.

[19] Bringing electricity to the island was a challenge that he relished. Keeping the battery system running for all those years made it Toby's mission to bring "light" to St. Catherines.

[20] Hollingsworth would fly his plane to the island on business and for pleasure. He survived three plane crashes (two on the island). He was not fazed by these crashes, and would salvage the plane and fly again.

[21] Loren Chapman Duffy now lives in California.

Chapter 16. Salvaging the Pinta

[1] Morgan's Inc., established in 1904, was a major supplier of marine equipment.

[2] The timing was important, since John still had the responsibility for supervising activities on the island.

[3] In an interview with Sonny Timmons, he described that even now, at the height of the oyster season, cars will line up in his driveway to get the oysters from him. He alludes to the fact that oysters are an aphrodisiac. He says that his costumers tease him by saying the oysters are not working their magic on them. Sonny says that they are not eating enough of them, and they will buy another bushel.

[4] John was reluctant to name anyone who "had trouble with the law." This individual is well known in the area. After serving his sentence, he came back and was a successful businessman who was elected mayor of Midway Georgia. I was amazed at the "forgiveness" of the local people with respect to people who have served time. A County Commissioner who had been convicted of a felony was also elected, and during the campaign I never heard anyone even mentioned it.

[5] Setback is also called Pitch or High-Low-Jack. Pitch can be played in a cutthroat way where every person determines his/her choices, or as a partner game with bidding. The Woods always played the partnered version.

[6] The GSA was started as a defense against environmental regulations that focused on saving turtles.

[7] This was the third boat that Danny Goodman had built, and it incorporated many state of the art features. Before it was sold (the asking price was $275,000), he had *The Amazing Grace* outfitted with a freezer processing unit.

Chapter 17. Life on the Mainland

[1] It is a frequent practice for archeologists to leave evidence of their excavations, so that if the site were ever to be excavated again, the previous disturbance would be evident.

[2] Grandma was a firm believer in the efficacy of Black Draught. Every evening she would give Jimp his daily dose. For Grandma it was a cure-all. John said that he was afraid to cough in her presence since it was a sure sign that you needed a dose of the draught, or worse, castor oil. Black Draught is still sold. It is a combination of magnesium and extracts from the senna plant. For you chemistry majors, the active ingredient in the plant is anthraquinone, which is a mild laxative.

Chapter 18. The Fish Story

[1] The annual event was organized by Roland Pedrick to raise funds for cystic fibrosis research. The 1992 event raised $30,000 for the foundation.

[2] The loblolly Pine (*P.taeda*) has a thick and scaly bark and reaches heights of 100 feet, with a trunk diameter as wide as three feet.

[3] Well into the third draft of the paper, John announced sheepishly that he had in fact "gassed up" at Yellow Bluff, but he had a legitimate explanation. He said that he occasionally towed stranded boaters to Yellow Bluff. John, ever the gentleman, has never accepted payment for his kindness. But when he would pull someone in to Yellow Bluff, Arthur Goodman would immediately top-off the tank on John's boats and told the towee that he put it on their bill. In July 2007, John towed my wife, Lynn Sibley, from near St. Catherines. I asked him if he had ever been towed. He said "never."He said that he has drifted, rowed, sailed and used a spare outboard motor that he frequently carries on his boats, but he has never been towed. Another "never" added to John's list of accomplishments.

[4] A new convenience store and gas station that is just seven miles away recently opened.

[5] Raburn's brother-in-law.

[6] Half-acre building lots with access to Yellow Bluff would now sell for $200,000. At $400,000 per acre, the potential profit would be in the range of $5-6 million.

[7] Mary Eugenia Youmans, who is now Mary Eugenia Coleman.

[8] The path roughly follows what is now known as Youmans Road, but in 1930s it followed a more circuitous route.

[9] Luther P. Youmans, "Doc," was a physician who married Hattie Bell. Roger was their only child. Gertrude Brown, "Doc" Youmans' niece, married Willie Bell, the brother of Hattie Bell Youmans. They had two children: Juanita and Mildred. Mildred eventually married Arthur Goodman (Groover 1987).

[10] Gefilte fish is a lightly seasoned ground fish rolled into a ball and cooked in a broth of carrots and onions.

[11] Mildred Bell.

[12] A Kings Grant, according to John, was the original grant that conveyed land and marsh. In the modern era, the ownership of the marshes was an important asset, since it gave ownership of the resources found in the mash and rivers that flowed through them. When ownership of the rivers was opened for use, the oysters were still controlled by the Kings Grantee and subsequent owners. Since the oyster business is no longer viable, the importance of having a Kings Grant has diminished, except for the "bragging rights" that go with it.

[13] John remembers that there were usually a dozen boats available during the time he was growing up.

[14] John claims that the decline in the oyster harvest began when pulp paper industry began operations in this area. Oyster harvests are restricted by the Georgia's DNR (Department of Natural Resources) because of pollution and toxins. Certain areas are open sporadically. The spots are not published but are available at the DNR office. A thriving oyster culture business has developed at Harris Neck.

[15] Uncle Ernest Youmans could build a bateaux in a day. This was before ply wood. Cypress planks were used since ell in water. The tighter fit made sealing seams unnecessary.

[16] Danny Goodman, another son, lives in Sunbury. Danny is a shrimper whose boat the 101-foot *Amazing Grace* is one of the largest shrimp boats on the southeastern coast. He is also the developer of the Village at Sunbury.

[17] The Tea Room also served as a site of many political meetings for the residents of Colonels Island.

[18] Parker said that when he sent his expense report to the Department of Transportation (DOT) for the cost an oxen driver and grain to feed the animals, they were perplexed. The DOT had specific job categories and Oxen Driver was not among them.

[19] There are sixteen homes at Camp Viking.

[20] There is a large condominium at Half Moon that represents one factor in the increase in population.

[21] A subdivision of 77 homes on 30 acres appears to be quite successful. Bob Vandegejuchte, the builder, said that it is planned like as old-fashioned neighborhood modeled after the Disney's Celebration. The houses will have large porches and will be spaced at "conversational distance" (Donahue 2004). I never realized while growing up in a Detroit suburb that the houses in our neighborhood weren't crowded but were just placed at a "conversational distance." Vandegejuchte does not mention the dissatisfaction that the inhabitants of Celebration have expressed regarding shoddy workmanship and some of the policies imposed by Disney (Ross 1999).

[22] He retired as president in 2006 and from the board in the same year. In his 41 years of service to Coastal Electric, he has not missed nor arrived later to a single meeting.

References Cited

AC

1869   An Italian Colony for Georgia. Atlanta Constitution, April 23, 1869. Pg. 1.

AC

1889   The Oyster Industry, and the Bill Which Comes Up Today, A matter of Great Importance to the State - The Present Status of the Industry and What Can be Accomplished - The Deep Fields. Atlanta Constitution, July 25, 1889. Pg. 4.

AC

1891   Crisp is a Busy Man. Atlanta Constitution. December 12, 1891. Pg. 1.

AC

1893a Can't Get His Vessel, Capt. Rauers Wants $500 Because a Scooner Went On His Land. Atlanta Constitution. October 20, 1893. Pg. 3.
1893b Etched and Sketched. Atlanta Constitution. February 2, 1893. Pg.15.

AC

1893c Hard on the Captain, Judge Falligant Says He Must Pay For Damages to the Beach. Atlanta Constitution. December 29, 1893. Pg. 2.

AC

1893d Much Damage in Savannah, May Lives Lost, Buildings wrecked and Vessels Big and Little Missing. Atlanta Constitution. August 30, 1893. Pg. 1.

AC

1893e Oyster Farming. The Oemler Company, of Savannah, Finds it Does Not Pay, Millions of Seed Oysters Killed, No Explanations of it Has Been Made, Even the Scientific President Being Puzzled-Other Savannah News. Atlanta Constitution, June 17, 1893. Pg. 3.

AC

1893f RUINS TRACK! All the Southern Coast Made Desolate by the Hurricane. Many a Good Vessel Was Thrown Up on the Shores. OTHERS UNDER THE WAVES, Years Entertained for the Staunch Steamship City of Savannah. Great LOSS AT HER HOME PORT, Charleston Was Racked, and Few Buildings Escaped-A Night of Terror on Sullivan's Island. Atlanta Constitution, August 30, 1893. Pg. 1.

AC

1894   Killed Nine Deer, Congressman Blanchard Has Splendid Luck on St. Catherines. Atlanta Constitution. January 1, 1894. Pg. 3.

AC

1897a The Flotilla Off Brunswick Takes the Inside Route from St. Catherines to Brunswick. Atlanta Constitution. December 6, 1897. Pg. 3.

AC

1897b Funeral of Mr. Colcord. Atlanta Constitution, August 7, 1897. Pg. 4.

AC

1898   Suing for an Island, The Government Finds a Determined Citizen in Possession. The Atlanta Constitution. March 18, 1898. Pg. 3.

AC

1899a Appraisers Make Report, Upon Damages to Rauer by Condemnation of Land. Atlanta Constitution. January 27, 1899. Pg. 3.

AC

1899b District Court Opens in Savannah. The Atlanta Constitution. January 10, 1899. Pg. 3.

AC

1899c Ordered Suit Withdrawn, Government Thinks Price too High for Lighthouse Site. Atlanta Constitution. February 21, 1899. Pg. 3.

AC

1901 In The Social Realm. Atlanta Constitution. December 20, 1901. Pg. 11.

AC

1902a Adams Goes on Supreme Court. Atlanta Constitution. September 9, 1902. Pg. 12.

AC

1902b Admiral Bags His First Deer, Face of Schley was Liberally Smeared with the Blood, Party Returns from St. Catherines Island , but Will Not Discuss Hunt for Fear of Getting in Trouble for Violating Game Law. Atlanta Constitution. January 19, 1902. Pg. 3.

AC

1902c Rauers Files His Answer, He Protests Against Uncle Sam Taking His Land. Atlanta Constitution. May 14, 1902. Pg. 4.

AC

1902d Schley Hunting The Deer, Admiral Goes to St. Catherines Island to Shoot with Friends. Atlanta Constitution. Januray 18, 1902. Pg. 7.

AC

1904a Aboard Boat wth Corpse. Living and Dead Negro Brought to Savannah. The Atlanta Constitution. December 7, 1904. Pg. 2.

AC

1904b Georgia's German Consul. Rauers Resigns After Service of Thirty-five Years. Atlanta Constitution. March 13, 1904. Pg. 11.

AC

1904c Mortuary, Death of Jacob Rauers. Atlanta Constitution, May 5, 1904. Pg. 4.

AC

1905a Government to Abandon Plan, Turns from St. Catherines to Blackbeards for Lighthouse. Atlanta Constitution. March 18, 1905. Pg. 3.

AC

1905b Rauers Island Case Dismissed, Judge Speer Orders Stopping the Proceedings. Atlanta Constitution. April 18, 1905. Pg. 5.

AC

1905c St. Catherine's Island Preserve The Paradise of Georgia Hunters. Atlanta Constitution, May 12, 1905. Pg. 8.

AC

1905f Tax Books Show $60,000, Value of St. Catherine's Island, as Given to Official. Atlanta Constitution. March 17, 1905. Pg. 11.

AC

1906a Again On Land Is Governor, Georgia's Chief Executive and Wife Land at Savannah. Atlanta Constitution. October 26, 1906. Pg. 6.

AC

AC 1906b Bones Those of Morgan. Atlanta Constittution. September 25, 1906. Pg. 8.

AC 1906c Capitol Gossip. Atlanta Constitution. October 26, 1906. Pg. 6.

AC 1906d Deer Killed By Governor, Gov. and Mrs. J. M. Terrrel Enjoyed Trip to St. Catherines Island. Atlanta Constitution. October 24, 1906. Pg. 7.

AC 1907 Adams Heads The Georgia Bar. Atlanta Constitution. June 1, 1907. Pg. 5.

AC 1911 Savannah Social News. Atlanta Constitution, March 11, 1911. Pg. 4.

AC 1917 Famous Capital Hunt Not On State Preserve. Atlanta Constitution. December 8, 1917. Pg. 18.

AC 1924a Atlantic Coastal Highway to Open Section Rich in Historical History. Atlanta Constitution. December 28, 1924. Pg. 7.

AC 1924b Cattle Dipping May Not Extend to Coast Islands. Atlanta Constitution. July 30, 1924. Pg. 15.

AC 1924c Georgia Opens Fight on Tick in Island Areas. Atlanta Consitution. September 3, 1924. Pg. 6.

AC 1924d Island Owners Plan Court Fight Over Dipping Laws. Atlanta Constitution. June 25, 1924. Pg. 10.

AC 1925 J. A. Langford Given 30 Days for Contempt, Continues Work of Dipping Horses and Mules Despite Injunction. Atlanta Constitution. July 23, 1925. Pg. 1.

AC 1929a Catherine's Isle, Off Georgia Coast, Bought by Three. Atlanta Constitution, April 7, 1929. Pg. 6.

AC 1929b English Descendant of Button Gwinnett to Visit Old Home. Atlanta Constitution. October 23, 1929. Pg. 7.

AC 1929c Englishwoman Visits Savannah Honme of Gwinnett. The Atlanta Constitution. October 24, 1929. Pg. 29.

AC 1929d Lindy, Anne Thought Honeymooning on Georgia Isle. Veracity is Lent Rumor by Barring of Newspapermen. Sapelo or Romantic St. Catherines Islands Believed Hiding Place of Famous Bridal Couple. Atlanta Constitution. June 1, 1929. Pg 1.

AC 1929e St. Catherine's Isle, Off Georgia Coast, Bought by Three. Atlanta Constitution, April 7, 1929. Pg. 6.

Ackerman, Sr., L. B.

    1938   Letter to J. J. Rauers. September 10, 1938. Georgia Historical Society. St. Catherine's Island Collection, MS.1696.

Adams, Sam B.

    1927   Letter to J. J. Rauers. August 27, 1927. Box 1, Folder 8. Georgia Historical Society. St. Catherine's Island Collection, MS.1696.

Alexander, Danielle

    2004   Forty Acres and a Mule; The Ruined Hope of Reconstruction. Humanities 25(1): http://www.neh.gov/news/humanities/2004-01/reconstruction.html.

American

    1820   Princeton. The American. October 3, 1820. Pg. 1.

Anon

    ND   Button Gwinnett, Man of Mystery, His Portrait in Oils Painted about 1757-1760. Papers in the Jenkins Collection. Friends Historical Library of Swarthmore College. Swartmore, PA.

Anon.

    1924   Absentee Ownership of Slaves in the United States in 1830. Journal of Negro History 9 (2):196-231.

Anon.

    1944   Edward J. Noble. Current Biography 4.

Aten, Lawrence E., and Jerald T. Milanich.

    2003   Clarence Bloomfield Moore: A Philadelphia Archaeologist in the Southeastern United States. *In* Philadelphia and the Development of Americanist Archaeology. D.D. Fowler and D.R. Wilcox., eds. Tuscaloosa: University of Alabama Press.

Baine, Rodney M.

    1992   Myths of Mary Musgrove. Georgia Historical Quarterly 76:428-435.

Baldwin, William P.

    1966   Report to David S. Smith. May 6, 1966. John T. Woods,II Collection.

Barnett, Claribel Ruth

    1928-1936   Arminius Oemler (1827-1897). *In* Dictionary of American Biography. American Council of Learned Societies.

Bauer-Mueller, Pamela

    2007   An Angry Drum Echoed: Mary Musgrove, Queen of the Creeks. El Paso: Piñata Publishing.

Bender, Marylin

    1965   Landed Gentry in Its Native Habitat Lures 800 Tourgoers To Greenwich. New York Times. June 11, 1965. Pg. 34.

Berlin, Ira, ed.

    1990   The Wartime Genesis of Free Labor: The Lower South. Cambridge and New York: Cambridge University Press.

Beven, M.S.S.

    1733   Oglethorpe's First Treaty with Lower Creeks at Savannah, no 36. In Juricek, John T. (1989) Early American Indian Documents:Treaties and laws, 1607-1789, Volume XI, Georgia Treaties, 1733-1763. Frederick, MD: University Publications of America. Pp. 15-17.

Bishop, Eleanor C.
    1989   Prints in the Sand : The U.S. Coast Guard Beach Patrol in World War II.
    Missoula, Mont.: Pictorial Histories Pub. Co.
BM
    1928   First National Bank & Trust Co. Port Chester, N.Y. In New Home. *In* Banker's
    Magazine. January 1928. 116, 1; APS Online. Pg153.
Bonaventure Historical Society
    2000   Bonaventure Cemetery, Savannah, Georgia. Index, Section A-H. . Savannah,
    Georgia: Bonaventure Historical Society.
Bosomworth, Mary
    1747   Mary Bosomworth's Memorial to Heron, August 10, 1747 Colonial Record of the
    State of Georgia XXXVI:256-273. Reprinted in Juricek, John T. (1989) Early American
    Indian Documents:Treaties and laws, 1607-1789, Volume XI, Georgia Treaties, 1733-
    1763. Frederick, Md: University Publications of America.
Boston Globe
    1905   NO ANNULMENT, Wife of Kid McCoy Said Marriage Was Illegal. Boston
    Globe, May 11, 1905. Pg. 6.
Braund, Kathryn E. Holland
    1991   The Creek Indians, Blacks, and Slavery. Journal of Southern History 57(4):601-
    636.
Bruce, Philip Alexander
    1905   The rise of the new South. Philadelphia: Printed for subscribers only by G. Barrie
    & Sons.
Burke, John
    2004   Historical Yellow Bluff sold, private development planned. *In* Savannah Morning
    News, August 19.
Calder, AC (Alexander)
    1952   Copy of Memo, December 15, 1952, transmitted by Edward J. Noble to John
    Toby Woods.
CD
    1902a   Schley Back from South, Savannah Bids Farewll to the Rear Admiral. Man who
    destroyed Cervera's Fleet on Way to Washington-Needs rest After Continuous Round of
    Hospitality-Strain of Public Receptions and Worry Over His Case Tells, Although He
    Appears Well-Affected by Welcome of Georgians. Chicago Daily. January 21, 1902. Pg.
    9.
CD
    1902b   Schley Is Given Key of Savannah, Southern City Welcomes Rear Admiral with
    Demonstrations at Station and in Street, Wild Scene in Theater. Chicago Daily. January
    11, 1902. Pg.1.
CD
    1902c   Schley To Go On Big Deer Hunt. Rear Admiral will Start on Friday for Game
    Preserve at St. Catherines. Chicago Daily.January 16, 1902. Pg. 2.
CD
    1902d   Schleys Loyal to The Schley. Chicago Daily. January 14, 1901. Pg.2.

CDT

    1902a Schley Ends Hunting Trip, Rear Admiral Says He Is Greatly Benefited by His Visit to St. Catherines Game Preserve. Chicago Daily Tribune. January 30, 1902. Pg. 5.

CDT

    1902b Schley Spends Quiet Sunday. Rear Admiral Attends Services at Historic Savannah Church-Plans an Active Week. Chicago Daily Tribune. January 13, 1902. Pg. 9.

CDT

    1905 Sorry She's Kid McCoy's Wife. Indiola Arnold Tells How She Married Prize Fighter Failed to Have Ceremony Annulled. Chicago Daily Tribune. June 1, 1905. Pg.3. .

CDT

    1958 Nixon Takes Vacation on Isle Off Georgia. *In* Chicagi Daily Tribune. June 1, 1958. Pg 2.

Chapman, Alger B., and Brady O. Bryson

    1943 Corporate Readjustments and the Excess Profits Credit Law and Contemporary Problems 10 (1):62-102.

Chapman, Dan

    2003a Georgia shrimpers try to carve out niche market. Atlanta Journal Constitution.

Chapman, Dan

    2003b Imports eating away at Georgians' livelihood. Atlanta Journal Constiution. February 26, 2003 Wednesday, Home Edition, p. 1F.

Chini

    1979 Harris Neck Battles U.S. Government. Southern Changes. Volume 2, Number 1, 1979 2 (1):14-17.

Cimbala, Paul A.

    1983 The Terms of Freedom: The Freedmen's Bureau and Reconstruction In Geogia, 1865-1870. Ph.D. Dissertation, Emory University

Cimbala, Paul A.

    1989 The Freedmen's Bureau, and Sherman's Grant in Reconstruction Georgia, 1865-1867. Journal of Southern History 55(4):597-632.

Clark, Alfred E.

    1979 Austin Igleheart Dies; Ex-General Foods Chairman. *In* New York Times. Ocyober 26, 1979. Pp. A29.

Clarke, Erskine

    2005 Dwelling place: a plantation epic. New Haven: Yale University Press.

Cohen, Gary

    2002 The Keystone Kommandos. The Atlantic 289(2).

Corn, Joseph J.

    1985 The Winged Gospel: America's Romance with Aviation, 1900–1950. New York: Oxford University Press.

Coulter, E. Merton

    1927 Mary Musgrove, 'Queen of the Creeks: a Chapter of Early Georgia Troubles. Georgia Historical Quarterly 11:1-30.

Coulter, E. Merton, ed.

    1937 Georgia's Disputed Ruins. Chapel Hill,: The University of North Carolina press.

Courson, Maxwell Taylor
    1999   Howard Earle Coffin, King of the Georgia Coast. Georgia Historical Quarterly 83:322-341.

Courson, Maxwell Taylor
    2003   Howard Coffin (1873-1937). New Georgia Encyclopedia. Retrieved December 15, 2006.

Cox, Vercie A.
    1979   The Story of George M. Waldburg. *In* Lane Library, Armstrong Atlantic State University, Special Collections, Savannah Biographies, V-Z, Volume 5. Savannah, Georgia .

Crane, Hart
    2006   Complete poems and selected letters. New York: Library of America : Distributed to the trade in the U.S. by Penguin Putnam.

CSM
    1929   Last of Georgia Coast Islands Pases Into the Hands of Rich Men. Christian Science Monitor. January 13, 1929. Pg. 4.

CSM
    1940   Noble Resigned From Government to Help Willkie. *In* The Christian Science Monitor. August 19, 1940. Pg.14.

Cunningham, Rauers
    1938a Telegram to Mrs. Eugene DuPont. September 12, 1938. Georgia Historical Society. St. Catherine's Island Collection, MS.1696.

Cunningham, Rauers
    1938b Telegram to Thomas B. McCabe. September 12, 1938. Georgia Historical Society. St. Catherine's Island Collection, MS.1696.

Cunningham, Rauers
    1939   Letter to Charles Francis Jenkins. May 3, 1939. Jenkins Collection. Friends Historical Library of Swarthmore College. Swartmore, PA.

Dasch, George John
    1959   Eight Spies against America. New York: Robert M. McBride Company.

Davis, Runnette
    1982   Mr. Wood's Garden. Sylvania Telephone. March 18, 1982. Pg 18.

Deane, Elizabeth, and Patricia Garcia Rios
    2004   Reconstruction: The Second Civil War, Part 2, Retreat. In PBS: The American Experience. Pp. 175 minutes. United States: Paramount Home Entertainment.

Deaton, Stan
    2006   Button Gwinnett (1735-1777). New Georgia Encyclopedia, http://www.georgiaencyclopedia.org/nge/Article.jsp?id=h-2543&hl=y.

Donahue, Patrick
    2004   New Sunbury development could start within month. *In* Coastal Courier, May 12.

Dorris, Henry N.
    1938   Noble Tells C.A.A. Aims. New York Times. August 7, 1938. Pg 139.

Drago, Edmund L.
    1982   Black Politicians and Reconstruction in Georgia : a splendid failure. Baton Rouge: Louisiana State University Press.

Dubin, Arthur D.
    2003   Coast To Coast By Rail and Air Classic Trains Winter 2003 20.
Duffus, R. L.
    1926   Obscure Gwinnett Flickers into Fame. New York Times. January 31. Pp. SM3.
Duncan, Russell
    1986   Freedom's shore : Tunis Campbell and the Georgia Freedmen. Athens: University of Georgia Press.
Duncan, Russell
    2004   Tunis Campbell (1812-1891). New Georgia Encyclopedia. Accessed June 14, 2004. http://www.georgiaencyclopedia.org/nge/Article.jsp?id=h-2903&sug=y.
DuPont, Mrs. Eugene
    1938   Telegram to Rauers Cunningham. September 13, 1938. Georgia Historical Society. St. Catherine's Island Collection, MS.1696. .
Durham, Roger S., and David Hurst Thomas
    1978   The History of St. Catherines Island after 1684. Anthropological Papers of the American Museum of Natural History 55(2):210-241.
E.P.B.
    1862   Off the Georgia Coast, The Shrewdness of Contabands-A Commotion on St Catherine's Island-The Nashville. New York Times, November 13. Pp. 3.
Egan, Leo
    1948   The Practical Men Around Thomas E. Dewey. New York Times. September 12, 1948.
Elia, Nada
    2003   Kum Buba Yali Kum Buba Tambe, Ameen, Ameen, Ameen" Did Some Flying Africans Bow To Allah? Callaloo 26(1):182-202.
Eltscher, Louis R., and Edward M. Young
    1998   Curtiss-Wright : Greatness and Decline. New York: Twayne Publishers.
Fisher, Clive
    2002   Hart Crane. New Haven: Yale University Press.
Fisher, Doris
    1990   Mary Musgrove: Creek Englishwoman. Ph.D., Emory University.
Fisher, Jerry M.
    1998   The pacesetter : the untold story of Carl G. Fisher. Ft. Bragg, CA: Lost Coast Press.
Fishman, Jane
    1999   At Yellow Bluff, life stays pretty much the same. Savannah Morning *Morning*, December 8, 1999.
Fitch, Clyde
    1902   Captain Jinks of the Horse Marines: A Fantastic Comedy in Three Acts. New York: Doubleday, Page & Company.
Floyd, Marmaduke
    1937   Certain tabby ruins on the Georgia coast. *In* Georgia's Disputed Ruins. E.M. Coulter, ed. Pp. 3-192. Chapel Hill: The University of North Carolina press.

Foster, Mark S.

2000   Castles in the sand : the life and times of Carl Graham Fisher. Gainesville, FL: University Press of Florida.

Foster, William

1960   James Jackson: Duelist and Militant Statesman. Athens: University of Georgia Press.

Frank, Andrew K.

2004   Mary Musgrove (ca. 1700-ca. 1763), Retrieved November 18, 2006. http://www.georgiaencyclopedia.org/nge/Article.jsp?id=h-688: New Georgia Encyclopedia.

Frazier, W. Franklin, Lilla M. Hawes, Thomas H. Gignilliat, H. Hansell Hillyer, and Edward A. Leonard

1959   The Burial Place of Button Gwinnett: A Report to the Mayor and Alderman of the City of Savannah. Savannah Georgia: Savannah-Chatham County Histroric and Monument Commission.

Gabriel, Daniel

2007   Hart Crane and the modernist epic: canon and genre formation in Crane, Pound, Eliot, and Williams. New York: Palgrave Macmillan.

Gamble, Thomas

1923   Savannah duels and duellists, 1733-1877. Savannah,: Review Publishing & Printing Co.

Gannaway, Evey, and Martin A Knoll

2007   Water Quality Studies of a Shallow Aquifer on St. Catherine's Island, Georgia. *In* Geological Society of America Abstracts with Programs, Vol. 39, No. 6, p. 323

Gannon, Michael

1990   Operation Drumbeat: The Dramatic True Story of Germany's First U-boat Attacks along the American Coast in World War II. New York: Harper & Row.

Garrison, Ervan G., Charles P. Giammona, Frank J. Kelly, Anthony R. Tripp, and Gary A. Wolff

1989   Historic Shipwrecks and Magnetic Anomalies of the Northern Gulf of Mexico. Reevaluation of Archaeological Resources Management Zone 1. Volume III: Appendicies. New Orleans: U. S. Department of interior Mineral Management Service.

Georgia Writers' Project. Savannah Unit.

1986   Drums and shadows : survival studies among the Georgia coastal Negroes. Athens: University of Georgia Press.

Georgia Historical Society

1984   Registers of Death in Savannah, Georgia. Volume II, 1807-July 1811. Savannah: Genealogical Committee of Georgia Historical Society.

Georgia Historical Society

1989   Registers of Death in Savannah, Georgia. Volume V, 1833-1847. Savannah: Genealogical Committee of Georgia Historical Society.

Georgia Historical Society

1993a   Marriages of Chatham County, Georgia. Volume I, 1748-1852. Savannah: Geneological Committee of Georgia Historical Society.

Georgia Historical Society

    1993b Marriages of Chatham County, Georgia. Volume II,1852-1877. Savannah: Geneological Committee of Georgia Historical Society.

Georgia Writers' Program.

    1940 Drums and shadows; survival studies among the Georgia coastal Negroes. Athens: University of Georgia Press.

Gilbert, Jess, Spencer D. Wood, and Gwen Sharp

    2002 Who Owns the Land? Agricultural land Ownership by Race/Ethnicity. Rural America 14(4):55-62.

Gillespie, Michele

    1997 The Sexual Politics of Race and Gender: Mary Musgrove and the Georgia Trustees,. *In* The Devil's Lane: Sex and Race in the Early South. C. Clinton and M. Gillespie, eds. New York:: Oxford University Press.

Glaser-Schmidt, Elisabeth

    1995 The Guggenheims and the Coming of the Great Depression in Chile, 1923-1934. Business and Economic History 24(1):176-185.

Goebel, William A.

    1952 Memo to E. J. Noble. St Catherine's Conference. July 29, 1952.

Gordon, John Steele

    2007 Nazi Saboteurs Land on Long Island. *In* American Heritage, Vol. June 27, 2007.

Gould, Jack

    1951 A. B. C., United Paramount Merge in $25,000,000 Deal. New York Times. May 24, 1951. Pg.1.

Graham, George Edward, and Winfield Scott Schley

    1902 Schley and Santiago; an historical account of the blockade and final destruction of the Spanish fleet under command of Admiral Pasquale Cervera, July 3, 1898. Chicago: W. B. Conkey Company.

Green, Michael D.

    2001 Mary Musgrove: Creating a New World. *In* Sifters: Native American Women's Lives. T. Perdue, ed. New York: Oxford University Press.

Groover, Robert Long

    1987 Sweet Land of Liberty: A History of Liberty County Georgia. Roswell, GA: W. H. Wolfe Associates.

Hamilton, Virginia

    1985 The People Could Fly: American Black Folktales. New York: Knopf.

Harden, William

    1969 A history of Savannah and South Georgia. Reprint of 1913 edition, Volume I, published by Lewis Publishing Company. Chicago. Atlanta: Cherokee Pub. Co.

Harvey, Steve

    1983 Rare Signature Now on Display. Atlanta Constitution. Pp. May 19, 1983, p. 40A.

Hawley, Marion

    1958a Letter to John Toby Woods. December 22, 1958. John T. Woods, II Collection.

Hawley, Marion

    1958b Letter to John Toby Woods. July 22, 1958. John T. Woods, II Collection.

Hawley, Marion
    1959   Letter to John Toby Woods. June 11, 1959. John T. Woods, II Collection.

Haygood, Tamara Miner
    1986   Cows, Ticks, and Disease: A Medical Interpretation of the Southern Cattle Industry. The Journal of Southern History 52(4):551-564.

Holmes, James, and Delma Eugene Presley
    1976   "Dr. Bullie's" notes : reminiscences of early Georgia and of Philadelphia and New Haven in the 1800s. Atlanta: Cherokee Pub. Co.

Hopkins, George E.
    1975   Transcontinental Air Transport, Inc. American Heritage Magazine 27(1).

Hulen, Bertram D.
    1940   Hopkins Resigns From Cabinet. New York Times. August 25, 1940. Pg. 34.

Ingham, John N.
    1983   Biographical Dictionary of American Business Leaders. N-U. Westport, Conn.: Greenwood Press.

J.H.C.
    1873   Reminiscence of the War of 1812, Continued-Peace. Georgia Weekly Telegraph. July 22, 1873. Pg.1.

Jenkins, Charles Francis
    1926   Button Gwinnett: Signer of the Declaration of Independence. Garden City, N.Y. : Doubleday.

Jenkins, Charles Francis
    1939a Letter To Rauers Cunnngham. May 8, 1939. Paper in the Jenkins Collection. Friends Historical Library of Swarthmore College. Swartmore PA.

Jenkins, Charles Francis
    1939b Letter To M. Rauers Cunnngham. Aoril 10, 1939. Paper in the Jenkins Collection. Friends Historical Library of Swarthmore College. Swartmore PA.

Jenkins, Charles Francis
    1941   Letter To Rauers Cunnngham. June 2, 1941. Paper in the Jenkins Collection. Friends Historical Library of Swarthmore College. Swartmore PA.

Jenkins, Charles Francis
    1943a Letter To Edward J. Noble. April 23, 1943. Paper in the Jenkins Collection. Friends Historical Library of Swarthmore College. Swartmore PA.

Jenkins, Charles Francis
    1943b Letter To Edward J. Noble. March10, 1943. Paper in the Jenkins Collection. Friends Historical Library of Swarthmore College. Swartmore PA.

Jenkins, Charles Francis
    1943c Letter To Edward J. Noble. March 25, 1943. Paper in the Jenkins Collection. Friends Historical Library of Swarthmore College. Swartmore PA.

Jenkins, Charles Francis
    ND   Button Gwinett Stone. Paper in the Jenkins Collection. Friends Historical Library of Swarthmore College. Swartmore PA.

Johnson, and Corish
    1942   Estate of Jacob Rauers, deceased. Bill for professional services. January 6, 1942. Box 1 Folder 9. St. Catherine's Island Collection, MS.1696. Georgia Historical Society.

Johnson, and Corish
    1943 Estate of Jacob Rauers, deceased. Bill for professional services. January 1, 1943.
    Georgia Historical Society. St. Catherine's Island Collection, MS.1696. Box 1 Folder 9
Johnson, H. Wiley
    1941 Letter to J. J. Rauers, Executer, Estate of Jacob Rauers. December 8,1941.
    Georgia Historical Society. St. Catherine's Island Collection, MS.1696. Box 1 Folder 10.
Johnson, Herbert Alan
    1997 The Chief Justiceship of John Marshall, 1801-1835. Columbia, S.C.: University
    of South Carolina Press.
Johnson, Thomas A.
    1979a 3 Rights Groups Aid A Colony of Blacks; Help Families Who Charge Ouster
    Years Ago From Their Lands. New York Times, May 2. Pp. A12.
Johnson, Thomas A.
    1979b 4 Blacks Are Sentenced to 30 days In Dispute Over Ownership. *In* The New York
    Times, May 5. Pp. 28.
Johnson, Thomas A.
    1979c On the Rural Coast of Georgia, Activist Blacks Pray and Plot Strategy in Land
    Dispute. *In* New York Times, May 7. Pp. A12.
Jones, Charles Colcock
    1878 The dead towns of Georgia. Pp. 263 p., [5] p. of plates. Savannah: Morning News
    Steam Printing House.
Jones, Charles Colcock
    1883 The history of Georgia. Boston, New York,: Houghton, Mifflin and Company.
Jones, Charles Colcock, and Robert Manson Myers
    1984 The Children of pride : selected letters of the family of the Rev. Dr. Charles
    Colcock Jones from the years 1860-1868, with the addition of several previously
    unpublished letters. New Haven: Yale University Press.
Juricek, John T.
    1989 Early American Indian Documents:Treaties and laws, 1607-1789, Volume XI,
    Georgia Treaties, 1733-1763. Frederick, Md: University Publications of America.
Keys, C. M.
    1901 Pets of the Poor. New York Times. October 27, 1901. Pg.SM5.
Keys, C. M.
    1902a Nests of Birds. New York Times. April 12, 1902. Pg. SM5.
Keys, C. M.
    1902b Omar in Wall Street. New York Tiomes. September 7, 1902. Pg SM4.
Keys, C. M.
    1902c Railroad Presidents. New York Times. August 10, 1902. Pg. SM5.
Keys, C. M.
    1902d Sea Birds of the Winter. New York Times. January 26, 1902. Pg. SM9.
Keys, C. M.
    1904 "Busted, B'Gosh!". Current Literature XXXVI(2):191.
Keys, C. M.
    1907 Harriman: Colossus of Roads. Characteristics of the Railroad Organized. Wall
    Street Journal. January 5, 1907. Pg. 6.

Keys, C. M.
    1913a The Buyers of Bargins. Los Angeles Times. August 1, 1913. Pg. 119.

Keys, C. M.
    1913b How to finance the building of a little home. Philadelphia: Issued by the Ladies'
    Home Journal.

Keys, C. M.
    1938a Letter to John J. Rauers. April 13, 1938. Georgia Historical Society. St.
    Catherine's Island Collection, MS.1696.

Keys, C. M.
    1938b Letter to John J. Rauers. August 10, 1938. Georgia Historical Society. St.
    Catherine's Island Collection, MS.1696. .

Keys, C. M.
    1938c Letter to John J. Rauers. August 30, 1938. Georgia Historical Society. St.
    Catherine's Island Collection, MS.1696.

Keys, C. M.
    1938d Letter to John J. Rauers. May 31, 1938. Georgia Historical Society. St.
    Catherine's Island Collection, MS.1696.

Keys, Mrs. C.M.
    1932   Letter to Toby Woods. June 28, 1932. John T. Woods, II Collection.

Lambright, Joe
    1958   Vice President Relaxes in Georgia, Talks Politics. Nixon Spends Holiday on St.
    Catherine's. Savannah News. June 6, 1958. Pg. 7A.

Lamplugh, George R.
    1989   Oh the Colossus! The Colossus!": James Jackson and the Jeffersonian Republican
    Party in Georgia, 1796-1806. Journal of the Early Republic 9(3):315-334.

Lamplugh, George R.
    2006   James Jackson (1757-1806). New Georgia Encyclopedia. February 20,
    2007.http://www.georgiaencyclopedia.org/nge/Article.jsp?id=h-1087.

LAT
    1958   E. J. Noble, Chairman of Life Savers, Dies. Los Angeles Times. December 29,
    1958. Pg.4.

Lee, Curtis
    1953   Letter to Mr, Edward J. Noble. March 28, 1953. John T. Woods, II Collection.

Lee, Martha
    1988   Newington Baptist Church Honored Mr. And Mrs. Woods. Sylvania Telephone.
    December 8, 1988. Pg 4.

Lethbridge, Cliff
    2006   The History of Cape Canaveral, Chapter 3. NASA Arrives (1959-Present).
    http://www.spaceline.org/capehistory/3a.html. Accessed April 10, 2007.

Liberator
    1862   The Negroes Good Fighters. *In* The Liberator. November 12, 1862. Pg. 187.

Liberty County
    1872   Indenture Between The Estate of Elizabeth H. Waldburg, Elizabeth C. Waldburg,
    J. Houston Clinch and Thomas M. Cunningham, executors and Anna M. Rodriguez.

December 5,1972. Recorded Liberty County, Georgia, Clerk's Office Superior Court. Book of Deeds Q, page 249, 250 and 251, December 5, 1872.

Liberty County
1876   Indenture Between Anna M. Rodriguez and Jacob Rauers. January 26, 1876. Recorded Liberty County, Georgia, Clerk's Office Superior Court. Book of Deeds R, page 267-268, January 26, 1876 . Box 1 Folder 4. St. Catherine's Island Collection, MS.1696. Georgia Historical Society

Liberty County
1893   Quit Claim Deed. Lancaster King to Jacob Rauers. January 27, 1893. Recorded Liberty County, Georgia, Clerk's Office Superior Court. Book of Deeds AA, page 149-150, January 30, 1893 . Box 1 Folder 6. St. Catherine's Island Collection, MS.1696. Georgia Historical Society

Liberty County
1918   Indenture Between Jacob Rauers and Augustus Oemler. September 18, 1900. Recorded Liberty County, Georgia, Clerk's Office Superior Court. Book of Deeds AO, page 408-409, May 9, 1929. Box 1 Folder 4. St. Catherine's Island Collection, MS.1696. Georgia Historical Society.

Liberty County
1929a   Bond of Titles between John J. Rauers and Samuel B. Adams, as Executors and Trustees under the Will Jacob Rauers and James C. Wilson. Recorded Liberty County, Georgia, Clerk's Office Superior Court. Book of Deeds, page 313, Aug. 5, 1929. Box 1 Folder 4. St. Catherine's Island Collection, MS.1696. Georgia Historical Society

Liberty County
1929b   Indenture Between John J. Rauers and S. B. Adams, Executors of the Jacob Rauers estate and C. Phillip Maggioni and Joseph G. Maggioni for lease of oyster rights. January 2, 1928. Recorded January 25, 1928. Liberty County, Georgia, Clerk's Office Superior Court. Book of Deeds AX, page 346-348, May 9, 1929 . Box 1 Folder 4. St. Catherine's Island Collection, MS.1696. Georgia Historical Society

Lichtman, Allan J.
1987   Tommy the Cork; the secret world of Washington's first modern lobbyist - Thomas G. Corcoran. Washington Monthly. February. Accessed October 6, 2007. http://findarticles.com/p/articles/mi_m1316/is_v19/ai_4696995.

Los AngelesTimes
1904   "Kid" M'Coy Married Los Angeles Times, January 18. Pp. 3.

Lowrey, Don
2000   Colonels Island Still a Hidden Treasure: Barrier Island Boast Wildlife and Solitude. Savannah Morning News, May 16.

Lynn, Vyvyan
2006   Gifts from the Sea: Shrimping the Georgia Coast. The Georgia Magazine 2006 (July):20-23.

Malone, Dumas
1954   The Men Who Signed the Declaration of Independence. New York Times. July 4. Pp. SM6,26-27.

Martin, Douglas
     2002   Charles E. Fraser, 73, Dies; Developer of Hilton Head. New York Times.
     December 19, 2002. pg. B.14.
Mayo, Charles W.
     1968   Mayo; the story of my family and my career. Garden City, N.Y.: Doubleday.
McILany, Dennis P.
     2007   The Horseshoe Curve: Sabotage and Subversion in the Railroad City.
     Hollidaysburg, PA: Seven Oaks Press.
McIlvaine, Paul Morton
     1971   The dead town of Sunbury, Georgia. Hendersonville, N.C.
McKean, David
     2004   Tommy the Cork : Washington's ultimate insider from Roosevelt to Reagan.
     Hanover, N.H.: Steerforth Press.
McMillem, Wheeler
     Ms   Nine Decades in the Human Race. Heterick Memorial Library. Ohio Northern
     University. http://www.onu.edu/library/onuhistory/mcmillen/contents.htm.
McMullen, Francis
     1930   Island Homes That Attract Men Weary of City Crowds, New York Times,
     September 7, 1930. pg.XII.
Michelmore, G. W.
     1932   Letter to C. F. Jenkins. February 18, 1932. Jenkins Collection. Friends Historical
     Library of Swarthmore College. Swartmore PA.
Miller, Page Putnam
     2006   Fripp Island : a history. Charleston, SC: History Press.
Mohr, Clarence L.
     1979   Before Sherman: Georgia Blacks and the Union War Effort, 1861-1864. Journal
     of Southern History XLV:331-352.
Moore, Clarence B.
     1898   Certain aboriginal mounds of the coast of South Carolina. Philadelphia: P. C.
     Stockhausen, printer.
Moore, Clarence B.
     1903   Certain aboriginal mounds of the Florida central west-coast. Philadelphia,: P.C.
     Stockhausen.
Moore, Clarence B., and Lewis H. Larson
     1998   The Georgia and South Carolina expeditions of Clarence Bloomfield Moore.
     Tuscaloosa: University of Alabama Press.
Moore, Clarence B., and Jean-François-Albert du Pouget Nadaillac
     1897   Certain aboriginal mounds of the Georgia coast. Philadelphia: P.C. Stockhausen.
Morgan, Philip D.
     1982   Work and Culture: The Task System and the World of Lowcountry Blacks, 1700-
     1800. William and Mary Quarterly XXXIX(August):399-420.
Morrison, Toni
     1977   Song of Solomon. New York: Plume.
MWT
     1865   Advertisement. Macon Weekly Telegraph. August 23, 1865. Pg1.

MWT
    1867   Restored Lands. *In* Macon Weekly Telegraph. April 5, 1867. Pg. 3.

New York State
    1929   Indenture Between James C. Willson and St. Catherines Corporation. April 18, 1929. Box 1 Folder 4. St. Catherine's Island Collection, MS.1696. Georgia Historical Society.

Nixon, Richard M.
    1978   RN : the memoirs of Richard Nixon. New York: Grosset & Dunlap.

Noble, Edward J.
    1940   War Strikes American Foreign Trade. American Academy of Political and Social Sciences 211(September):111-116.

Noble, Edward J.
    1943a Letter to Charles F. Jenkins. March 17, 1943. Jenkins Collection. Friends Historical Library of Swarthmore College. Swarthmore PA.

Noble, Edward J.
    1943b Letter to Charles F. Jenkins. March 31, 1943. Jenkins Collection. Friends Historical Library of Swarthmore College. Swarthmore PA.

Noble, Edward J.
    1943c Letter to Savannah Bank & Trust. February 13, 1943. Georgia Historical Society. St. Catherine's Island Collection, MS.1696. Box 1 Folder 10.

Noble, Edward J.
    1947   Profit and Loss Work Sheet. John T. Woods, II Collection.

Noble, Edward J.
    1948a Letter to John Toby Wood, Sr. November 19, 1948. John T. Woods, II Collection.

Noble, Edward J.
    1948b Letter to John Toby Wood, Sr. November 29, 1948. John T. Woods, II Collection.

Noble, Edward J.
    1952a Letter to J. T. Woods. October 13, 1952. John T. Woods, II Collection.

Noble, Edward J.
    1952b Letter to J. Tobias Wood, Sr. April 15, 1952. John T. Woods, II Collection.

Noble, Edward J.
    1952c Letter to J. Tobias Wood, Sr. December 8, 1952. John T. Woods, II Collection.

Noble, Edward J.
    1952d Letter to J. Tobias Woods. October 8, 1952. John T. Woods, II Collection.

Noble, Edward J.
    1952e Letter to John Toby Wood, Sr. December 3, 1952. John T. Woods, II Collection.

Noble, Edward J.
    1953   Letter to J. Tobias Woods. March 4, 1953. John T. Woods, II Collection.

Noble, Edward J.
    1955   Letter to J. Tobias Wood, Sr. August 24, 1955. John T. Woods, II Collection.

Noble, Edward J.
    1956a Letter to J. Tobias Wood, Sr. February 16, 1956. John T. Woods, II Collection.

Noble, Edward J.
    1956b Letter to J. Tobias Wood, Sr. January 18, 1956. John T. Woods, II Collection.

Nolan, Peggy
    1999   The spy who came in from the sea. Sarasota, Fla.: Pineapple Press.
Noonan, John Thomas
    1977   The Antelope : the ordeal of the recaptured Africans in the administrations of
    James Monroe and John Quincy Adams. Berkeley: University of California Press.
NWR
    1819   Weekly Register. Niles Weekly Register. February 20, 1819. Pg. 23. See page
    449, Law Library of Congress (U.S.), and Library of Congress. National Digital Library
    Program. 1998 A century of lawmaking for a new nation: U.S. Congressional documents
    and debates, 1774-1875. Washington, D.C.: Library of Congress.
NYT
    1866   Georgia, Miscellaneous Matters-The Blacks and Whites. New York Times,
    August 13. Pp. 5. .
NYT
    1892   Sea Islands Changing Hands. Most of them Now owned by Northern Men. New
    York Times, November 24. Pp. 1.
NYT
    1902   Schley's First Deer, He was Excited When He Pulled the Trigger-To Start North
    Today. New York Times. January 30, 1902. Pg. 1.
NYT
    1905   Mr. M'Coy, Engaged, Now Reads Chaucer. Tennyson, Longfellow, and Browning
    Also Delight the Pugilist. New York Times, May 29, 1905. Pg. 9.
NYT
    1925   Boldt Castle Is Sold. Thousand Islands Estate, Valued at $5,000,000, Passes to E.
    J. Noble. New York Times. June 28,1925. Pg. 5.
NYT
    1927   Site in Connecticut Bought for House. New Yourk Time, November 22,1927. Pp.
    52.
NYT
    1928   New Hotel Planned for Montauk Beach. *In* New York Times. May 13, 1928. Pg.
    42.
NYT
    1929   Buys 23000-acre Islands. *In* New York Times, April 12. Pp. 54.
NYT
    1930   J. C. Willson Blocks Separation Suit, Wife's Action Dismissed here on Ground
    Aviation Financier is a Kentucky Resident. New York Times, August 15, 1930. Pg.22.
NYT
    1931   Perry Martin Dies. Last Negro Driver of Deer on Georgia Island a Stroke Victim.
    New York Times. July 27, 1931. Pg. 14.
NYT
    1932   "Golden Isles" Along Course. New York Times. December 24, 1932. Pg. 4.
NYT
    1934   Buys Tract in Greenwich. Edward J. Noble Takes Over 45 Acres from Mrs.
    Ashforth. New York Times. July 27, 1934. Pg. 32.

NYT

    1935   Greenwich Festive as New Year Arrives; 500 attend Hungarian Ball at the Round Hill Club-Many Large Dances are Held. New York Times, January 1. Pp. 33.

NYT

    1936   Afghan Oil Rights Won by Americans. New York Times, December 31. Pp. 23.

NYT

    1937a Club in Greenwich Plans Movie Fete: "Hollywood Party" to be held at Round Hill on a New Year's Eve Feature. New York Times, December 26. Pp. 65.

NYT

    1937b H. E. Coffin Found Dead From Bullet Industrialist, 64, Is Killed in Georgia on Eve of Hunt-Rifle Beside His Body. New York Times, November 22, 1937. pg.1.

NYT

    1937c Sees Her Jewels Stolen. Mrs. E. J. Noble of Greenwich is Too Scared to Scream. *In* The New York Times. June 2, 1937. Pg. 8.

NYT

    1938a C. M. Keys Heads Montauk Company. New York Times. January 14, 1938. Pg. 36.

NYT

    1938b Greenwich Realty Assessment Rise. New York Times. September 11, 1938. Pg. I-75.

NYT

    1939a Boldt Castle Tower Burns. New York Times. August 8, 1939. Pg. 15.

NYT

    1939b Noble Enters New Post. Sworn in as First Undersecretary of Commerce. New York Times. June 10, 1939. Pg. 36.

NYT

    1940a Candy Official a Bank Director. New York Times. October 18, 1940. Pg.43.

NYT

    1940b E. J. Noble To Back Willkie Campaign. Under-Secertary of Commerce Who Resigned Wednesday Announces his Support. Wants to Aid Defence. New York Times. August 17, 1940. Pg. 7.

NYT

    1940c Noble Not Seeking Senate Seat, He Says. New York Times. August 22, 1940. Pg.15.

NYT

    1940d Noble Quits Post as Hopkins Aide. Republican who created CAA Says He Has Fulfilled Roosevelt's Assignments. New York Times. August 15, 1940. Pg. 14.

NYT

    1940e Senate Race is Reported. New York Times. August 15, 1940. Pg. 14.

NYT

    1941   Buying at Montauk, Nine Sales Closed and Four New Dwellings Being Erected. New York Times. March 30, 1941. Pg. E2.

NYT

    1942a Boldt Castle Will Yield Scrap. New York Times. September 27, 1942. Pg 40.

NYT

1942b Coast Guard Calls For Horse Marines, Wants Steed Owners, Riders for Mounted Patrol on Atlantic and Gulf. No Women are Allowed,The Captain Jinkes Must Supply Harness and Pay for Stabling Their Animals.New York Times. August 2, 1942. Pg. 17.

NYT

1942c Coast Guard is planning Horse Maines. New York Times. Julu 26, 1942. Pg. 17.

NYT

1942d Sea-Horses on Shore. New York Times. July 28, 1942. Pg.16.

NYT

1943a Flamm Suit Seeks to Get Back WMCA. New York Times. August 14, 1943. Pg. 9.

NYT

1943b New Yorker Buys an Island. New York Times. March 7, 1943. Pg. 14.

NYT

1943c Noble Purchases the Blue Network. Sarnoff Reveals Completion of Deal for Radio Chain, Involving $8,000,000. New York Times. July 31, 1943. Pg. 17.

NYT

1944a Miss Sally Noble. New York Times. Febuary 10, 1944. Pg.15.

NYT

1944b WMCA Charges Hit By Nobles Lawyer. New York Times. February 11, 1944. Pg. 13.

NYT

1944c WMCA Sale Upheld By House Inquiry. New York Times. January 11, 1945. Pg. 14.

NYT

1946a $2,925,000 Trial Starts. Damage Suit Involving Sale of Station WMCA Opens. New York Times. February 20, 1946. Pg. 20.

NYT

1946b $350, 000 Awarded in Flamm's Suit. . New York Times. March 2, 1946. Pg. 9.

NYT

1947a E. J. Noble Gets Scroll. Honored by the Salvation Army, will Lead its 1948 Drive. *In* The New York Times. October 3, 1947. Pg. 27.

NYT

1947b Flamm Wins Rise in WMCA Payment. State Appeals Court Reverses Lower Tribunals. Gives Him $107,508 in Interest. New York Times. April 22, 1947. Pg. 54.

NYT

1948 James C. Willson, Plane Financier, Ex-head of Investment Firm Who Aided Merger of Curtis Wright Interest Dies. New York Times. May 3, 1948. Pg. 21

NYT

1949a 8-Year Fight Ended Over Sale of WMCA. New York Times. October 8, 1949. Pg. 28.

NYT

1949b ABC Moving up, but Stock in a "speculation" because of TV, Chairman Tells Stockholders. New York Times. April 13, 1949. Pg. 49.

NYT

1949c Dulles Campaign Opens Tomorrow. New York Times. September 18, 1948. Pg. 74.

NYT

1950a A. B. Chapman Runs Republican Drive; Lawyer Who Directed Dewey's Campaign in 1946 is Chosen for Third-Term Contest. New York Times. September 12, 1950. Pg. 19.

NYT

1950b Merger in Effect for Blair Rollins. New York Times. January 17. Pp. 38.

NYT

1950c Radio Executive Takes Thousand Island Club. The New York Times. March 23, 1950. Pg. 48.

NYT

1953 Gift of $2,000,000 Made to Noble Foundation. The New York Times. December 14, 1953. Pg. 37.

NYT

1954a Noble Gives Again to His Foundation. Executive Adds $5,000,000 to Last Years $2,000,000 for Philanthropies. New York Times. December 30, 1954. Pg. 34.

NYT

1954b St. Lawrence U. Board Elects. New York Times. June 6, 1954. Pg30.

NYT

1956a $600,000 Donated to St. Lawrence. New York Times. January 30, 1956. Pg. 25.

NYT

1956b Life Savers Plan To Join Beech-Nut. New York Times. June 7, 1956. Pg.43.

NYT

1958 Edward J. Noble, A Financier, Dead. Chairman of Beech-Nut Life Savers Served US- Bought Blue Network. New York Times. December 29, 1958. Pg. 15.

NYT

1959a ABC-Paramount Fills Board. New York Times. May 20, 1959. Pg. 49.

NYT

1959b State Treasurer of G. O. P. Resigns. New York Times. January 19, 1959. Pg. 17.

NYT

1960 Savannah Won't Part With Historical Bones. New York Times. April 5, 1960. Pg.24.

NYT

1965 Maj. Gen. Arthur Carter Dies; Senior Partner in Haskins & Sells. New York Times, January 4. Pp. 33.

NYT

1967 Theodore Montague Dies at 69: Executive Added Products, Employed Elsie the Cow to Build Warm Image. New York Times, August 14. Pp. 31.

NYT

1968a John M. Lovejoy is Dead at 79; Retired Seaboard Oil Chairman. New York Tines, November 11. Pp. 47.

NYT

    1968b Medley G. B. Whelpley, 75, Dies; Officer in Guggenheims' Mines. New York Times, March 25. Pp. 41.

NYT

    1969   Amos J. Peaslee, Ex-Enovy, IS Dead. New York Times. August 30, 1969. Pg. 21.

NYT

    1971   Earl E. Anderson, Business Adviser: Ex-Aide with Beech-Nut Life Savers Dies at 85. New York Times, January 9, 1971, pg. 31.

NYT

    1973   Warren H. Snow Sr., Investment Banker.New York Times, May 8. Pp. 39.

NYT

    1976   William T. Taylor, Ex-Chairman of ACF Industries, Dead at 75. New York Times, March 17. Pp. 44.

NYT

    1979   Evicted Colony Claims Wildlife Refuge in Georgia. New York Times. Pp. A16.

Oemler, A.

    1883   Truck-farming at the South: a Guide to the Raising of Vegetables for Northern Markets. New York: Orange Judd.

Oemler, A.

    1889   The Life History, Propagation and Protection of the American Oyster; an Essay Read Before the Georgia Historical Society. Savannah, GA: The Morning News Print (YA Pamphlet Collection, Library of Congress)

Orren, Karren

    1998   "A War Between Officers": The Enforcement of Slavery in the Northern United States, and of the Republic for Which it Stands, Before the Civil War. Studies in American Political Development 12(2):343-382.

Pate, Suzanne

    1992   Woods, Collins and Son Win at Yellow Bluff Shark Tournament. Update, A Coastal EMC Bi-Weekly News Letter, August 7. Hinesville.

Peaslee, Amos Jenkins

    1942   A Permanent United Nations. New York: G. P. Putnam's sons.

Peaslee, Amos Jenkins

    1943   Future Fundamentals. Swarthmore, Pa.,.

Peaslee, Amos Jenkins

    1945   United Nations Government. New York: Justice house.

Peaslee, Amos Jenkins

    1956   Constitutions of Nations; the First Compilation in the English language of the Texts of the Constitutions of the Various Nations of the World, Together with Summaries, Annotations, Bibliographies, and Comparative Tables. The Hague: M. Nijhoff.

Peaslee, Amos Jenkins, and Dorothy Peaslee Xydis

    1961   International Governmental Organizations: Constitutional Documents. The Hague: M. Nijhoff.

Peason, Drew

    1948   Line-up of the Dewey "Team." Washington Post. November 3, 1948. Pg.B15.

Phillips, Cabell
    1951   Stassen Running Again, For Whom Is Not Clear. He is Surely a Candidate but He
    Also is in Favor of Eisenhower Draft. New York Times. December 2, 1951. Pg. 184.
Piechocinski, Elizabeth Carpenter
    1999   The Old Burying Ground : Colonial Park Cemetery, Savannah, Georgia, 1750-
    1853. Savannah, Ga.: Oglethorpe Press.
Porter, Jr. A. E.
    ND   Manual of the U. S. Coast Guard Beach Patrol (Restricted). Charleston, SC: Sixth
    Naval Distruct.
Rasmussen, Frederick N.
    2006   Brady Oliver Bryson, 90, Lawyer at Nuremberg Trail. Baltimore Sun. February
    16, 2006. Pg. 6B.
Rauers, J. J.
    1938   Letter to C. M. Keys. September 1, 1938. Georgia Historical Society. St.
    Catherine's Island Collection, MS.1696.
Rauers, Jacob
    1876a   Agreement to Purchase Personal Property from Anna M. Rodriquez. Box 1 Folder
    3. St. Catherine's Island Collection, MS.1696. Georgia Historical Society.
Rauers, Jacob
    1876b   Promissory Note to Anna M. Rodriquez. Box 1 Folder 3. St. Catherine's Island
    Collection, MS.1696. Georgia Historical Society.
Rawson, Edward K., and Robert H. Woods
    1897   Official Records of the Union and Confederate Navies in the War of the
    Rebellion. Series 1,Volume 6. Atlantic Blockading Squadron from July 16 to October 29,
    1861. North Atlantic Blockading Squadron from October 29, 1861 to March 8, 1862.
    Washington: Government Printing Office.
Reed, Brian
    2006   Hart Crane: after His Lights. Tuscaloosa: University of Alabama Press.
Riddle, Lyn
    1996   The Visionary Pioneer of Hilton Head Island, S.C. New York Times. May 5,
    1996. Section 9, Pg. 7.
Riddle, Lyn
    2001   Upscale Homes for S. Carolina Woods. New York Times, October 14. Pp. 11.
Rippen, Charles
    1977   The Harris Neck Army Air Field 1941-1944. Coastal Quarterly 3(2):23-27.
Robertson, William J.
    1946   Rare Button Gwinnett. The Georgia Historical Quarterly 30(4):297-307.
Ross, Andrew
    1999   The Celebration Chronicles: Life, Liberty and the Pursuit of Property Values in
    Disney's New Town. New York: Ballantine Books.
Ryan, Edward F.
    1948   Dewey Believes in Well Paid Aides. Washington Post. June 29, 1948. Pg. 3.
Saffro, Richard, Jim Smith, Don Shaw, Ralph Roberts, George Sanders, and Helen Sanders
    1994   The Sanders Price Guide to Autographs. Alexander, NC: Alexander Books.

SALR
    1943   Bill of Lading. Seaboard Air Line Railway. Papers in the Jenkins Collection. Friends Historical Library of Swarthmore College. Swartmore PA.

Sanderson, John
    1822   Biography of the Signers to the Declaration of Independence. Philadelphia: R.W. Pomeroy.

Saxon, Wolfgang
    1983a A. B. Chapman Dies; A Leader of G. O. P., Lawyer and Squibb Chairman Ran New York Campaigns-Associate of Dewey. New York Times. November 5, 1983. Pg. 34.

Saxon, Wolfgang
    1983b A. B. Chapman Dies; A Leader of the G. O. P. *In* New York Times, November 5. Pp. 34.

Schneider, Kent A., and Donald L. Crusoe
    1976   Joseph Ralston Caldwell, 1916-1973. American Antiquity, Vol. 41, No. 3 (Jul., 1976), pp. 303-307 41(3):303-307.

See, Alonzo B.
    1928   Schools. Philadelphia: The Ferguson press.

SEP
    1861   Villerroi's Submarine Propeller. *In* Saturday Evening Post. May 25, 1861. Page 3.

Shelton, Stacy
    2006   Ossabaw Cabins Offer Peek Into Slave Life. If Walls could Talk. Atlanta Journal Constitution. November 27, 2006. Pg.1.

Smith, Jean Edward
    1996   John Marshall: Definer of a Nation. New York: H. Holt & Co.

Smith, Jean Edward
    2001   The Face of Justice: Portraits of John Marshall. Huntington, WV: Huntington Museum of Art.

Smith, Liz
    1999   When Love Was the Adventure. The Five Romances That, for Better or Worse, Captured Our Imagination this Century. Anne Morrow and Charles Lindberg. Time Magazine. May 14, 1999. http://www.time.com/time/time100/heroes/romances/index.html.

Smith, Llewellyn M.
    2004   Reconstruction: The Second Civil War, Part 1, Revolution. In The American Experience. Pp. 175 minutes. United States: Paramount Home Entertainment.

Smith, Mike
    2006   Alligator:The Forgotten Torchbearer of the U. S. Submarine Force. Undersea Warfare 8(3).

Sparks, Andrew
    1955   We Searched for the Lost Grave of Button Gwinnett. Atlanta Journal and The Atlanta Constitution Magazine. Pp. 6-7, 11, Vol. July 3, 1955.

State of Georgia
    1918   An Act fror the Protection of the Owners of Sea Islands in Georgia. State of Georgia Act of 1918. Pg.262. .

Sullivan, Buddy
    1990   Early Days on the Georgia Tidewater: the Story of McIntosh County & Sapelo:
    Being a Documented Narrative Account, with Particular Attention to the County's
    Waterway and Maritime Heritage; Plantation Culture and Uses of the Land in the 19th
    Century; and a Detailed Analysis of the History of Sapelo Island. Darien, Ga: McIntosh
    County Board of Commissioners.

Sullivan, Buddy
    2002   Sapelo Island. New Georgia Encyclopedia. Accessed February 3, 2006.

Sullivan, Buddy
    2003   Blackbeard Island. New Georgia Encyclopedia. Accessed June 5, 2006.
    http://www.newgeorgiaencyclopedia.org/nge/Article.jsp?id=h-929.

Sullivan, Patricia
    2005   Rose Mary Woods Dies; Loyal Nixon Secretary. Washington Post. January 24,
    2005. Pg. B04

Swanberg, W. A.
    1970   The Spies Who Came in From The Sea. *In* American Heritage Magazine, Vol. 21
    (3).

Sweet, George D.
    1815   Home Intelligence. Remarkable Additions to the Great Ogeechee Church, In
    Georgia. The Massachusett Baptist Missionary Magazine. December 1815. Pg.4.8.

Sweet, Julia Anne
    2005   Negotiating for Georgia: British-Creek Relations in the Trustee Era, 1733-1752.
    Athens: University of Georgia Press.

Tempkin, William F.
    1927   Letter to J. J. Rauers. August 26, 1927. Box 1, Folder 8. Georgia Historical
    Society. St. Catherine's Island Collection, MS.1696

Thomas, David Hurst
    1987   The Archaeology of Mission Santa Catalina de Guale. 1, Search and discovery.
    Anthropological Papers of the AMNH 63(2):47-161.

Thomas, David Hurst, Grant D. Jones, Roger S. Durham, and Clark Spencer Larsen
    1978   The Anthropology of St. Catherines Island. 1. Natural and Cultural History.
    Anthropological Papers of the American Museum of Natural History 55(2):157-248.

Thomas, David Hurst, Stanley A. South, and Clark Spencer Larsen
    1977   Rich man, poor men: observations on three antebellum burials from the Georgia
    coast. Anthropological papers of the American Museum of Natural History 54(3):395-
    420.

Time
    1939   Life Saver. *In* Time Magazine. April 24, 1939.

Time
    1956   New Wrapper. *In* Time Magazine. January 18, 1956.
    http://www.time.com/time/printout/0,8816,862268,00.html#.

Todd, Helen
    1981   Mary Musgrove, Georgia Indian princess. Savannah, Ga.: Seven Oaks.

Toepke, Alvaro, and Angel Serrano
    1998   The Language You Cry In: Story of a Mende Song. San Francisco: California Newsreel.
TrentonTimes
    1905   Divorce Granted Kid M'Coy's Wife. Trenton Times, April 5, 1905. Pp. 9.
Turner, Lorenzo Dow
    1949   Africanisms in the Gullah dialect. Chicago: University of Chicago Press.
Tuten, Sarah Beth F.
    1959   Letter to John Toby Woods. May 31, 1959. John T. Woods, II Collection.
Updegraff, Robert
    1999   The Subconscious Mind in Business:
    http://www.dreamsalive.com/subconmind.htm. Retrieved January 15, 2007.
USG
    1861   Report of the Secretary of Navy in Message of the President of The United States to the Two Houses of Congress at the Commencement of the Second Session of the Thirty-Seventh Conggress. Volume III. Washington D. C.: United States Printing Office.
Van der Linden, F. Robert
    2002   Airlines and Air Mail: The Post Office and the Birth of the Commercial Aviation Industry. Lexington, Ky.: University Press of Kentucky.
VanMarter, James Gilbert
    1904   An Island Deer Hunt. Outing, An Illustrated Monthly Magazine of Recreation XLIII:441-448.
Vidal, Gore
    1985   Love of Flying. The New York Review of Books 31(21&22).
White, George
    1849   Statistics of the state of Georgia: including an account of its natural, civil, and ecclesiastical history; together with a particular description of each county, notices of the manners and customs of its aboriginal tribes, and a correct map of the state. Savannah: W. Thorne Williams.
White, T. D., and Pieter A. Folkens
    2005   The human bone manual. Amsterdam ; Boston: Elsevier Academic.
Whiteside, Thomas
    1977   Tomato. New Yorker. January 24 1977. Pg 37-61.
Williams, Roger M.
    1966   Who's Got Button's Bones? American Heritage Magazine 17(2):28-32,102-103.
Willoughby, Malcolm Francis
    1980   The U.S. Coast Guard in World War II. New York: Arno Press.
Witt, M.D. , and H.D. Knudsen.
    1993   Milkweed Cultivation for Floss Production. In New Crops. J. Janick and J.E. Simon, eds. Pp. 428-431. New York: Wiley.
Wood, Betty
    1974   Thomas Stephens and the Introduction of Black Slavery in Georgia. Georgia Historical Quarterly 58.
Wood, Betty
    1984   Slavery in Colonial Georgia, 1730-1775 Athens: University of Georgia Press.

Wood, Betty

    2002   Slavery in Colonial Georgia. Retrieved on November 13,
2006.http://www.georgiaencyclopedia.org/nge/Article.jsp?id=h-685: New Georgia
Encyclopedia.

Wood, Betty, and Ralph Gray

    1976   The Transition from Indentured to Involuntary Servitude in Colonial Georgia.
Explorations in Economic History 13(4).

Woods, J. T.

    1948   Letter to Edward J. Noble. February 6, 1948. John T. Woods, II Collection.

Woods, J. T.

    1949   Letter to E. J. Noble. October 5, 1949. John T. Woods, II Collection.

Woods, John Toby

    1944   Day Book. John T. Woods, II Collection.

Woods, John Toby

    1945   Cattle Inventory. John T. Woods, II Collection.

Woods, John Toby

    1946   Cattle Inventory. John T. Woods, II Collection.

Woods, John Toby

    1947   Profit and Loss Work Sheet. John T. Woods, II Collection.

Woods, John Toby

    1950   Federal Income Tax Return. John T. Woods, II Collection.

Woods, John Toby

    1952a Cattle Inventory. John T. Woods, II Collection.

Woods, John Toby

    1952b Federal Income Tax Return. John T. Woods, II Collection.

Woods, John Toby

    1954a Cattle Inventory. John T. Woods, II Collection.

Woods, John Toby

    1954b Day Book. John T. Woods, II Collection.

Woods, John Toby

    1955a Cattle Inventory. John T. Woods, II Collection.

Woods, John Toby

    1955b Day Book. John T. Woods, II Collection.

Woods, John Toby

    1956   Cattle Inventory. John T. Woods, II Collection.

Woods, John Toby

    1957   Cattle Inventory. John T. Woods, II Collection.

Woods, John Toby

    1958a Cattle Inventory. John T. Woods, II Collection.

Woods, John Toby

    1958b Day Book. John T. Woods, II Collection.

Woods, John Toby

    1958c Federal Income Tax Return. John T. Woods, II Collection.

Woods, John Toby

    1959a Day Book. John T. Woods, II Collection.

Woods, John Toby

    1959b Federal Income Tax Return. John T. Woods, II Collection.

WP

    1894   Anglers in Congress, Popular Statesmen Are Fond of Rod and Gun, Tom Murrey Writes Them Up. About Two Hundred of the Entire Membership Are True Sportsmen-Two-Thirds of Senators Are Anglers-These Are Men that Never Introduce Insane or Idiotic Legislative Measures-Senator Pehffer's Whiskers Responsible. Washington Post. October 1, 1894. Pg.12.

WP

    1902   Schley Talks to Blacks, Enthusiastic Welcome by Pupils of Georgia Agricultural College. Admiral Tells His Hearers that Their Comfort and Happiness Lie in Development of Mind and Hand. Washington Post. January 15, 1902. Pg. 3.

WP

    1936   Allen Vice President of Union Bag & Paper. Washington Post. November 25, 1936. Pg X7.

WP

    1938a Air Authority Open Inquiry on Mail Rates. Washington Post. August 26, 1938. Pg. 1.

WP

    1938b Candy Magnate, Edward Noble, to Co-ordinate Civil Flying. Washington Post. July 8, 1938. Pg. X1.

WP

    1939   Noble Call Chest Citadel of Democracy, Social Consciousmess is Vital to American System, He Declares. Washington Post. November 10, 1939. Pg.3.

WP

    1958   Millionaire Noble, Promoted Life Saver. Washington Post and Times Hearld. December 29, 1958. Pg.B2.

WSJ

    1932   C. M. Keys Retires. Wall Street Journal. January 8, 1932, Pg. 1.

WSJ

    1938   Union Bag Stockholder Agree to Waive Rights to Stock.Bond Offerings. Wall Stree Journal. April 12, 1938. Pg.8.

WSJ

    1956   New Beech-Nut Life Savers Names E. J. Noble Chairman. Wall Street Journal. July 9, 1956. Pg. 13.

WSJ

    1964   Beech-Nut Expands its Operations to Nonfoods. Wall Street Journal. August 27, 1964. Pg13.

WSJ

    1966   Beech-Nut, Dobbs Agree in Principle on Plan to Merge. Wall Street Journal. March 23, 1966. Pg. 4.

WSJ

    1967   Beech-Nut Says Vote for Olin Unit Merger Totaled More than 80%. Ratification of the Consolidation with Squibb & Sons Is Delayed Pending a Favorable Tax Ruling. Wall Street Journal. September 29, 1967. Pg.10.

WSJ

    1974   Squibb Chairman Resigns, Becomes a Political Aide. Wall Street Journal. August 16, 1974. Pg. 15.

Young, Edward M.

    1992   Clement M. Keys. Encyclopedia of American Business History and Biography: The Airline Industry. W.M. Leary, ed. Pp. 258-266. New York: Bruccoli Clark Layman.

Index

285

CPSIA information can be obtained at www.ICGtesting.com
Printed in the USA
LVOW031116240612

287161LV00002B/2/P

9 780985 345501